YUMA COUNTY LIBRAR

P9-CKB-725

DISCARDED

AMERICAN MILITARY HISTORY

★ ★ ★ ★ ★ ★ ★ ★ ★ ★ ★

VOLUME 1: 1775-1902

AMERICAN MILITARY HISTORY

★ ★ ★ ★ ★ ★ ★ ★ ★ ★ ★ ★ ★

VOLUME 1: 1775-1902

Edited by
Maurice Matloff

355.00973 A512 1996 v.1 AME

CX0037656001

COMBINED BOOKS
Pennsylvania

PUBLISHER'S NOTE

Combined Books, Inc., is dedicated to publishing books of distinction in history and military history. We are proud of the quality of writing and the quantity of information found in our books. Our books are manufactured with style and durability and are printed on acid-free paper. We like to think of our books as soldiers: not infantry grunts, but well dressed and well equipped avant garde. Our logo reflects our commitment to the modern and yet historic art of bookmaking.

We call ourselves Combined Books because we view the publishing enterprise as a "combined" effort of authors, publishers and readers. And we promise to bridge the gap between us—a gap which is all too seldom closed in contemporary publishing.

We would like to hear from our readers and invite you to write to us at our offices in Pennsylvania with your reactions, queries, comments, even complaints. All of your correspondence will be answered directly by a member of the Editorial Board or by the author.

We encourage all of our readers to purchase our books from their local booksellers, and we hope that you let us know of booksellers in your area that might be interested in carrying our books. If you are unable to find a book in your area, please write us.

For information, address:
COMBINED BOOKS., INC.
151 East 10th Avenue
Conshohocken, PA 19428

This edition of *American Military History* includes Chapters 1-28 from the 1989 edition, several of which have been partially revised, plus a new chapter dealing with the period after 1975, two new appendices, and some additions to the Suggested Readings.

Copyright© revised material 1996 by Combined Books.

All rights reserved. No part of this publication may be reproduced, stored in a retrieval system or transmitted in any form or by any means, electrical, mechanical or otherwise without first seeking the written permission of the publisher.

Library of Congress Cataloguing-in-Publication Data
American military history / edited by Maurice Matloff.
     p.   cm.
    Includes bibliographical references and index.
    Contents: v. 1. 1775-1902 -- v. 2. 1902-1996.
    ISBN 0-938289-72-1 (v. 1 : hc : alk. paper). -- ISBN 0-938289-70-5
(v. 2 : pb). -- ISBN 0-938289-73-X (v. 2 : hc : alk. paper). -- ISBN
0-938289-71-3 (v. 2. : pb)
    1. United States--History, Military. I. Matloff, Maurice, 1915- .

E181.A44   1973
355'.00973--dc20
                         96-7108
                            CIP

Printed in the United States of America.

Contributors

BELL, WILLIAM GARDNER (Chapter 14), a graduate of the Cavalry School and a former editor of the *Cavalry Journal* and *Armor Magazine,* has written frequently on the frontier Army and the American West.

COAKLEY, ROBERT W. (Chapters 2, 3, 4, and 23), Ph.D. (Virginia), is coauthor of the two *Global Logistics and Strategy* volumes in the U.S. Army in World War II series and author of *The Role of Federal Military Forces in Domestic Disorders* in the Historical Studies series.

CONN, STETSON (Chapter 19), Ph.D. (Yale), was coauthor of *The Framework of Hemisphere Defense* and *Guarding the United States and Its Outposts,* both in the U.S. Army in World War II series.

COOLING, BENJAMIN F., III (Chapters 10 and 11), Ph.D. (Pennsylvania), is author of, among others, *Forts Henry and Donelson: The Key to the Confederate Heartland* and editor of *New American State Papers—Military Affairs.*

DEMMA, VINCENT H. (Chapter 28), M.A. (Wisconsin), is a CMH historian specializing in the study of the role of the Army in the Vietnam conflict.

HERMES, WALTER G. (Chapters 26 and 27), Ph.D. (Georgetown), is author of *Truce Tent and Fighting Front* in the U.S. Army in the Korean War series.

JONES, VINCENT C. (Chapters 15 and 16), Ph.D. (Wisconsin), is author of *Manhattan: The Army and the Atomic Bomb* in the U.S. Army in World War II series.

MACDONALD, CHARLES B. (Chapters 17, 18, and 22), B.A., Litt.D. (Presbyterian), is author of, among others, *Company Commander,* and of *Three Battles, The Siegfried Line Campaign,* and *The Last Offensive,* volumes in the U.S. Army in World War II series.

MACGREGOR, MORRIS J., JR. (Chapters 5 and 6), M.A. (Catholic), is author of *The Integration of the Armed Forces, 1940–1965* in the Defense Studies series and coauthor of *Soldier-Statesmen of the Constitution* and *Blacks in the United States Armed Forces.*

MATLOFF, MAURICE (Chapters 1, 20, and 21), Ph.D. (Harvard), is coauthor of *Strategic Planning for Coalition Warfare, 1941–1942* and author of *Strategic Planning for Coalition Warfare, 1943–1944* in the U.S. Army in World War II series.

MAYO, LIDA (Chapters 7 and 8), B.A. (Randolph-Macon), was author of *The Ordnance Department: On Beachhead and Battlefront* and coauthor of *The Ordnance Department: Procurement and Supply* and *The Corps of Engineers: The War Against Germany,* all in the U.S. Army in World War II series.

MOSSMAN, B.C. (Chapters 24 and 25), B.A. (Nebraska State), is author of *Ebb and Flow,* a volume in the U.S. Army in the Korean War series, and coauthor of *The Last Salute: Civil and Military Funerals, 1921–1969.*

ROMANUS, CHARLES F. (Chapters 9 and 12), M.A. (Illinois), was coauthor of the three volumes on the China-Burma-India Theater and of *The Quartermaster Corps: Operations in the War Against Germany,* all in the U.S. Army in World War II series.

SCHEIPS, PAUL J. (Chapter 13), Ph.D. (American), is coauthor of *Bayonets in the Streets* and author of *Hold the Fort* and numerous other works, principally on the frontier Army and the use of troops in domestic disturbances.

NOFI, ALBERT A. (Chapter 29), Ph.D. (CUNY), is author *The '98 Campaign, The Spanish American War,* and coauthor of *Dirty Little Secrets of World War II* and *Deceit.*

Contents

Maps

Preface to the 1969 Edition

The Office of the Chief of Military History has prepared this historical survey of the organization and accomplishments of the United States Army primarily for use in the American Military History course usually given in the sophomore year of the Reserve Officers' Training Corps program in civilian colleges and universities. The aim has been to present a balanced history of the Army from its beginnings through the year 1967, with appropriate attention to peacetime as well as wartime achievements.

In describing military operations through the Civil War the contributors have pointed out, more than in later chapters, the application (or violation) of the principles of war that are discussed in the introductory chapter. In the interest of getting on with the narrative, they have necessarily omitted many other illustrations that will undoubtedly occur to the thoughtful reader. The century since the Civil War receives greater attention in this text than in its predecessor, both through chronological extension and by the inclusion of additional chapters on the post-Civil War period and World War I. Inevitably the story from World War II onward has a broader perspective than the record of the Army's earlier experiences, since in recent decades the Army's history has become increasingly intermingled with that of the other armed services and with that of the higher echelons of government directing the national defense.

In preparing this work, the contributors used as a point of departure the earlier ROTC text, *American Military History, 1607–1958*; but in the present volume half of the chapters are new or completely rewritten, and the remainder have been extensively revised. It is nevertheless only proper to acknowledge the work of previous contributors who wrote some of the basic texts of chapters used in the revision: Dr. Byron Fairchild, now with the Department of State Historical Office; the late Dr. Kent Roberts Greenfield, former Chief Historian; Dr. Richard M. Leighton, now with the faculty of the Industrial College of the Armed Forces; Dr. Leo J. Meyer, now retired; the late Dr. John Miller, jr., former Deputy Chief Historian; Professor Louis Morton of Dartmouth College; Brig. Gen. Paul McD. Robinett, USA (Ret.); and Mr. Robert R. Smith, recently returned to the OCMH staff. A major change has been the inclusion in the present work of an annotated general bibliography and detailed chapter bibliographies. Quotations have been used more generously than before, but it is hoped with sufficient identification in the text to justify the decision against documentation.

The planning for this work and the preparation of its preliminary draft were carried out under the supervision of Dr. Matloff. The draft was then reviewed by a panel with the undersigned as chairman, and consisting otherwise, in addition to four other contributors, of Professor Stephen E. Ambrose of The Johns Hopkins University; Mr. Detmar Finke, Chief, Reference Branch, OCMH; Maj. James A. Garnett, Assistant Professor of Military Science at the University of Virginia; Mr. Ralph W. Hampton of the United States Continental Army Command; Dr. Leighton; and Col. Wolfred K. White, Chief, Histories Division, OCMH. Additionally, the Continental Army Command circulated a number of copies of the draft to the ROTC departments of representative colleges and universities. Both panel and outside review comments aided materially in the final revision of the volume for publication. The Editor in Chief, Mr. Friedman, worked continuously with the contributors throughout the period of preparation and supervised the final editing of the manuscript by staff members of OCMH's Editorial Branch, including its chief, Mr. David Jaffé, and senior editor, Mrs. Loretto C. Stevens.

The forty-seven maps in this volume include five newly prepared by Mr. Mossman and one by Mr. Bell plus forty-one retained from those prepared by Maj. James P. Holly for the 1959 version. The photographs were selected by Miss Ruth A. Phillips, and the index was prepared by Mr. Nicholas J. Anthony.

Although the United States Continental Army Command is charged with setting up the guidelines for the ROTC American Military History course, its officials have gladly accepted the suggestions and comments presented by the historians of this office insofar as preparation of the present work is concerned. The contributors assume full responsibility for what appears in the following pages, including any errors of omission or commission.

Washington, D.C.
2 December 1968

STETSON CONN
Chief Historian

Preface to the Revised Edition

This new edition continues the history of the U.S. Army through the post-Vietnam era. Chapter 28 and the Suggested Readings are entirely new. The Index has been partially revised. The Contributors list (p. v) indicates the authorship of all parts of this textbook. Howell C. Brewer, Jr., and Linda M. Cajka prepared three new maps for the chapter on Vietnam.

Washington, D.C.   MORRIS J. MacGREGOR
15 August 1988   Acting Chief Historian

Preface to the 1996 Edition

This new edition continues the history of the U.S. Army from the post-Vietnam era to the end of the Gulf War. Chapter 29 is entirely new. The index, readings and some post-Vietnam material have been revised to reflect recent developments. Paul Dangel prepared two new maps for the section on the Gulf War in Chapter 29.

Conshohocken, PA   ALBERT A. NOFI
22 February 1996   Editor, 1996 Edition

CHAPTER 1

Introduction

The history of the United States Army lies in the mainstream of modern Western military development. Heir to European traditions, the American Army has both borrowed from and contributed to that main current. Molded by the New World environment, a product of democratic and industrial revolutions, it has at the same time evolved, along with the nation it serves, uniquely. To the present generation of Americans faced by complex challenges to their national security, the role that force and military institutions have played in American history becomes of increasing interest and importance. This volume is an introduction to the story of the U.S. Army, and of American military history, of which that story is an integral part.

What Is Military History?

Narrowly defined, the term *military history* used to connote conflicts in arms—campaigns and battles. In the eighteenth century, when the American Army was born and before the French Revolution introduced the modern concept of the "nation in arms," such eruptions in the Western World usually involved clashes by soldiers of the opposing armies and left the civilian masses largely unaffected. Until the latter part of that century, wars were relatively simple and restricted in area, forces, and objectives. The wars of the French Revolution and of Napoleon became mass conflicts of whole nations in arms. With the spread of the industrial revolution, warfare grew more complex and exerted an ever-increasing influence on society. This new era in warfare coincided with the evolution of the United States as an independent nation. In the first half of the twentieth century the effects of large-scale wars became so pervasive that they were felt not only by the combatant nations but throughout the entire world, now grown more compact. The outcome in those wars was no longer measured in terms of the preservation of national honor or the winning of territory, familiar in eighteenth century warfare, but in terms of national survival. Thus, as warfare in the past two centuries has broadened to involve more and more people and more and more of the energies and resources of society to fight it—or in more recent days, to deter it—the definition has had to be extended to encompass more activities.

Broadly defined, military history lies on the frontier between general history and military art and science. It deals with the confluence and interaction of military affairs with diplomatic, political, social, economic, and intellectual trends in society. To understand it therefore requires some knowledge of both general history and military art. In its American context it represents many interrelated facets. Certainly it involves wars—all kinds of wars. It may surprise Americans, who traditionally have regarded themselves as a peaceable and unmilitary people, to learn that the range of warfare in their national experience has been quite wide, and the incidence quite frequent. Born in a revolution, a violent struggle often considered a prelude to other "peoples' wars," the United States has since endured a bitter Civil War and participated in seven international wars. In American national experience war itself has undergone considerable change and oscillation from one mode to another. The American Revolution was a limited war of the eighteenth century variety; the War of 1812 and the Korean conflict of 1950–53 were two later models of limited conflict. The Civil War introduced the age of total war to which World Wars I and II added their bloody chapters. War cut deeper and deeper into the life of the nation. Since World War II, under the shadow of nuclear weapons that threaten all civilization with annihilation, warfare has returned to earlier forms. Guerrilla wars, foreshadowed in American experience by the long-continuing Indian wars and the Philippine Insurrection of 1899–1902, have come into vogue again and American forces have become engaged in counterinsurgency warfare, notably in Vietnam.

Wars used to be regarded as clearly definable exercises in violence when diplomacy failed and statesmen handed over to soldiers the burden of achieving victory. They were usually marked by formal ceremonies—a declaration at the beginning and a surrender and peace treaty at the end. Since World War II these formalities are no longer the fashion. War and peace have become blurred. Neither in Korea nor in Vietnam was war declared. No peace treaty followed the surrender of Germany in World War II, or the truce in Korea in 1953. While this change in the nature of warfare has affected the conduct of war and the role of the military and society in it, participation in organized violence in all its forms is a component of military history that must be treated. Not only must the traditional three C's of warfare—causes, conduct, and consequences—be studied, but as the line between war and peace becomes more indistinct, the periods between the wars gain in interest to students of military history.

Besides war in the broad sense, there is another major facet that military history must deal with and that military historians of this generation have found more and more integral to their subject. To apply force, armies are organized. Reflecting the national culture and varying in their impact on it, armies are institutions, social entities in themselves. Some armies have close relations with the societies from which they are drawn; others are separate and a class apart. For example, in much of United States history the Army was scattered in frontier posts and physically isolated from the rest of society. But in the period since World War II, as in the founding era, civil-military relations have been close. As institutions, armies take form and character. Their institutional outlines are manifested in a number of ways, some overt, some subtle: their organization and administration, system of training, mode of supply, planning for mobilization and the conduct of war, methods of fighting on the battlefield, weaponry and utilization of technology, system of command and control, selection of manpower and leaders, and relations with the civilian population and authorities. The whole host of policies, doctrines, customs, traditions, values, and practices that have grown up about armies are an important part of the institutional story. All of these facets represent histories in themselves and reflect change in the nature of warfare, technology, the country's internal development, and external responsibilities. A shift in one component will inevitably have impact within the institutional structure. For example, a fundamental change in weaponry, equipment, or technology, be it the adoption of gunpowder, the rifle musket, the airplane, the tank, or the atomic bomb, will affect the traditional modes of fighting and reverberate throughout the institutional framework. The phenomenon of cultural lag evident in other human institutions applies to military organizations too, and some armies have been slower to adopt changes than others, often with fatal results in the test of battle.

While the U.S. Army as a social entity has evolved to meet its primary mission—to fight—in its American institutional context military history must also treat the Army as a social force in peace. From the beginning the Army has played a role in developing the country—in exploring, guarding the frontier, and constructing roads, in engineering, transportation, communication, sanitation and medicine, and in flood control. At the same time the Army has served as a vehicle for social mobility of certain disadvantaged groups—for example, European immigrants in the 1840's and 1850's and Negroes in the 1950's and 1960's. The mixture of the European legacy, native environment, democratic ideals and values, and national experience in war and peace have combined to mold the Army into a distinct institution in American life—a unique blend of professional and civilian elements. Indeed, as Russell F. Weigley, a student of the Army's institutional history, has well expressed it, the story of the American Army is really a history of "two armies"—"a Regular Army of professional soldiers and a citizen army of various components variously known as militia, National Guards, Organized Reserves, selectees."

It has been said that every generation rewrites its history. Its own needs and problems inevitably make it take fresh looks at its own past for light, understanding, guidance, and alternative courses of action. Nowhere is this necessity more evident than in the field of American military history today— broadly conceived. During most of the national existence of the United States the liberal democratic tradition and geographic isolation combined to subordinate in the public mind the role of force and military institutions in its history. Blessed by relatively weak neighbors on the north and south and safe behind its ocean barriers, the United States could define its security in terms of its own boundaries and frontiers. The military factor in its heritage, birth, and development tended to be discounted. But when scientists began to conquer space and time in the twentieth century, and the European system that had maintained order in the nineteenth century began to crumble under the impact of two world wars, Americans began to find their security bound up with the fate of other countries. The nation that began the twentieth century with a strong sense of security by mid-century began to feel insecure. As George F. Kennan, former director of the Policy Planning Staff of the Department of State, put it, "A country which in 1900 had no thought that its prosperity and way of life could in any way be threatened by the outside world had arrived by 1950 at a point where it seemed to be able to think of little else but this danger." Not since the era of the founding fathers has survival in a dangerous world become such an urgent issue and the foundations of national security of such concern.

Theory and Practice of War

The question of whether warfare should be treated as science or art has long interested students of military affairs. In the eighteenth century, the age of enlightenment, when the systematic study of war began, military theory regarded warfare as "mathematical" and "scientific." A general who knew mathematics and topography, the theorists optimistically maintained, could conduct campaigns with geometrical precision and win wars without bloody battles. The violent shock of Napoleonic warfare put a rude end to the notion of war as a purely scientific or mathematical game. But insofar as the application of physical pressure upon the enemy involves the use of mechanical tools under certain predictable or calculable conditions, it is possible to speak in terms of military science. The systematic application of science to the development of weapons and to technology in general is a comparatively recent development. Since World War II, techniques of research and analysis have been enlisted from scientific fields to make calculations and choices among complex weapon systems and in the management of huge defense programs more exact. Over and above the techniques, the successful conduct of war at all levels of command requires assessing unpredictable variables and taking calculated risks under circumstances for which no precise precedent exists. Since the "fog of war" still holds and wars involve men as well as machines, warfare remains in many ways what it has always been essentially— an art.

Military theorists have long searched for the principles underlying the art of war. They have sought to distill from the great mass of military experience over the centuries simple but fundamental truths to guide commanders through the fog of war. The lists of principles they have evolved have been derived from an analysis of the campaigns and the writings of the great captains of war, such as Caesar, Frederick the Great, Napoleon, von Moltke; occasionally the masters have provided their own set of precepts. Foremost among the analysts have been Jomini, Clausewitz, Ardant duPicq, Mahan, Foch, Douhet, Liddell Hart, and Fuller. Almost 2,500 years ago, in 500 B.C., Sun Tzu, a Chinese general, set down thirteen principles. The axioms range from the Confederate General Nathan B. Forrest's oft-quoted advice, "Git thar fustest with the mostest men," to Napoleon's 115 maxims. The lists differ in emphasis as well as in number. Some theorists have stressed that the battle is all and the defeat of the enemy's armed forces the correct objective; others, that the best path to victory is by indirect methods and approaches, by what has been termed obliquity.

Today, all great nations recognize principles of war and incorporate them in army doctrine. The lists vary from nation to nation. In their modern dress in the Western World, the accepted principles are essentially a post-Napoleonic conception, advanced by Clausewitz, the great Prussian philosopher of war in the early nineteenth century, and his contemporary, Jomini, the well-known French general and theorist. Since the United States shares a common military heritage and a common body of military thought with Europe, American students of war have also sought to reduce the conduct of war to certain essential premises. The United States Army recognizes nine principles and includes them in its *Field Service Regulations*. Their proper application, the Army holds, is essential to the exercise of effective command and to the successful conduct of military operations. The Russians and Chinese have a principle of annihilation and the British a principle of flexibility that do not appear on the American list. Indeed, Mao Tse-tung and his disciples in their philosophy of protracted conflict have given the principles a new twist and have challenged conventional Western doctrine.

Despite differences over their precise number and meaning, principles of war are taught in military schools throughout the world. Some cautions are usually attached to the American Army set. The principles are not absolute and have been successfully violated at times for special reasons that have been carefully considered beforehand. The principles are interrelated. They do not operate with equal force under all circumstances. In particular cases they may reinforce each other or be in conflict. They are applied in combination to specific situations. The combinations will vary according to the factors that influence operations, such as the nature of the terrain, the relative strength of the opposing forces, the effect of weather, and the mission of the command. The art of generalship, consequently, is to be found in the proper application of the principles.

The nine principles are concisely stated as objective, offensive, mass, economy of force, maneuver, unity of command, security, surprise, and simplicity. They are set forth in *Field Manual 100–5* as follows:

Objective. Every military operation must be directed toward a clearly defined, decisive, and attainable objective. The ultimate military objective of war is the destruction of the enemy's armed forces and his will to fight. The objective of each operation must contribute to this ultimate objective. Each intermediate objective must be such that its attainment will most directly, quickly, and economically contribute to the purpose of the operation. The selection of an objective is based upon consideration of the means available, the enemy, and the area of operations. Every commander must understand and clearly define his objective and consider each contemplated action in light thereof.

Offensive. Offensive action is necessary to achieve decisive results and to maintain freedom of action. It permits the commander to exercise initiative and impose his will upon the enemy; to set the pace and determine the course of battle; to exploit enemy weaknesses and rapidly changing situations, and to meet unexpected developments. The defensive may be forced on the commander, but it should be deliberately adopted only as a temporary expedient while awaiting an opportunity for offensive action or for the purpose of economizing forces on a front where a decision is not sought. Even on the defensive the commander seeks every opportunity to seize the initiative and achieve decisive results by offensive action.

Mass. Superior combat power must be concentrated at the critical time and place for a decisive purpose. Superiority results from the proper combination of the elements of combat power. Proper application of the principle of mass, in conjunction with the other principles of war, may permit numerically inferior forces to achieve decisive combat superiority.

Economy of Force. Skillful and prudent use of combat power will enable the commander to accomplish the mission with minimum expenditure of resources. This principle is the corollary of the principle of mass. It does not imply husbanding but rather the measured allocation of available combat power to the primary task as well as secondary tasks such as limited attacks, the defense, deception, or even retrograde action in order to insure sufficient combat power at the point of decision.

Maneuver. Maneuver is an essential ingredient of combat power. It contributes materially in exploiting successes and in preserving freedom of action and reducing vulnerability. The object of maneuver is to dispose a force in such a manner as to place the enemy at a relative disadvantage and thus achieve results which would otherwise be more costly in men and materiel. Successful maneuver requires flexibility in organization, administrative support, and command and control. It is the antithesis of permanence of location and implies avoidance of stereotyped patterns of operation.

Unity of Command. The decisive application of full combat power requires unity of command. Unity of command obtains unity of effort by the coordinated action of all forces toward a common goal. While coordination may be attained by cooperation, it is best achieved by vesting a single commander with the requisite authority.

Security. Security is essential to the preservation of combat power. Security is achieved by measures taken to prevent surprise, preserve freedom of action, and deny the enemy information of friendly forces. Since risk is inherent in war, application of the principle of security does not imply undue caution and the avoidance of calculated risk. Security frequently is enhanced by bold seizure and retention of the initiative, which denies the enemy the opportunity to interfere.

Surprise. Surprise can decisively shift the balance of combat power. By surprise, success out of proportion to the effort expended may be obtained. Surprise results from striking an enemy at a time, place, and in a manner for which he is not prepared. It is not essential that the enemy be taken unaware but only that he becomes aware too late to react effectively. Factors contributing to surprise include speed, deception, application of unexpected combat power, effective intelligence and counterintelligences, to include communication and electronic security, and variations in tactics and methods of operation.

Simplicity. Simplicity contributes to successful operations. Direct, simple plans and clear, concise orders minimize misunderstanding and confusion. If other factors are equal, the simplest plan is preferred.

Many examples of the successful employment or of the violation of these principles can be cited in American military history and illustrations will be given in appropriate places in the text. Each case requires careful study in its own context. Here, we may note briefly that the proper objective has often eluded commanders in war. The British in the American Revolution, for example, were never clear as to what their prime objective was, whether to capture strategic positions, to destroy the Continental Army, or simply to try by an appropriate show of force to woo the Americans back to their allegiance to the Crown. As a result, their victories over Washington's army in the field seldom had much meaning. Not until after many years of fighting the elusive Seminoles in the Florida swamps did Col. William J. Worth realize that the destruction of their villages and sources of supply would end the conflict. In the Civil War the North's infatuation with the "On to Richmond" strategy long obscured what proved to be the real objective, the destruction of the enemy forces and control of the principal lines of communications. In the limited wars since 1945, however, the United States has sought to achieve objectives short of the total destruction of the enemy or his productive capacity. The traditional concept of "victory" and "winning" has taken on a different meaning in the new political context of warfare in the nuclear age. Force has been applied with restraint. Fresh support has been given to Clausewitz' reminder that a successful war is one in which the political objectives for which it is waged are achieved by suitable means and at appropriate cost.

No principle has been more ingrained in American military thinking than the belief that only offensive action can achieve decisive results. Many examples can be cited: Washington's brilliant attacks at Trenton, Princeton, and Yorktown, Grant's and Sherman's campaigns of 1864–65, Pershing's insistence on attack by American units in France in 1918, and Eisenhower's invasion of Normandy in 1944. But opponents of the principle argue that the defense has in certain cases more advantages than the offensive. In Sir Edward Creasy's *The Fifteen Decisive Battles of the World,* ten were won by the defending commander. Some of the most notable actions in American military history have involved the defense—Jackson's stand at New Orleans, the retreat of Chief Joseph and the Nez Perces, McAuliffe at Bastogne, and Ridgway's spoiling tactics on the stabilized front in Korea.

The principle of mass, often called concentration, probably offers more examples of successful and unsuccessful application than any other. Washington at Trenton and Eisenhower in Normandy are two obvious illustrations of how application resulted in success. Conversely, Lee on the second day at Gettysburg, Custer at the Little Bighorn, the Huertgen Forest battle in Germany in World War II, and the Viet Cong in the Ia Drang valley battle show a failure to apply the proper amount of force at the proper place and time. No principle has been more successfully violated by great generals than that of mass. Lee's division of his army at Chancellorsville is a classic case. However inadvertent, dispersal, not concentration, during American airborne operations in Sicily and Normandy during World War II led to a disruption of German communications and tactics. Indeed, the one airborne landing deemed a virtual failure, in Operation MARKET-GARDEN in the Netherlands in 1944, involved the greatest concentration of troops.

The successful application of economy of force has usually resulted in brilliant gains. Lee's battle at Chancellorsville, MacArthur's bypassing of the Japanese stronghold at Rabaul in World War II, and his decision in Korea not to reinforce in great strength Lt. Gen. Walton H. Walker's troops on the Pusan perimeter in order to conserve forces for the Inch'on landing are notable cases in point. No principle of war is probably more important today, in this era of limited war, than restraint in the use of force.

No one would deny the necessity of maneuver to success in military operations. Brilliant examples have occurred throughout American military history: Morgan at Cowpens, Scott at Cerro Gordo, Grant before Vicksburg, Eisenhower in Normandy, Patton's shift of the Third Army's offensive from an east-west axis into Germany to a north-south axis into Luxembourg during the Battle of the Bulge, and MacArthur at Inch'on. Attempts at direct assault, rather than maneuver, have often led to bloody and indecisive actions: Gage at Bunker Hill, Burnside at Fredericksburg, Hodges in the Huertgen Forest. Even a successful maneuver can be subject to criticism—witness the controversy over Eisenhower's decision to advance across Europe along a continuous broad front rather than permit one of his major forces to thrust deep into Germany.

Unity of command was successfully achieved for the Union under Grant in 1864, for the Allies under Marshal Foch in World War I, and for the Allied forces under General Eisenhower in the European Theater of Operations in World War II. Divided command of British forces in America played an important role in leading to the surrender at Saratoga. The lack of unity of command or even effective co-operation between Admiral Halsey's Third Fleet and MacArthur's landing force in Leyte might have cost American forces dearly in 1944. The interservice conflicts between MacArthur and Nimitz during World War II indicate that this principle can in some respects be violated and military victory gained. For the armchair critic, an interesting case in divided command was MacArthur's failure to place X Corps of the United Nations forces under the command of the Eighth Army in Korea during the fall and early winter of 1950.

Security and surprise are obvious necessities and closely related. The Antietam battle saw security violations on both sides—by Lee whose courier allowed the operations plan to fall into Union hands and by McClellan who failed to reconnoiter the approaches to the battlefield before the action took place. Elaborate security precautions taken by the Allies before the Normandy invasion permitted them to deceive the Germans as to the precise time and place of the attack. The success of the Chinese Communist intervention in Korea resulted both from a United Nations' security failure and from a carefully planned deception by the Communist forces. From the time Washington trapped the Hessians at Trenton to the time MacArthur caught the Koreans unaware at Inch'on the principle of surprise has been an effective weapon of commanders. But there have been occasions when commanders have openly flaunted their power in order to demoralize an enemy. Thus, Henry Bouquet marched into the Ohio country in 1764 with a show of British power to impress the Indians engaged in the Pontiac conspiracy.

Of all the principles of war none is now probably harder to follow above the battalion level than the principle of simplicity. Modern warfare, involving mechanization, electronic equipment, and airborne and seaborne operations, is inherently not simple. Even the ostensibly easy movement of a small tank-infantry-artillery team cannot be termed "simple." In counterinsurgency operations the integration of military with political, economic, sociological, and psychological factors often leads to a high degree of complexity. But operations sometimes can become too complex for the commanders to execute. Washington's plan for the attack on the British at Germantown in 1777, involving convergence of four columns of inexperienced troops moving over different roads at night, proved too complicated for successful execution.

The growing complexity and variety of modern warfare have led students of military affairs to take a fresh look at the principles. Since World War II a debate has been raging in military literature over the precise meaning and application of the principles, a debate fed by the new circumstances of nuclear and counterinsurgency warfare. The discussion revolves around three major questions: Are the present principles too exclusive? Are they too inclusive? Does modern insurgent and nuclear warfare make them obsolete? To some extent this is a debate over semantics. The defenders point out that the principles are as valid in modern as in ancient warfare; that each age must make its own applications of the "fundamental truths." Critics argue that they are not immutable scientific laws of universal applicability; that they require constant re-examination; that no two military situations are ever completely alike; that the principles are merely methods and common-sense procedures adopted by great captains in the past and that changes in the conditions of war alter their relative importance; that the new weapons have destroyed whatever infallibility remained; that the principles are not pat formulas for victories to be followed rigidly. They argue that the new conditions of warfare do not allow for the traditional Napoleonic concepts embodied in the principles; that limited conflicts restrict the principles of the offensive and the objective; that in any future nuclear conflict the principle of mass will be severely limited and that dispersion, not concentration of men and equipment, will become critical on the battlefield. The principles, these critics conclude, are no substitute for imaginative thinking, logical analysis, broad professional knowledge, and highly developed qualities of leadership.

Perhaps the key point to be remembered, whatever the outcome of the present debate among the theorists, is that war remains fundamentally an art. Dennis Hart Mahan, famed West Point professor and teacher of the Civil War generals, put it well: "In war, as in every other art based upon settled principles, there are exceptions to all general rules. It is in discovering these cases that the talent of the general is shown." Even the defenders of the principles stress that the art of war lies in their interpretation and application. Within limits, the principles of war nevertheless remain a useful tool for analysis, a general frame of reference, and a checklist, for examining past campaigns. Themselves an inheritance from the past, these adages offer no substitute for real historical inquiry or for thinking and action on the part of the officer. They represent generalizations and premises rather than fixed immutable rules. They provide general guides to conduct, guides that on the whole have in the past led to military success. Nuclear and counterinsurgency operations undoubtedly will demand a modification or application different from so-called conventional warfare. As in the past, the victorious captain will have to adapt concepts or improvise others most suitable to the particular circumstances facing him.

All theorists agree that, in the final analysis, the art of war is what men make it. To quote Mahan again, "No soldier who has made himself conversant with the resources of his art, will allow himself to be trammelled by an exclusive system." He must be flexible. He must learn to deal with men. Napoleon stated that in war, "The moral is to the physical as three to one." The ability to penetrate the fog of war and make the correct decision is the heart of leadership. Indeed, flexibility and leadership might well be added as tenth and eleventh principles, basic concepts inherent in all the others. It is not surprising therefore that the qualities that make for good leadership have long interested the Army and that a whole body of literature has grown up about the theoretical and practical foundations of this phase of the military art.

The military profession, like other professions, has developed its own language to make for easy communication. Aside from the principles of war, it is useful for the student of military history to become familiar with other terms commonly encountered in the literature. In the theory of warfare, strategy and tactics have usually been put into separate categories. Strategy deals with both the preparation for and the waging of war and has often been defined as the art of projecting and directing campaigns. To tactics, its close partner, military jargon has reserved the art of executing plans and handling troops in battle. Strategy is usually regarded as the prelude to the battlefield; tactics the action on the battlefield. As society and warfare have grown more complex, the term *strategy* has been gradually broadened from its eighteenth century connotation as the "art of the general," far beyond its original, narrow military meaning. In the nineteenth century, and even more in the twentieth, distinctions began to be blurred between strategy as a purely military phenomenon and national strategy of a broader variety involving a combination of political, economic, technological, and psychological factors, along with the military elements, in the management of national policy. As a result, the term *grand strategy* (or *higher strategy*) has come to connote the art of employing all the resources of a nation, or coalition of nations, to achieve the objects of war (and peace). The broad policy decisions governing the over-all conduct of war, or its deterrence, are the prerogative of the chief of state and his principal advisers. The strategist, whether in the narrower or broader sense, deals in many uncertainties and his art is the art of the calculated risk. At the opposite end of the scale are *minor tactics,* the term used to describe the maneuver of small units.

Despite distinctions in theory, strategy and tactics cannot always be easily separated in practice. The language of strategic maneuver—putting one's army into the most favorable position to engage the enemy and depriving the enemy of freedom of movement—is also largely the language of tactics. Thus, *envelopment* is an attack on an enemy's flank and toward his rear, usually accompanied by an attack on his front. A *turning movement* is a wide enveloping maneuver, passing around the side of the enemy's main forces and attacking him from the rear. *Double envelopment* involves an attack on both flanks of the enemy while his center is held in check. A *penetration* is an attack on the enemy's front by driving a wedge into it or piercing it completely. It may be followed by an enveloping attack on one or both flanks. In connection with these four basic forms of attack, two terms often are used: *main effort*—concentrating on the critical point in the enemy's position—and *holding attack*—pinning down the remainder of the enemy. To *refuse* a flank is to draw the flank of a line or command to the rear in order to prevent an envelopment by an enemy.

Linking strategy and tactics and attracting more and more attention among the theorists is a third field, *logistics,* simply defined as the art of planning and carrying out the movement and maintenance of forces. This field too has been greatly broadened as warfare has expanded and grown more technological and complex. Logistics deals with the deployment of military forces and their equipment to the area of war, and with innumerable services, such as feeding, clothing, supplying, transporting, and housing troops. The connecting links, the network of railways, waterways, roads, and air routes by which an armed force in the field is reinforced and supplied from its base of operations in the home or friendly area, are called the *lines of communications.* The *theater of operations* comprises the combat zone as well as the supply and administration area directly connected with military operations.

In modern warfare the major divisions of the military art—strategy, logistics, and tactics—are closely interdependent. One field merges into the other, and changes in one inevitably lead to changes in the others. Sometimes weapons have appeared on the battlefield before military theory and planning have fully absorbed them, and adjustments throughout the art have been slow to follow. In the Civil War, for example, the widespread use of the rifle musket upset the relation among the combat arms; the range and accuracy of these weapons in the hands of defending infantry shattered the effectiveness of the concentrated attack in which Napoleonic strategy culminated. But, as often has been observed in the history of warfare, armaments and weapons are more readily changed than ideas. Napoleon's principles continued to be held, sometimes with disastrous consequences on the battlefield. An oft-cited case of the appalling repercussions of holding concepts too long or rigidly is the French offensive spirit in World War I. It is small wonder in light of the carnage of World Wars I and II that the coming of the atomic bomb has caused strategy in the Western World to focus on the deterrence of war and fostered tactics to seek means of dispersal on the battlefield.

It is clear that in modern warfare theory and practice have not always been the same. Wars, particularly in the great coalition conflicts of the twentieth century, are simply not run by rules or theories. Once joined, modern war has had a way of breeding its own strategy, tactics, and weapons. For successful commanders more than ever flexibility has become the only sure guide. World War I, beginning as a war of mass offensives, was a classic case of arrested strategy requiring new tactics and weapons to dig the war out of the trenches. Anglo-American strategy against Germany in World War II proved a compromise of the theory of mass and concentration upheld by the U.S. Army and Winston Churchill's peripheral theory. Despite attention to "principles," Allied strategy in World War II was a hybrid product hammered out largely on the "anvil of necessity." In war, moreover, military strategy varies with political direction and goals. In this vein Clausewitz had argued that military strategy must respond to national policy and political aims. Perhaps he best summed up the political context of modern war in his assertion, "War is not merely a political act, but also a real political instrument, a continuation of policy carried out by other means." "War," he concluded, "admittedly has its own grammar, but not its own logic."

The American Military System

To organize for national security, each nation adopts the military system most suited to its culture, needs, and policies. Some nations have traditionally tended to concentrate significant segments of their economy on the maintenance of huge military forces and to determine national policies largely in terms of their military implications. While the United States shares with Europe a legacy of military thought and practice, whose roots lie deep in the past, its military system has grown out of its own national experience.

The form of government, the traditions of the people, the nature of the country, and its geographical position in relation to other powers have had a profound influence upon American military institutions. In turn, those institutions are a reflection of the American culture and way of life. Indeed, the Army is essentially an institutional form adapted by American society to meet military requirements. The American military system has been developed so as to place a minimum burden upon the people and give the nation a reasonable defense without sacrificing its fundamental values. From the beginning, the United States has sought to reconcile individual liberty with national security without becoming a nation in arms.

Chief among the characteristics of American culture that have a bearing on its military system are the value placed upon human beings as individuals; life, liberty, and the pursuit of happiness and peace as basic goals; the desire to achieve decisive results quickly; a talent for the design and use of machinery; highly developed productive capacity and managerial skills; and great material wealth. These characteristics underline the American penchant for absolutes— the sharp distinction between war and peace, the insistence on complete victory and on short, decisive, offensive action in warfare. They help account for the traditional American attitude toward war as an aberration in which the bully who disturbed the peace must be soundly and quickly thrashed so that American society can return to normality. They also point to the vital importance of public opinion in a democracy in raising and supporting armed forces and to the reason why wars against disturbers of the peace are apt to take on the character of moral crusades. They help explain the traditional rhythm of sharp expansion of the armed forces in wartime and precipitate contraction immediately thereafter.

In turn, these characteristics and attitudes have shaped the Army in its organizational relationships and in its philosophy of operations. They account also for such distinctive Army features as the development of great mechanical power, the stress on firepower rather than sheer manpower, and the concentration on victory by offensive operations.

Throughout its existence the United States has been compelled to provide for military security. The degree to which the provisions were made has varied with the nature and magnitude of the particular threat. Until technology reduced the distance separating the United States from the Old World, the forces in being could be, and were, small. At the same time the deep-seated American reluctance to devote a large proportion of the national wealth to the support of a standing military force played an important part in the development of a system based upon a small professional nucleus that could be expanded in time of need by the induction of citizen soldiers. This initial system took advantage of the ocean barriers favoring the United States and the balance of power existing in Europe. In accord with Washington's injunction, it held forth the possibility of acquiring greater strength by temporary alliances in extraordinary emergencies. Since World War II the rise of new foes and the destruction of the balance of power in Europe and the Far East have caused a drastic change in the American military system. Accordingly, the United States now maintains large air, land, and sea forces ready for immediate action and for co-operation with forces of its many allies.

The American Army as it exists today has evolved through a historical process paralleling the social, economic, and political development of the United States. Its evolution may in general be divided into three periods: colonial, continental expansion, and overseas operations. During the colonial period (1607-1775) the militia of the various colonies defended the settlers while they were establishing themselves in America, and helped England eliminate the French from North America. This was the period of roots and origins, of the transplanting of military institutions from abroad, particularly from England, and of their modification in the New World. During the era of continental expansion (1775-1898) the militia and volunteers and the Continental Army and its successor, the Regular Army, played a significant role in bringing the United States into being, in winning important extensions of national territory, in saving the nation from internal destruction, and in exploring, policing, and governing vast regions of the west. This was the period of national independence and consolidation. In the wars of this era, the Army's activities were concentrated on problems vital to the establishment, maintenance, and expansion of a nation based on new concepts of individual freedom and representative government. Only once in this period did the Army fight with the help of allies—during the Revolutionary War—and then on a temporary basis.

The year 1898, which saw the outbreak of the Spanish-American War, the symbol of "looking outward," was an important turning point. It marked the emergence of the United States as a world power. In the third period (1898 to the present) the Army has carried the flag to the four corners of the earth. Its assigned role has been to serve as a principal instrument for promoting American policies and American interests overseas and protecting the nation against the menace of tyrannical power. In the two great world wars of the twentieth century, and in Korea and Vietnam, it has fought alongside associated

or allied nations, and in the increasing complexity of modern war its operations have become inseparably intertwined with those of the Navy and the
Air Force. In the history of the nation and the Army in the twentieth century,
World War II marked an important dividing line whose full implications are
still not entirely clear. Since World War II the revolution in the strategic
position of the United States, its emergence as leader of the free world and
of allies in military combination, the cold war, and the nuclear age, have
presented unprecedented challenges to traditional American concepts and
institutions in national security. Under the nuclear threat the spectrum of
war has broadened and theorists have been engaged in great debate on the
future of war and military institutions. Berlin, Korea, Cuba, and Vietnam
are symbols of the pressures confronting the nation and its army in the new
phase of world power, in which the role of force appears to be taking on new
meaning and new functions.

The Whatever its future contribution, it is as an instrument of force—the
primary mission of an army—that the United States Army has played its
major role in American history. From desperate hand-to-hand engagements
with savages to vast battles with motorized and armored forces, from revolutionary war to world war, civil to foreign war, guerrilla to counterguerrilla
war, from hot to cold war, the Army has figured prominently in the nation's
conflicts. And the Army has also made important contributions to the general
welfare and to the preservation of domestic order in peacetime.

The leaders of the U.S. Army have consistently adhered to the principle
basic in the American military system, that the Army is an instrument of civilian
authority. This principle, firmly established in practice by General Washington
during the Revolutionary War, was embodied in the Constitution of the United
States as a fundamental safeguard of republican institutions. The supremacy
of civilian authority is the American solution to the problem of forestalling
any possible danger from a standing army. Until recently, American military
policy has also been based upon the maintenance of very small Regular forces
and reliance on citizen soldiers in case of national emergency. In the colonial
period almost every able-bodied man was a member of the militia and could
be called out in case of need, and this system continued in force at least
theoretically during the first century of national existence. It was usually,
nonetheless, the citizen volunteer who swelled the Army's ranks in earlier
wars. Both the militia and the volunteer principle gave way in the wars of
the twentieth century to the idea of universal obligation for military duty
under selective service in time of national emergency.

In an age when forces in being may determine the outcome of a war or an emergency action in peacetime, the principle of reliance on masses of citizen soldiers appears to be giving way to the concept of large, efficient professional forces supported by a selected body of trained reserves. The increasing complications of modern warfare, the great rapidity with which attacks can be launched with modern weapons, and the extensive overseas commitments of the United States have negated the traditional American habit of preparing for wars after they have begun. But whatever the future composition of the Army, it will still have to incorporate the historic principle, ingrained in the nation's military system, of being representative of the people and subject to civilian control.

To be truly progressive, a military system, like most evolving human institutions, must operate in two planes of time, the present and the future. In the field of national security, the choices in the twentieth century have never been easy and in a world in ferment since the end of World War II are likely to be crucial. The citizen and the soldier cannot know what path to follow unless they are aware of the breadth of alternatives that have been accepted or rejected in the past. Santayana's dictum that those who ignore the past are condemned to repeat its mistakes is nowhere more apt than in military history. At the same time the blend of the historical with the military art reinforces the caution that no two periods or operations are precisely alike, that the easy analogy and the false comparison must be avoided, that the past must be interpreted in proper context and depth, and that the soldier must not "be trammelled by any exclusive system." For the fledgling officer, as well as the citizen, American military history provides a laboratory of experience, an accumulation of continuities and disparities, a rich storehouse of courage, sacrifice, and knowledge, and a source of inspiration and wisdom. It is to the multifaceted story of the American Army—how it originated and developed, and what it contributed to the nation in war and peace—that we now turn.

CHAPTER 2

The Beginnings

The United States as a nation was, in its origins, a product of English expansion in the New World in the seventeenth and eighteenth centuries—a part of the general outward thrust of western European peoples in this epoch. British people and institutions, transplanted to a virgin continent and mixed with people of different origins, underwent changes that eventually produced a distinctive American culture. In no area was the interaction of the two influences—European heredity and American environment—more apparent than in the shaping of the military institutions of the new nation.

The European Heritage

The European military heritage reaches far back into the dim recesses of history. Many centuries before the birth of Christ, organized armies under formal discipline and employing definite systems of battlefield tactics appeared in the empires of the Near East, rivaling in numbers and in the scope of their conflicts anything that was to appear in the Western World before the nineteenth century. In the fourth century B.C., Alexander the Great of Macedonia brought all these empires and dominions, in fact most of civilization known to the Western World, under his suzerainty in a series of rapid military conquests. In so doing, he carried to the highest point of development the art of war as it was practiced in the Greek city-states. He utilized the phalanx—a solid mass infantry formation using pikes as its cutting edge—as the Greeks had long done, but put far greater emphasis on heavy cavalry and contingents of archers and slingers to increase the maneuverability of his armies.

The Romans eventually fell heir to most of Alexander's empire and extended their conquests westward and northward to include present-day Spain, France, Belgium, and England, bringing these areas within the pale of Roman civilization. The Romans built on the achievements of Alexander and brought the art of war to its zenith in the ancient world. They perfected, in the legion, a tactical military unit of great maneuverability comparable in some respects to the modern division, performed remarkable feats of military engineering, and developed elaborate systems of fortification and siegecraft.

For all their achievements, the Romans made no real progress in the development of new weapons, and Roman military institutions, like Roman political organization and economy, underwent progressive decay after the second century A.D. The Roman Empire in the west was succeeded first by a congeries of barbarian kingdoms and eventually by a highly decentralized political system known as feudalism, under which a multitude of warring nobles exercised authority over local areas of varying size. The art of war underwent profound change with the armored knight on horseback succeeding to the battlefield supremacy that, under the Greeks and Romans, had belonged to disciplined formations of infantry. Society in the Middle Ages was highly stratified, and a rigid division existed between the knightly or ruling noble class and the great mass of peasants who tilled the soil, most of them as serfs bound to the nobles' estates. Warfare became for the most part a monopoly of the ruling classes, for only men of substance could afford horse and armor. Every knight owed a certain number of days of military service to his lord each year in a hierarchical or pyramid arrangement, the king at the apex and the great mass of lesser knights forming the base. But lords who were strong enough defied their superiors. Fortified castles with moat and drawbridge, built on commanding points of terrain, furnished sanctuaries where lesser lords with inferior forces could defy more powerful opponents.

Wherever freemen were found, nonetheless, in town or countryside, they continued to bear arms on occasion as infantry, often as despised adjuncts to armies composed of heavy cavalry. This yeoman class was always stronger in England than on the Continent, except in such remote or mountainous areas as Switzerland and the Scandinavian countries. Even after the Norman conquest had brought feudal institutions to England, the ancient Saxon tradition of the fyrd that required every freeman between sixteen and sixty to bear arms in defense of his country remained alive. In 1181 the English King Henry II declared in his Assize of Arms that every freeman should keep and "bear these arms in his [the king's] service according to his order and in allegiance to the lord King and his realm."

Vestiges of feudal institutions survived well into the twentieth century, nowhere more prominently than in European military organizations where the old feudal nobility long dominated the officer ranks and continued its traditions of honor and chivalry. At the other end of the scale, the militia system, so prominent in British and American history, owed much to medieval precedents, for the Saxon fyrd and Henry II's Assize of Arms underlay the militia tradition transplanted from England to America.

Between the fourteenth and sixteenth centuries the feudal order as the basic political organization of European society gave way gradually to new national states under the dynastic rule of royal families. The growth of towns with their merchant and artisan classes and the consequent appearance of a money economy enabled ambitious kings to levy taxes and borrow money to raise and support military forces and to unify and rule their kingdoms. The Protestant Reformation shattered the religious unity of Western Christendom. A long series of bloody wars ensued in which the bitter animosity of Protestant and Catholic was inextricably mixed with dynastic and national ambition in provoking conflict.

Changes in military organization, weapons, and tactics went hand in hand with political, social, and economic change. In the later Middle Ages formations of disciplined infantry using longbow, crossbow, pike, and halberd (a long-handled ax with a pike head at the end), reasserted their superiority on the battlefield. The introduction of gunpowder in the fourteenth century began a process of technological change in weapons that was to enhance that superiority; more immediately, gunpowder was used in crude artillery to batter down the walls of medieval castles. The age of the armored knight and the castle gave way to an age of mercenary infantry.

In the religious and dynastic wars of the sixteenth and seventeenth centuries, as mercenary armies came more and more to be national armies, various weapons employing gunpowder gradually replaced pike and halberd as the standard infantry weapons, and armor gradually disappeared from the bodies of both infantry and cavalry soldiers. At first musketeers were employed alongside pikemen in square formations, the pikemen protecting the musketeers while they reloaded. As the wheel lock musket succeeded the harquebus as a shoulder arm and the flintlock in turn supplanted the wheel lock, armies came to rely less and less on the pike, more and more on firepower delivered by muskets. By 1700, with the invention of a socket bayonet that could be fitted onto the end of the flintlock musket without plugging the barrel, the pike disappeared entirely and along with it the helmet and body armor that had primarily been designed for protection against pikes. Meanwhile, commanders learned to maneuver large bodies of troops on the battlefield and to employ infantry, cavalry, and artillery in combination. National armies composed of professional soldiers came once again to resemble the imperial forces that had served Alexander the Great and the Roman emperors.

In the destructive Thirty Years' War in Germany (1618–48), religious passions finally ran their course. European warfare would henceforth be a matter of clashes of dynastic and national rather than local or religious interests.

After the chaos and destruction that had attended the religious wars, rulers and ruling classes in all countries sought stability and order. Beginning with the wars of Louis XIV of France in 1660, dynastic rivalries were to be fought out by professional armies within the framework of an established order which, in its essentials, none sought to disturb. The eighteenth century European military system that resulted constituted an important part of the world environment in the period the United States came into being.

Eighteenth Century European Warfare

In contrast to the great world wars of the twentieth century, eighteenth century warfare was limited in character, fought by rival states for restricted territorial gains and not for the subjugation of whole peoples or nations. It was conducted by professional armies and navies without the mobilization of men, economic resources, and popular opinion of entire nations that has characterized twentieth century war, and without the passion and hatred of the religious wars. Except in areas where military operations took place, the people in the warring nations carried on their everyday life as usual.

The professional armies employed in this "formal" warfare reflected the society from which they sprang. Although Europe's titled nobles no longer exercised political power independent of their kings, they remained the dominant privileged class, proprietors of the great estates and leaders of the national armies. The great masses of people remained for the most part without property or voice in the government, either tilling the soil on the nobles' estates or working in the shops and handicraft industries in the towns. Absolute monarchy was the prevailing form of government in every European country save England and certain smaller states on the Continent. In England, where the constitutional power of Parliament had been successfully established over the king, Parliament was by no means a democratic institution but one controlled by the landed gentry and wealthy merchants.

The military distinction nobles had formerly found in leading their own knights in battle they now sought as officers in the armies of their respective kings. Princes, counts, earls, marquises, and barons, men who held position by hereditary right, royal favor, or purchase, filled the higher commands, while "gentlemen" of lesser rank usually served as captains and lieutenants. Advancement to higher ranks depended as much on wealth and influence at court as on demonstrated merit on the battlefield. Eighteenth century officers were hardly professionals in the modern sense of the word, for they might well first enter the service as mere boys through inheritance or purchase of a commission, and, except for technical specialists in artillery and engineering, they were not required to attend a military school to train for their duties.

As the officers came from the highest classes, so the men in the ranks came from the lowest. They were normally recruited for long terms of service, sometimes by force, from among the peasants and the urban unemployed, and more than a sprinkling of paupers, ne'er-do-wells, convicts, and drifters were in the ranks. Since recruiting extended across international boundaries, foreign mercenaries formed part of every European army. Discipline, not patriotic motivation, was the main reliance for making these men fight. Penalties for even minor offenses ran as high as a thousand lashes, and executions by hanging or firing squad were frequent. The habit of obedience inculcated on the drill ground carried over into battle where, it has often been said, the men advanced because they preferred the uncertainties of combat to the certainty of death if orders were disobeyed.

Most of the significant European wars of the period were fought over terrain that was open, relatively flat, and thickly populated. Normally, fighting took place only during favorable weather and during daylight hours; rain or darkness quickly called a halt to a battle, and by December opposing armies usually retired to winter quarters where they awaited spring to resume hostilities. Road and river transportation systems were, for the time, highly developed, facilitating the movement of men and supplies. Food for men and forage for horses were usually available in the areas of military operations, but all supplies were customarily obtained by systematic and regular procedures, not by indiscriminate plunder. Each nation set up a series of fortresses or magazines along the line of march of its army in which replacement supplies and foodstuffs could be stored.

Eighteenth century armies were composed predominantly of infantry, with cavalry and artillery as supporting elements. Because battles were usually fought in open country, cavalry could be employed to full advantage. As for artillery, it was used in both attack and defense, either in campaigns of maneuver or in siege warfare. Some eighteenth century commanders used the three arms skillfully in combination, but it was the clash of infantry that usually decided the issue. In the eighteenth century infantry was truly the "Queen of Battle."

The standard infantry weapon of the time was the flintlock musket with bayonet. Probably the most famous model was Brown Bess, the one used in the British Army. Brown Bess had a smoothbore barrel 3 feet 8 inches long with a 14-inch bayonet and fired a smooth lead ball about three-quarters of an inch in diameter. The musket was highly inaccurate since the barrel had no rifling and the charge necessarily fitted loosely, permitting the escape of gas and reducing the effect of the propelling charge. It misfired occasionally and was useless when the powder in the priming pan got wet. The rate of fire was, at best, about three rounds per minute. When the ball hit within its effective range, 150 to 200 yards, its impact was terrific, tearing ghastly holes in flesh and shattering bone, but the inaccuracy of the weapon practically precluded its use, even for volley fire, at ranges greater than 50 to 100 yards. The inefficiency of the smoothbore musket as a firearm made its attached bayonet almost as important as its firepower, and infantry relied on the bayonet for shock action against an enemy softened by musketry fire.

Cavalrymen were variously armed with pistol and lance, carbine and sword, depending on the country and the time. Pistol and carbine were discharged at close range against the ranks of opposing infantry or cavalry, while lance and sword were used for close-in shock action.

There were many different kinds of artillery. The larger pieces were mainly for siege warfare and were relatively immobile. Artillery used in the field was lighter and mounted on wheeled carriages pulled by men or horses. Whether siege or field, these artillery pieces were, like the muskets, smoothbore muzzle-loaders, very limited in range and highly inaccurate. Loading and firing were even slower than in the case of the musket, for the cannon barrel had to be swabbed out after each round to prevent any residue of burning powder from causing a premature explosion. There was no traverse and the whole carriage had to be moved to change the direction of fire. Cannon fired mainly solid iron balls, or at shorter ranges, grapeshot and canister. Grapeshot was a cluster of small iron balls attached to a central system (thus resembling a bunch of grapes) and dispersed by the explosion of a propellent charge; canister consisted of loose pellets placed in a can and when fired had even greater dispersion than grape.

The nature of the soldiers, their weapons, and the terrain go far to explain the tactics used. These tactics were usually designated *linear* tactics to distinguish them from earlier mass formations such as the Spanish Square and the column formations employed later by Napoleon. Linear tactics were first used by Gustavus Adolphus, the Swedish king and military innovator, in the Thirty Years' War, and they came into general use in European armies in the later dynastic wars of Louis XIV of France with the invention of the socket bayonet. Frederick the Great of Prussia carried them to their ultimate state of perfection, and his armies were the most methodically ordered in Europe. In the mid-eighteenth century the Frederician system was the model that others imitated.

In the employment of linear tactics, troops marched onto the battlefield in columns and then deployed into line. A line consisted of a number of battalions or regiments—the terms were then practically synonymous—formed three or more ranks deep. In the ranks the men stood shoulder to shoulder and delivered their fire. Loading, firing, and bayonet charge were all performed at command in a drill involving many separate motions. Firing, insofar as officers were able to maintain rigid discipline, was entirely by volley, the purpose being to achieve the greatest mass of firepower over a given area. The goal was always the "perfect volley." Individual, aimed fire, given the characteristics of the flintlock musket, was deemed to be of little value.

Artillery was deployed in the line with the infantry, cavalry on the flanks or in the rear. Usually commanders also kept an infantry force in reserve for use at a critical point in the battle. In the traditional eighteenth century battle, both forces would be drawn up in similar formation, and the battle would be opened by artillery fire from both sides. In the midst of this fire, the attacking infantry would move forward, maintaining the rigid linear formation in which it was trained, stopping as frequently as necessary to dress its lines. At a range of 50 to 100 yards, the attacking line would halt on the command of its officers. At a second command, a volley would be fired and answered by the opposing line; or there might be a great deal of jockeying over who should fire first, for it was considered an advantage to take, not to give, the first volley and to deliver one's own answering volley at closer range. In any case, the exchange of volleys would continue until one side determined to try to carry the field by bayonet or cavalry charge, usually committing its reserves in this action. If either side was able to carry the field, the victorious commander then sought to execute a successful pursuit, destroying the enemy's army; the defeated commander attempted to withdraw his force in a semblance of order to a fortress or other defensive position, there to re-form and fight another day.

Eighteenth century battles were bloody affairs. At Zorndorf in 1758, for instance, the victorious army of Frederick lost 38 percent of its effectives, the defeated Russians about half of theirs. Professional soldiers were difficult to replace for there was no national reservoir of trained manpower to draw on, and it took two years or more to train a recruit properly. Commanders, therefore, sparing of the blood of their soldiers, sought to avoid battle and to overcome the enemy by a successful series of maneuvers against his line of communications. They also tried to take advantage of terrain features and of fortified positions, to strike by surprise or against the flanks of the enemy, forcing him to realign his forces while fighting, and to employ artillery and cavalry to the greatest advantage in paving the way for infantry assault. Fortresses, normally constructed along the frontiers to impede the advance of an invading army, played a vital role in these maneuvers. It was considered axiomatic that no army could leave a fortress in its rear athwart its line of communications, that any major fortified point had to be reduced by siege. By 1700 the arts of both fortification and siegecraft had been reduced to certain geometric principles by Marshal Sebastien Vauban, a distinguished soldier and engineer in the service of Louis XIV of France.

Vauban's fortresses were star-shaped, with walls partially sunk in the earth and covered with earthen ramparts on which cannon could be mounted; projections or bastions with mutually supporting fields of fire jutted forth from the main walls; a ditch was dug around the whole and a second smaller wall erected in front of it, with earth also sloped against it to absorb the shock of cannon balls.

Vauban's system for attacking this or any other type of fortified position was known as an approach by parallel lines. Once a fortress had been surrounded and outside aid cut off, batteries of siege artillery were brought up within about 600 yards of the fortress walls, the guns being so placed as to rake the lengths of the bastions with enfilade fire; behind these guns the first parallel trench was dug to protect the gunners and assault troops. Zigzag approach trenches were then dug forward about 200 yards to the points from which a second parallel was constructed, then the same process was repeated and a third parallel was dug. Infantry and siege artillery were moved forward as each parallel was completed until, in the third, they were beneath the outer wall of the fortress. From this vantage point the artillery could breach the main wall and the infantry could take the fortress by storm, but usually the fortress commander surrendered to avoid further bloodshed. Under Vauban's system the capture of a fortress by a superior besieging force was usually only a matter of time, and the siege was conducted, often in leisurely fashion, along lines as rigidly fixed as those of the formal battle in the open field.

Perhaps the most indelible picture of formal eighteenth century warfare that has survived is one of French and British officers at the Battle of Fontenoy in 1746, bowing politely to each other and each inviting the other side to fire the first volley, thus starting the carnage that was to follow. This picture has a certain ludicrous quality about it, but there was method in their madness as there was in eighteenth century warfare generally. The eighteenth century army was adapted to the European environment of the time, to the political and social climate as well as to the geography and terrain. Men knowledgeable in military matters at the time firmly believed that no body of semitrained citizens, however numerous and inspired, could stand before the disciplined ranks of professionals. If today we can see many of the weaknesses in the eighteenth century military system that were not so obvious to contemporaries—

its basic lack of flexibility, a paucity of true professional leadership, and its failure effectively to mobilize national resources for war—these perceptions result from a vastly different social and political environment.

The Colonial Scene

The environment in the British colonies of North America was different from that of Europe. America was a new continent, heavily forested and sparsely populated. The main enemy with whom the English colonists had first to contend was the primitive and savage Indian, who neither knew the rules of formal warfare nor cared to learn them. Colonial society from its very beginnings developed along more democratic and individualistic lines than society in England or continental Europe. Military institutions and practices, though heavily influenced by English patterns, also evolved in the seventeenth and eighteenth centuries along different lines. It would be a mistake to call the society that took form in the thirteen English colonies in North America a new society, for in most respects it followed the English pattern of social, economic, and political organization. But England itself had stronger democratic traditions than existed on the Continent, and important differences in the environment gave these English traditions much stronger force in America. Here there was no titled nobility exercising a monopoly on governmental office or holding a vested title to most of the land. While an aristocracy of wealth soon appeared, it was never able to exercise the same prerogatives as a titled nobility. Besides, it was far easier to move from the poorer to the wealthier class, since acquisition of landed wealth was easier in a country where land was plentiful and labor to work it scarce. If older settled areas tended to develop something approaching the pattern of European class distinction, new frontiers were constantly opening up where dissatisfied individuals could move and find new opportunities. Life under these conditions bred a spirit of individualism and self-reliance.

In political life, this spirit found expression in the popular assemblies that played an increasingly important part in the government of each of the colonies. Each colony had a government modeled generally on England's. Though there were variations in the pattern, the prevailing form consisted of a royal governor appointed by the British Crown, a council appointed by the governor from the ranks of the colonial aristocracy, and a popular assembly elected by the landholders. Modeled on the British House of Commons, these popular assemblies in the colonies rested on a much broader democratic base, since property ownership—the main qualification for voting in Britain and America in this age—

was far more widespread in the colonies. The colonial assemblies claimed the same prerogatives vis-à-vis the royal governor that the British Parliament exercised in its relations with the Crown, including control of the purse and regulation of the military establishment of the colony.

The Indian method of warfare in the forest, perforce adopted by the white man also, was the most significant influence in developing and preserving the spirit of individualism and self-reliance in the military sphere. When the white man came, the Indian relied on bow and spear, or tomahawk and knife, but he soon learned the value of the white man's muskets and was not long in obtaining them in trade for his valuable furs. With bow or musket, his method of fighting was the same. Indian tribes had no organized system of war; warriors simply formed voluntary bands under war chiefs and took off on the warpath. In battle each Indian fought a separate opponent without regard for his fellows. Indians avoided pitched battle whenever possible, instead seeking victory by surprise and carefully utilizing cover and concealment. Only when they had the advantage did they close in for hand-to-hand combat. In such combat the Indian brave lacked neither skill nor courage. Since he cared little about the rules of civilized warfare, he slaughtered men, women, and children indiscriminately. The favorite Indian tactic was a surprise raid on an isolated settlement. When the settlers organized a pursuit, the Indians lay in wait and ambushed them.

The white man soon adapted his tactics to the Indian's, quickly learning the value of surprise and stealth himself. To avoid ambush he sent out scouts as the Indians did, frequently employing friendly Indians in the role. Instead of fighting in the closed formations of Europe, he too adopted the open formation and fought from behind trees, rocks, and fences. In such fighting more depended on individual initiative and courage than on strict discipline and control.

The white settler learned to benefit from some of the enemy's weaknesses. For all their cunning, the Indians never learned the lesson of proper security and did not post guards at night. Nor did they like to fight in winter. Expeditions into the Indian country used as their favorite technique an attack on an Indian village at dawn and in the winter season. This attack almost invariably came as a surprise, and the white man, imitating the savagery of his opponent, burned the Indian's villages and sometimes slaughtered braves, squaws, and papooses.

The settlers tried to provide some permanent protection for their frontiers by erecting forts along the westernmost line of settlement in each colony, moving them forward as the line of settlement moved. These forts were not the elaborate earth and masonry structures of Europe, but simple rectangular inclosures, their walls constructed of upright pointed logs. Usually there were wooden blockhouses at each corner. These rude frontier forts served as points to which settlers and their families could retreat for protection in time of Indian troubles. Having no artillery, the Indians found the forts hard to take and could rely only on burning arrows to set them afire, on surprise attack, or on direct frontal assault. From the last alternative they almost invariably shrank. Their war chiefs possessed no power to order any group of braves to undertake an assault in which they would suffer heavy casualties for the sake of gaining an objective.

Colonial Militia

For fighting Indians, colonial governments were in no position to form professional armies, even had the nature of Indian warfare lent itself to such a practice. Instead they fell back on the ancient British tradition of the militia. This tradition took on new vitality in America at the same time that it was declining in England where, after Oliver Cromwell's time, England's wars were fought on the sea and in foreign lands. The British Government came to rely on its Regular Army and Navy just as other European states did, despite a continuing tradition of opposition to a standing army. Each of the thirteen colonies, except for Pennsylvania where Quaker influence was dominant, enacted laws providing for a compulsory militia organization, generally based on the principle of the Saxon fyrd that every able-bodied free male from sixteen to sixty should render military service. Each member of the militia was obligated to appear for training at his county or town seat a certain number of days each year, to provide himself with weapons, and to hold himself in readiness for call in case of Indian attack or other emergency.

Each colony maintained its separate militia establishment, and each concentrated on the problems of protecting or extending its own frontiers; co-operation among the militias of the various colonies was confined to specific expeditions in which two or more colonies had an interest. The militia was by and large a local institution, administered in county and town or township under the general militia laws of each colony. It was closely integrated with the social and economic structure of colonial society. Though the royal governors or colonial assemblies appointed the general officers and the colonels who commanded militia districts, the companies in each locality elected their own officers. This practice seemingly put a premium on popularity rather than wealth or ability, but rank in the militia generally corresponded with social station in the community.

Each individual militiaman was expected to provide his own weapon—usually a smoothbore musket—and ammunition, clothing, and food for a short expedition, just as the British knight had been required to provide his own horse, armor, and suitable weapons for feudal warfare. Local authorities maintained reserve supplies of muskets to arm those too poor to buy them and collected stores of ammunition and sometimes small cannon that could be dragged along through the wilderness. For really long campaigns, the colonial government had to take charge, the assembly appropriating the money for supplies and designating the supply officers or contractors to handle purchasing and distribution.

Although the militia was organized into units by county or township, it hardly ever fought that way. Instead the local unit served as a training and mobilization base from which individuals could be selected for active operations. When a particular area of a colony was threatened, the colonial government would direct the local militia commander to call out his men and the commander would mobilize as many as he could or as he thought necessary, selecting the younger and more active men for service. For expeditions into the Indian country, individuals from many localities were usually selected and formed into improvised units for the occasion. Selection was generally by volunteering, but local commanders could draft both men and property if necessary. Drafted men were permitted the option of hiring substitutes, a practice that favored the well to do. Volunteer, drafted man, and substitute alike insisted on the militiaman's prerogative to serve only a short period and return to home and fireside as quickly as possible.

As a part-time citizen army, the militia was naturally not a well-disciplined, cohesive force comparable to the professional army of the age. Moreover, its efficiency, even for Indian fighting, varied from colony to colony and even from locality to locality within the same colony, depending on the ability and determination of commanders and the presence or absence of any threat. When engaged in eliminating an Indian threat to their own community, militiamen might be counted on to make up in enthusiasm what they lacked in discipline and formal training, but when the Indian threat was pushed westward there was a tendency for people along the seaboard to relax. Training days, one a week in the early days of settlement, fell to one a month or even one a year. Festivities rather than military training increasingly became the main purpose of many of the gatherings, and the efficiency of the militia in these regions declined accordingly. In some towns and counties, however, the military tradition was kept alive by volunteers who formed units of their own, purchased distinctive uniforms, and prepared themselves to respond in case of war or emergency. These units became known as the volunteer militia and were the predecessors of the National Guard of the United States. In Pennsylvania, which lacked a militia law until 1755 and then passed one that made militia service voluntary rather than compulsory, all units were composed of volunteers.

On the frontier, where Indian raids were a constant threat, training days were more frequent and militia had to be ready for instant action. Except on the frontier, where proficiency in this sort of warfare was a matter of survival, it is doubtful that colonial militia in general were really adept in forest fighting. Training days were devoted not to the techniques of fighting Indians but to learning the drill and motions required on a European battlefield.

The Colonies in the World Conflict, 1689–1783

While England was colonizing the eastern seaboard from Maine to Georgia, France was extending its control over Canada and Louisiana and asserting its claim to the Great Lakes region and the Mississippi Valley in the rear of the British colonies. (*Map 1*) Spain held Florida, an outpost of its vast colonial domains in Mexico, Central and South America, and the West Indies. England

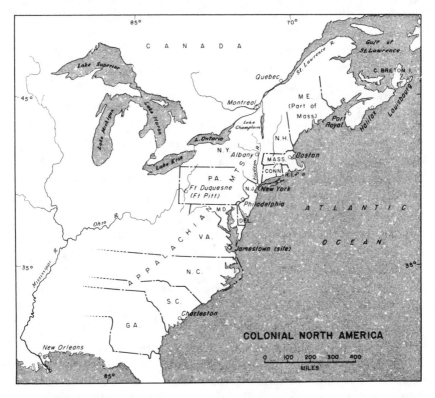

MAP 1

and France were invariably on opposite sides in the four great dynastic coalition wars fought in Europe between 1689 and 1763. Spain was allied with France in the last three of these conflicts. Each of these European wars had its counterpart in a struggle between British and French and Spanish colonists in America, intermingled with a quickening of Indian warfare all along the frontiers as the contestants tried to use the Indian tribes to their advantage. Americans and Europeans called these wars by different names. The War of the League of Augsburg (1689–97) was known in America as King William's War, the War of Spanish Succession (1701–13) as Queen Anne's War, the War of Austrian Succession (1744–48) as King George's War, and the final and decisive conflict, the Seven Years' War (1756–63), as the French and Indian War. In all of these wars one of the matters involved was the control of the North American continent; in the last of them it became the principal point at issue in the eyes of the British Government.

The main centers of French strength were along the St. Lawrence River in Canada—Quebec and Montreal—and the strategic line along which much of the fighting took place in the colonies lay between New York and Quebec, either on the lake and river chain that connects the Hudson with the St. Lawrence in the interior or along the seaways leading from the Atlantic up the St. Lawrence. In the south, the arena of conflict lay in the area between South Carolina and Florida and Louisiana. In 1732 the British Government established the colony of Georgia primarily as a military outpost in this region.

In the struggle for control of North America, the contest between England and France was the vital one, the conflict with Spain, a declining power, important but secondary. This latter conflict reached its height in the "War of Jenkins' Ear," a prelude to the War of Austrian Succession, which began in 1739 and pitted the British and their American colonists against the Spanish. In the colonies the war involved a seesaw struggle between the Spanish in Florida and the West Indies and the English colonists in South Carolina and Georgia. Its most notable episode, however, was a British expedition mounted in Jamaica against Cartagena, the main port of the Spanish colony in Colombia. The mainland colonies furnished a regiment to participate in the assault as British Regulars under British command. The expedition ended in disaster, resulting from climate, disease, and the bungling of British commanders, and only about 600 of over 3,000 Americans who participated ever returned to their homes. The net result of the war itself was indecisive.

The first three wars with the French were also indecisive. The nature of the fighting in them was much the same as that in the Indian wars. Although the French maintained garrisons of Regulars in Canada, they were never sufficient to bear the brunt of the fighting. The French Canadians also had their militia, a more centralized and all-embracing system than that in the English colonies, but the population of the French colonies was sparse, scarcely a twentieth of that of the British colonies in 1754. The French relied heavily on Indian allies, whom they equipped with firearms. They were far more successful than the British in influencing the Indians, certainly in part because their sparse population posed little threat to Indian lands. The French could usually count on the support of the Indian tribes in the Great Lakes and Ohio Valley regions, though the British colonists did maintain greater influence with the powerful Iroquois confederacy in New York. The French constructed forts at strategic points and garrisoned them with small numbers of Regulars, a few of whom they usually sent along with militia and Indian raiding parties to supervise operations. Using guerrilla methods, the French gained many local successes and indeed kept the frontiers of the English colonies in a continual state of alarm, but they could achieve no decisive results because of the essential weakness of their position.

The British and their colonists usually took the offensive and sought to strike by land and sea at the citadels of French power in Canada. The British Navy's control of the sea made possible the mounting of sea expeditions against Canada and at the same time made it difficult for the French to reinforce their small Regular garrisons. In 1710 a combined British and colonial expedition captured the French fort at Port Royal on Nova Scotia, and by the treaty of peace in 1713 Nova Scotia became an English possession. In 1745 an all-colonial expedition sponsored by Massachusetts captured Louisbourg on Cape Breton Island in what was perhaps the greatest of colonial military exploits, only to have the stronghold bargained away in 1748 for Madras, a post the French had captured from the British in India.

While militia units played an important part in the colonial wars, colonial governments resorted to a different device to recruit forces for expeditions outside their boundaries such as that against Louisbourg. This was the volunteer force, another institution that was to play an important part in all American wars through the end of the nineteenth century. Unlike the militia units, volunteer forces were built from the top down. The commanding officers were first chosen by one of the colonial governors or assemblies and the men were enlisted by them. The choice of a commander was made with due regard for his popularity in the colony since this was directly related to his ability to persuade officers and men to serve under him. While the militia was the main base for recruitment, and the officers were almost invariably men whose previous experience was in the militia, indentured servants and drifters without military obligation were also enlisted. The enlistment period was only for the duration of a campaign, at best a year or so, not for long periods as in European armies. Colonial assemblies had to vote money for pay and supplies, and assemblies were usually parsimonious as well as unwilling to see volunteer forces assume any of the status of a standing Regular Army. With short enlistments, inexperienced officers, and poor discipline by European standards, even the best of these colonial volunteer units were, like the militia, often held in contempt by British officers.

The only positive British gain up to 1748 was Nova Scotia. The indecisive character of the first three colonial wars was evidence of the inability of the English colonies to unite and muster the necessary military forces for common action, of the inherent difficulty of mounting offensives in unsettled areas, and of a British preoccupation with conflicts in Europe and other areas. Until 1754 the British Government contented itself with maintaining control of the seas and furnishing Regulars for sea expeditions against French and Spanish strongholds; until 1755 no British Regulars took part in the war in the interior, though small "independent companies" of indifferent worth were stationed continuously in New York and occasionally in other colonies. No colony, meanwhile, was usually willing to make any significant contribution to the common cause unless it appeared to be in its own interest. Efforts to form some kind of union, the most notable of which was a plan advanced by Benjamin Franklin in a colonial congress held at Albany in 1754, all came to naught.

Between 1748 and 1754 the French expanded their system of forts around the Great Lakes and moved down into the Ohio Valley, establishing Fort Duquesne at the junction of the Allegheny and Monongahela Rivers in 1753 and staking a claim to the entire region. In so doing, they precipitated the final and decisive conflict which began in America two years before the outbreak of the Seven Years' War in Europe. In 1754 Governor Robert Dinwiddie of Virginia sent young George Washington at the head of a force of Virginia militia to compel the French to withdraw from Fort Duquesne. Washington was driven back and forced to surrender. The British Government then sent over two understrength regiments of Regulars under Maj. Gen. Edward Braddock, a soldier of some forty-five years' experience on continental battlefields, to accomplish the task in which the militia had failed. Accustomed to the parade ground tactics and the open terrain of Europe, Braddock placed all his faith in disciplined Regulars and close order formations. He filled his regiments with American recruits and early in June 1755 set out on the long march through the wilderness to Fort Duquesne with a total force of about

2,200, including a body of Virginia and North Carolina militiamen. (*Map 2*)
George Washington accompanied the expedition, but had no command role.

Braddock's force proceeded westward through the wilderness in traditional
column formation with 300 axmen in front to clear the road and a heavy baggage
train of wagons in the rear. The heavy wagon train so slowed his progress that
about halfway he decided to let it follow as best it could and went ahead with
about 1,300 selected men, a few cannon, wagons, and packhorses. As he approached Fort Duquesne, he crossed the Monongahela twice in order to avoid
a dangerous and narrow passage along the east side where ambush might be
expected. He sent Lt. Col. Thomas Gage with an advance **guard to secure the**
site of the second crossing, also deemed a most likely spot for an ambush. Gage
found no enemy and the entire force crossed the Monongahela the second
time on the morning of July 9, 1755, then confidently took up the march toward
Fort Duquesne, only seven miles away.

About three quarters of a mile past the Monongahela crossing, Gage's
advance guard suddenly came under fire from a body of French and Indians
concealed in the woods. Actually it was a very inferior force of 70 French

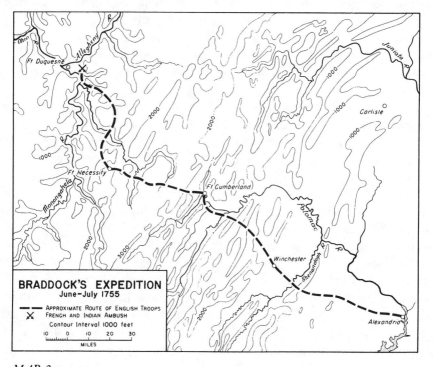

MAP 2

Regulars, 150 Canadian militia (many mere boys), and 650 Indians who had just arrived on the scene after a hasty march from Fort Duquesne. Some authorities think Gage might have changed the whole course of the battle had he pushed forward, forcing the enemy onto the open ground in their rear. Instead he fell back on the main body of Braddock's troops, causing considerable confusion. This confusion was compounded when the French and Indians slipped into the forests on the flanks of the British troops, pouring their fire into a surprised and terrified mass of men who wasted their return volleys on the air. "Scarce an officer or soldier," wrote one of the participants, "can say they ever saw at one time six of the Enemy and the greatest part never saw a single man. . . ."

None of the training or experience of the Regulars had equipped them to cope with this sort of attack, and Braddock could only exhort them to rally in conventional formation. Two-thirds of his officers fell dead or wounded. The militia, following their natural instincts, scattered and took positions behind trees, but there is no evidence they delivered any effective fire, since French and Indian losses for the day totaled only 23 killed and 16 wounded. The few British cannon appear to have been more telling. Braddock, mortally wounded himself, finally attempted to withdraw his force in some semblance of order, but the retreat soon became a disordered flight. The panic-stricken soldiers did not stop even when they reached the baggage wagons many miles to their rear.

Despite the completeness of their victory, the French and Indians made no attempt to follow it up. The few French Regulars had little control over the Indians, who preferred to loot the battlefield and scalp the wounded. The next day the Indians melted back into the forest, and the French commandant at Duquesne noted in his official report: "If the enemy should return with the 1,000 fresh troops that he has in reserve in the rear, at what distance we do not know, we should perhaps be badly embarrassed." The conduct of the battle was not so reprehensible as the precipitate retreat of the entire force back to the safety of the settled frontiers, when no enemy was pursuing it.

Although Braddock had been aware of the possibilities of ambush and had taken what he thought were necessary precautions, in the broader sense he violated the principles of security and maneuver; for when the ambush came he had little idea how to cope with Indian tactics in the forest. As he lay dying on the wagon that transported him from the battlefield, the seemingly inflexible old British general is alleged to have murmured, "Another time we shall know better how to deal with them."

BRADDOCK'S DEFEAT

Braddock could not profit from his appreciation of the lesson but the British Army did. "Over the bones of Braddock," writes Sir John Fortescue, the eminent historian of the British Army, "the British advanced again to the conquest of Canada."

After a series of early reverses, of which Braddock's disastrous defeat was only one, the British Government under the inspired leadership of William Pitt was able to achieve a combination of British and colonial arms that succeeded in overcoming the last French resistance in Canada and in finally removing the French threat from North America. In this combination British Regular troops, the British Navy, British direction, and British financial support were the keys to victory; the colonial effort, though considerable, continued to suffer from lack of unity.

As an immediate reaction to Braddock's defeat, the British Government sought to recruit Regulars in America to fight the war, following the precedent set in the Cartagena expedition. Several American regiments were raised, the most famous among them Col. Henry Bouquet's Royal Americans. On the whole, however, the effort was a failure, for most Americans preferred short service in the militia or provincial volunteer forces to the long-term service and rigid discipline of the British Army. After 1757 the British Government under Pitt, now convinced that America was the area in which the war would be won or lost, dispatched increasing numbers of Regulars from England—a total of 20,000 during the war. The British Regulars were used in conjunction with short-term militia and longer term volunteer forces raised in the service of the various individual colonies. The British never hit upon any effective device to assure the sort of colonial co-operation they desired and the burdens of the war were unequally divided since most colonies did not meet the quotas for troops, services, and supplies the British Government set. Massachusetts, Connecticut, and New York furnished about seven-tenths of the total colonial force employed. The British found it necessary to shoulder the principal financial burden, reimbursing individual colonies for part of their expenses and providing the pay and supply of many of the colonial volunteer units in order to insure their continued service.

Braddock's defeat was not repeated. In no other case in the French and Indian War was an inferior guerrilla force able to overcome any substantial body of Regulars. The lessons of the debacle on the Monongahela, as the British properly understood, were not that Regular forces or European methods were useless in America or that undisciplined American militia were superior to Regular troops. They were rather that tactics and formations had to be adapted to terrain and the nature of the enemy and that Regulars, when employed in the forest, would have to learn to travel faster and lighter and take advantage of cover, concealment, and surprise as their enemies did. Or the British could employ colonial troops and Indian allies versed in this sort of warfare as auxiliaries, something the French had long since learned to do.

The British adopted both methods in the ensuing years of the French and Indian War. Light infantry, trained as scouts and skirmishers, became a permanent part of the British Army organization. When engaged in operations in the forest, these troops were clad in green or brown clothes instead of the traditional red coat of the British soldier, their heads shaved and their skins sometimes painted like the Indians'. Special companies, such as Maj. Robert Rogers' Rangers, were recruited among skilled woodsmen in the colonies and placed in the Regular British establishment.

Despite this employment of light troops as auxiliaries, the British Army did not fundamentally change its tactics and organization in the course of the war in America. The reduction of the French fortress at Louisbourg in 1758 was conducted along the classic lines of European siege warfare. The most decisive single battle of the war was fought in the open field on the Plains of Abraham before the French citadel of Quebec. In a daring move, Maj. Gen. James Wolfe and his men scaled the cliffs leading up to the plain on the night of September 12, 1759, and appeared in traditional line of battle before the city the next morning. Major General the Marquis de Montcalm, the able French commander, accepted the challenge, but his troops, composed partly of militia levies, proved unable to withstand the withering "perfect volleys" of Wolfe's exceptionally well-disciplined regiments.

The ultimate lesson of the colonial wars, then, was that European and American tactics each had its place, and either could be decisive where conditions were best suited to its use. The colonial wars also proved that only troops possessing the organization and discipline of Regulars, whatever their tactics, could actually move in, seize, and hold objectives, and thus achieve decisive results.

Other important lessons lay in the realm of logistics, where American conditions presented difficulties to which European officers were unaccustomed. The impediments to supply and transport in a vast, undeveloped, and sparsely populated country limited both the size and variety of forces employed. The settled portions of the colonies produced enough food, but few manufactured goods. Muskets, cannon, powder, ball, tents, camp kettles, salt, and a variety of other articles necessary for even the simple military operations of the period almost all had to come from Europe. Roads, even in the settled areas, were poor and inadequate; forces penetrating into the interior had to cut their roads as they went, as Braddock did. These logistical problems go far to explain why the fate of America was settled in battles involving hardly one-tenth the size of forces engaged in Europe in the Seven Years' War, and why cavalry was almost never employed and artillery to no great extent except in fixed fortifications and in expeditions by sea when cannon could be transported on board ship. The limited mobility of large Regular forces, whatever the superiority of their organization and tactics, put a premium both on small bodies of trained troops familiar with the terrain and on local forces, not so well trained, already in an area of operations. Commanders operating in America would ignore these logistical limitations at their peril.

The American Rifle

By the end of the French and Indian War, a new weapon had appeared on the frontier in Pennsylvania and to the southward, one far better suited to guerrilla warfare than the musket. This weapon was later to become renowned as the Kentucky rifle. The effects of rifling a gun barrel, that is, of making spiral grooves that imparted a spinning effect to the bullet, giving it greater range and accuracy, had been known for some centuries in Germany and Switzerland. But the early rifles made there were too heavy and slow to load to be of military use. The Germans who settled in Pennsylvania developed, around 1750, a much

NOT TRUE!

lighter model, far easier and <u>faster to</u> load. They used a bullet smaller than the bore and a greased patch to keep the fit tight. This early American rifle could, in proper hands, hit a target the size of a man's head at 200 yards.

Despite its superior range and accuracy, the rifle was to undergo almost a hundred years of development before it would supplant the musket as the standard infantry weapon. At first each individual piece was handmade and each required a separate bullet mold. The standard bayonet would fit none of them. The rifle was effective only in the hands of an expert trained in its use. The rate of fire was only about one-third that of the musket, and therefore, without bayonet, the rifle could hardly be used by troops in the line. For the guerrilla tactics of the frontier, where men did not fight in line but from behind trees, bushes, and rocks, it was clearly a superior weapon. Thus, like the tactics of the American forest, it would have its place in any future war fought in America.

The Colonial Heritage

In the Indian wars and the colonial wars with France, Americans gained considerable military experience, albeit much of it in guerrilla warfare that did not require the same degree of organized effort and professional competence as the European style of warfare. The major effort against the French in Canada had, after all, been directed by the British Government. Many colonials later to become famous in the Revolution had served their military apprenticeship as officers of middle rank in the French and Indian War: George Washington, Israel Putnam, Philip Schuyler, and John Stark, for instance, in provincial forces; Charles Lee, Horatio Gates, and Richard Montgomery in the British Army.

Certain traditions had been established that were to influence American military policy and practice right down to the two great world wars of the twentieth century. One of these was primary reliance on the militia for defense and on volunteer forces for special emergencies and expeditions. Another was that relatively permanent volunteer units should be formed within the militia. The fear of a standing army of professionals, an English heritage, had become an even stronger article of faith in America. The colonial experience also established a strong tradition of separatism among the colonies themselves, for each had for a long period of years run its own military establishment. Within each colony, too, the civilian authority represented in the popular assembly had always kept a strict rein on the military, another tradition that was to have marked effect on American military development.

Certain characteristics of the American soldier that were to be fairly constant throughout all future wars had also made their appearance. The American soldier was inclined to be highly individualistic and to resent discipline and the inevitable restrictions of military life; he sought to know why he should do things before he would put his heart into doing them; and if in the end he accepted discipline and order as a stern necessity he did so with the idea of winning victory as quickly as possible so that he could return to his normal civilian pursuits.

These traditions and these characteristics were the product of a society developing along democratic lines. The military strengths and weaknesses they engendered were to be amply demonstrated when the American soldier took up arms against his erstwhile comrade, the British Regular, in the American Revolution.

CHAPTER 3

The American Revolution: First Phase

The American Revolution came about, fundamentally, because by 1763 the English-speaking communities on the far side of the Atlantic had matured to an extent that their interests and goals were distinct from those of the ruling classes in the mother country. British statesmen failed to understand or adjust to the situation. Ironically enough, British victory in the Seven Years' War set the stage for the revolt, for it freed the colonists from the need for British protection against a French threat on their frontiers and gave free play to the forces working for separation.

In 1763 the British Government, reasonably from its point of view, moved to tighten the system of imperial control and to force the colonists to contribute to imperial defense, proposing to station 10,000 soldiers along the American frontiers and to have the Americans pay part of the bill. This imperial defense plan touched off the long controversy about Parliament's right to tax that started with the Stamp and Sugar Acts and ended in December 1773, when a group of Bostonians unceremoniously dumped a cargo of British tea into the city harbor in protest against the latest reminder of the British effort to tax. In this 10-year controversy the several British ministries failed to act either firmly enough to enforce British regulations or wisely enough to develop a more viable form of imperial union, which the colonial leaders, at least until 1776, insisted that they sought. In response to the Boston Tea Party, the king and his ministers blindly pushed through Parliament a series of measures collectively known in America as the Intolerable Acts, closing the port of Boston, placing Massachusetts under the military rule of Maj. Gen. Sir Thomas Gage, and otherwise infringing on what the colonists deemed to be their rights and interests.

Since 1763 the colonial leaders, in holding that only their own popular assemblies, not the British Parliament, had a right to levy taxes on Americans, had raised the specter of an arbitrary British Government collecting taxes in America to support red-coated Regulars who might be used not to protect the frontiers but to suppress American liberties. Placing Massachusetts under military rule gave that specter some substance and led directly to armed revolt.

The Outbreak

The First Continental Congress meeting at Philadelphia on September 5, 1774, addressed respectful petitions to Parliament and king but also adopted nonimportation and nonexportation agreements in an effort to coerce the British Government into repealing the offending measures. To enforce these agreements, committees were formed in almost every county, town, and city throughout the colonies, and in each colony these committees soon became the effective local authorities, the base of a pyramid of revolutionary organizations with revolutionary assemblies, congresses, or conventions, and committees of safety at the top. This loosely knit combination of *de facto* governments superseded the constituted authorities and established firm control over the whole country before the British were in any position to oppose them. The *de facto* governments took over control of the militia, and out of it began to shape forces that, if the necessity arose, might oppose the British in the field.

In Massachusetts, the seat of the crisis, the Provincial Congress, eyeing Gage's force in Boston, directed the officers in each town to enlist a third of their militia in minutemen organizations to be ready to act at a moment's warning, and began to collect ammunition and other military stores. It established a major depot for these stores at Concord, about twenty miles northwest of Boston.

General Gage learned of the collection of military stores at Concord and determined to send a force of Redcoats to destroy them. His preparations were made with the utmost secrecy. Yet so alert and ubiquitous were the patriot eyes in Boston that when the picked British force of 700 men set out on the night of April 18, 1775, two messengers, Paul Revere and William Dawes, preceded them to spread the alarm throughout the countryside. At dawn on the 19th of April when the British arrived at Lexington, the halfway point to Concord, they found a body of militia drawn up on the village green. Some nervous finger—whether of British Regular or American militiaman is unknown to this day—pressed a trigger. The impatient British Regulars, apparently without any clear orders from their commanding officer, fired a volley, then charged with the bayonet. The militiamen dispersed, leaving eight dead and ten wounded on the ground. The British column went on to Concord, destroyed such of the military stores as the Americans had been unable to remove, and set out on their return journey.

By this time, the alarm had spread far and wide, and both ordinary militia and minutemen had assembled along the British route. From behind walls, rocks, and trees, and from houses they poured their fire into the columns of Redcoats, while the frustrated Regulars found few targets for their accustomed volleys or bayonet charges. Only the arrival of reinforcements sent by Gage enabled the British column to get back to the safety of Boston. At day's end the British counted 273 casualties out of a total of 1,800 men engaged; American casualties numbered 95 men, including the toll at Lexington. What happened was hardly a tribute to the marksmanship of New England farmers—it has been estimated 75,000 shots poured from their muskets that day—but it did testify to a stern determination of the people of Massachusetts to resist any attempt by the British to impose their will by armed force.

The spark lit in Massachusetts soon spread throughout the rest of the colonies. Whatever really may have happened in that misty dawn on Lexington Green, the news that speedy couriers, riding horses to exhaustion, carried through the colonies from New Hampshire to Georgia was of a savage, unprovoked British attack and of farmers rising in the night to protect their lives, their families, and their property. Lexington, like Fort Sumter and Pearl Harbor, furnished an emotional impulse that led all true patriots to gird themselves for battle. From the other New England colonies, militia poured in to join the Massachusetts men and together they soon formed a ring around Boston. Other militia forces under Ethan Allen of Vermont and Benedict Arnold of Connecticut seized the British forts at Ticonderoga and Crown Point, strategic positions on the route between New York and Canada. These posts yielded valuable artillery and other military stores. The Second Continental Congress, which assembled in Philadelphia on May 10, 1775, found itself forced to turn from embargoes and petitions to the problems of organizing, directing, and supplying a military effort.

Before Congress could assume control, the New England forces assembled near Boston fought another battle on their own, the bloodiest single engagement of the entire Revolution. After Lexington and Concord, at the suggestion of Massachusetts, the New England colonies moved to replace the militia gathered before Boston with volunteer forces, constituting what may be loosely called a New England army. Each state raised and administered its own force and appointed a commander for it. Discipline was lax and there was no single chain of command. Though Artemas Ward, the Massachusetts commander, exercised over-all control by informal agreement, it was only because the other commanders chose to co-operate with him, and decisions were made in council. While by mid-June most of the men gathered were volunteers, militia units continued to come and go. The volunteers in the Connecticut service were enlisted until December 10, 1775, those from the other New England states until the end of the year. The men were dressed for the most part in homespun clothes and armed with muskets of varied types; powder and ball were short and only the barest few had bayonets.

Late in May Gage received limited reinforcements from England, bringing his total force to 6,500 rank and file. With the reinforcements came three major generals of reputation—Sir William Howe, Sir Henry Clinton, and Sir John Burgoyne—men destined to play major roles in England's loss of its American colonies. The newcomers all considered that Gage needed more elbowroom and proposed to fortify Dorchester Heights, a dominant position south of Boston previously neglected by both sides. News of the intended move leaked to the Americans, who immediately countered by dispatching a force onto the Charlestown peninsula, where other heights, Bunker Hill and Breed's Hill, overlooked Boston from the north. (*Map 3*) The original intent was to fortify Bunker Hill, the eminence nearest the narrow neck of land connecting the peninsula with the mainland, but the working party sent out on the night of June 16, 1775, decided instead to move closer in and construct works on Breed's Hill—a tactical blunder, for these exposed works could much more easily be cut off by a British landing on the neck in their rear.

The British scorned such a tactic, evidently in the mistaken assumption that the assembled "rabble in arms" would disintegrate in the face of an attack by disciplined British Regulars. On the afternoon of the 17th, Gage sent some 2,200 of his men under Sir William Howe directly against the American positions, by this time manned by perhaps an equal force. Twice the British advanced on the front and flanks of the redoubt on Breed's Hill, and twice the Americans, holding their fire until the compact British lines were at close range, decimated the ranks of the advancing regiments and forced them to fall back and re-form. With reinforcements, Howe carried the hill on the third try but largely because the Americans had run short of ammunition and had no bayonets. The American retreat from Breed's Hill was, for inexperienced volunteers and militia, an orderly one and Howe's depleted regiments were unable to prevent the Americans' escape. British casualties for the day totaled a staggering 1,054, or almost half the force engaged, as opposed to American losses of about 440.

The Battle of Bunker Hill (for it was Bunker that gave its name to a battle actually fought on Breed's Hill) has been aptly characterized as a "tale of great blunders heroically redeemed." The American command structure violated the principle of unity of command from the start, and in moving onto Breed's Hill the patriots exposed an important part of their force in an indefensible position, violating the principles of concentration of force, mass, and maneuver. Gage and Howe, for their parts, sacrificed all the advantages the American blunders gave

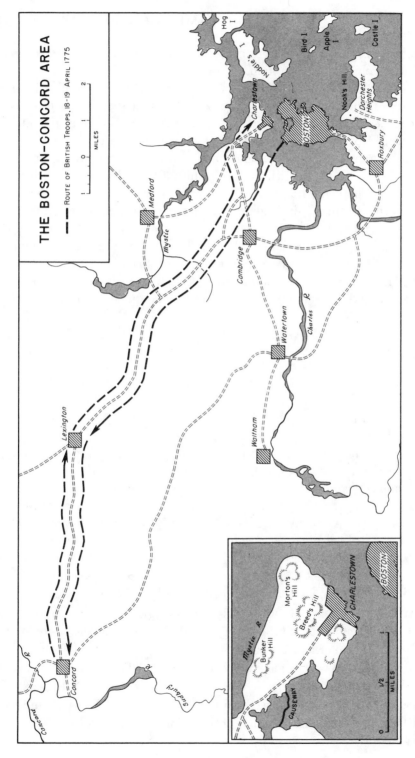

THE BOSTON–CONCORD AREA

— — — ROUTE OF BRITISH TROOPS, 18-19 APRIL 1775

MILES

Hog I.
Noddle's I.
Bird I.
Apple I.
Castle I.
Charlestown
BOSTON
Nook's Hill
Dorchester Heights
Roxbury

Medford
Mystic R.
Cambridge
Watertown
Charles R.
Waltham

Lexington
Concord
Concord R.
Sudbury R.

Mystic R.
Bunker Hill
Morton's Hill
Breed's Hill
CHARLESTOWN
BOSTON
CAUSEWAY
MILES

MAP 3

them, violating the principles of maneuver and surprise by undertaking a suicidal attack on a fortified position.

Bunker Hill was a Pyrrhic victory, its strategic effect practically nil since the two armies remained in virtually the same position they had held before. Its consequences, nevertheless, cannot be ignored. A force of farmers and townsmen, fresh from their fields and shops, with hardly a semblance of orthodox military organization, had met and fought on equal terms with a professional British Army. On the British this astonishing feat had a sobering effect, for it taught them that American resistance was not to be easily overcome; never again would British commanders lightly attempt such an assault on Americans in fortified positions. On the Americans, the effect was hardly sobering, and in the long run was perhaps not salutary. Bunker Hill, along with Lexington and Concord, went far to create the American tradition that the citizen soldier when aroused is more than a match for the trained professional, a tradition that was to be reflected in American military policy for generations afterward.

Formation of the Continental Army

The response of George III and his ministers to the events at Lexington, Concord, and Bunker Hill was a determined effort to subdue the rebellious colonists by force. It took time to mount this effort, and after Bunker Hill the Americans enjoyed a respite lasting almost a year. During most of this period the Second Continental Congress, though forced by events in New England to take on itself the leadership of an armed revolt, proceeded hesitantly, still seeking a formula for reconciliation that would preserve American rights. Military preparations were designed for a short struggle, to endure no longer than the end of the year 1776. Nevertheless the Americans took advantage of the respite to create a national army, to consolidate their hold on the governmental machinery throughout the thirteen colonies, to invade Canada, and finally to force the British to evacuate Boston.

The creation of a Continental Army was in the long run perhaps their most significant achievement. Some time before Bunker Hill the Massachusetts Provincial Congress, aware of the necessity of enlisting the support of all the colonies in the struggle against the British, appealed to the Continental Congress to adopt the New England army. Although there is no formal record of the action, Congress evidently did vote to adopt it on June 14, 1775—the accepted birthday of the U.S. Army. On the same day it voted to raise ten companies of riflemen—the first soldiers to be enlisted directly in the Continental service—in Pennsylvania, Maryland, and Virginia, to march north to join the army before Boston.

The next day, June 15, Congress chose George Washington, a Virginian, to be Commander in Chief. The choice was made for geographical and political as much as for military reasons. The New Englanders felt that in order to enlist the support of the southern colonies, a southerner should be chosen for the post of command. Washington's military experience was perhaps greater than that of any other southerner, and he came from the largest and most important of the southern colonies. His impressive appearance, quiet and confident manner, and good work in the military committees of Congress had impressed all.

The choice proved fortunate. Washington himself recognized, when he accepted the command, that he lacked the requisite experience and knowledge in handling large bodies of men. His whole military experience had been in frontier warfare during the French and Indian War. But experience as a political leader in his native Virginia and in directing the business affairs of his large plantation at Mount Vernon also stood him in good stead. He brought to the task traits of character and abilities as a leader that in the end more than compensated for his lack of professional military experience. Among these qualities were a determination and a steadfastness of purpose rooted in an unshakable conviction of the righteousness of the American cause, a scrupulous sense of honor and duty, and a dignity that inspired respect and confidence in those around him. Conscious of his own defects, he was always willing to profit by experience. From the trials and tribulations of eight years of war he was to learn the essentials of strategy, tactics, and military organization.

Congress also appointed four major generals and eight brigadiers to serve under Washington, set up a series of staff offices closely resembling those in the British Army, prescribed a pay scale and standard ration, and adopted Articles of War to govern the military establishment. The same mixture of geographical, political, and military considerations governed the choice of Washington's subordinates. Two-thirds of them came from New England, in recognition of the fact that the existing army was a New England army. Three others—Charles Lee, Horatio Gates, and Richard Montgomery—were chosen because of their experience in the British Army. Lee, in particular, who had come from England to the colonies in 1773, was in 1775 deemed the foremost military expert in America, and he was for a time to be Washington's first assistant.

The army of which Washington formally took command on July 3, 1775, he described as "a mixed multitude of people . . . under very little discipline, order or government." Out of this "mixed multitude," Washington set out to create an army shaped in large part in the British image. Basing his observations on his experience with British Regulars during the French and Indian War, he wrote: "Discipline is the soul of an army. It makes small numbers formidable;

GENERAL WASHINGTON (*center*) WITH MAJ. GEN. ARTEMAS WARD (*right*) and an aide (*left*) visiting the field, July 1775.

procures success to the weak and esteem to all." Employing Gates, his experienced adjutant general, to prepare regulations and orders, the Commander in Chief set out to inculcate discipline. A strenuous effort was made to halt the random comings and goings of officers and men and to institute regular roll calls and strength returns. Suspicious of the "leveling" tendencies of the New Englanders, Washington made the distinction between officers and enlisted men more rigid. Various punishments were introduced—lash, pillory, wooden horse, and drumming out of camp—and courts-martial sat almost constantly.

While establishing discipline in the existing army, Washington had at the same time to form a new one enlisted directly in the Continental service. Out of conferences with a Congressional committee that visited camp in September 1775 emerged a plan for such an army, composed of 26 regiments of infantry of 728 men each, plus one regiment of riflemen and one of artillery, 20,372 men in all, to be uniformly paid, supplied, and administered by the Continental Congress and enlisted to the end of the year 1776. Except for the short term of enlistment, it was an excellent plan on paper, but Washington soon found he could not carry it out. Both officers and men resisted a reorganization that cut across the lines of the locally organized units in which they were accustomed to serve. The men saw as their first obligation their families and farms at home, and they were reluctant to re-enlist for another year's service. On December 10, despite pressures and patriotic appeals, most of the Connecticut men went home and militia from New Hampshire and Massachusetts had to be brought in to fill their places in the line. Others, who had jeered and hooted when the Connecticut men left, also went home when their enlistment expired only three weeks later. On January 1, 1776, when the army became "Continental in every respect," Washington found that he had only slightly more than 8,000 enlistments instead of the 20,000 planned. Returns in early March showed only a thousand or so more. "I have often thought how much happier I would have been," wrote a sorely tried commander, "if, instead of accepting a command under such circumstances, I had taken up musket on my shoulder and entered the ranks, or, if I could have justified the measure to posterity and my own conscience, had retired to the back country and lived in a Wigwam."

With enlistments falling short, the only recourse was to continue to use short-term militia to fill the gaps in the lines. A Continental Army had been formed, but it fell far short of the goals Washington and Congress had set for it. This army was enlisted for but a year and the whole troublesome process would have to be repeated at the end of 1776. The short term of enlistment was, of course, a cardinal error, but in 1775 everyone, including Washington, anticipated only a short campaign.

While organizing and disciplining his army, Washington had also to maintain the siege of Boston and overcome his deficiencies in supply. In these efforts he was more successful. Congress and the individual colonies sponsored voyages to the West Indies, where the French and Dutch had conveniently exported quantities of war materials. Washington put some of his troops on board ship and with an improvised navy succeeded in capturing numerous British supply ships. He sent Col. Henry Knox, later to be his Chief of Artillery, to Ticonderoga, and Knox in the winter of 1775–76 brought some fifty pieces of captured cannon to Cambridge over poor or nonexistent roads in icebound New York and New England. By March 1776, despite deficiencies in the number of Continentals, Washington was ready to close in on Boston.

The Invasion of Canada and the Fall of Boston

The major military operations of 1775 and early 1776 were not around Boston but in far-distant Canada, which the Americans tried to add as a fourteenth colony. Canada seemed a tempting and vulnerable target. To take it would eliminate a British base at the head of the familiar invasion route along the lake and river chain connecting the St. Lawrence with the Hudson. Congress, getting no response to an appeal to the Canadians to join in its cause, in late June 1775 instructed Maj. Gen. Philip Schuyler of New York to take possession of Canada if "practicable" and "not disagreeable to the Canadians."

Schuyler managed to get together a force of about 2,000 men from New York and Connecticut, thus forming the nucleus of what was to become known as the Northern Army. In September 1775 Brig. Gen. Richard Montgomery set out with this small army from Ticonderoga with the objective of taking Montreal. To form a second prong to the invasion, Washington detached a force of 1,100 under Col. Benedict Arnold, including a contingent of riflemen under Capt. Daniel Morgan of Virginia, to proceed up the Kennebec River, across the wilds of Maine, and down the Chaudière to join with Montgomery before Quebec. (*Map 4*)

Montgomery, advancing along the route via Lake George, Lake Champlain, and the Richelieu River, was seriously delayed by the British fort at St. Johns but managed to capture Montreal on November 13. Arnold meanwhile had arrived opposite Quebec on November 8, after one of the most rugged marches in history. One part of his force had turned back and others were lost by

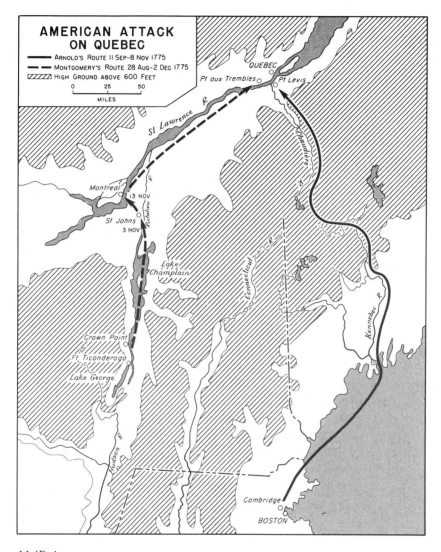

AMERICAN ATTACK
ON QUEBEC

— ARNOLD'S ROUTE II SEP-8 NOV 1775
— — MONTGOMERY'S ROUTE 28 AUG-2 DEC 1775
////// HIGH GROUND ABOVE 600 FEET

0   25   50
MILES

MAP 4

starvation, sickness, drowning, and desertion. Only 600 men crossed the St. Lawrence on November 13, and in imitation of Wolfe scaled the cliffs and encamped on the Plains of Abraham. It was a magnificent feat, but the force was too small to prevail even against the scattered Canadian militia and British Regulars who, unlike Montcalm, shut themselves up in the city and refused battle in the open. Arnold's men were finally forced to withdraw to Point aux Trembles, where they were joined by Montgomery with all the men he could spare from the defense of Montreal—a total of 300. Nowhere did the Canadians show much inclination to rally to the American cause; the French *habitants* remained indifferent, and the small British population gave its loyalty to the governor general. With the enlistments of about half their men expiring by the new year, Arnold and Montgomery undertook a desperate assault on the city during the night of December 30 in the middle of a raging blizzard. The Americans were outnumbered by the defenders, and the attack was a failure. Montgomery was killed and Arnold wounded.

The wounded Arnold, undaunted, continued to keep up the appearance of a siege with the scattered remnants of his force while he waited for reinforcements. The reinforcements came—Continental regiments raised in New York, New Jersey, and Pennsylvania—but they came in driblets and there were never enough to build a force capable of again taking the offensive, though a total of 8,000 men were eventually committed to the Canadian campaign. Smallpox and other diseases took their toll and never did the supply line bring in adequate food, clothing, or ammunition. Meanwhile, the British received reinforcements and in June 1776 struck back against a disintegrating American army that retreated before them almost without a fight. By mid-July the Americans were back at Ticonderoga where they had started less than a year earlier, and the initiative on the northern front passed to the British.

While the effort to conquer Canada was moving toward its dismal end, Washington finally took the initiative at Boston. On March 4, 1776, he moved onto Dorchester Heights and emplaced his newly acquired artillery in position to menace the city; a few days later he fortified Nook's Hill, standing still closer in. On March 17 the British moved out. It would be presumptuous to say that their exit was solely a consequence of American pressure. Sir William Howe, who succeeded Gage in command, had concluded long since that Boston was a poor strategic base and intended to stay only until the transports arrived to take his army to Halifax in Nova Scotia to regroup and await reinforcements. Nevertheless, Washington's maneuvers hastened his departure, and the reoccupation of Boston was an important psychological victory for the Americans, balancing the disappointments of the Canadian campaign. The stores of cannon and ammunition the British were forced to leave behind were a welcome addition indeed to the meager American arsenal.

The New Nation

The Declaration of Independence on July 4, 1776, established a new nation and transformed a limited revolt to secure rights within the British empire into a far-reaching one, aimed at complete independence from British control. Since the king and his ministers had determined to restore British rule, the Americans now faced a long, hard struggle for independence requiring a sustained national effort such as they had not expected in 1775.

The new nation was still a weak confederation of thirteen independent states. Such national feeling as existed was a new phenomenon growing out of common opposition to British measures. Colonial tradition, divided loyalties, the nature of the economy, and the spirit of a revolt born in opposition to the use of military force to suppress popular liberties, all worked against the creation of any new strong central authority capable of mobilizing resources effectively for the long struggle that lay ahead.

The thirteen states proclaiming their independence in 1776 possessed a total population of about two and a half million people, but not all the males of military age were part of the military potential. About 20 percent were Negro slaves who except under special circumstances were not eligible for service, though Negroes did serve in the Revolution and not in segregated units. Perhaps one-third of the "politically active" Americans remained loyal to the British Government. As in any society there were also the apathetic and indifferent who swayed with the tide. The genuine patriots still provided a far larger potential of military manpower than the British could possibly transport and supply across the Atlantic, but most of the men of military age were farmers who married young and immediately started large families. Whatever their patriotic sentiments, few were ready to undertake long terms of military service, fearing that if they did their farms and families at home would suffer. Accustomed to the tradition of short-term militia service under local commanders, they infinitely preferred it to long-term service in the Continental Army.

The economy of the thirteen new states was neither self-sufficient nor truly national. The states were essentially a collection of separate agricultural communities, accustomed to exchanging their agricultural surplus for British manufactured goods and West Indian products. Manufacturing was still in its infancy and America produced few of the essentials of military supply. Despite diligent efforts to promote domestic production during the war years, the Continental Army had to rely primarily on captures and imports from Europe and the West Indies, run through a British blockade, for much of its military hardware and even for clothing. While the country produced food-stuffs in ample quantity, transport from one area to another was difficult. The normal avenues of commerce ran up and down the rivers, not overland; roads running north and south were few and inadequate. There was always a shortage of wagons, boats, and other means of transportation. Under these circumstances, it was far easier to support local militia for a few days or weeks than any sizable and continuously operating national army in the field.

The governmental machinery created after the Declaration was characterized by decentralization and executive weakness. The thirteen new "free and independent states" transformed their existing *de facto* revolutionary governments into legal state governments by adopting constitutions. Almost invariably, these constitutions vested most of the powers of government in the state legislatures, successors to the popular assemblies of the colonial period, and severely restricted the executive authority of the governors. At the national level, the same general distrust of strong authority was apparent, and the existing Continental Congress essentially a gathering of delegates chosen by the state legislatures and without either express powers of its own or an executive to carry out its enactments, was continued as the only central governing body. Articles of Confederation stipulating the terms of union and granting Congress specific but limited powers were drawn up shortly after the Declaration, but jealousies among the states prevented ratification until 1781. In the interim, Congress exercised most of the powers granted it under the Articles, but they did not include either the right to levy taxes or the power to raise military forces directly under its auspices. Congress could only determine the Confederation's need for troops and money to wage war and set quotas for the states to meet in proportion to their population and wealth. It had no means of insuring that the states met their quotas, and indeed they seldom did.

The decentralized structure provided no adequate means of financing the war. The state legislatures, possessing the power to tax that Congress lacked, hesitated to use it extensively in the face of popular opposition to taxation, and were normally embarrassed to meet even their own expenses. Congress very early took unto itself the power to issue paper money and to negotiate domestic and foreign loans, but it shared these powers with the states, which also printed paper money in profusion and borrowed both at home and abroad to the extent they could. The paper money was a useful expedient in the early part of the war; indeed the Revolution could not have been carried on without it. But successive issues by Congress and the states led to first gradual and then galloping inflation, leaving the phrase "not worth a Continental" as a permanent legacy to the American language. The process of depreciation and the exhaustion of credit gradually robbed both the states and Congress of the power to pay troops, buy supplies, and otherwise meet the multitudinous expenses of war.

Evolution of the Continental Army

Under these circumstances it is not surprising that Washington never got the kind of army, molded in the British image, that he desired. The experience before Boston in 1775 was repeated many times, as local militia had to be called in continually to give the American Army a numerical superiority in the field. The Continental Army, nevertheless, became the center of American resistance, and its commander, Washington, the symbol of the patriot cause. The extent to which militia could be expected to rally to that cause was very largely determined by the Continental Army's success or failure in the field.

Though the militia belonged to the states, the Continental Army was a creation of the Continental Congress. Congress prescribed its size and composition, chose its generals, and governed the system for its administration and supply. Suspicious on principle of a standing army and acutely aware of historic examples of seizure of political power by military leaders, its members kept a watchful eye on the Army's commanders and insisted they defer to civilian authority. Washington countered these suspicions by constantly deferring to Congressional wishes, and he was rewarded by the assiduity with which Congress usually adopted his recommendations.

Lacking an executive, Congress had to rely on committees and boards to carry out its policies—unwieldy devices at best and centers of conflicting interest and discord at worst. In June 1776 it set up a Board of War and Ordnance, consisting of five of its members, the lineal ancestor of the War Department. In 1777 Congress changed the composition of the board, directing that it henceforth be made up of persons outside Congress who could devote full time to their military duties. Neither of these devices really worked well, and Congress continually handled administrative matters by action of the entire membership or by appointment of special committees to go to camp. In 1781 the board was replaced by a single Secretary at War.

Under the Articles of Confederation the states were responsible for raising troops for the Continental Army, for organizing and equipping them, and for appointing officers through the rank of colonel. State authorities called out militia sometimes at the request of Congress and sometimes on their own initiative. When they joined the main army, militia normally shared in its supplies and equipment. The states, however, maintained an interest in supplying and administering the troops of their own "lines" as well as their militia, and the Continental agents had continually to enlist state assistance in their own efforts. Lines of authority crisscrossed at every turn.

It was an inefficient military system for an organized national effort. Washington could never depend on having enough trained men or supplies. He continually inveighed against sending militia to fight his battles and by early 1776 had concluded that he needed an army enlisted for the duration of the war. Congress did not, as has often been charged, ignore his wishes. In October 1776 it voted a new establishment, superseding the plan developed for the army before Boston in 1775 and haphazard arrangements made in the interim for raising Continental regiments in various states. This establishment was to contain 88 battalions of infantry, or about 60,000 men, enlisted to serve three years or "during the present war," with each state assigned a quota in proportion to its population under the system set up in the Articles. After the disastrous retreat across New Jersey in December 1776, Congress went further and authorized an additional 22 battalions to be recruited by Washington's officers directly into the Continental service. These 110 battalions remained the authorized strength of the Continental Army until 1781, when Congress cut it to 59.

Neither the 88 battalions, nor the 110, nor even the 59 ever existed except on paper. The Continental Army never had as many as 30,000 men at any one time, and very rarely was Washington able to muster as many as 15,000 effectives in the field. The states were simply unable to meet their quotas. By the winter of 1777–78, the effort to enlist men for three years or the duration collapsed, and the following spring, with the sanction of Washington, Congress reverted to a system of one-year enlistments and recommended to the states that they institute a system of drafting men from the militia for one year's service. This first American wartime draft was applied irregularly in the various states and succeeded no better than had earlier methods in filling the Continental ranks. Bounties, instituted by both the states and the Congress very early in the war and progressively increased one step behind the pace of inflation, also produced only temporary and irregular results.

The coin did have another side. In reality the shortage of arms and ammunition and of facilities for producing them limited the number of men who could be kept continuously in the field as effectively as did the failure of enlistment drives. The militia system enabled many able-bodied males to perform part-time military service and still remain most of the time in the labor force that kept the economy going. It is doubtful whether the American economy could have sustained such an army as Washington and Congress proposed in 1776, even had there been a central administration with adequate power. As it was, the small Continental Army that did remain in the field intermittently suffered extreme hardship and near starvation. On the other hand, American ability to raise local armies in any threatened region helped to balance the strategic mobility that the British Fleet gave to the British Army. Although militia generally did not perform well in regular warfare, when highly motivated and ably led, they could fight well on terrain suited to their capabilities. Given the conditions under which the Revolution was fought, the American military system was more effective than its critics have recognized, though it failed to provide adequately for a sustained military effort over a period of years.

Perhaps Washington's greatest achievement was simply in maintaining the Continental Army continuously in the field. Despite its many vicissitudes, that army did take shape during the war as the first distinctively American military organization, neither quite a replica of the professional British Army on which it was modeled nor yet the type of national army raised by conscription that was to appear in France after the Revolution of 1789.

The Continental Army operated in three main territorial divisions or departments—the main army under Washington largely in the Middle States, the Northern Army in northern New York, and the Southern Army in the Carolinas and Georgia. Although Washington was Commander in Chief of the whole, the commanders of the Northern and Southern Armies still operated with a considerable measure of independence. Congress, rather than Washington, named their commanders and communicated directly with them. Of the two "separate armies," the Northern Army was by far the most important until 1777 and the Southern Army existed largely on paper; by 1780 the situation was reversed as the British transferred their main effort to the southern states.

The Continental Army was composed mainly of infantry and artillery, with very little cavalry. The basic unit of infantry organization was the regiment or battalion composed of eight companies. Organization above this level was highly flexible. A brigade was usually formed of several regiments and was commanded by a brigadier general; a division consisted of a similar grouping of several brigades commanded by a major general. Artillery was organized into a brigade of four regiments under a Chief of Artillery, Brig. Gen. Henry Knox, but the various companies were distributed among the infantry battalions. There was a small corps of engineers and an even smaller contingent of artificers, who handled the servicing and repair of ordnance.

Washington was provided with a staff generally corresponding to that of the British Army. The most important staff officer was the Quartermaster General, responsible not only for **transportation** and delivery of supplies but also for arranging the camp, regulating marches, and establishing the order of battle of the army. There were also an Adjutant General, a Judge Advocate

General, a Paymaster General, a Commissary General of Musters, a Commissary General of Provisions, a Clothier General, a Chief Surgeon, and a Chief Engineer. Each of the separate armies also usually had staff officers in these positions, designated as deputies to those of the main army.

All these staff officers had primarily administrative and supply functions. The modern concept of a general staff that acts as a sort of collective brain for the commander had no real counterpart in the eighteenth century. For advice on strategy and operations, Washington relied on a Council of War made up of his principal subordinate commanders, and, conforming to his original instructions from Congress, he usually consulted the council before making major decisions.

Both organization and staff work suffered from the ills that afflicted the whole military system. Regiments were constantly understrength, were organized differently by the various states, and employed varying systems of drill, discipline, and training. In the promotion of officers in the state lines, Continental commanders shared authority with the states, and the confused system gave rise to all sorts of rivalries, jealousies, and resentment, leading to frequent resignations. Staff officers were generally inexperienced, and few had the patience and perseverance to overcome the obstacles posed by divided authority, inadequate means, and poor transportation and communication facilities. The supply and support services of the Continental Army never really functioned efficiently, and with the depreciation in the currency they came close to collapse.

The British Problem

Whatever the American weaknesses, the British Government faced no easy task when it undertook to subdue the revolt by military force. Even though England possessed the central administration, stable financial system, and well-organized Army and Navy that the Americans so sorely lacked, the whole establishment was ill-prepared in 1775 for the struggle in America. A large burden of debt incurred in the wars of the preceding century had forced crippling economies on both Army and Navy. British administrative and supply systems, though far superior to anything the Americans could improvise, were also characterized by division and confusion of authority, and there was much corruption in high places.

To suppress the revolt, Britain had first to raise the necessary forces, then transport and sustain them over 3,000 miles of ocean, and finally use them effectively to regain control of a vast and sparsely populated territory. Recruiting men for an eighteenth century army was most difficult. The British Government had no power to compel service except in the militia in defense of the homeland, and service in the British Army overseas was immensely unpopular. To meet Sir William Howe's request for 50,000 men to conduct the campaign in 1776, the ministry resorted to hiring mercenaries from the small German states, particularly Hesse-Cassell (hence Hessians). These German states were to contribute almost 30,000 men to the British service during the war—complete organizations with their own officers up to the rank of major general and schooled in the system of Frederick the Great. Howe did not get his 50,000 men but by midsummer 1776 his force had passed 30,000 British and Hessians, and additional reinforcements were sent to Canada during the year. Maintaining a force of this size proved to be virtually impossible. The attrition rate in America from battle losses, sickness, disease, and desertion was tremendously high. English jails and poorhouses were drained of able-bodied men, bounties were paid, patriotic appeals were launched throughout England, Scotland, and Ireland, and all the ancient methods of impressment were tried, but the British were never able to recruit enough men to meet the needs of their commanders in America.

Providing adequate support for this army over a long ocean supply line was equally difficult. Even for food and forage, the British Army had to rely primarily on sea lines of supply. Transports were in short supply, the hardships of the 2- to 4-month voyage terrible, and the loss of men and supplies to natural causes heavy. Moreover, though the Americans could muster no navy capable of contesting British control of the seas, their privateers and the ships of their infant navy posed a constant threat to unprotected troop and supply transports. British commanders repeatedly had to delay their operations, awaiting the arrival of men and supplies from England.

Once in America, British armies could find no strategic center or centers whose capture would bring victory. Flat, open country where warfare could be carried on in European style was not common; and woods, hills, and swamps suited to the operations of militia and irregulars were plentiful. A British Army that could win victories in the field over the Continentals had great difficulty in making those victories meaningful. American armies seemed to possess miraculous powers of recuperation, while a British force, once depleted or surrendered, took a tremendous effort to replace.

As long as they controlled the seas, the British could land and establish bases at nearly any point on the long American coast line. The many navigable rivers dotting the coast also provided water avenues of invasion well into the interior. But to crush the revolt the British Army had to cut loose from coastal bases and rivers. When it did so its logistical problems multiplied and its lines of communications became vulnerable to constant harassment. British armies almost inevitably came to grief every time they moved very far from the areas where they could be nurtured by supply ships from the homeland. These difficulties, a British colonel asserted in 1777, had "absolutely prevented us this whole war from going fifteen miles from a navigable river."

The British could not, in any case, ever hope to muster enough strength to occupy with their own troops the vast territory they sought to restore to British rule. Their only real hope of meaningful victory was to use American loyalists as an instrument for controlling the country, as one British general put it, to help "the good Americans to subdue the bad." There were many obstacles to making effective use of the Tories. Patriot organization, weak at the center, was strong at the grass roots, in the local communities throughout America, whereas the Tories were neither well organized nor energetically led. The patriots seized the machinery of local government in most communities at the outset, held it until the British Army appeared in their midst, and then normally regained it after the British departed. Strong local control enabled the patriots to root out the more ardent Tories at the very outset, and by making an example of them to sway the apathetic and indifferent. British commanders were usually disappointed in the number of Tories who flocked to their standards and even more upset by the alacrity with which many of them switched their allegiance when the British Army moved out. They found the Tories a demanding, discordant, and puzzling lot, and they made no really earnest effort to enlist them in British forces until late in the war. By 1781 they had with their armies some 8,000 "provincial rank and file"; perhaps 50,000 in all served the British in some military capacity during the war.

On the frontiers the British could also expect support from the Indian tribes who almost inevitably drifted into the orbit of whatever power controlled Canada. But support of the Indians was a two-edged sword, for nothing could raise frontier enthusiasm for battle like the threat of an Indian attack.

Finally, the British had to fight the war with one eye on their ancient enemies in Europe. France, thirsting for revenge for defeat in the Seven Years' War, stood ready to aid the American cause if for no other purpose than to weaken British power, and by virtue of a Family Compact could almost certainly carry Spain along in any war with England. France and Spain could at the very least provide badly needed money and supplies to sustain the American effort and force the British to divert their forces from the contest in America. At most the combined Franco-Spanish fleet might well prove a match for the British Fleet and neutralize that essential control of the seas needed by the British to carry on the American war.

Of Strategy

The story of the American Revolution can hardly be told in terms of long-term strategy and its success or failure. Neither side ever had any really consistent plan for the conduct of the war. The British, who retained the strategic initiative most of the time, failed to use it to great advantage. They were highly uncertain about their objective; plans were laid from year to year and seldom co-ordinated even for a single year. Blame for this uncertain approach falls in almost equal part on the administration in England and the commanders in America. If King George III, Lord North, his Prime Minister, and Lord George Germain, Secretary of State for the American Department—the three British officials mainly responsible for the conduct of the war—never provided the timely guidance that might have been expected of them, their inability to do so came about in part because the commanders in the field never furnished accurate enough predictions of what to expect and differed so much among themselves as to the proper course to pursue. In assessing blame in this fashion, one must keep in mind the difficulties of logistics and communications under which the British labored, for these difficulties made it virtually impossible to co-ordinate plans over great distances or to assemble men and materials in time to pursue one logical and consistent plan.

American strategy was primarily defensive and consequently had to be shaped largely in terms of countering British moves. Uncertainties as to the supply of both men and materials acted on the American side even more effectively to thwart the development of a consistent plan for winning the war. Yet Washington was never so baffled by the conditions of the war or uncertain of his objective as were the various British commanders. After some early blunders, he soon learned both his own and the enemy's strengths and weaknesses and did his best to exploit them. Though unable to develop a consistent plan, he did try to develop a consistent line of action. He sought to maintain his principal striking force in a central position blocking any British advance into the interior; to be neither too bold nor too timid in seeking battle for limited objectives; to avoid the destruction of his army at all costs; and to find some means of concentrating a sufficient force to strike a decisive offensive blow whenever the British overreached themselves. He showed a better appreciation than the British commanders of the advantages in mobility their Navy gave them, and after 1778, when the French entered the war, he clearly saw that the decisive blow he desired could be struck only by a combined effort of the Continental Army and the French Fleet.

The British Offensive in 1776

If the British ever had a single strategic objective in the war, it was the Hudson River–Lake Champlain line. By taking and holding this line the British believed they could separate New England, considered to be the principal center of the rebellion, from the more malleable colonies to the southward. Howe proposed to make this the main objective of his campaign in 1776 by landing at New York, securing a base of operations there, and then pushing north. He wanted to concentrate the entire British force in America in New York, but the British Government diverted part of it to Canada in early 1776 to repel the American invasion, laying the groundwork for the divided command that was so to plague British operations afterward.

After the evacuation of Boston, Howe stayed at Halifax from March until June, awaiting the arrival of supplies and reinforcements. While he tarried, the British Government ordered another diversion in the south, aimed at encouraging the numerous loyalists who, according to the royal governors watching from their havens on board British warships, were waiting only for the appearance of a British force to rise and overthrow rebel rule. Unfortunately for the British, the naval squadron sent from England under Admiral Sir Peter Parker was delayed and did not arrive off the American coast until late in May. By this time all hopes of effective co-operation with the Tories had been dashed. Loyalist contingents had been completely defeated and dispersed in Virginia, North Carolina, and South Carolina. Parker, undeterred by these developments, determined to attack Charleston, the largest city in the south. There South Carolina militia and newly raised Continentals had prepared and manned defenses under the guidance of Maj. Gen. Charles Lee, whom Washington had dispatched south to assist them. The South Carolinians, contrary to Lee's advice, centered their defenses in Fort Moultrie, a palmetto log fort constructed on Sullivan's Island, commanding the approach to the harbor. It was an unwise decision, somewhat comparable to that at Bunker Hill, but fortunately for the defenders the British had to mount an un-co-ordinated attack in haste. Clinton's troops were landed on nearby Long Island, but on the day the Navy attacked, June 28, the water proved too deep for them to wade across to Sullivan's Island as expected. The British Army consequently sat idly by while the gunners in Fort Moultrie devastated the British warships. Sir Peter Parker suffered the ultimate indignity when his pants were set afire.

The battered British Fleet hastily embarked the British soldiers and sailed northward to join Howe, for it was already behind schedule. For three years following the fiasco at Charleston the British were to leave the south unmolested and the Tories there, who were undoubtedly numerous, without succor.

Howe was meanwhile beset by other delays in the arrival of transports from England, and his attack did not get under way until late August—leaving insufficient time before the advent of winter to carry through the planned advance along the Hudson–Lake Champlain line. He therefore started his invasion of New York with only the limited objective of gaining a foothold for the campaign the following year.

The British commander had, when his force was all assembled, an army of about 32,000 men; it was supported by a powerful fleet under the command of his brother, Admiral Richard Howe. To oppose him Washington had brought most of his army down from Boston, and Congress exerted its utmost efforts to reinforce him by raising Continental regiments in the surrounding states and issuing a general call for the militia. Washington was able to muster a paper strength of roughly 28,500 men, but only about 19,000 were present and fit for duty. As Christopher Ward remarks, "The larger part of them were raw recruits, undisciplined and inexperienced in warfare, and militia, never to be assuredly relied upon."

Washington and Congress made the same decision the South Carolinians had made at Charleston—to defend their territory in the most forward positions—and this time they paid the price for their mistake. The geography of the area gave the side possessing naval supremacy an almost insuperable advantage. The city of New York stood on Manhattan Island, surrounded by the Hudson, Harlem, and East Rivers. (*Map 5*) There was only one connecting link with the mainland, Kingsbridge across the Harlem River at the northern tip of Manhattan. Across the East River on Long Island, Brooklyn Heights stood in a position dominating the southern tip of Manhattan. With the naval forces at their disposal, the Howes could land troops on either Long Island or Manhattan proper and send warships up either the East or Hudson Rivers a considerable distance.

Washington decided he must defend Brooklyn Heights on Long Island if he was to defend Manhattan; he therefore divided his army between the two places—a violation of the principle of mass and the first step toward disaster. For all practical purposes command on Long Island was also divided. Maj. Gen. Nathanael Greene, to whom Washington first entrusted the command, came down with malaria and was replaced by Maj. Gen. John Sullivan. Not completely satisfied with this arrangement, at the last moment Washington placed Maj. Gen. Israel Putnam over Sullivan, but Putnam hardly had time to become acquainted with the situation before the British struck. The forces on Long

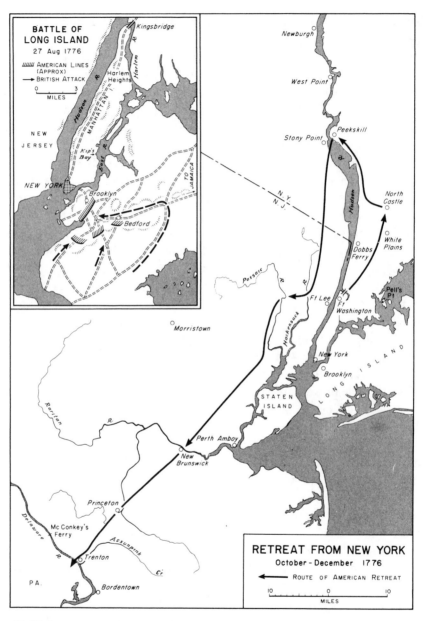

BATTLE OF
LONG ISLAND
27 Aug 1776

////// AMERICAN LINES
(APPROX)
⟶ BRITISH ATTACK

0   3
MILES

NEW
JERSEY

Kingsbridge

Harlem
Heights

MANHATTAN

Hudson R

Harlem R

Kip's
Bay

East R

NEW YORK

Brooklyn

Bedford

TO JAMAICA

Newburgh

West Point

Stony Point

Peekskill

North
Castle

White
Plains

Dobbs
Ferry

N.Y.
N.J.

Hudson

Pell's
Pt

Passaic R

R

Ft Lee

Ft
Washington

Hackensack R

Morristown

New York

Brooklyn

LONG ISLAND

STATEN
ISLAND

Raritan

R

Perth Amboy

New
Brunswick

Princeton

McConkey's
Ferry

Delaware R

Assunpink

Trenton

Cr

P.A.

Bordentown

RETREAT FROM NEW YORK
October - December 1776

⟵ ROUTE OF AMERICAN RETREAT

10   0   10
MILES

MAP 5

Island, numbering about 10,000, were disposed in fortifications on Brooklyn
Heights and in forward positions back of a line of thickly wooded hills that
ran across the southern end of the island. Sullivan was in command on the left

of the forward line, Brig. Gen. William Alexander (Lord Stirling) on the right. Four roads ran through the hills toward the American positions. (*inset, Map 5*) Unfortunately Sullivan, in violation of the principle of security, left the Jamaica-Bedford road unguarded.

Howe was consequently able to teach the Americans lessons in maneuver and surprise. On August 22 he landed a force of 20,000 on the southwestern tip of Long Island and, in a surprise attack up the Jamaica-Bedford road against the American left flank, crumpled the entire American position. Stirling's valiant fight on the right went for naught, and inexperienced American troops fled in terror before the British and Hessian bayonets, falling back to the fortifications on Brooklyn Heights. It seems clear that had Howe pushed his advantage immediately he could have carried the heights and destroyed half the American Army then and there. Instead he halted at nightfall and began to dig trenches, signaling an intent to take the heights by "regular approaches" in traditional eighteenth century fashion. Washington managed to evacuate his forces across the East River on the night of August 29. According to one theory, wind and weather stopped the British warships from entering the river to prevent the escape; according to another, the Americans had placed impediments in the river that effectively barred their entry. In any case, it was a narrow escape, made possible by the skill, bravery, and perseverance of Col. John Glover's Marblehead Regiment, Massachusetts fishermen who manned the boats.

Washington had two weeks to prepare his defenses on Manhattan before Howe struck again, landing a force at Kip's Bay above the city of New York (now about 34th Street) on September 15. Raw Connecticut militia posted at this point broke and ran "as if the Devil was in them," defying even the efforts of a raging Washington to halt them. Howe once again had an opportunity to split the American Army in two and destroy half, but again he delayed midway across the island to wait until his entire force had landed. General Putnam was able to bring the troops stationed in the city up the west side of Manhattan to join their compatriots in new fortifications on Harlem Heights. There the Americans held out for another month, and even won a skirmish, but this position was also basically untenable.

In mid-October Howe landed again in Washington's rear at Pell's Point. The American commander then finally evacuated the Manhattan trap via Kingsbridge and took up a new position at White Plains, leaving about 6,000 men behind to man two forts, Fort Washington and Fort Lee, on opposite sides of the Hudson. Howe launched a probing attack on the American position at White Plains and was repulsed, but Washington, sensing his inability to meet the British in battle on equal terms, moved away to the north toward the New

York highlands. Again he was outmaneuvered. Howe quickly moved to Dobbs Ferry on the Hudson between Washington's army and the Hudson River forts. On the advice of General Greene (now recovered from his bout with malaria), Washington decided to defend the forts. At the same time he again split his army, moving across the Hudson and into New Jersey with 5,000 men and leaving General Lee and Maj. Gen. William Heath with about 8,000 between them to guard the passes through the New York highlands at Peekskill and North Castle. On November 16 Howe turned against Fort Washington and with the support of British warships on the Hudson stormed it successfully, capturing 3,000 American troops and large quantities of valuable munitions. Greene then hastily evacuated Fort Lee and by the end of November Washington, with mere remnants of his army, was in full retreat across New Jersey with Lord Charles Cornwallis, detached by Howe, pursuing him rapidly from river to river.

While Washington was suffering these disastrous defeats, the army that had been gathered was slowly melting away. Militia left by whole companies and desertion among the Continentals was rife. When Washington finally crossed the Delaware into Pennsylvania in early December, he could muster barely 2,000 men, the hard core of his Continental forces. The 8,000 men in the New York highlands also dwindled away. Even more appalling, most enlistments expired with the end of the year 1776 and a new army would have to be raised for the following year.

Yet neither the unreliability of the militia nor the short period of enlistment fully explained the debacle that had befallen the Continental Army. Washington's generalship was also faulty. Criticism of the Commander in Chief, even among his official family, mounted, centering particularly on his decision to hold Fort Washington. General Lee, the ex-British colonel, ordered by Washington to bring his forces down from New York to join him behind the Delaware, delayed, believing that he might himself salvage the American cause by making incursions into New Jersey. He wrote Horatio Gates, ". . . *entre nous,* a certain great man is most damnably deficient. . . ."

There was only one bright spot in the picture in the autumn of 1776. While Howe was routing Washington around New York City, other British forces under Sir Guy Carleton were attempting to follow up the advantage they had gained in repulsing the attack on Canada earlier in the year. Carleton rather leisurely built a flotilla of boats to carry British forces down Lake Champlain and Lake George, intending at least to reduce the fort at Ticonderoga before winter set in. Benedict Arnold countered by throwing together a much weaker flotilla of American boats with which he contested the British passage. Arnold lost this naval action on the lakes, but he so delayed Carleton's advance that the British commander reached Ticonderoga too late in the year to consider undertaking a siege. He returned his army to winter quarters in Canada, leaving the British with no advance base from which to launch the next year's campaign.

Although its consequences were to be far reaching, this limited victory did little to dispel the gloom that fell on the patriots after Washington's defeats in New York. The British, aware that Continental enlistments expired at the end of the year, had high hopes that the American Army would simply fade away and the rebellion collapse. Howe halted Cornwallis' pursuit of Washington and sent Clinton with a detachment of troops under naval escort to seize Newport, Rhode Island. He then dispersed his troops in winter quarters, establishing a line of posts in New Jersey at Perth Amboy, New Brunswick, Princeton, Trenton, and Bordentown, and retired himself to New York. Howe had gained the object of the 1776 campaign, a strong foothold, and possibly, as he thought at the time, a great deal more.

Trenton and Princeton

While Howe rested comfortably in New York, Washington desperately sought to reconcentrate his forces and redeem the defeat in New York. General Lee had the misfortune to fall into British hands on December 12, and his 2,000 remaining men then made haste to join Washington. Eight decimated regiments were also pulled from the Northern Army, and with some Pennsylvania militia Washington was able to assemble a force totaling about 7,000 by the last week of December 1776. If he was to use this force, he would have to do so before the enlistments expired on December 31. With great boldness, Washington formulated a plan to strike by surprise at the Hessian garrisons at Trenton and Bordentown on Christmas night, when the troops might be expected to relax their guard for holiday revelry. A Continental force of 2,400 men under Washington's personal command was to cross the Delaware at McConkey's Ferry above Trenton and then proceed in two columns by different routes, converging on the opposite ends of the main street of Trenton in the early morning of December 26. (*Map 6*) A second force, mainly militia, under Col. John Cadwalader was to cross below near Bordentown to attack the Hessian garrison there; a third, also militia, under Brig. Gen. James Ewing, was to cross directly opposite Trenton to block the Hessian route of escape across Assunpink Creek.

Christmas night was cold, windy, and snowy and the Delaware River was filled with blocks of ice. Neither Cadwalader nor Ewing was able to fulfill his part of the plan. Driven on by Washington's indomitable will, the main force did cross as planned and the two columns, commanded respectively by Greene and Sullivan, converged on Trenton at eight o'clock in the morning of December 26,

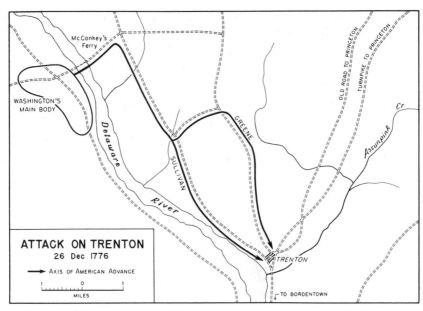

MAP 6

taking the Hessians completely by surprise. A New England private noted in his diary for the 26th: "This morning at 4 a clock we set off with our Field pieces and Marched 8 miles to Trenton whare we ware attacked by a Number of Hushing and we Toock 1000 of them besides killed some. Then we marched back and got to the River at Night and got over all the Hushing." This rather undramatic description of a very dramatic event was not far wrong, except in attributing the attack to the "Hushings." The Hessians surrendered after a fight lasting only an hour and a half. Forty were killed and the prisoner count was 918. Only 400 escaped to Bordentown, and these only because Ewing was not in place to block their escape. The Americans lost only 4 dead and 4 wounded.

Encouraged by this success, Washington determined to make another foray. By an impassioned appeal to the patriotism of the men, supplemented by an offer of a $10 bounty in hard money, he was able to persuade at least part of his old army to remain for six more weeks. With a force of around 5,000 Washington again crossed the Delaware on the night of December 30–31. By this time Cornwallis had hastily gathered together the scattered British garrisons in New Jersey, and took up a position confronting Washington at Trenton on January 2, 1777. Convinced that he had the Americans in a trap, he put off battle until the next day because of the exhausted state of his troops. In the night Washington slipped away, leaving campfires burning brightly to deceive the British. The

ALEXANDER HAMILTON'S ARTILLERY AT TRENTON, *with a 6-pounder brass field gun in the foreground.*

next morning he struck another surprise blow at Princeton, inflicting heavy losses on two British regiments just leaving the town to join Cornwallis. Washington then went into winter quarters in the hills around Morristown, New Jersey. Cornwallis did not pursue. The British had had enough of winter warfare, and Howe drew in his outposts in New Jersey to New Brunswick and Perth Amboy.

Trenton and Princeton not only offset the worst effects of the disastrous defeats in New York but also restored Washington's prestige as a commander with friend and foe alike. In the execution of the two strokes east of the Delaware, Washington had applied the principles of offensive, surprise, and maneuver with great success and finally achieved stature as a military commander. If these victories did not assure him that he could recruit such an army as Congress had voted, they did at least guarantee that he would be able to field a force the following year. Sir William Howe found that, despite his smashing rout of the Americans in New York, he was left with little more than that city, a foothold in New Jersey, and the port of Newport in Rhode Island.

CHAPTER 4

The Winning of Independence
1777-1783

The year 1777 was most critical for the British. The issue, very plainly, was whether they could score such success in putting down the American revolt that the French would not dare enter the war openly to aid the American rebels. Yet it was in this critical year that British plans were most confused and British operations most disjointed. The British campaign of 1777 provides one of the most striking object lessons in military history of the dangers of divided command.

The Campaign of 1777

With secure bases at New York and Newport, Howe had a chance to get the early start that had been denied him the previous year. His first plan, advanced on November 30, 1776, was probably the most comprehensive put forward by any British commander during the war. He proposed to maintain a small force of about 8,000 to contain Washington in New Jersey and 7,000 to garrison New York, while sending one column of 10,000 from Newport into New England and another column of 10,000 from New York up the Hudson to form a junction with a British force moving down from Canada. On the assumption that these moves would be successful by autumn, he would next capture Philadelphia, the rebel capital, and then make the southern provinces the "objects of the winter." For this plan, Howe requested 35,000 men, 15,000 more effective troops than he had left at the end of the 1776 campaign. Sir George Germain, the American Secretary, could promise him only 8,000. Even before receiving this news, but evidently influenced by Trenton and Princeton, Howe changed his plan and proposed to devote his main effort in 1777 to taking Philadelphia. On March 3, 1777, Germain informed Howe that the Philadelphia plan was approved, but that there might be only 5,500 reinforcements. At the same time Germain and the king urged a "warm diversion" against New England.

Meanwhile, Sir John Burgoyne, who had succeeded in obtaining the separate military command in Canada, submitted his plan calling for an advance southward to "a junction with Howe." Germain and the king also approved this plan on March 29, though aware of Howe's intention to go to Philadelphia. They seem to have expected either that Howe would be able to form his junction by the "warm diversion," or else that he would take Philadelphia quickly and then turn north to aid Burgoyne. In any case, Germain approved two separate and un-co-ordinated plans, and Howe and Burgoyne went their separate ways, doing nothing to remedy the situation. Howe's Philadelphia plan did provide for leaving enough force in New York for what its commander, General Clinton, called "a damn'd starved offensive," but Clinton's orders were vague. Quite possibly Burgoyne knew before he left England for Canada that Howe was going to Philadelphia, but ambitious "Gentleman Johnny" was determined to make a reputation in the American war, and evidently believed he could succeed alone. Even when he learned certainly on August 3, 1777, that he could not expect Howe's co-operation, he persisted in his design. As Howe thought Pennsylvania was filled with royalists, Burgoyne cherished the illusion that legions of Tories in New York and western New England were simply awaiting the appearance of the king's troops to rally to the colors.

Again in 1777 the late arrival of Howe's reinforcements and stores ships gave Washington time that he sorely needed. Men to form the new Continental Army came in slowly and not until June did the Americans have a force of 8,000. On the northern line the defenses were even more thinly manned. Supplies for troops in the field were also short, but the arrival of the first three ships bearing secret aid from France vastly improved the situation. They were evidence of the covert support of the French Government; a mission sent by Congress to France was meanwhile working diligently to enlist open aid and to embroil France in a war with England. The French Foreign Minister, the Comte de Vergennes, had already decided to take that risk when and if the American rebels demonstrated their serious purpose and ability to fulfill it by some signal victory in the field.

With the first foreign material aid in 1777, the influx of foreign officers into the American Army began. These officers were no unmixed blessing. Most were adventurers in search of fortune or of reputation with little facility for adjusting themselves to American conditions. Few were willing to accept any but the highest ranks. Nevertheless, they brought with them professional military knowledge and competence that the Continental Army sorely needed. When the misfits were culled out, this knowledge and competence were used to considerable advantage. Louis DuPortail, a Frenchman, and Thaddeus Kosciuszko, a Pole, did much to advance the art of engineering in the Continental Army; Casimir Pulaski, another Pole, organized its first genuine cavalry contingent; Johann de Kalb and Friedrich Wilhelm von Steuben, both Germans, and the Marquis de Lafayette, an influential French nobleman who financed his own way, were all to make valuable contributions as trainers and leaders. On the Continental Army of 1777, however, these foreign volunteers had little effect and it remained much as it had been before, a relatively untrained body of inexperienced enlistees.

When Howe finally began to stir in June 1777, Washington posted his army at Middlebrook, New Jersey, in a position either to bar Howe's overland route to Philadelphia or to move rapidly up the Hudson to oppose an advance northward. Washington confidently expected Howe to move northward to form a junction with Burgoyne, but decided he must stay in front of the main British Army wherever it went. Following the principle of economy of force, he disposed a small part of his army under General Putnam in fortifications guarding the approaches up the Hudson, and at a critical moment detached a small force to aid Schuyler against Burgoyne. The bulk of his army he kept in front of Howe in an effort to defend Philadelphia. Forts were built along the Delaware River and other steps taken to block the approach to the Continental capital by sea.

In the effort to defend Philadelphia Washington again failed, but hardly so ignominiously as he had the year before in New York. After maneuvering in New Jersey for upward of two months, Howe in August put most of his army on board ship and sailed down the coast and up the Chesapeake Bay to Head of Elk (a small town at the head of the Elk River) in Maryland, putting himself even further away from Burgoyne. (*Map 7*) Though surprised by Howe's movement, Washington rapidly shifted his own force south and took up a position at Chad's Ford on Brandywine Creek, blocking the approach to Philadelphia. There on September 11, 1777, Howe executed a flanking movement not dissimilar to that employed on Long Island and again defeated Washington. The American commander had disposed his army in two main parts, one directly opposite Chad's Ford under his personal command and the other under General Sullivan guarding the right flank upstream. While Lt. Gen. Wilhelm von Knyphausen's Hessian troops demonstrated opposite the ford, a larger force under Lord Cornwallis marched upstream, crossed the Brandywine, and moved to take Sullivan from the rear. Washington lacked good cavalry reconnaissance, and did not get positive information on Cornwallis' movement until the eleventh hour. Sullivan was in the process of changing front when

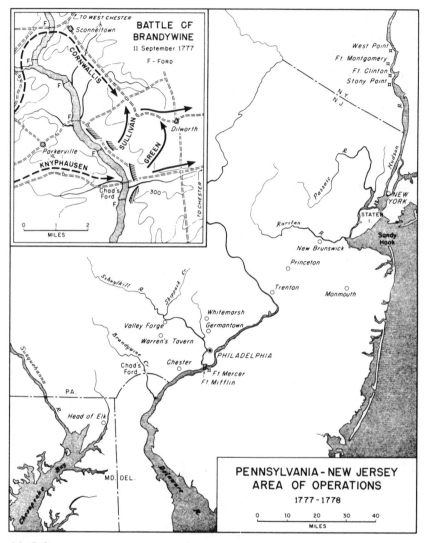

MAP 7

the British struck and his men retreated in confusion. Washington was able to salvage the situation by dispatching General Greene with two brigades to fight a valiant rear-guard action, but the move weakened his front opposite Kynp-hausen and his forces also had to fall back. Nevertheless, the trap was averted and the Continental Army retired in good order to Chester.

Howe followed with a series of maneuvers comparable to those he had executed in New York, and was able to enter Philadelphia with a minimum of fighting on September 26. A combined attack of British Army and Navy forces shortly afterward reduced the forts on the Delaware and opened the river as a British supply line.

On entering Philadelphia, Howe dispersed his forces, stationing 9,000 men at Germantown north of the city, 3,000 in New Jersey, and the rest in Philadelphia. As Howe had repeated his performance in New York, Washington sought to repeat Trenton by a surprise attack on Germantown. The plan was much like that used at Trenton but involved far more complicated movements by much larger bodies of troops. Four columns—two of Continentals under Sullivan and Greene and two of militia—moving at night over different roads were to converge on Germantown simultaneously at dawn on October 4. (*Map 8*) The plan violated the principle of simplicity, for such a maneuver was

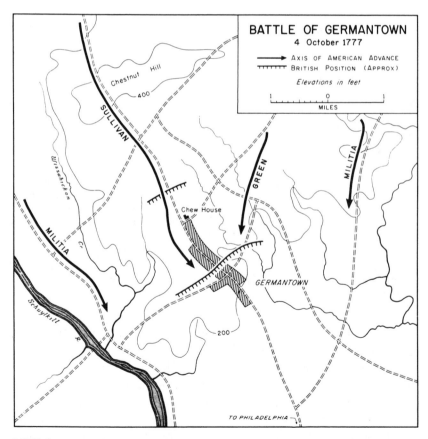

MAP 8

difficult even for well-trained professionals to execute. The two columns of Continentals arrived at different times and fired on each other in an early morning fog. The two militia columns never arrived at all. British fire from a stone house, the Chew Mansion, held up the advance while American generals argued whether they could leave a fortress in their rear. The British, though surprised, had better discipline and cohesion and were able to re-form and send fresh troops into the fray. The Americans retreated about 9:00 a.m., leaving Howe's troops in command of the field.

After Germantown Howe once again concentrated his army and moved to confront Washington at Whitemarsh, but finally withdrew to winter quarters in Philadelphia without giving battle. Washington chose the site for his own winter quarters at a place called Valley Forge, twenty miles northwest of the city. Howe had gained his objective but it proved of no lasting value to him. Congress fled west to York, Pennsylvania. No swarms of loyalists rallied to the British standards. And Howe had left Burgoyne to lose a whole British army in the north.

Burgoyne set out from Canada in June, his object to reach Albany by fall. (*Map 9*) His force was divided into two parts. The first and largest part—7,200 British and Hessian Regulars and 650 Tories, Canadians, and Indians, under his personal command—was to take the route down Lake Champlain to Ticonderoga and thence via Lake George to the Hudson. The second—700 Regulars and 1,000 Tories and Indian braves under Col. Barry St. Leger—was to move via Lake Ontario to Oswego and thence down the Mohawk Valley to join Burgoyne before Albany. In his preparations, Burgoyne evidently forgot the lesson the British had learned in the French and Indian War, that in the wilderness troops had to be prepared to travel light and fight like Indians. He carried 138 pieces of artillery and a heavy load of officers' personal baggage. Numerous ladies of high and low estate accompanied the expedition. When he started down the lakes, Burgoyne did not have enough horses and wagons to transport his artillery and baggage once he had to leave the water and move overland.

At first Burgoyne's American opposition was very weak—only about 2,500 Continentals at Ticonderoga and about 450 at old Fort Stanwix, the sole American bulwark in the Mohawk Valley. Dissension among the Americans was rife, the New Englanders refusing to support Schuyler, the aristocratic New Yorker who commanded the Northern Army, and openly intriguing to replace him with their own favorite, Maj. Gen. Horatio Gates. Ticonderoga fell to Burgoyne on June 27 all too easily. American forces dispersed and Burgoyne pursued the remnants down to Skenesborough. Once that far along, he decided to continue overland to the Hudson instead of returning to Ticonderoga to float his force

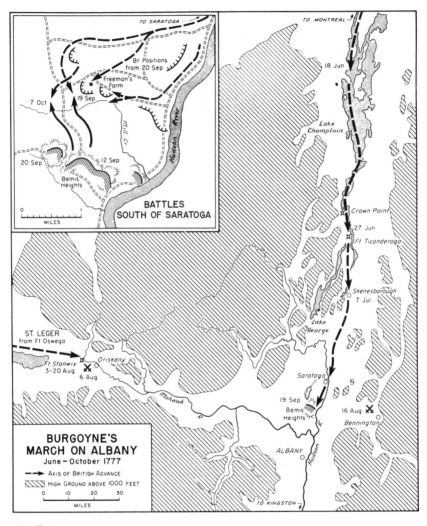

MAP 9

down Lake George, though much of his impedimenta still had to be carried by boat down the lake.

The overland line of advance was already a nightmare, running along wilderness trails, through marshes, and across wide ravines and creeks that had been swollen by abnormally heavy rains. Schuyler adopted the tactic of making it even worse by destroying bridges, cutting trees in Burgoyne's path, and digging trenches to let the waters of swamps onto drier ground. The British were able to move at a rate of little more than a mile a day and took until July 29 to reach Fort Edward on the Hudson. By that time Burgoyne was desperately short of horses, wagons, and oxen. Yet Schuyler, with a unstable force of 4,500 men discouraged by continual retreats, was in no position to give battle.

Washington did what he could to strengthen the Northern Army at this juncture. He first dispatched Maj. Gen. Benedict Arnold, his most aggressive field commander, and Maj. Gen. Benjamin Lincoln, a Massachusetts man noted for his influence with the New England militia. On August 16 he detached Col. Daniel Morgan with 500 riflemen from the main army in Pennsylvania and ordered them along with 750 men from Putnam's force in the New York highlands to join Schuyler. The riflemen were calculated to furnish an antidote for Burgoyne's Indians who, despite his efforts to restrain them, were terrorizing the countryside.

It was the rising militia, rather than Washington, who were to provide the Northern Army with its main reinforcements. Nothing worked more to produce this result than Burgoyne's employment of Indians. The murder and scalping of a beautiful white woman, Jane McCrea, dramatized the Indian threat as nothing else probably could have done. New England militiamen now began to rally to the cause, though they still refused to co-operate with Schuyler. New Hampshire commissioned John Stark, a disgruntled ex-colonel in the Continental Army and a veteran of Bunker Hill and Trenton, as a brigadier general in the state service (a rank denied him by Congress), and Stark quickly recruited 2,000 men. Refusing Schuyler's request that he join the main army, Stark took up a position at Bennington in southern Vermont to guard the New England frontier. On August 11 Burgoyne detached a force of 650 men under Hessian Col. Friedrich Baum to forage for cattle, horses, and transport in the very area Stark was occupying. At Bennington on August 16 Stark nearly annihilated Baum's force, and reinforcements sent by Burgoyne arrived on the field just in time to be soundly thrashed in turn. Burgoyne not only failed to secure his much-needed supplies and transport but also lost about a tenth of his command.

Meanwhile, St. Leger with his Tories and Indians had appeared before Fort Stanwix on August 2. The garrison, fearing massacre by the Indians, determined to hold out to the bitter end. On August 4, the Tryon County militia under Brig. Gen. Nicholas Herkimer set out to relieve the fort but were ambushed by the Indians in a wooded ravine near Oriskany. The militia, under the direction of a mortally wounded Herkimer, scattered in the woods and fought a bloody afternoon's battle in a summer thunderstorm. Both sides suffered heavy losses, and though the militia were unable to relieve Stanwix the losses discouraged St. Leger's Indians, who were already restless in the static siege operation at Stanwix.

Despite his own weak position, when Schuyler learned of the plight of the Stanwix garrison, he courageously detached Benedict Arnold with 950 Continentals to march to its relief. Arnold devised a ruse that took full advantage of the dissatisfaction and natural superstition of the Indians. Employing a half-wit Dutchman, his clothes shot full of holes, and a friendly Oneida Indian as his messengers, Arnold spread the rumor that the Continentals were approaching "as numerous as the leaves on the trees." The Indians, who had special respect for any madman, departed in haste, scalping not a few of their Tory allies as they went, and St. Leger was forced to abandon the siege.

Bennington and Stanwix were serious blows to Burgoyne. By early September he knew he could expect help from neither Howe nor St. Leger. Disillusioned about the Tories, he wrote Germain: "The great bulk of the country is undoubtedly with Congress in principle and zeal; and their measures are executed with a secrecy and dispatch that are not to be equalled. Wherever the King's forces point, militia in the amount of three or four thousand assemble in twenty-four hours; they bring with them their subsistence, etc., and the alarm over, they return to their farms. . . ." Nevertheless, gambler that he was, Burgoyne crossed the Hudson to the west side during September 13 and 14, signaling his intention to get to Albany or lose his army. While his supply problem daily became worse, his Indians, with a natural instinct for sensing approaching disaster, drifted off into the forests, leaving him with little means of gaining intelligence of the American dispositions.

The American forces were meanwhile gathering strength. Congress finally deferred to New England sentiment on August 19 and replaced Schuyler with Gates. Gates was more the beneficiary than the cause of the improved situation, but his appointment helped morale and encouraged the New England militia. Washington's emissary, General Lincoln, also did his part. Gates understood Burgoyne's plight perfectly and adapted his tactics to take full advantage of it. He advanced his forces four miles northward and took up a position, surveyed and prepared by the Polish engineer, Kosciusko, on Bemis Heights, a few miles below Saratoga. Against this position Burgoyne launched his attack on September 19 and was repulsed with heavy losses. In the battle, usually known as Freeman's Farm, Arnold persuaded Gates to let him go forward to counter the British attack, and Colonel Morgan's riflemen, in a wooded terrain well suited to the use of their specialized weapon, took a heavy toll of British officers and men.

After Freeman's Farm, the lines remained stable for three weeks. Burgoyne had heard that Clinton, with the force Howe had left in New York, had started north to relieve him. Clinton, in fact, stormed Forts Clinton and Montgomery on the Hudson on October 6, but, exercising that innate caution characteristic of all his actions, he refused to gamble for high stakes. He simply sent an advance guard on to Kingston and he himself returned to New York.

Burgoyne was left to his fate. Gates strengthened his entrenchments and calmly awaited the attack he was sure Burgoyne would have to make. Militia reinforcements increased his forces to around 10,000 by October 7. Meanwhile Burgoyne's position grew more desperate. Food was running out; the meadows were grazed bare by the animals; and every day more men slipped into the forest, deserting the lost cause. With little intelligence of American strength or dispositions, on October 7 he sent out a "reconnaissance in force" to feel out the American positions. On learning that the British were approaching, Gates sent out a contingent including Morgan's riflemen to meet them, and a second battle developed, usually known as Bemis Heights. The British suffered severe losses, five times those of the Americans, and were driven back to their fortified positions. Arnold, who had been at odds with Gates and was confined to his tent, broke out, rushed into the fray, and again distinguished himself before he was wounded in leading an attack on Breymann's Redoubt.

Two days after the battle, Burgoyne withdrew to a position in the vicinity of Saratoga. Militia soon worked around to his rear and cut his supply lines. His position hopeless, Burgoyne finally capitulated on October 17 at Saratoga. The total prisoner count was nearly 6,000 and great quantities of military stores fell into American hands. The victory at Saratoga brought the Americans out well ahead in the campaign of 1777 despite the loss of Philadelphia. What had been at stake soon became obvious. In February 1778 France negotiated a treaty of alliance with the American states, tantamount to a declaration of war against England.

Valley Forge

The name of Valley Forge has come to stand, and rightly so, as a patriotic symbol of suffering, courage, and perserverance. The hard core of 6,000 Continentals who stayed with Washington during that bitter winter of 1777–78 indeed suffered much. Some men had no shoes, no pants, no blankets. Weeks passed when there was no meat and men were reduced to boiling their shoes and eating them. The wintry winds penetrated the tattered tents that were at first the only shelter.

The symbolism of Valley Forge should not be allowed to obscure the fact that the suffering was largely unnecessary. While the soldiers shivered and went hungry, food rotted and clothing lay unused in depots throughout the country. True, access to Valley Forge was difficult, but little determined effort was made to get supplies into the area. The supply and transport system broke down. In mid-1777, both the Quartermaster and Commissary Generals resigned along with numerous subordinate officials in both departments, mostly merchants who found private trade more lucrative. Congress, in refuge at York, Pennsylvania, and split into factions, found it difficult to find replacements. If there was not, as most historians now believe, an organized cabal seeking to replace Washington with Gates, there were many, both in and out of the Army, who were dissatisfied with the Commander in Chief, and much intrigue went on. Gates was made president of the new Board of War set up in 1777, and at least two of its members were enemies of Washington. In the administrative chaos at the height of the Valley Forge crisis, there was no functioning Quartermaster General at all.

Washington weathered the storm and the Continental Army was to emerge from Valley Forge a more effective force than before. With his advice, Congress instituted reforms in the Quartermaster and Commissary Departments that temporarily restored the effectiveness of both agencies. Washington's ablest subordinate, General Greene, reluctantly accepted the post of Quartermaster General. The Continental Army itself gained a new professional competence from the training given by the Prussian, Friedrich Wilhelm von Steuben.

Steuben appeared at Valley Forge in February 1778 arrayed in such martial splendor that one private thought he had seen Mars, the god of war, himself. He represented himself as a baron, a title he had acquired in the service of a small German state, and as a former lieutenant general on the staff of Frederick the Great, though in reality he had been only a captain. The fraud was harmless, for Steuben had a broad knowledge of military affairs and his remarkable sense of the dramatic was combined with the common touch a true Prussian baron might well have lacked.

Washington had long sensed the need for uniform training and organization, and after a short trial he secured the appointment of Steuben as Inspector General in charge of a training program. Steuben carried out the program during the late winter and early spring of 1778, teaching the Continental Army a simplified but effective version of the drill formations and movements of European armies, proper care of equipment, and the use of the bayonet, a weapon in which British superiority had previously been marked. He attempted to consolidate the understrength regiments and companies and organized light

STEUBEN TRAINING AMERICAN FORCES AT VALLEY FORGE

infantry companies as the elite force of the Army. He constantly sought to impress upon the officers their responsibility for taking care of the men. Steuben never lost sight of the difference between the American citizen soldier and the European professional. He early noted that American soldiers had to be told why they did things before they would do them well, and he applied this philosophy in his training program. His trenchant good humor and vigorous profanity, almost the only English he knew, delighted the Continental soldiers and made the rigorous drill more palatable. After Valley Forge, Continentals would fight on equal terms with British Regulars in the open field.

First Fruits of the French Alliance

While the Continental Army was undergoing its ordeal and transformation at Valley Forge, Howe dallied in Philadelphia, forfeiting whatever remaining chance he had to win a decisive victory before the effects of the French alliance were felt. He had had his fill of the American war and the king accepted his resignation from command, appointing General Clinton as his successor. As Washington prepared to sally forth from Valley Forge, the British Army and the Philadelphia Tories said goodbye to their old commander in one of the most lavish celebrations ever held in America, the *Mischianza*, a veritable Belshazzar's feast. The handwriting on the wall appeared in the form of orders, already in Clinton's hands, to evacuate the American capital. With the French in the war, England had to look to the safety of the long ocean supply line to America and to the protection of its possessions in other parts of the world. Clinton's orders were to detach 5,000 men to the West Indies and 3,000 to Florida, and to return the rest of his army to New York by sea.

As Clinton prepared to depart Philadelphia, Washington had high hopes that the war might be won in 1778 by a co-operative effort between his army and the French Fleet. The Comte d'Estaing with a French naval squadron of eleven ships of the line and transports carrying 4,000 troops left France in May to sail for the American coast. D'Estaing's fleet was considerably more powerful than any Admiral Howe could immediately concentrate in American waters. For a brief period in 1778 the strategic initiative passed from British hands, and Washington hoped to make full use of it.

Clinton had already decided, before he learned of the threat from d'Estaing, to move his army overland to New York prior to making any detachments, largely because he could find no place for 3,000 horses on the transports. On June 18, 1778, he set out with about 10,000 men. Washington, who by that time had gathered about 12,000, immediately occupied Philadelphia and then took up the pursuit of Clinton, undecided as to whether he should risk an attack on the British column while it was on the march. His Council of War was divided, though none of his generals advised a "general action." The boldest, Brig. Gen. Anthony Wayne, and the young major general, the Marquis de Lafayette, urged a "partial attack" to strike at a portion of the British Army while it was strung out on the road; the most cautious, General Lee, who had been exchanged and had rejoined the army at Valley Forge, advised only guerrilla action to harass the British columns. On June 26 Washington decided to take a bold approach, though he issued no orders indicating an intention to bring on a "general action." He sent forward an advance guard composed of almost half his army to strike at the British rear when Clinton moved out of Monmouth Court House on the morning of June 27. Lee, the cautious, claimed the command from Lafayette, the bold, when he learned the detachment would be so large.

In the early morning, Lee advanced over rough ground that had not been reconnoitered and made contact with the British rear, but Clinton reacted quickly and maneuvered to envelop the American right flank. Lee, feeling that his force was in an untenable position, began a retreat that became quite confused. Washington rode up amidst the confusion and, exceedingly irate to find the advance guard in retreat, exchanged harsh words with Lee. He then assumed direction of what had to be a defense against a British counterattack. The battle that followed, involving the bulk of both armies, lasted until nightfall on a hot, sultry day with both sides holding their own. For the first time the Americans fought well with the bayonet as well as with the musket and rifle, and their battlefield behavior generally reflected the Valley Forge training. Nevertheless, Washington failed to strike a telling blow at the British Army, for Clinton slipped away in the night and in a few days completed the retreat to New York. Lee demanded and got a court-martial at which he was judged, perhaps unjustly, guilty of disobedience of orders, poor conduct of the retreat, and disrespect for the Commander in Chief. As a consequence he retired from the Army, though the controversy over his actions at Monmouth was to go on for years.

Washington, meanwhile, sought his victory in co-operation with the French Fleet. D'Estaing arrived off the coast on July 8 and the two commanders at first agreed on a combined land and sea attack on New York, but d'Estaing feared he would be unable to get his deep-draft ships across the bar that extended from Staten Island to Sandy Hook, in order to get at Howe's inferior fleet. They then decided to transfer the attack to the other and weaker British stronghold at Newport, Rhode Island—a city standing on an island with difficult approaches. A plan was agreed on whereby the French Fleet would force the passage on the west side of the island and an American force under General Sullivan would cross over and mount an assault from the east. The whole scheme soon went awry. The French Fleet arrived off Newport on July 29 and successfully forced the passage; Sullivan began crossing on the east on August 8 and d'Estaing began to disembark his troops. Unfortunately at this juncture Admiral Howe appeared with a reinforced British Fleet, forcing d'Estaing to re-embark his troops and put out to sea to meet Howe. As the two fleets maneuvered for advantage, a great gale scattered both on August 12. The British returned to New York to refit, and the French Fleet to Boston, whence d'Estaing decided he must move on to tasks he considered more pressing in the West Indies. Sullivan was left to extricate his forces from an untenable position as best he could, and the first experiment in Franco-American co-operation came to a disappointing end with recriminations on both sides.

The fiasco at Newport ended any hopes for an early victory over the British as a result of the French alliance. By the next year, as the French were forced to devote their major attention to the West Indies, the British regained the initiative on the mainland, and the war entered a new phase.

The New Conditions of the War

After France entered the war in 1778, it rapidly took on the dimensions of a major European as well as an American conflict. In 1779 Spain declared war against England, and in the following year Holland followed suit. The necessity of fighting European enemies in the West Indies and other areas and of standing guard at home against invasion weakened the British effort against the American rebels. Yet the Americans were unable to take full advantage of Britain's embarrassments, for their own effort suffered more and more from war weariness, lack of strong direction, and inadequate finance. Moreover, the interests of European states fighting Britain did not necessarily coincide with American interests. Spain and Holland did not ally themselves with the American states at all, and even France found it expedient to devote its major effort to the West Indies. Finally, the entry of ancient enemies into the fray spurred the British to intensify their effort and evoked some, if not enough, of that characteristic tenacity that has produced victory for England in so many wars. Despite their many new commitments, the British were able to maintain in America an army that was usually superior in numbers to the dwindling Continental Army, though never strong enough to undertake offensives again on the scale of those of 1776 and 1777.

Monmouth was the last general engagement in the north between Washington's and Clinton's armies. In 1779 the situation there became a stalemate and remained so until the end of the war. Washington set up a defense system around New York with its center at West Point, and Clinton made no attempt to attack his main defense line. The British commander did, in late spring 1779, attempt to draw Washington into the open by descending in force on unfinished American outpost fortifications at Verplanck's Point and Stony Point, but Washington refused to take the bait. When Clinton withdrew his main force to New York, the American commander retaliated by sending Maj. Gen. Anthony Wayne on July 15, 1779, with an elite corps of light infantry, on a stealthy night attack on Stony Point, a successful action more notable for demonstrating the proficiency with which the Americans now used the bayonet than for any important strategic gains. Wayne was unable to take Verplanck's, and Clinton rapidly retook Stony Point. Thereafter the war around New York became largely an affair of raids, skirmishes, and constant vigilance on both sides.

Clinton's inaction allowed Washington to attempt to deal with British-inspired Indian attacks. Although Burgoyne's defeat ended the threat of invasion from Canada, the British continued to incite the Indians all along the frontier to bloody raids on American settlements. From Fort Niagara and Detroit they sent out their bands, usually led by Tories, to pillage, scalp, and burn in the Mohawk Valley of New York, the Wyoming Valley of Pennsylvania, and the new American settlements in Kentucky. In August 1779 Washington detached General Sullivan with a force to deal with the Iroquois in Pennsylvania and New York. Sullivan laid waste the Indians' villages and defeated a force of Tories and Indians at Newtown on August 29.

In the winter of 1778-79, the state of Virginia had sponsored an expedition that struck a severe blow at the British and Indians in the northwest. Young Lt. Col. George Rogers Clark with a force of only 175 men, ostensibly recruited for the defense of Kentucky, overran all the British posts in what is today Illinois and Indiana. Neither he nor Sullivan, however, was able to strike at the sources of the trouble—Niagara and Detroit. Indian raids along the frontiers continued, though they were somewhat less frequent and severe.

British Successes in the South

Late in 1778 the British began to turn their main effort to the south. Tory strength was greater in the Carolinas and Georgia and the area was closer to the West Indies, where the British Fleet had to stand guard against the French. The king's ministers hoped to bring the southern states into the fold one by one, and from bases there to strangle the recalcitrant north. A small British force operating from Florida quickly overran thinly populated Georgia in the winter of 1778-79. Alarmed by this development, Congress sent General Benjamin Lincoln south to Charleston in December 1778 to command the Southern Army and organize the southern effort. Lincoln gathered 3,500 Continentals and militiamen, but in May 1779, while he maneuvered along the Georgia border, the British commander, Maj. Gen. Augustine Prevost, slipped around him to lay siege to Charleston. The city barely managed to hold out until Lincoln returned to relieve it. (*Map 10*)

In September 1779 d'Estaing arrived off the coast of Georgia with a strong French Fleet and 6,000 troops. Lincoln then hurried south with 1,350 Americans to join him in a siege of the main British base at Savannah. Unfortunately, the Franco-American force had to hurry its attack because d'Estaing was unwilling to risk his fleet in a position dangerously exposed to autumn storms. The French and Americans mounted a direct assault on Savannah on October 9, abandoning their plan to make a systematic approach by regular parallels. The British in strongly entrenched positions repulsed the attack in what was essentially a Bunker Hill in reverse, the French and Americans suffering

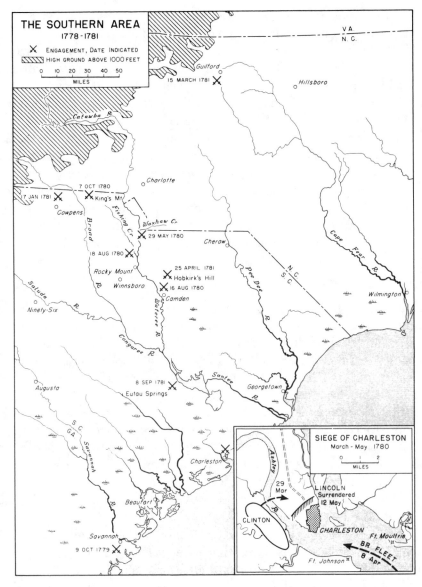

MAP 10

staggering losses. D'Estaing then sailed away to the West Indies, Lincoln returned to Charleston, and the second attempt at Franco-American co-operation ended in much the same atmosphere of bitterness and disillusion as the first.

Meanwhile Clinton, urged on by the British Government, had determined to push the southern campaign in earnest. In October 1779 he withdrew the British garrison from Newport, pulled in his troops from outposts around New York, and prepared to move south against Charleston with a large part of his force. With d'Estaing's withdrawal the British regained control of the sea along the American coast, giving Clinton a mobility that Washington could not match. While Clinton drew forces from New York and Savannah to achieve a decisive concentration of force (14,000 men) at Charleston, Washington was able to send only piecemeal reinforcements to Lincoln over difficult overland routes. Applying the lessons of his experience in 1776, Clinton this time carefully planned a co-ordinated Army-Navy attack. First, he landed his force on John's Island to the south, then moved up to the Ashley River, investing Charleston from the land side. Lincoln, under strong pressure from the South Carolina authorities, concentrated his forces in a citadel defense on the neck of land between the Ashley and Cooper Rivers, leaving Fort Moultrie in the harbor lightly manned. On April 8 British warships successfully forced the passage past Moultrie, investing Charleston from the sea. The siege then proceeded in traditional eighteenth century fashion, and on May 12, 1780, Lincoln surrendered his entire force of 5,466 men, the greatest disaster to befall the American cause during the war. Meanwhile, Col. Abraham Buford with 350 Virginians was moving south to reinforce the garrison. Lt. Col. Banastre Tarleton with a force of British cavalry took Buford by surprise at the Waxhaws, a district near the North Carolina border, and slaughtered most of his men, refusing to honor the white flag Buford displayed.

After the capture of Charleston, Clinton returned to New York with about a third of his force, leaving General Cornwallis with 8,000 men to follow up the victory. Cornwallis established his main seaboard bases at Savannah, Beaufort, Charleston, and Georgetown, and in the interior extended his line of control along the Savannah River westward to Ninety-Six and northward to Camden and Rocky Mount. Cornwallis' force, however, was too small to police so large an area, even with the aid of the numerous Tories who took to the field. Though no organized Continental force remained in the Carolinas and Georgia, American guerrillas, led by Brig. Gens. Thomas Sumter and Andrew Pickens and Lt. Col. Francis Marion, began to harry British posts and lines of communications and to battle the bands of Tories. A bloody, ruthless, and confused civil war ensued, its character determined in no small degree by Tarleton's action at the Waxhaws. In this way, as in the Saratoga campaign, the American grass roots strength began once again to assert itself and to deny the British the fruits of military victory won in the field.

On June 22, 1780, two more understrength Continental brigades from Washington's army arrived at Hillsboro, North Carolina, to form the nucleus of a new Southern Army around which militia could rally and which could serve as the nerve center of guerrilla resistance. In July Congress, without consulting Washington, provided a commander for this army in the person of General Gates, the hero of Saratoga. Gates soon lost his northern laurels. Gathering a force of about 4,000 men, mostly militia, he set out to attack the British post at Camden, South Carolina. Cornwallis hurried north from Charleston with reinforcements and his army of 2,200 British Regulars made contact with Gates outside Camden on the night of August 15. In the battle that ensued the following morning, Gates deployed his militia on the left and the Continentals under Maj. Gen. Johann de Kalb on the right. The militia were still forming in the hazy dawn when Cornwallis struck, and they fled in panic before the British onslaught. De Kalb's outnumbered Continentals put up a valiant but hopeless fight. Tarleton's cavalry pursued the fleeing Americans for 30 miles, killing or making prisoner those who lagged. Gates himself fled too fast for Tarleton, reaching Hillsboro, 160 miles away, in three days. There he was able to gather only about 800 survivors of the Southern Army. To add to the disaster, Tarleton caught up with General Sumter, whom Gates had sent with a detachment to raid a British wagon train, and virtually destroyed his force in a surprise attack at Fishing Creek on August 18. Once more South Carolina seemed safely in British hands.

Nadir of the American Cause

In the summer of 1780 the American cause seemed to be at as low an ebb as it had been after the New York campaign in 1776 or after the defeats at Ticonderoga and Brandywine in 1777. Defeat in the south was not the only discouraging aspect of patriot affairs. In the north a creeping paralysis had set in as the patriotic enthusiasm of the early war years waned. The Continental currency had virtually depreciated out of existence, and Congress was impotent to pay the soldiers or purchase supplies. At Morristown, New Jersey, in the winter of 1779–80 the army suffered worse hardships than at Valley Forge. Congress could do little but attempt to shift its responsibilities onto the states, giving each the task of providing clothing for its own troops and furnishing certain quotas of specific supplies for the entire Army. The system of "specific supplies" worked not at all. Not only were the states laggard in furnishing supplies, but when they did it was seldom at the time or place they were needed. This breakdown in the supply system was more than even General Greene, as Quartermaster General, could cope with, and in early 1780, under heavy criticism in Congress, he resigned his position.

Under such difficulties, Washington had to struggle to hold even a small Army together. Recruiting of Continentals, difficult to begin with, became almost impossible when the troops could neither be paid nor supplied adequately and had to suffer such winters as those at Morristown. Enlistments and drafts from the militia in 1780 produced not quite half as many men for one year's service as had enlisted in 1776 for three years or the duration. While recruiting lagged, morale among those men who had enlisted for the longer terms naturally fell. Mutinies in 1780 and 1781 were suppressed only by measures of great severity.

Germain could write confidently to Clinton: "so very contemptible is the rebel force now . . . that no resistance . . . is to be apprehended that can materially obstruct . . . the speedy suppression of the rebellion . . . the American levies in the King's service are more in number than the whole of the enlisted troops in the service of the Congress." The French were unhappy. In the summer of 1780 they occupied the vacated British base at Newport, moving in a naval squadron and 4,000 troops under the command of Lieutenant General the Comte de Rochambeau. Rochambeau immediately warned his government: "Send us troops, ships and money, but do not count on these people nor on their resources, they have neither money nor credit, their forces exist only momentarily, and when they are about to be attacked in their own homes they assemble . . . to defend themselves." Another French commander thought only one highly placed American traitor was needed to decide the campaign.

Clinton had, in fact, already found his "highly placed traitor" in Benedict Arnold, the hero of the march to Quebec, the naval battle on the lakes, Stanwix, and Saratoga. "Money is this man's God," one of his enemies had said of Arnold earlier, and evidently he was correct. Lucrative rewards promised by the British led to Arnold's treason, though he evidently resented the slights Congress had dealt him, and he justified his act by claiming that the Americans were now fighting for the interests of Catholic France and not their own. Arnold wangled an appointment as commander at West Point and then entered into a plot to deliver this key post to the British. Washington discovered the plot on September 21, 1780, just in time to foil it, though Arnold himself escaped to become a British brigadier.

Arnold's treason in September 1780 marked the nadir of the patriot cause. In the closing months of 1780, the Americans somehow put together the in-gredients for a final and decisive burst of energy in 1781. Congress persuaded

Robert Morris, a wealthy Philadelphia merchant, to accept a post as Superintendent of Finance, and Col. Timothy Pickering, an able administrator, to replace Greene as Quartermaster General. Greene, as Washington's choice, was then named to succeed Gates in command of the Southern Army. General Lincoln, exchanged after Charleston, was appointed Secretary at War and the old board was abolished. Morris took over many of the functions previously performed by unwieldy committees. Working closely with Pickering, he abandoned the old paper money entirely and introduced a new policy of supplying the army by private contracts, using his personal credit as eventual guarantee for payment in gold or silver. It was an expedient but, for a time at least, it worked.

Greene's Southern Campaign

It was the frontier militia assembling "when they were about to be attacked in their own homes" who struck the blow that actually marked the turning point in the south. Late in 1780, with Clinton's reluctant consent, Cornwallis set out on the invasion of North Carolina. He sent Maj. Patrick Ferguson, who had successfully organized the Tories in the upcountry of South Carolina, to move north simultaneously with his "American Volunteers," spread the Tory gospel in the North Carolina back country, and join the main army at Charlotte with a maximum number of recruits. Ferguson's advance northward alarmed the "over-mountain men" in western North Carolina, southwest Virginia, and what is now east Tennessee. A picked force of mounted militia riflemen gathered on the Catawba River in western North Carolina, set out to find Ferguson, and brought him to bay at King's Mountain near the border of the two Carolinas on October 7. In a battle of patriot against Tory (Ferguson was the only British soldier present), the patriots' triumph was complete. Ferguson himself was killed and few of his command escaped death or capture. Some got the same "quarter" Tarleton had given Buford's men at the Waxhaws.

King's Mountain was as fatal to Cornwallis' plans as Bennington had been to those of Burgoyne. The North Carolina Tories, cowed by the fate of their compatriots, gave him little support. The British commander on October 14, 1780, began a wretched retreat in the rain back to Winnsboro, South Carolina, with militia harassing his progress. Clinton was forced to divert an expedition of 2,500 men sent to establish a base in Virginia to reinforce Cornwallis.

The frontier militia had turned the tide, but having done so, they returned to their homes. To keep it moving against the British was the task of the new commander, General Greene. When Greene arrived at Charlotte, North Carolina, early in December 1780, he found a command that consisted of 1,500 men

1 THE WINNING OF INDEPENDENCE, 1777-1783 91

fit for duty, only 949 of them Continentals. The army lacked clothing and provisions and had little systematic means of procuring them. Greene decided that he must not engage Cornwallis' army in battle until he had built up his strength, that he must instead pursue delaying tactics to wear down his stronger opponent. The first thing he did was to take the unorthodox step of dividing his army in the face of a superior force, moving part under his personal command to Cheraw Hill, and sending the rest under Brig. Gen. Daniel Morgan west across the Catawba over 100 miles away. It was an intentional violation of the principle of mass. Greene wrote:

I am well satisfied with the movement . . . . It makes the most of my inferior force, for it compels my adversary to divide his, and holds him in doubt as to his own line of conduct. He cannot leave Morgan behind him to come at me, or his posts at Ninety-Six and Augusta would be exposed. And he cannot chase Morgan far, or prosecute his views upon Virginia, while I am here with the whole country open before me. I am as near to Charleston as he is, and as near Hillsborough as I was at Charlotte; so that I am in no danger of being cut off from my reinforcements.

Left unsaid was the fact that divided forces could live off the land much easier than one large force and constitute two rallying points for local militia instead of one. Greene was, in effect, sacrificing mass to enhance maneuver.

Cornwallis, an aggressive commander, had determined to gamble everything on a renewed invasion of North Carolina. Ignoring Clinton's warnings, he depleted his Charleston base by bringing almost all his supplies forward. In the face of Greene's dispositions, Cornwallis divided his army into not two but three parts. He sent a holding force to Camden to contain Green, directed Tarleton with a fast-moving contingent of 1,100 infantry and cavalry to find and crush Morgan, and with the remainder of his army moved cautiously up into North Carolina to cut off any of Morgan's force that escaped Tarleton.

Tarleton caught up with Morgan on January 17, 1781, west of King's Mountain at a place called the Cowpens, an open, sparsely forested area six miles from the Broad River. (*Map 11*) Morgan chose this site to make his stand less by design than necessity, for he had intended to get across the Broad. Nevertheless, on ground seemingly better suited to the action of Regulars, he achieved a little tactical masterpiece, making the most effective use of his heterogeneous force, numerically equal to that of Tarleton but composed of three-fourths militia. Selecting a hill as the center of his position, he placed his Continental infantry on it, deliberately leaving his flanks open. Well out in front of the main line he posted militia riflemen in two lines, instructing the first line to fire two volleys and then fall back on the second, the combined line to fire until the British pressed them, then to fall back to the rear of the Continentals and re-form as a reserve. Behind the hill he placed Lt. Col. William Washing-

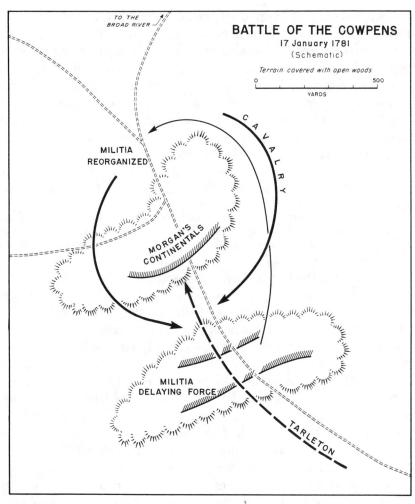

MAP 11

ton's cavalry detachment, ready to charge the attacking enemy at the critical moment. Every man in the ranks was informed of the plan of battle and the part he was expected to play in it.

On finding Morgan, Tarleton ordered an immediate attack. His men moved forward in regular formation, were momentarily checked by the militia rifles, but, taking the retreat of the first two lines to be the beginning of a rout, rushed headlong into the steady fire of the Continentals on the hill. When the British were well advanced, the American cavalry struck them on the right flank and the militia, having re-formed, charged out from behind the hill to hit the British left. Caught in a clever double envelopment, the British surrendered after suffering heavy losses. Tarleton managed to escape with only a small force of cavalry he had held in reserve. It was on a small scale, and with certain significant differences, a repetition of the classic double envelopment of the Romans by a Carthaginian army under Hannibal at Cannae in 216 B.C., an event of which Morgan, no reader of books, probably had not the foggiest notion.

Having struck his fatal blow against Tarleton, Morgan still had to move fast to escape Cornwallis. Covering 100 miles and crossing two rivers in five days, he rejoined Greene early in February. Cornwallis by now was too heavily committed to the campaign in North Carolina to withdraw. Hoping to match the swift movement of the Americans, he destroyed all his superfluous supplies, baggage, and wagons and set forth in pursuit of Greene's army. The American general retreated, through North Carolina, up into southern Virginia, then back into North Carolina again, keeping just far enough in front of his adversary to avoid battle with Cornwallis' superior force. Finally on March 15, 1781, at Guilford Court House in North Carolina, on ground he had himself chosen, Greene halted and gave battle. By this time he had collected 1,500 Continentals and 3,000 militia to the 1,900 Regulars the British could muster. The British held the field after a hard-fought battle, but suffered casualties of about one-fourth of the force engaged. It was, like Bunker Hill, a Pyrrhic victory. His ranks depleted and his supplies exhausted, Cornwallis withdrew to Wilmington on the coast, and then decided to move northward to join the British forces General Clinton had sent to Virginia.

Greene, his army in better condition than six months earlier, pushed quickly into South Carolina to reduce the British posts in the interior. He fought two battles—at Hobkirk's Hill on April 25, and at Eutaw Springs on September 8—losing both but with approximately the same results as at Guilford Court House. One by one the British interior posts fell to Greene's army, or to militia and partisans. By October 1781 the British had been forced to withdraw to their port strongholds along the coast—Charleston and Savannah. Greene had lost battles, but won a campaign. In so doing, he paved the way for the greater victory to follow at Yorktown.

Yorktown: The Final Act

As Howe and Burgoyne went their separate ways in 1777, seemingly determined to satisfy only their personal ambitions, so Clinton and Cornwallis in 1781 paved the road to Yorktown by their disagreements and lack of co-ordination. Clinton was Cornwallis' superior in this case, but the latter enjoyed the confidence of Germain to an extent that Clinton did not. Clinton, believing that without large reinforcements the British could not operate far from coastal bases, had opposed Cornwallis' ventures in the interior of the Carolinas, and when Cornwallis came to Virginia he did so without even informing his superior of his intention.

Since 1779 Clinton had sought to paralyze the state of Virginia by conducting raids up its great rivers, arousing the Tories, and establishing a base in the Chesapeake Bay region. (*Map 12*) He thought this base might eventually be used as a starting point for one arm of a pincers movement against Pennsylvania for which his own idle force in New York would provide the other. A raid conducted in the Hampton Roads area in 1779 was highly successful, but when Clinton sought to follow it up in 1780 the force sent for the purpose had to be diverted to Charleston to bail Cornwallis out after King's Mountain. Finally in 1781 he got an expedition into Virginia, a contingent of 1,600 under the American traitor, Benedict Arnold. In January Arnold conducted a destructive raid up the James River all the way to Richmond. His presence soon proved to be a magnet drawing forces of both sides to Virginia.

In an effort to trap Arnold, Washington dispatched Lafayette to Virginia with 1,200 of his scarce Continentals and persuaded the French to send a naval squadron from Newport to block Arnold's escape by sea. The plan went awry when a British fleet drove the French squadron back to Newport and Clinton sent another 2,600 men to Virginia along with a new commander, Maj. Gen. William Phillips. Phillips and Arnold continued their devastating raids, which Lafayette was too weak to prevent. Then on May 20 Cornwallis arrived from Wilmington and took over from Phillips. With additional reinforcements sent by Clinton he was able to field a force of about 7,000 men, approximately a quarter of the British strength in America. Washington sent down an additional reinforcement of 800 Continentals under General Wayne, but even with Virginia militia Lafayette's force remained greatly outnumbered.

Cornwallis and Clinton were soon working at cross-purposes. Cornwallis proposed to carry out major operations in the interior of Virginia, but Clinton saw as little practical value in this tactic as Cornwallis did in Clinton's plan to establish a base in Virginia for a pincers movement against Pennsylvania. Cornwallis at first turned to the interior and engaged in a fruitless pursuit of Lafayette north of Richmond. Then, on receiving Clinton's positive order to return to the coast, establish a base, and return part of his force to New York, Cornwallis moved back down the Virginia peninsula to take up station at Yorktown, a small tobacco port on the York River just off Chesapeake Bay. In the face of

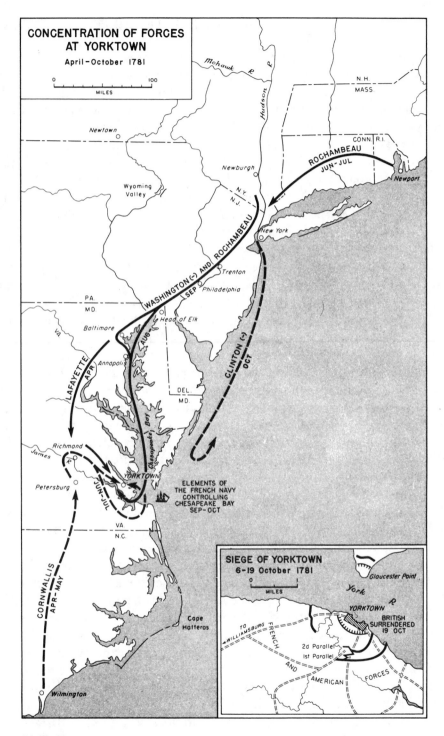

CONCENTRATION OF FORCES AT YORKTOWN
April–October 1781

```
0          100
├─┬─┬─┬─┬─┤
    MILES
```

Mohawk R.

N.H.
MASS.

Newtown

Hudson R.

Newburgh

CONN. R.I.

ROCHAMBEAU
JUN–JUL

Newport

Wyoming Valley

N.Y.
N.J.

New York

WASHINGTON (–) AND ROCHAMBEAU

Trenton

1 SEP   Philadelphia

PA.
MD.

Head of Elk

CLINTON (–)
OCT

Baltimore

AUG

Annapolis

LAFAYETTE APR.

DEL.
MD.

Chesapeake Bay

Richmond

James R.

YORKTOWN

Petersburg

JUN–JUL

ELEMENTS OF
THE FRENCH NAVY
CONTROLLING
CHESAPEAKE BAY
SEP–OCT

VA.
N.C.

CORNWALLIS
APR–MAY

Cape Hatteras

Wilmington

SIEGE OF YORKTOWN
6–19 October 1781

```
0
├─┬─┬─┤
  MILES
```

Gloucester Point

York R.

YORKTOWN

TO WILLIAMSBURG

FRENCH

2d Parallel
1st Parallel

BRITISH
SURRENDERED
19 OCT

AND

AMERICAN

FORCES

MAP 12

Cornwallis' insistence that he must keep all his troops with him, Clinton vacillated, reversing his own orders several times and in the end granting Cornwallis' request. Lafayette and Wayne followed Cornwallis cautiously down the peninsula, lost a skirmish with him at Green Spring near Williamsburg on July 6, and finally took up a position of watchful waiting near Yorktown.

Meanwhile, Washington had been trying to persuade the French to co-operate in a combined land and naval assault on New York in the summer of 1781. Rochambeau brought his 4,000 troops down from Newport in April and placed them under Washington's command. The prospects were still bleak since the combined Franco-American force numbered but 10,000 against Clinton's 17,000 in well-fortified positions. Then on August 14 Washington learned that the French Fleet in the West Indies, commanded by Admiral Francois de Grasse, would not come to New York but would arrive in the Chesapeake later in the month and remain there until October 15. He saw immediately that if he could achieve a superior concentration of force on the land side while de Grasse still held the bay he could destroy the British army at Yorktown before Clinton had a chance to relieve it.

The movements that followed illustrate most effectively a successful application of the principles of the offensive, surprise, objective, mass, and maneuver. Even without unified command of Army and Navy forces, Franco-American co-operation this time was excellent. Admiral Louis, Comte de Barras, immediately put out to sea from Newport to join de Grasse. Washington sent orders to Lafayette to contain Cornwallis at Yorktown and then, after making a feint in the direction of New York to deceive Clinton, on August 21 started the major portion of the Franco-American Army on a rapid secret movement to Virginia, via Chesapeake Bay, leaving only 2,000 Americans behind to watch Clinton.

On August 30, while Washington was on the move southward, de Grasse arrived in the Chesapeake with his entire fleet of twenty-four ships of the line and a few days later debarked 3,000 French troops to join Lafayette. Admiral Thomas Graves, the British naval commander in New York, meanwhile had put out to sea in late August with nineteen ships of the line, hoping either to intercept Barras' squadron or to block de Grasse's entry into the Chesapeake. He failed to find Barras, and when he arrived off Hampton Roads on September 5 he found de Grasse already in the bay. The French admiral sallied forth to meet Graves and the two fleets fought an indecisive action off the Virginia capes. Yet for all practical purposes the victory lay with the French for, while the fleets maneuvered at sea for days following the battle, Barras' squadron slipped into the Chesapeake and the French and American troops got past into the James River. Then de Grasse got back into the bay and joined Barras, con-

SURRENDER OF CORNWALLIS

fronting Graves with so superior a naval force that he decided to return to New York to refit.

When Washington's army arrived on September 26, the French Fleet was in firm control of the bay, blocking Cornwallis' sea route of escape. A decisive concentration had been achieved. Counting 3,000 Virginia militia, Washington had a force of about 9,000 Americans and 6,000 French troops with which to conduct the siege. It proceeded in the best traditions of Vauban under the direction of French engineers. Cornwallis obligingly abandoned his forward position on September 30, and on October 6 the first parallel was begun 600 yards from the main British position. Artillery placed along the trench began its destructive work on October 9. By October 11 the zigzag connecting trench had been dug 200 yards forward, and work on the second parallel had begun. Two British redoubts had to be reduced in order to extend the line to the York River. This accomplished, Cornwallis' only recourse was escape across the river to Gloucester Point where the American line was thinly held. A storm on the night of October 16 frustrated his attempt to do so, leaving him with no hope but relief from New York. Clinton had been considering such relief for days, but he acted too late. On the very day, October 17, that Admiral Graves set sail from New York with a reinforced fleet and 7,000 troops for the relief of Yorktown, Cornwallis began negotiations on terms of surrender. On October 19 his entire army marched out to lay down its arms, the British band playing an old tune called "The World Turned Upside Down."

So far as active campaigning was concerned, Yorktown ended the war. Both Greene and Washington maintained their armies in position near New York and Charleston for nearly two years more, but the only fighting that occurred was some minor skirmishing in the South. Cornwallis' defeat led to the overthrow of the British cabinet and the formation of a new government that decided the war in America was lost. With some success, Britain devoted its energies to trying to salvage what it could in the West Indies and in India. The independence for which Americans had fought thus virtually became a reality when Cornwallis' command marched out of its breached defenses at Yorktown.

The Summing Up: Reasons, Lessons, and Meaning

The American victory in the War of the Revolution was a product of many factors, no one of which can be positively assigned first importance. Washington, looking back on the vicissitudes of eight years, could only explain it as the intervention of "Divine Providence." American historians in the nineteenth century saw that "Divine Providence" as having been manifested primarily in the character and genius of the modest Commander in Chief himself. Washington's leadership was clearly one of the principal factors in American success; it seems fair to say that the Revolution could hardly have succeeded without him. Yet in many of the events that led to victory—Bennington, Saratoga, King's Mountain, and Cowpens, to name but a few—his personal influence was remote.

Today many scholars stress not the astonishment that Washington felt at the victory of a weak and divided confederation of American states over the greatest power of the age, but the practical difficulties the British faced in suppressing the revolt. These were indeed great but they do not appear to have been insuperable if one considers military victory alone and not its political consequences. The British forfeited several chances for military victory in 1776–77, and again in 1780 they might have won had they been able to throw 10,000 fresh troops into the American war. American military leaders were more resourceful and imaginative than the British commanders, and they proved quite capable of profiting from British blunders. In addition to Washington, Nathanael Greene, Henry Knox, Daniel Morgan, and Benedict Arnold showed remarkable military abilities, and of the foreign volunteers Steuben and the young Lafayette were outstanding. The resourcefulness of this extraordinary group of leaders was matched by the dedication of the Continental rank and file to the cause. Only men so dedicated could have endured the hardships of the march to Quebec, the crossing of the Delaware, Valley Forge, Morristown, and Greene's forced marches in the southern campaign. British and Hessian professionals never showed the same spirit; their virtues were exhibited principally in situations where discipline and training counted most.

The militia, the men who fought battles and then went home, also exhibited this spirit on many occasions. The militiamen have been generally maligned as useless by one school of thought, and glorified by another as the true victors in the war. In any balanced view it must be recognized that their contributions were great, though they would have counted for little without a Continental Army to give the American cause that continued sustenance that only a permanent force in being could give it. It was the ubiquity of the militia that made British victories over the Continentals in the field so meaningless. And the success with which the militia did operate derived from the firm political control the patriots had established over the countryside long before the British were in any position to challenge it—the situation that made the British task so difficult in the first place.

For all these American virtues and British difficulties and mistakes, the Americans still required French aid—money, supplies, and in the last phase military force—to win a decisive and clear-cut military victory. Most of the muskets, bayonets, and cannon used by the Continental Army came from France. The French contested the control of the seas that was so vital to the British, and compelled them to divert forces from the American mainland to other areas. The final stroke at Yorktown, though a product of Washington's strategic conception, was possible only because of the temporary predominance of French naval power off the American coast and the presence of a French army.

French aid was doubly necessary because the American war effort lacked strong national direction. The Revolution showed conclusively the need for a central government with power to harness the nation's resources for war. It is not surprising that in 1787 nearly all those who had struggled so long and hard as leaders in the Continental Army or in administrative positions under the Congress were to be found in the ranks of the supporters of a new constitution creating such a central government with a strong executive and the power to "raise armies and navies," call out the militia, and levy taxes directly to support itself.

Strictly military lessons of the Revolution were more equivocal. Tactical innovations were not radical but they did represent a culmination of the trend, which started during the French and Indian War, toward employment of light troops as skirmishers in conjunction with traditional linear formations. By the end of the war both armies were fighting in this fashion. The Americans strove to develop the same proficiency as the British in regular line-of-battle tactics, while the British adapted to the American terrain and tactics by themselves employing skirmishers and fighting when possible from behind cover. Washington was himself a military conservative, and Steuben's training program was designed to equip American troops to fight in European fashion with modifications to provide for the increased use of light infantry. The guerrilla tactics that characterized many actions, principally those of the militia, were no product of the design of Washington or his leading subordinates but of circumstances over which they had little control. The American rifle, most useful in guerrilla actions or in the hands of skirmishers, played no decisive role in the Revolution. It was of great value in wooded areas, as at Saratoga and King's Mountain, but for open-field fighting its slow rate of fire and lack of a bayonet made it inferior to the musket.

Since both militia and Continentals played roles in winning the war, the Revolutionary experience provided ammunition for two diametrically opposed schools of thought on American military policy: the one advocating a large Regular Army, the other reliance on the militia as the bulwark of national defense. The real issue, as Washington fully recognized, was less militia versus Regulars—for he never believed the infant republic needed a large standing army—than the extent to which militia could be trained and organized to form a reliable national reserve. The lesson Washington drew from the Revolution was that the militia should be "well regulated," that is, trained and organized under a uniform national system in all the states and subject to call into national service in war or emergency.

The lesson had far greater implications for the future than any of the tactical changes wrought by the American Revolution. It balanced the rights of freedom and equality, proclaimed in the Declaration of Independence, with a corresponding obligation of all citizens for military service to the nation. This concept, which was to find explicit expression in the "nation in arms" during the French Revolution, was also implicit in the American, and it portended the end of eighteenth century limited war, fought by professional armies officered by an aristocratic class. As Steuben so well recognized, American Continentals were not professional soldiers in the European sense, and militia even less so. They were, instead, a people's army fighting for a cause. In this sense then, the American Revolution began the "democratization of war," a process that was eventually to lead to national conscription and a new concept of total war for total victory.

CHAPTER 5

The Formative Years, 1783–1812

On September 24, 1783, four days after the signing of the Treaty of Paris formally ended the war, Congress directed General Washington to discharge "such parts of the Federal Army now in Service as he shall deem proper and expedient." For the time being Washington retained the force facing the British at New York, discharging the rest of the Continentals. After the British quit New York, he kept only one infantry regiment and a battalion of artillery, 600 men in all, to guard the military supplies at West Point and other posts.

The period leading up to this demobilization was a stormy one for the Congress. During the winter of 1782 the Army had grown impatient, and rumors that it would take matters into its own hands gained credence when several anonymous addresses were circulated among the officers at Newburgh urging them not to fight if the war continued or not to lay down their arms if peace were declared and their pay accounts left unsettled. In an emotional speech to his old comrades, Washington disarmed this threat. He promised to intercede for them, and in the end, Congress did give in to the officers' demands, agreeing to award the men their back pay and to grant the officers full pay for five years in lieu of half pay for life. Demobilization then proceeded peacefully, but it was against the background of these demands and threats that Congress wrestled with a major postwar problem, the size and character of the peacetime military establishment. In the way of most governments, Congress turned the problem over to a committee, this one under Alexander Hamilton, to study the facts and make recommendations for a military establishment.

The Question of a Peacetime Army

Congress subscribed to the prevailing view that the first line of defense should be a "well-regulated and disciplined militia sufficiently armed and accoutered." Its reluctance to create a standing army was understandable; a permanent army would be a heavy expense, and it would complicate the struggle between those who wanted a strong national government and those who preferred the existing loose federation of states. Further, the recent threats of the

Continental officers strengthened the popular fear that a standing army might be used to coerce the states or become an instrument of despotism.

General Washington, to whom Hamilton's committee turned first for advice, echoed the prevailing view. He pointed out that a large standing army in time of peace had always been considered "dangerous to the liberties of a country" and that the nation was "too poor to maintain a standing army adequate to our defense." The question might also be considered, he continued, whether any surplus funds that became available should not better be applied to "building and equipping a Navy without which, in case of War we could neither protect our Commerce, nor yield that assistance to each other which, on such an extent of seacoast, our mutual safety would require." He believed that America should rely ultimately on an improved version of the historic citizens' militia, a force enrolling all males between 18 and 50 liable for service to the nation in emergencies. He also recommended a volunteer militia, recruited in units, periodically trained, and subject to United States rather than state control. At the same time Washington did suggest the creation of a small Regular Army "to awe the Indians, protect our Trade, prevent the encroachment of our Neighbors of Canada and the Floridas, and guard us at least from surprises; also for security of our magazines." He recommended a force of four regiments of infantry and one of artillery, totaling 2,630 officers and men.

Hamilton's committee also listened to suggestions made by General von Steuben, Major General Louis le Bèque Du Portail, Chief Engineer of the Army, and Benjamin Lincoln, Secretary at War. On June 18, 1783, it submitted a plan to Congress similar to Washington's, but with a more ambitious militia program. Congress, however, rejected the proposal. Sectional rivalries, constitutional questions, and, above all, economic objections were too strong to be overcome.

The committee thereupon revised its plan, recommending an even larger army that it hoped to provide at less expense by decreasing the pay of the regimental staff officers and subalterns. Washington when asked admitted that detached service along the frontiers and coasts would probably require more men than he had proposed, but he disagreed that a larger establishment could be provided more economically than the one he had recommended. A considerable number of the delegates to Congress had similar misgivings, and when the committee presented its revised report on October 23, Congress refused to accept it. During the winter of 1783 the matter rested. Under the Articles of Confederation an affirmative vote of the representatives of nine states was required for the exercise of certain important powers, including military matters, and on few occasions during this winter were enough states represented for Congress to renew the debate.

In the spring of 1784 the question of a permanent peacetime army became involved in the politics of state claims to western lands. The majority of men in the remaining infantry regiment and artillery battalion were from Massachusetts and New Hampshire, and those states wanted to be rid of the financial burden of providing the extra pay that they had promised the men on enlistment. Congress refused to assume the responsibility unless the New England states would vote for a permanent military establishment. The New England representatives, led by Elbridge Gerry of Massachusetts, insisted that Congress had no authority to maintain a standing army, but at the same time they wanted the existing troops to occupy the western forts, situated in land claimed by the New England states. New York vigorously contested the New England claims to western lands, particularly in the region around Oswego and Niagara, and refused to vote for any permanent military establishment unless Congress gave it permission to garrison the western forts with its own forces.

The posts that had been the object of concern and discussion dominated the Great Lakes and the St. Lawrence River. (*Map 13*) Located on American

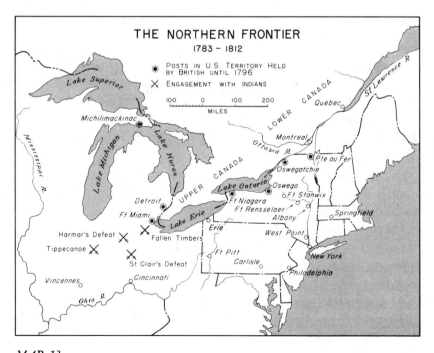

MAP 13

territory south of the boundary established by the peace treaty of 1783, the posts were in the hands of British troops when the war ended, but by the terms of the treaty they were to be turned over to the United States as speedily as possible. Congress agreed that a force should be retained to occupy the posts as soon as the British left. The problem was how and by whom the troops were to be raised. A decision was all the more urgent because the government was in the midst of negotiating a treaty with the Indians of the Northwest, and, as Washington had suggested, a sizable force "to awe the Indians" would facilitate the negotiations. But the deadlock between the New England states and New York continued until early June 1784.

Finally, on the last two days of the session, Congress rushed through a compromise. It ordered the existing infantry regiment and battalion of artillery disbanded, except for 80 artillerymen retained to guard military stores at West Point and Fort Pitt. It tied this discharge to a measure providing for the immediate recruitment of a new force of 700 men, a regiment of eight infantry and two artillery companies, which was to become the nucleus of a new Regular Army. By not making requisitions on the states for troops, but merely recommending that the states provide them from their militia, Congress got rid of most of the New England opposition on this score; by not assigning a quota for Massachusetts and New Hampshire, Congress satisfied the objections of most of the other states.

Four states were called upon to furnish troops: 260 men from Pennsylvania, 165 from Connecticut, 165 from New York, and 110 from New Jersey. Lt. Col. Josiah Harmar of Pennsylvania was appointed commanding officer. By the end of September 1784 only New Jersey and Pennsylvania had filled their quotas by enlisting volunteers from their militia.

Congress had meanwhile learned that there was little immediate prospect that the British would evacuate the frontier posts. Canadian fur traders and the settlers in Upper Canada had objected so violently to this provision of the peace treaty that the British Government secretly directed the Governor-General of Canada not to evacuate the posts without further orders. The failure of the United States to comply with a stipulation in the treaty regarding the recovery of debts owed to loyalists provided the British with an excuse to postpone the evacuation of the posts for twelve more years. So the New Jersey contingent of Colonel Harmar's force was sent to Fort Stanwix, in upstate New York, to assist in persuading the Iroquois to part with their lands, while the remainder of the force moved to Fort MacIntosh, thirty miles down the Ohio River from Fort Pitt, where similar negotiations were carried on with the Indians of the upper Ohio.

Toward a More Perfect Union

Postwar problems revealed a number of serious defects in the Articles of Confederation. The federal government lacked a separate executive branch and a judiciary, and although Congress exercised a certain amount of executive as well as legislative power, it lacked the power to tax. To some of the delegates the conflicts and dissension between the states over the western lands seemed to carry the seeds of civil war. Rioting and disturbances in Massachusetts throughout the fall and winter of 1786 strengthened the pessimism of those who feared the collapse of the new nation. A severe commercial depression following on the heels of an immediate postwar boom was causing particular distress among the back-country farmers. Angry mobs gathered in the Massachusetts hills, broke up the meetings of the courts, harried lawyers and magistrates out of the villages, and began to threaten the government arsenal in Springfield.

On October 20, 1786, Congress responded to the threat by calling on several states to raise a 1,340-man force to serve for three years. This time the New England states did not object to Congressional action, but before any of the soldiers voted by Congress could reach the scene, local militiamen repulsed an attack on the Springfield Arsenal led by Daniel Shays in late January 1787, and a few days later a large reinforcement from the eastern part of the state arrived at Springfield and put an end to the disorders. Recruiting for the force authorized by Congress continued until the following April. By then about 550 men had been enlisted and the question of expense was becoming bothersome. Congress therefore directed the states to stop recruiting and to discharge the troops already raised, except those in two artillery companies retained to guard West Point and the Springfield Arsenal. Shays' Rebellion was thus responsible for the first augmentation of the federal Army. More important, it helped persuade Americans that a stronger government was needed.

Rising concern over the ineffectiveness of the federal government, particularly in matters of finance and commercial regulation, finally led to the convening of a Constitutional Convention in the spring of 1787. To strengthen the military powers of the government was one of the principal tasks of the convention, a task no less important than establishing its financial and commercial authority. The general problem facing the convention, that of power and the control of power, came into sharp focus in the debates on military matters, since the widespread suspicion of a strong central government and the equally widespread fear of a standing army were merged in the issue of the government's military powers. Those who mistrusted a powerful government argued against a broad grant of authority not only in the fields of taxation and commercial regulation, but, and with especial force, in military matters as well. Even those, like Hamilton, who wanted to give the central government wide latitude in handling both purse and sword were also somewhat wary of standing armies. They too were concerned over the possible usurpation of political power by a military force or its use by officeholders as an instrument for perpetuating their personal power. The Hamiltonians nevertheless were willing to have the country run the risk of being less free in order to be more safe. In the final compromise the problem of the military powers of the central government was resolved through the system of checks and balances built into the new Constitution.

The Constitution clothed the central government with adequate authority to raise and maintain an army without calling upon the states. By giving Congress power to levy taxes, the Constitution provided the central government with the necessary financial means; by creating a separate executive branch, the Constitution made it possible for the daily business of the government to be conducted without constant reference to the states. The Constitution gave the power to declare war, raise armies, and provide for a navy exclusively to Congress. It also empowered Congress to call forth the militia "to execute the Laws of the Union, suppress Insurrections and repel Invasions." But authority over the militia was a shared power. Congress could provide for organizing, arming, and disciplining the militia and governing "such Part of them as may be employed in the Service of the United States," but the Constitution specifically reserved to the states the authority to appoint militia officers and to train the militia "according to the discipline prescribed by Congress."

The new Constitution introduced an important innovation by assigning all executive power to the President. The Secretary of War, therefore, became directly responsible to the President and not to Congress. The Constitution specifically provided that the President should be Commander in Chief of the Army and Navy. As such, his powers were exclusive, limited only "by their nature and by the principles of our institutions." The President had the right to assume personal command of forces in the field, but he could also delegate that right. As Commander in Chief he was responsible for the employment and disposition of the armed forces in time of peace and for the general direction of military and naval operations in war.

Washington became the first President under the new Constitution in April 1789, and on August 7 Congress created the Department of War. There was no change, however, in either the policy or the personnel of the department. General Knox, who had succeeded Washington as commander of the Army and had been handling military affairs under the old form of government, remained in charge. Since there was no navy, a separate department was unnecessary, and at first the War Department included naval affairs under its jurisdiction. Harmar, who had been given the rank of brigadier general during the Confederation period, was confirmed in his appointment, as were his officers, and the existing miniscule Army was taken over intact by the new government. In August 1789 this force amounted to about 800 officers and men. All the troops, except the two artillery companies retained after Shays' Rebellion, were stationed along the Ohio River in a series of forts built after 1785.

So small an Army required no extensive field organization to supply its needs. In keeping with the accepted military theory that the Quartermaster was a staff officer necessary only in time of war, the Confederation Congress had included the Quartermaster General and his assistants among the others discharged in 1783 and placed the military supply system under civilian control. It had made the civilian Secretary responsible for the transport, safekeeping, and distribution of military supplies and the Board of Treasury responsible for procuring and purchasing all military stores, including food and clothing. Except during a brief period in which the Secretary of War was allowed to execute contracts for Army clothing and subsistence, the new federal government retained the Confederation system, adding in 1792 a civilian Office of the Quartermaster General to transport supplies to the frontier posts during the Indian expeditions. In 1794 Congress established the Office of the Purveyor of Public Supplies in the Treasury and the Office of Superintendent of Military Stores in the War Department to continue the same broad supply functions established in the Confederation period. This organization of military supply remained in effect with only slight modification until 1812.

The contract system used by the Purveyor of Public Supplies for the procurement of food and equipment operated much as it did in colonial times. Contracts were awarded to the lowest bidder who agreed to deliver and issue authorized subsistence at a fixed price to troops at a given post. The contractor was obliged to have on hand sufficient rations to feed the troops at all times, providing subsistence for at least six months in advance at the more distant posts. The procurement, storage, and distribution of all other supplies for the Army were centralized in Philadelphia where the Purveyor contracted for all clothing, camp utensils, military stores, medicines, and hospital stores, and the Superintendent of Military Stores collected and issued them when needed by the troops. The contract system was supposed to be more economical and efficient than direct purchase, but its weaknesses were soon apparent. The quality of the supplies and the promptness of their delivery were dictated by the contractor's profit interest.

The method of arms procurement was a variation of the contract purchase system. Convinced that the development of a domestic arms industry was essential to independence, Hamilton had urged as early as 1783 "the public manufacture of arms, powder, etc." A decade later Secretary Knox reported to Congress that although arms could be purchased more cheaply in Europe the bargain price was of little significance "compared with the solid advantages which would result from extending and perfecting the means upon which our safety may ultimately depend." Congress responded by expanding the number of U.S. arsenals and magazines for the stockpiling of weapons and by establishing national armories for the manufacture of weapons. The first national armory was established at Springfield, Massachusetts, in 1794, and a second the same year at Harpers Ferry, Virginia. Despite these developments the government still purchased most of its armament abroad, and many years would pass before domestic industry could supply the government's needs.

The Militia

Time and again Washington pointed out that the only alternative to a large standing army was an effective militia, yet his efforts and those of Knox and Hamilton to make the militia more effective by applying federal regulation failed. Congress passed the basic militia law in May 1792. It called for the enrollment of "every able-bodied white male citizen" between 18 and 45 and the organization of the militia into divisions, brigades, regiments, battalions, and companies by the individual states, each militiaman providing his own "arms, munitions, and other accouterments." The law that survived the legislative process bore little resemblance to the one proposed by Washington and Knox. It left compliance with its provisions up to the states and in the end did little more than give federal recognition to the colonial militia organization that had plagued Washington during the Revolution. Despite these limitations, the act did preserve the idea of a citizen soldiery, a concept of profound importance to the future of the country, and it also provided for the creation of special volunteer units to supplement the obligatory mass system. The volunteers, organized into companies, met regularly for military training under elected officers. With antecedents in the organized military associations of the colonial era, this volunteer force later became the National Guard.

Training and discipline were the key to an effective militia, but after the act of 1792 the militia was to be neither disciplined nor well trained. When permitted to fight in less standardized fashion—either from behind fortifications or as irregulars—militiamen could give a good account of themselves, but only highly trained troops could be expected to employ successfully the complicated, formal linear tactics of the day. Strictly interpreting the constitutional provision that reserved to the states the authority to train the militia, Congress left the extent and thoroughness of training completely to the states and merely prescribed General von Steuben's system of discipline and field exercises as the rules to be followed.

The limitations placed on the length of tours of duty and the circumstances for which it might be called into federal service further impaired the usefulness of the militia. No militiaman could be compelled to serve more than three months in any one year, nor could the President order the militia to duty outside the United States. The effect of these limitations would be readily apparent during the War of 1812.

The President first exercised his authority to employ militia for suppressing insurrection and executing the laws of Congress in 1794 when Washington sent a large force of militia under Maj. Gen. Henry Lee into western Pennsylvania during the Whiskey Rebellion. Lee encountered no resistance. As a show of force, the demonstration was impressive; as an indication of the military value of the militia in an emergency, it was inconclusive.

Military Realities in the Federalist Period

The military policies of the new nation evolved realistically in response to foreign and domestic developments. First, there was little actual military threat to the United States from a foreign nation. Britain had no desire or design to reconquer its lost colonies, although both Britain and Spain sought to curb the United States from expanding beyond the borders established by the treaty of 1783. The military alliance that bound the United States to England's arch rival, France, was a potential source of danger, but England and France were at peace until 1793. Second, the jealousy of the individual states toward one another and toward the federal government made it difficult to establish a federal Army at all and defeated efforts to institute federal regulation of the militia beyond the minimum permitted by the Constitution. Third, the federal government, plagued by financial problems, had to pare expenditures to the bone. Fourth, there was extreme reluctance on the part of Americans to serve in the Army, either as Regulars or as volunteers, for more than a brief period. At no time could the government recruit enough men to bring the Regular Army up to authorized strength. In view of these drawbacks, a larger military establishment was not feasible, even though a well-trained militia to take its place was lacking.

The Indian Expeditions

Free of the threat of foreign invasion, the young republic nevertheless faced a serious security problem in the West where the new settlers demanded protection against the Indians as well as an equitable administration of the vast new territories won in the peace of 1783. The Indian problem was an old one. Under the relentless pressure of the pioneers and because of the grants made to Continental soldiers, the frontier was rapidly receding. The Confederation Congress had tried to cope with the situation by concluding a series of treaties with the various Indian groups, but the treaties failed to keep pace with the expansion of the frontier boundaries, and the Indians, supported by British arms and the British presence in the Northwest, ferociously resisted the incursions of the settlers. In the years of the Confederation, they killed or captured over 1,500 settlers in the Kentucky Territory alone.

The Indians fought the settlers all along the frontier, but several factors militated against federal intervention in the Southwest during the first years of Washington's administration. In 1790 the United States concluded a treaty with the Creeks, the most powerful of the Southwest tribes, a treaty that the Spanish in Louisiana, eager to maintain their profitable trade with the Indians, would be likely to support. Georgia and South Carolina introduced a further argument against intervention when they objected to the presence of federal forces within their borders.

The situation was entirely different in the Northwest. There federal troops had been chiefly occupied in driving squatters out of the public domain and protecting the Indian's treaty rights, a type of duty that neither endeared them to the settlers nor trained them in the art of war. Since the enactment of the Northwest Ordinance in 1787, settlers had been pouring into the Ohio country and were demanding federal protection. Their demands carried a veiled threat: ignore their plight and they would turn to Spain and England for succor. The federal union could be destroyed in its infancy.

Tardily and somewhat inadequately, the new government groped for a response to the West's challenge. In his first annual message to Congress President Washington called for the defense of the frontier against the Indians, and Congress responded by raising the authorized strength of Regulars to

1,283. Aware that this force was inadequate to protect the entire frontier, Secretary Knox planned to call on the militia to join the Regulars in an offensive to chastise the Miami Indian group as a show of force. In June 1790 he ordered General Harmar, in consultation with Arthur St. Clair, governor of the Northwest Territory, to lead the expedition. Under an authorization given him the preceding fall, St. Clair called on Pennsylvania and Kentucky to send 1,500 militiamen to Harmar at Fort Washington (now Cincinnati). (*See Map 13.*)

The untrained and undisciplined militia was a weak reed on which to lean in a sustained campaign against the Indians, but Knox knew the militia's strengths as well as its weaknesses. Depending on the fast-striking, mounted militiamen to support the Regulars, Knox wanted Harmar to conduct a "rapid and decisive" maneuver, taking advantage of the element of surprise, to find and destroy the Indian forces and their food supplies. But the two-phased operation concocted by Harmar and St. Clair bore little resemblance to Knox's proposed tactics. Harmar planned a long march northward from Fort Washington to the Miami villages concentrated at the headwaters of the Wabash River. A second column under Maj. John Hamtramck would ascend the Wabash from Fort Vincennes, Indiana, destroying villages along the way and finally joining with Harmar's column after a 150-mile march.

The expedition failed. Hamtramck left Vincennes with 330 Regulars and Virginia militia on September 30, but after an 11-day march during which a few Indian villages were burned, the militia refused to advance farther. Harmar also set out on September 30. After struggling through the wilderness for more than two weeks with a force of 1,453 men, including 320 Regulars, he reached the neighborhood of the principal Indian village near what is now Fort Wayne, Indiana. Instead of pushing on with his entire strength, Harmar on three successive occasions sent forward unsupported detachments of about 200 to 500 militiamen plus 50 or 60 Regulars. The undisciplined militia could not be restrained from scattering in search of Indians and plunder, and, after two of the detachments suffered heavily in brushes with the Indians, Harmar took the rest of his army back to Fort Washington. His conduct was severely criticized, but a court of inquiry, noting the untrained troops with which Harmar had been provided and the lateness of the season, exonerated him.

Secretary Knox's injunctions for a "rapid and decisive" maneuver were again ignored when the government decided to send another expedition against the Northwest Indians in 1791. Congress raised the size of the invasion force, adding a second infantry regiment to the Regular Army and authorizing the President to raise a corps of 2,000 men for a term of six months, either by calling for militia or by enlisting volunteers into the service of the United States. The President commissioned Governor St. Clair a major general and placed him in command of the expedition. So slowly did recruiting and the procuring of supplies proceed that St. Clair was unable to set out before September 17, and only by calling on the neighboring states for militia was he able to bring his force up to strength. When St. Clair's force finally marched out of Fort Washington, it consisted of about 600 Regulars, almost all the actual infantry strength of the U.S. Army, in addition to about 800 enlisted "levies" and 600 militiamen.

By November 3 St. Clair had advanced about 100 miles northward from Cincinnati, and most of his force, now numbering about 1,400 effectives, encamped for the night near the headwaters of the Wabash. Neglecting the principle of security, St. Clair had not sent out scouts, and just before dawn a horde of about 1,000 Indians fell upon the unsuspecting troops. Untrained, low in morale as a result of inadequate supplies, and led by a general who was suffering from rheumatism, asthma, and "colic," the army was thrown into confusion by the sudden assault. St. Clair and less than half his force survived unscathed—637 were killed and 263 wounded.

The United States was alarmed and outraged over St. Clair's defeat. Some urged that the government abandon the Indian wars and accept the British proposal for an Indian buffer state in the Northwest, but Washington well understood the strategic implications of such a scheme and decided instead to mount a third expedition. He appointed Anthony Wayne, the dashing commander of the Pennsylvania Line during the Revolution, a major general to succeed St. Clair, and Congress doubled the authorized strength of the Army by providing for three additional regiments, two of which were to be infantry and the other a composite regiment of infantry and light dragoons. It tried to avoid the bad effects of short-term enlistment by adding the new regiments to the Regular Army as a temporary augmentation to be "discharged as soon as the United States shall be at peace with the Indian tribes." Congress also agreed to Secretary of War Knox's proposed reorganization of the Army into a "Legion," a term widely used during the eighteenth century and which had come to mean a composite organization of all combat arms under one command. Instead of regiments, the Army was composed of four "sub-legions," each commanded by a brigadier general and consisting of two infantry battalions, one battalion of riflemen, one troop of dragoons (cavalrymen trained to fight either mounted or dismounted), and one company of artillery.

Egotistical, blustery, and cordially disliked by many of his contemporaries, General Wayne nevertheless displayed little of his celebrated "madness" during the expedition. His operation was skillfully planned. Correcting previous mistakes, he insisted on rigid discipline and strict training, and conscious of the welfare of his men, he saw to it that supplies were adequate and equipment satisfactory. These military virtues finally won for the United States its elusive victory.

In the spring of 1793 General Wayne took the Legion down the river to Cincinnati where he tried to persuade the Indians to submit peacefully. When negotiations broke down, the Legion followed the route that Harmer and St. Clair had taken. Wayne was in even poorer health than St. Clair, but more determined. Like St. Clair he moved slowly and methodically, building a series of forts and blockhouses along his line of march. Despite his efforts to improve morale, he found desertion as serious a problem as had his predecessors.

Reinforced by mounted militia in July 1794, Wayne led about 3,000 men to within a few miles of Fort Miami, a post recently established by the British on the site of what is now Toledo. There, on August 20, 1794, almost within sight of the British guns, the Indians attacked. The Americans held their ground and then with a furious bayonet charge drove the enemy out of the cover of fallen trees that gave the Battle of Fallen Timbers its name. In the open prairie the Indians were at the mercy of Wayne's mounted volunteers, and in less than an hour the rout was complete.

Ignoring the protest of the British commander at Fort Miami, Wayne remained for several days, burning the Indian villages and destroying crops before leading the Legion back to Cincinnati. The western tribes, their resistance broken, finally agreed on August 3, 1795, in the Treaty of Greenville to make peace and cede their lands in Ohio to the United States. Their submission had been hastened by news that England was about to evacuate the frontier posts.

In the years following the Battle of Fallen Timbers settlers pushed rapidly into Ohio and beyond into lands still claimed by the Indians. To resist these encroachments, Tecumseh, chief of the Shawnees, and his brother, the Prophet, organized a tribal confederacy aimed at keeping the settlers out. Urged on by the settlers, Governor William Henry Harrison of the Indiana Territory decided in the summer of 1811 to strike at the Indians before they could descend on the settlements. Secretary of War William Eustis approved Harrison's scheme and placed 300 Regulars under Harrison's command in addition to his approximately 650 militia, including mounted riflemen. Moving north from Vincennes at the end of September, Harrison built a fort on the edge

BATTLE OF FALLEN TIMBERS

of the Indian country and then continued to the neighborhood of Tecumseh's principal village on Tippecanoe Creek. (*See Map 13.*) On November 6 he halted about a mile west of the village, encamping his force in the form of a trapezoid around the wagons and baggage on a piece of high-wooded ground that rose above the marshy prairies.

The Indians struck just before dawn. Harrison's situation was very similar to that of St. Clair, and for a time his force seemed about to suffer the same fate. Furious hand-to-hand combat followed the Indians' wild charge that carried them into the camp itself. Although taken by surprise, the soldiers rallied and then counterattacked. The end came when the mounted riflemen charged in on the Indians and drove them from the field. Harrison lost 39 men killed and missing and had 151 wounded, of whom 29 died. The engagement by no means solved the frontier problem in the Northwest, but this problem was soon overshadowed by the outbreak of war with England. Its most permanent legacy was a tradition that helped Harrison win the Presidency in 1841.

The Perils of Neutrality

While the United States was launching a new government and defending the frontier, France had undergone a revolution, which within a few years led to a general European war. Britain joined the coalition against France in 1793 and in the first year of the war instituted a blockade, seizing at least 300 American merchant vessels. In 1794 Jay's treaty eased the mounting crisis in Anglo-American relations. By acquiescing in the British doctrine of contraband, the United States obtained a settlement of some long-standing questions, including evacuation of the frontier posts, but only at the expense of domestic unity and peaceful relations with the French. Regarding Jay's treaty as evidence of a pro-British policy on the part of the United States, France retaliated by seizing American vessels that were trading with the British, by sending secret agents to stir up the Creek Indians along the southern frontier, and by meddling in American politics in an attempt to bring about the defeat of the "pro-British" administration. These were the new and serious problems that President Washington bequeathed to his successor, John Adams, in 1797.

Adams inherited a military establishment with an authorized strength of about 3,300 officers and men. In 1797 Congress dropped the legion type of organization that had served well in the frontier fighting, and the Army returned to a regimental type of organization with four regiments of infantry, a Corps of Artillerists and Engineers, and two companies of light dragoons more appropriate to the duties of border defense. During 1796 and early 1797 there had been some redeployment into the Southwest, so that by 1797 nine companies of infantry, about two companies of artillery, and the entire force of dragoons were stationed along the southwestern frontier. Up in the old Northwest there were five infantry companies at Detroit and smaller detachments at a dozen scattered forts elsewhere in the territory. Fort Washington was the major installation. There were also small garrisons at the important seaports, which had been fortified after 1794 by French technicians, émigrés of the recent revolution. The rest of the Army was stationed along the Canadian border from the lakes eastward and at the older posts, like West Point, Carlisle, and Fort Pitt.

The Quasi War With France

When the French continued to attack American vessels and refused to receive the newly appointed American Minister, President Adams called Congress into special session to consider national defense. He particularly urged that immediate steps be taken to provide a navy. He also recommended that harbor defenses be improved, additional cavalry be raised, the Militia Act of 1792 be revised to provide for better organization and training, and the President be authorized to call an emergency force, although he saw no immediate need for the last. Congress approved the naval recommendations, but except for a modest appropriation for harbor defenses and an act authorizing the

President to call out 80,000 militia for a maximum term of three months, it voted down the military recommendations.

By the spring of 1798 France's actions had thoroughly aroused the country. President Adams again recommended an expanded defense program, which this time fared somewhat better in Congress. Congress passed the recommended naval increases and created a separate Navy Department. Of the three regiments the administration recommended adding to the Regular Army, Congress authorized the additional artillery but not the cavalry. With respect to the infantry regiment, the Secretary of War proposed to Congress that it might act in the double capacity of marines and infantrymen. Instead, Congress voted the U.S. Marine Corps into existence, making it part of the Army or Navy, according to whether the marines served on land or on shipboard. Congress also increased the number of companies in each of the 4 Regular infantry regiments from 8 to 10; voted a sizable sum for harbor defenses and ordnance; and authorized a Provisional Army, the emergency force that Adams had suggested the year before.

Again Congress tried to avoid the defects of short-term enlistments by setting the duration of the "existing differences between the United States and the French Republic" as the term of enlistment for the Provisional Army. Reluctant to abandon its traditional reliance on short-term militia volunteers, Congress turned down another Presidential request for an increase in the Regular Army, giving him instead the authority to accept privately armed and equipped volunteer units for short-term service. Adams never made use of this authority, but went ahead with the plans to raise the twelve infantry regiments and one cavalry regiment that made up the Provisional Army. He persuaded Washington to come out of retirement to accept command as lieutenant general, and at Washington's request appointed Alexander Hamilton senior major general. By the beginning of 1799 the officers had been appointed and in May 1799 recruiting began. By the time the Provisional Army was disbanded in June 1800, about 4,100 men had been mobilized, assembled in camps, and given from six to twelve months' training. Hamilton directed the preparation of new drill regulations to replace Steuben's, but before the task was finished the French crisis had ended and the Provisional Army was discharged.

The possibility that the United States might ally itself with Britain helped persuade the French to agree to negotiations. Furthermore, the French had been pressing Spain to return Louisiana as a step toward restoring their colonial empire in America, and for this venture peace with the United States was necessary. On September 30, 1800, a treaty was signed in which France agreed to recognize American neutrality, thus formally ending the alliance of 1778, and to refrain from seizing American vessels that were not carrying contraband. On the very next day, October 1, 1800, France and Spain signed a secret treaty turning Louisiana over to France, and a few months later England and her allies made peace with France.

Defense Under Jefferson

President Jefferson took office in 1801 committed to a policy of peace and economy. With Europe at peace and American relations with France and England better than they had been for ten years past, Congress proceeded to economize. It sold the Navy that had acquitted itself so well in the quasi war with France, retaining only the frigates and a few of the other larger ships. The Army did not feel the effect of the economy drive until March 1802. Until then the military establishment was much as Adams had left it after the Provisional Army troops had been discharged, with an authorized strength of 5,438 officers and men and an actual strength of about 4,000. In the reduction of March 1802 Congress cut back the total strength of the Army to 3,220 men, approximately what it had been in 1797 when Adams took office. It was more than 50 percent stronger in artillery, but the more expensive cavalry was eliminated.

Congress also abolished the Office of the Quartermaster General when it reduced the size of the Army and in its place instituted a system of contract agents. It divided the country into three military departments with a military agent in each who, with his assistants, was responsible for the movement of supplies and troops within his department. Since the assistant agents were also appointed by the President, the three military agents had no way to enforce accountability on their subordinates. This system soon led to large property losses.

Since the Revolution the Army had suffered from a lack of trained technicians, particularly in engineering science, and had depended largely upon foreign experts. As a remedy Washington, Knox, Hamilton, and others had recommended the establishment of a military school. During Washington's administration, Congress had added the rank of cadet in the Corps of Artillerists and Engineers with two cadets assigned to each company for instruction. But not until the Army reorganization of 1802 did Congress create a separate Corps of Engineers, consisting of 10 cadets and 7 officers, and assign it to West Point to serve as the staff of a military academy. Within a few years the U.S. Military Academy became a center of study in military science and a source of trained officers. By 1812 it listed 89 graduates, 65 of them still serving in the Army and playing an important role in operations and the construction of fortifications.

The Army and Westward Expansion

Not long after Thomas Jefferson became President, rumors reached America that France had acquired Louisiana from Spain. The news was upsetting. Many Americans, including Jefferson, had believed that when Spain lost its weak hold on the colonies the United States would automatically fall heir to them. But, with a strong power like France in possession, it was useless to wait for the colonies to fall into the lap of the United States. The presence of France in North America also raised a new security problem. Up to this time the problem of frontier defense had been chiefly one of pacifying the Indians, keeping the western territories from breaking away, and preventing American settlers from molesting the Spanish. Now, with a strong, aggressive France as backdoor neighbor, the frontier problem became tied up with the question of security against possible foreign threats. The transfer of Louisiana to France also marked the beginning of restraints on American trade down the Mississippi. In the past, Spain had permitted American settlers to send their goods down the river and to deposit them at New Orleans. Just before transferring the colony, however, it revoked the American right of deposit, an action which made it almost impossible for Americans to send goods out by this route.

These considerations persuaded Jefferson in 1803 to inquire about the possibility of purchasing New Orleans from France. When Napoleon, anticipating the renewal of the war in Europe, offered to sell the whole of Louisiana, Jefferson quickly accepted, suddenly doubling the size of the United States. The Army, after taking formal possession of Louisiana on December 20, 1803, established small garrisons at New Orleans and the other former Spanish posts on the lower Mississippi. Jefferson later appointed Brig. Gen. James Wilkinson, who had survived the various reorganizations of the Army to become senior officer, first governor of the new territory. (*Map 14*)

Before the Louisiana Purchase, Jefferson had persuaded Congress to support an exploration of the unknown territory west of the Mississippi. The acquisition of this territory now made such an exploration even more desirable. To lead the expedition, Jefferson chose Capt. Meriwether Lewis and Lt. William Clark, both of whom had served under General Wayne in the Northwest. Leaving St. Louis in the spring of 1804 with twenty-seven men, Lewis and Clark traveled up the Missouri River, crossed the Rocky Mountains, and followed the Columbia River down to the Pacific, which they reached after much

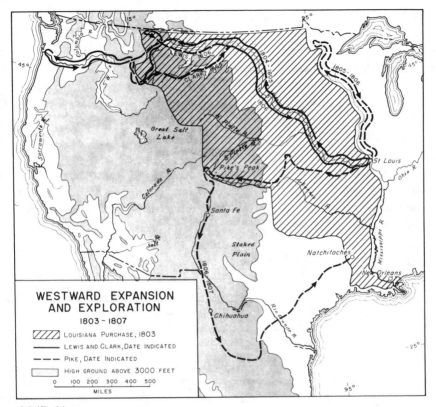

MAP 14

hardship in November 1805. On the return journey, the party explored the region of central Montana and returned to St. Louis in September 1806.

While Lewis and Clark were exploring beyond the Missouri, General Wilkinson sent out Capt. Zebulon M. Pike on a similar expedition to the headwaters of the Mississippi. In 1807 Wilkinson organized another expedition. This time he sent twenty men under Captain Pike westward into what is now Colorado. After exploring the region around the peak that bears his name, Pike encountered some Spaniards who, resentful of the incursion, escorted his party to Santa Fe. From there the Spanish took the Americans into Mexico and then back across Texas to Natchitoches, once more in American territory. The Lewis and Clark expedition and those of Captain Pike contributed much to the geographic and scientific knowledge of the country, and today remain as great epics of the West.

To march across the continent might seem the manifest destiny of the Republic, but it met with an understandable reaction from the Spanish. The dispute over the boundary between Louisiana and Spain's frontier provinces and the question of the two Floridas became burning issues during Jefferson's second administration. Tension mounted in 1806 as rumors reached Washington of the dispatch of thousands of Spanish Regulars to reinforce the mounted Mexican militiamen in east Texas. Jefferson reacted to the rumors by calling up the Orleans and Mississippi Territories' militia and sending approximately 1,000 Regulars to General Wilkinson to counter the Spanish move. The rumors proved unfounded; at no time did the Spanish outnumber the American forces in the area. A series of cavalry skirmishes occurred along the Sabine River, but the opposing commanders prudently avoided war by agreeing to establish a neutral zone between the Arroyo Hondo and the Sabine River. The two armies remained along this line throughout 1806, and the neutral zone served as a *de facto* boundary until 1812.

American Reaction to the Napoleonic Wars

The second round of the great conflict between England and France began in 1803, shortly after the purchase of Louisiana. It was a much more serious affair than the earlier one. Both Britain and France adopted policies under which American merchant shipping, whether carrying contraband or not, was subject to search and seizure. The Napoleonic Wars and the consequent depredations on American commerce were less a threat to national security than a blow to national pride. Jefferson responded to the challenge by withdrawing American shipping from the seas. Madison adopted the even riskier policy of economic coercion. Jefferson's Embargo Act of 1807 prohibited trade with all foreign countries. It was replaced by the Non-Intercourse Act of 1809, which prohibited trade only with England and France. The Non-Intercourse Act was, in turn, replaced by an act in May 1810, known as Macon's Bill No. 2, which reopened trade with England and France but provided that, if either of those countries repealed its restrictive measures and the other failed to follow suit, the Non-Intercourse Act would be put into effect against the nation that continued its restrictions.

The legislation failed to keep the United States from becoming embroiled in the war and was unsuccessful in forcing England and France to respect neutral trade. Neither Jefferson nor Madison recognized that under the new scheme of economic warfare being waged by both England and France the American measures were in effect provocative acts, likely to bring the United States into the war on one side or the other. The Embargo Act and, to a lesser extent, the Non-Intercourse Act of 1809 did cripple American trade, something that neither Britain nor France had succeeded in doing. As a result, the American people, already divided by sectional jealousies and by the French crisis during Adams' administration, were so thoroughly disunited that the government could not count on the loyalty and support of a sizable part of the population.

International tension was so great in the months after the embargo went into effect that Congress, while rejecting Jefferson's proposal for recruiting a 24,000-man volunteer force, authorized the recruitment of 6,000 men as a temporary addition to the Army. In the last month of his administration President Jefferson sent more than 2,000 of these men to General Wilkinson to defend "New Orleans and its dependencies" against an expected English invasion. The invasion never materialized, but poor leadership and bureaucratic mismanagement bordering on the criminal combined with the tropical heat to accomplish what no British invasion could have done. Over 1,000 men, half of Wilkinson's army, died in Louisiana.

By January 1810 relations with Britain had so deteriorated that President Madison recommended the recruitment of a volunteer force of 20,000. Congress, apparently satisfied with the existing militia system, again refused to vote a volunteer force; not until January 1812 did it increase the Army's strength when it added thirteen additional regiments, totaling about 25,700 men, and authorized the President to call 50,000 militiamen into service.

The additional men would soon be needed. On June 18, 1812, Congress declared war against England. At the same time a Senate proposal to declare war against France failed by only two votes.

CHAPTER 6

The War of 1812

To Great Britain the War of 1812 was simply a burdensome adjunct of its greater struggle against Napoleonic France. To the Canadians it was clearly a case of naked American aggression. But to the Americans it was neither simple nor clear. The United States entered the war with confused objectives and divided loyalties and made peace without settling any of the issues that had induced the nation to go to war.

Origins of the War

The immediate origins of the war were seizure of American ships, insults and injuries to American seamen by the British Navy, and rapid expansion of the American frontier. The British outrages at sea took two distinct forms. One was the seizure and forced sale of merchant ships and their cargoes for allegedly violating the British blockade of Europe. Although France had declared a counterblockade of the British Isles and had seized American ships, England was the chief offender because its Navy had greater command of the seas. The second, more insulting, type of outrage was the capture of men from American vessels for forced service in the Royal Navy. The pretext for impressment was the search for deserters, who, the British claimed, had taken employment on American vessels.

The reaction in the United States to impressment differed from that aroused by the seizure of ships and cargoes. In the latter case the maritime interests of the eastern seaboard protested vigorously and demanded naval protection, but rather than risk having their highly profitable trade cut off by war with England they were willing to take an occasional loss of cargo. Impressment, on the other hand, presented no such financial hardship to the shipowners, whatever the consequences for the unfortunate seamen, and the maritime interests tended to minimize it.

To the country at large the seizure of American seamen was much more serious than the loss of a few hogsheads of flour or molasses. When a British naval vessel in June 1807 attacked and disabled the USS *Chesapeake* and impressed several members of the crew, a general wave of indignation rose in which even the maritime interests joined. This was an insult to the flag, and had Jefferson chosen to go to war with England he would have had considerable support. Instead he decided to clamp an embargo on American trade. In New England scores of prosperous shipowners were ruined, and a number of thriving little seaports suffered an economic depression from which few recovered. While the rest of the country remembered the *Chesapeake* affair and stored up resentment against Britain, maritime New England directed its anger at Jefferson and his party.

The seat of anti-British fever was in the Northwest and the lower Ohio Valley, where the land-hungry frontiersmen had no doubt that their troubles with the Indians were the result of British intrigue. Stories were circulated after every Indian raid of British Army muskets and equipment being found on the field. By 1812 the westerners were convinced that their problems could best be solved by forcing the British out of Canada.

While the western "war hawks" urged war in the hope of conquering Canada, the people of Georgia, Tennessee, and the Mississippi Territory entertained similar designs against Florida, a Spanish possession. The fact that Spain and England were allies against Napoleon presented the southern war hawks with an excuse for invading Florida. By this time, also, the balance of political power had shifted south and westward; ambitious party leaders had no choice but to align themselves with the war hawks, and 1812 was a Presidential election year.

President Madison's use of economic pressure to force England to repeal its blockade almost succeeded. The revival of the Non-Intercourse Act against Britain, prohibiting all trade with England and its colonies, coincided with a poor grain harvest in England and with a growing need of American provisions to supply the British troops fighting the French in Spain. As a result, on June 16, 1812, the British Foreign Minister announced that the blockade would be relaxed on American shipping. Had there been an Atlantic cable, war might have been averted. President Madison had sent a message to Congress on June 1 listing all the complaints against England and asking for a declaration of war. Dividing along sectional lines the House had voted for war on June 4, but the Senate approved only on June 18 and then by only six votes.

The Opposing Forces

At the outbreak of the war the United States had a total population of about 7,700,000 people. A series of border forts garrisoned by very small Regular Army detachments stretched along the Canadian boundary: Fort Michilimackinac, on the straits between Lake Michigan and Lake Huron; Fort Dearborn, on the site of what is now Chicago; Fort Detroit; and Fort Niagara, at the mouth of the Niagara River on Lake Ontario. (*Map 15*) The actual strength of the Regular Army in June 1812 totaled approximately 11,744 officers and men, including an estimated 5,000 recruits enlisted for the additional force authorized the preceding January, in contrast to an authorized strength of 35,600. The Navy consisted of 20 vessels: the 3 large 44-gun frigates, 3 smaller frigates of the *Constellation* class rated at 38 guns, and 14 others.

Congress did not lack the will to prepare for war. In March 1812 it had tried to place the Army's supply system on a more adequate footing by establishing a Quartermaster Department on the military staff in place of the inefficient and costly military agent system. At the same time Congress created the Office of the Commissary General of Purchases in the War Department, and for the first time since the Revolution the Army's supply system was placed under the exclusive control of the Secretary of War. In May Congress had made provision for an Ordnance Department, responsible for the inspection and testing of all ordnance, cannon balls, shells, and shot, the construction of gun carriages and ammunition wagons, and the preparation and inspection of the "public powder." It enlarged the Corps of Engineers by adding a company of bombardiers, sappers, and miners, and expanded and reorganized the Military Academy at West Point. In addition to increasing the Regular Army, Congress had authorized the President to accept volunteer forces and to call upon the states for militia. The difficulty was not planning for an army, but raising one.

One of the world's major powers was ranged against the United States, but on the basis of available resources the two belligerents were rather evenly matched. Most of Britain's forces were tied up in the war against Napoleon, and for the time being very little military and naval assistance could be spared for the defense of Canada. At the outbreak of the war, there were approximately 7,000 British and Canadian Regulars in Upper and Lower Canada (now the provinces of Ontario and Quebec). With a total white population of only about half a million, Canada itself had only a small reservoir of militia to draw upon. When the war began, Maj. Gen. Isaac Brock, the military commander and civil governor of Upper Canada, had 800 militiamen available in addition to his approximately 1,600 Regulars. In the course of the war, the two provinces put a total of about 10,000 militia in the field, whereas in the United States probably 450,000 of the militia saw active service, although not more than half of them ever got near the front. The support of Indian tribes gave Canada one source of manpower that the United States lacked. After the Battle of Tippe-

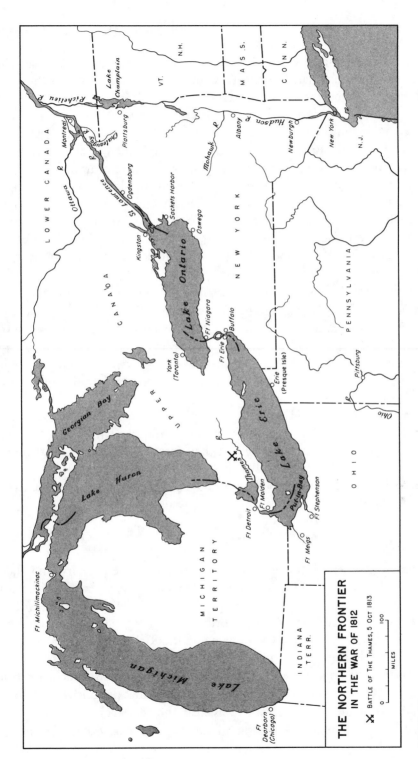

THE NORTHERN FRONTIER
IN THE WAR OF 1812

✗ BATTLE OF THE THAMES, 5 OCT 1813

0   100
MILES

MAP 15

canoe, Tecumseh had led his warriors across the border into Canada, where, along with the Canadian Indians, they joined the forces opposing the Americans. Perhaps 3,500 Indians were serving in the Canadian forces during the Thames River campaign in the fall of 1813, probably the largest number that took the field at any one time during the war.

The bulk of the British Navy was also fighting in the war against Napoleon. In September 1812, three months after the outbreak of war with the United States, Britain had no more than eleven ships of the line, thirty-four frigates, and about an equal number of smaller naval vessels in the western Atlantic. These were all that could be spared for operations in American waters, which involved the tremendous task of escorting British merchant shipping, protecting the St. Lawrence River, blockading American ports, and at the same time hunting down American frigates.

A significant weakness in the American position was the disunity of the country. In the New England states public opinion ranged from mere apathy to actively expressed opposition to the war. A good many Massachusetts and Connecticut shipowners fitted out privateers—privately owned and armed vessels that were commissioned to take enemy ships—but New England contributed little else to the prosecution of the war, and continued to sell grain and provisions to the British.

Canada was not faced with the same problem. Nevertheless, many inhabitants of Upper Canada were recent immigrants from the United States who had no great desire to take up arms against their former homeland, and there were other Canadians who thought that the superiority of the United States in men and material made any defense hopeless. That General Brock was able to overcome this spirit of defeatism is a tribute to his leadership.

The Strategic Pattern

The fundamental strategy was simple enough. The primary undertaking would be the conquest of Canada. The United States also planned an immediate naval offensive, whereby a swarm of privateers and the small Navy would be set loose on the high seas to destroy British commerce. The old invasion route into Canada by way of Lake Champlain and the Richelieu River led directly to the most populous and most important part of the enemy's territory. The capture of Montreal would cut the line of communications upon which the British defense of Upper Canada depended, and the fall of that province would then be inevitable. But this invasion route was near the center of disaffection in the United States, from which little local support could be expected. The west, where enthusiasm for the war ran high and where the Canadian forces were weak, offered a safer theater of operations though one with fewer strategic opportunities. Thus, in violation of the principles of objective and economy of force, the first assaults were delivered across the Detroit River and across the Niagara River between Lake Erie and Lake Ontario.

The war progressed through three distinct stages. In the first, lasting until the spring of 1813, England was so hard pressed in Europe that it could spare neither men nor ships in any great number for the conflict in North America. The United States was free to take the initiative, to invade Canada, and to send out cruisers and privateers against enemy shipping. During the second stage, lasting from early 1813 to the beginning of 1814, England was able to establish a tight blockade but still could not materially reinforce the troops in Canada. In this stage the American Army, having gained experience, won its first successes. The third stage, in 1814, was marked by the constant arrival in North America of British Regulars and naval reinforcements, which enabled the enemy to raid the North American coast almost at will and to take the offensive in several quarters. At the same time, in this final stage of the war, American forces fought their best fights and won their most brilliant victories.

The First Campaigns

The first blows of the war were struck in the Detroit area and at Fort Michilimackinac. President Madison gave Brig. Gen. William Hull, governor of the Michigan Territory, command of operations in that area. Hull arrived at Fort Detroit on July 5, 1812, with a force of about 1,500 Ohio militiamen and 300 Regulars, which he led across the river into Canada a week later. (*See Map 15.*) At that time the whole enemy force on the Detroit frontier amounted to about 150 British Regulars, 300 Canadian militiamen, and some 250 Indians led by Tecumseh. Most of the enemy were at Fort Malden, about twenty miles south of Detroit, on the Canadian side of the river. General Hull had been a dashing young officer in the Revolution, but by this time age and its infirmities had made him cautious and timid. Instead of moving directly against Fort Malden, Hull issued a bombastic proclamation to the people of Canada and stayed at the river landing almost opposite Detroit. He sent out several small raiding detachments along the Thames and Detroit Rivers, one of which returned after skirmishing with the British outposts near Fort Malden. In the meantime General Brock, who was both energetic and daring, sent a small party of British Regulars, Canadians, and Indians across the river from Malden to cut General Hull's communications with Ohio. By that time Hull was discouraged by the loss of Fort Michilimackinac, whose sixty defenders had quietly surrendered on July 17 to a small group of British Regulars supported by a motley force of fur traders and Indians that, at Brock's suggestion, had swiftly marched from St. Joseph Island, forty miles to the north. Hull also knew that the enemy in Fort Malden had received reinforcements (which he overestimated tenfold) and feared that Detroit would be completely cut off from its base of supplies. On August 7 he began to withdraw his force across the river into Fort Detroit. The last American had scarcely returned before the first men of Brock's force appeared and began setting up artillery opposite Detroit. By August 15 five guns were in position and opened fire on the fort, and the next morning Brock led his troops across the river. Before Brock could launch his assault, the Americans surrendered. Militiamen were released under parole; Hull and the Regulars were sent as prisoners to Montreal. Later paroled, Hull returned to face a court-martial for his conduct of the campaign, was sentenced to be shot, and was immediately pardoned.

On August 15, the day before the surrender, the small garrison at distant Fort Dearborn, acting on orders from Hull, had evacuated the post and started out for Detroit. The column was almost instantly attacked by a band of Indians who massacred the Americans before returning to destroy the fort.

With the fall of Michilimackinac, Detroit, and Dearborn, the entire territory north and west of Ohio fell under enemy control. The settlements in Indiana lay open to attack, the neighboring Indian tribes hastened to join the winning side, and the Canadians in the upper province lost some of the spirit of defeatism with which they had entered the war.

Immediately after taking Detroit, Brock transferred most of his troops to the Niagara frontier where he faced an American invasion force of 6,500 men. Maj. Gen. Stephen van Rensselaer, the senior American commander and a New York militiaman, was camped at Lewiston with a force of 900 Regulars and about 2,300 militiamen. Van Rensselaer owed his appointment not to any active military experience, for he had none, but to his family's position in New York. Inexperienced as he was in military art, van Rensselaer at least fought the enemy, which was more than could be said of the Regular Army commander in the theater, Brig. Gen. Alexander Smyth. Smyth and his 1,650 Regulars and nearly 400 militiamen were located at Buffalo. The rest of the American force, about 1,300 Regulars, was stationed at Fort Niagara.

Van Rensselaer planned to cross the narrow Niagara River and capture Queenston and its heights, a towering escarpment that ran perpendicular to the river south of the town. From this vantage point he hoped to command the area and eventually drive the British out of the Niagara peninsula. Smyth, on the other hand, wanted to attack above the falls, where the banks were low and the current less swift, and he refused to co-operate with the militia general. With a force ten times that of the British opposite him, van Rensselaer decided to attack alone. After one attempt had been called off for lack of oars for the boats, van Rensselaer finally ordered an attack for the morning of October 13. The assault force numbered 600 men, roughly half New York militiamen; but several boats drifted beyond the landing area, and the first echelon to land, numbering far less than 500, was pinned down for a time on the river bank below the heights until the men found an unguarded path, clambered to the summit, and, surprising the enemy, overwhelmed his fortified battery and drove him down into Queenston.

The Americans repelled a hastily formed counterattack later in the morning, during which General Brock was killed. This, however, was the high point of van Rensselaer's fortunes. Although 1,300 men were successfully ferried across the river under persistent British fire from a fortified battery north of town, less than half of them ever reached the American line on the heights. Most of the militiamen refused to cross the river, insisting on their legal right to remain on American soil, and General Smyth ignored van Rensselaer's request for Regulars. Meanwhile, British and Canadian reinforcements arrived in Queenston, and Maj. Gen. Roger Sheaffe, General Brock's successor, began to advance on the American position with a force of 800 troops and 300 Indian skirmishers. Van Rensselaer's men, tired and outnumbered, put up a stiff resistance on the heights but in the end were defeated—300 Americans were killed or wounded and nearly 1,000 were captured.

After the defeat at Queenston, van Rensselaer resigned and was succeeded by the unreliable Smyth, who spent his time composing windy proclamations. Disgusted at being marched down to the river on several occasions only to be marched back to camp again, the new army that had assembled after the battle of Queenston gradually melted away. The men who remained lost all sense of discipline, and finally at the end of November the volunteers were ordered home and the Regulars were sent into winter quarters. General Smyth's request for leave was hastily granted, and three months later his name was quietly dropped from the Army rolls.

Except for minor raids across the frozen St. Lawrence, there was no further fighting along the New York frontier until the following spring. During the Niagara campaign the largest force then under arms, commanded by Maj. Gen. Henry Dearborn, had been held in the neighborhood of Albany, more than 250 miles from the scene of operations. Dearborn had had a good record in the Revolutionary War and had served as Jefferson's Secretary of War. Persuaded to accept the command of the northern theater, except for Hull's forces, he was in doubt for some time about the extent of his authority over the Niagara front. When it was clarified he was reluctant to exercise it. Proposing to move his army, which included seven regiments of Regulars with artillery and dragoons, against Montreal in conjunction with a simultaneous operation across the Niagara River, Dearborn was content to wait for his subordinates to make the first move. When van Rensselaer made his attempt against Queenston, Dearborn, who was still in the vicinity of Albany, showed no sign of marching toward Canada. At the beginning of November he sent a large force north to Plattsburg and announced that he would personally lead the army into Montreal, but most of his force got no farther than the border. When his advanced guard was driven back to the village of Champlain by Canadian militiamen and Indians, and his Vermont and New York volunteers flatly refused to cross the border, Dearborn quietly turned around and marched back to Plattsburg, where he went into winter quarters.

If the land campaigns of 1812 reflected little credit on the Army, the war at sea brought lasting glory to the infant Navy. Until the end of the year the American frigates, brigs-of-war, and privateers were able to slip in and out of harbors and cruise almost at will, and in this period they won their most brilliant victories. At the same time, American privateers were picking off English merchant vessels by the hundreds. Having need of American foodstuffs, Britain was at first willing to take advantage of New England's opposition to the war by not extending the blockade to the New England coast, but by the beginning of 1814 it was effectively blockading the whole coast and had driven most American naval vessels and privateers off the high seas.

The Second Year, 1813

On land, the objects of the American plan of campaign for 1813 were the recapture of Detroit and an attack on Canada across Lake Ontario. (*See Map 15.*) For the Detroit campaign, Madison picked Brig. Gen. William H. Harrison, governor of the Indian Territory and hero of Tippecanoe. The difficulties of a winter campaign were tremendous, but the country demanded action. Harrison therefore started north toward Lake Erie at the end of October 1812 with some 6,500 men. In January 1813 a sizable detachment, about 1,000, pushed on to Frenchtown, a small Canadian outpost on the Raisin River twenty-six miles south of Detroit. There the American commander, Brig. Gen. James Winchester, positioned his men, their backs to the river with scant natural protection and their movements severely hampered by deep snow. A slightly larger force of British Regulars, militiamen, and Indians under Col. Henry Proctor soundly defeated the Americans, killing over 100 Kentucky riflemen and capturing approximately 500. The brutal massacre of wounded American prisoners by their Indian guards made "Remember the Raisin" the rallying cry of the Northwestern Army, but any plans for revenge had to be postponed, for Harrison had decided to suspend operations for the winter. He built Forts Meigs and Stephenson and posted his army near the Michigan border at the western end of Lake Erie.

The Ontario campaign was entrusted to General Dearborn, who was ordered to move his army from Plattsburg to Sackett's Harbor, where Commodore Isaac Chauncey had been assembling a fleet. Dearborn was to move across the lake to capture Kingston and destroy the British flotilla there, then proceed to York (now Toronto), the capital of Upper Canada, to capture military stores, and finally he was to co-operate with a force from Buffalo in seizing the forts on the Canadian side of the Niagara River.

The American strategy was sound. The capture of Kingston, the only tenable site for a naval station on the Canadian side of Lake Ontario, would give the United States control of the lake and, by cutting the British lines of communications, frustrate enemy plans for operations in the west. After the fall of Kingston, the operations against York and the Niagara forts would be simple mopping-up exercises. When the time came to move, however, Dearborn and Chauncey, hearing a rumor that the British forces in Kingston had been reinforced, decided to bypass that objective and attack York first. About 1,700 men were embarked and sailed up Lake Ontario without incident, arriving off York before daybreak on April 27. Dearborn, who was in poor health, turned over the command of the assault to Brig. Gen. Zebulon Pike, the explorer of the Southwest. The landing, about four miles west of the town, was virtually unopposed. The British garrison of about 600 men, occupying a fortification about halfway between the town and the landing, was overwhelmed after sharp resistance, but just as the Americans were pushing through the fort toward the town, a powder magazine exploded, killing or disabling many Americans and a number of British soldiers. Among those killed was General Pike. Remnants of the garrison fled toward Kingston, 150 miles to the east. The losses were heavy on both sides—almost 20 percent of Dearborn's forces had been killed or wounded. With General Dearborn incapacitated and General Pike dead, the troops apparently got out of hand. They looted and burned the public buildings and destroyed the provincial records. After holding the town for about a week, they recrossed the lake to Niagara to join an attack against the forts on the Canadian side of the Niagara River.

Meanwhile, Sackett's Harbor had been almost stripped of troops for the raid on York and for reinforcing the army at Fort Niagara. At Kingston, across the lake, Sir George Prevost, the Governor-General of Canada, had assembled a force of 800 British Regulars in addition to militia. Taking advantage of the absence of Chauncey's fleet, which was at the other end of the lake, Prevost launched an attack on Sackett's Harbor with his entire force of Regulars on the night of May 26. The town was defended by about 400 Regulars and approximately 750 militiamen, under the command of Brig. Gen. Jacob Brown of the New York militia. Brown posted his men in two lines in front of a fortified battery to cover a possible landing. Coming ashore under heavy fire the British nevertheless pressed rapidly forward, routed the first line, and pushed the second back into the prepared defenses. There the Americans held. The British then tried two frontal assaults, but were repulsed with heavy losses. While they were re-forming for a third attack, General Brown rallied the militia and sent them toward the rear of the enemy's right flank. This was the turning point. Having suffered serious losses and in danger of being cut off, the British hurriedly withdrew to their ships.

On the same day that Prevost sailed against Sackett's Harbor, General Dearborn at the western end of Lake Ontario was invading Canada with an army of 4,000 men. The operation began with a well-executed and stubbornly resisted amphibious assault led by Col. Winfield Scott and Commander Oliver Hazard Perry, USN, with Chauncey's fleet providing fire support. Outnumbered more than two to one, the British retreated, abandoning Fort George and Queenston to the Americans. (*Map 16*) An immediate pursuit might have sealed the victory, but Dearborn, after occupying Fort George, waited several days and then sent about 2,000 men after the enemy. The detachment advanced to within ten miles of the British and camped for the night with slight regard for security and even less for the enemy's audacity. During the night a force of about 700 British attacked the camp and thoroughly routed the Americans. Dearborn withdrew his entire army to Fort George. About two weeks later, a 500-man detachment ventured fifteen miles outside the fort and surrendered to a force of British and Indians that was half as large. After these reverses there was no further action of consequence on the Niagara front for the remainder of the year. Dearborn, again incapacitated by illness, resigned his commission in early July. Both armies were hard hit by disease, and the

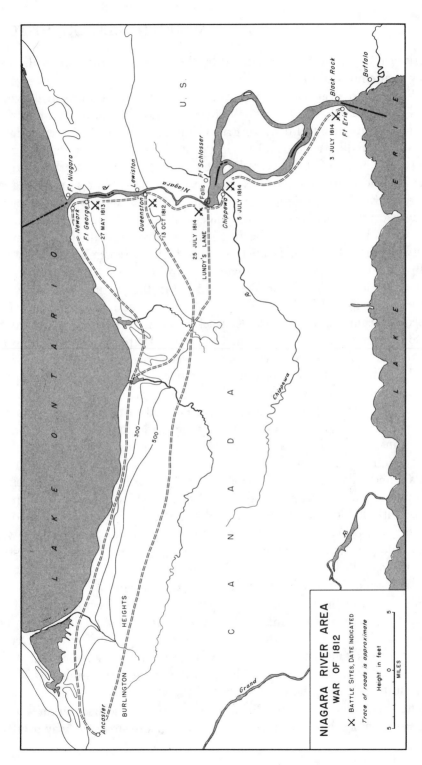

NIAGARA RIVER AREA
WAR OF 1812

X BATTLE SITES, DATE INDICATED

Trace of roads is approximate

Height in feet

5   0   5
|————————————|————————————|
MILES

MAP 16

American forces were further reduced by the renewal of the war in the west and by an attempt against Montreal.

Hull's disaster at Detroit in 1812 and Harrison's unsuccessful winter campaign had clearly shown that any offensive action in that quarter depended upon first gaining control of Lake Erie. Commander Perry had been assigned the task of building a fleet and seizing control of the lake. Throughout the spring and summer of 1813, except for the time he had joined Dearborn's force, the 27-year-old Perry had been busy at Presque Isle assembling his fleet, guns, and crews. By the beginning of August his force was superior to that of the British in every respect except long-range armament. Sailing up the lake, he anchored in Put-in-Bay, near the line still held by General Harrison in the vicinity of Forts Meigs and Stephenson, and there on September 10 Perry met the British Fleet, defeated it, and gained control of Lake Erie.

As soon as the damage to Perry's ships and the captured British vessels had been repaired, Harrison embarked his army and sailed against Fort Malden. A regiment of mounted Kentucky riflemen under Col. Richard M. Johnson moved along the shore of the lake toward Detroit. Vastly outnumbered on land and now open to attack from the water, the British abandoned both Forts Malden and Detroit and retreated eastward. Leaving a detachment to garrison the forts, Harrison set out after the enemy with the Kentucky cavalry regiments, five brigades of Kentucky volunteers, and a part of the 27th Infantry, a force of about 3,500 men. On October 5 he made contact with the British on the banks of the Thames River about eighty-five miles from Malden. (*See Map 15.*) The enemy numbered about 2,900, of whom about 900 were British Regulars and the remainder Indians under Tecumseh. Instead of attacking with infantry in the traditional line-against-line fashion, Harrison ordered a mounted attack. The maneuver succeeded completely. Unable to withstand the charging Kentuckians, the British surrendered in droves. The Indians were routed, and Tecumseh, who had brought so much trouble to the western frontier, was killed. Among those who distinguished themselves on that day was Commander Perry, who had ridden in the front rank of Johnson's charge.

As a result of the victory, which illustrated successful employment of the principles of offensive and mass, Lake Erie became an American lake. The Indian confederacy was shattered. The American position on the Detroit frontier was re-established, a portion of Canadian territory was brought under American control, and the enemy threat in that sector was eliminated. There was no further fighting here for the rest of the war.

The small remnant of the British force that had escaped capture at the Thames—no more than 250 soldiers and a few Indians—made its way overland to the head of Lake Ontario. Harrison, after discharging his Kentucky volunteers and arranging for the defenses of the Michigan Territory, sailed after it with the remainder of his army. He arrived at the Niagara frontier at an opportune time, since the American forces in that theater were being called upon to support a 2-pronged drive against Montreal.

The expedition against Montreal in the fall of 1813 was one of the worst fiascoes of the war. It involved a simultaneous drive by two forces: one, an army of about 4,000 men assembled at Plattsburg on Lake Champlain under the command of Brig. Gen. Wade Hampton and another, of about 6,000 men under the command of Maj. Gen. James Wilkinson, which was to attack down the St. Lawrence River from Sackett's Harbor. Hampton and Wilkinson were scarcely on speaking terms, and there was no one on the spot to command the two of them. Neither had sufficient strength to capture Montreal without the other's aid; each lacked confidence in the other, and both suspected that the War Department was leaving them in the lurch. At first contact with the British, about halfway down the Chateaugay River, Hampton retreated and, after falling back all the way to Plattsburg, resigned from the Army. Wilkinson, after a detachment of about 2,000 men was severely mauled in an engagement just north of Ogdensburg, also abandoned his part of the operation and followed Hampton into Plattsburg.

In the meantime, during December 1813 the British took advantage of the weakened state of American forces on the Niagara frontier to recapture Fort George and to cross the river and take Fort Niagara, which remained in British hands until the end of the war. Before evacuating Fort George the Americans had burned the town of Newark and part of Queenston. In retaliation the British, after assaulting Fort Niagara with unusual ferocity, loosed their Indian allies on the surrounding countryside and burned the town of Buffalo and the nearby village of Black Rock.

During 1813 a new theater of operations opened in the south. Andrew Jackson, an ardent expansionist and commander of the Tennessee militia, wrote the Secretary of War that he would "rejoice at the opportunity of placing the American eagle on the ramparts of Mobile, Pensacola, and Fort St. Augustine." (*Map 17*) For this purpose Tennessee had raised a force of 2,000 men to be under Jackson's command. Congress, after much debate, approved only an expedition into that part of the gulf coast in dispute between the United States and Spain, and refused to entrust the venture to the Tennesseans. Just before he went north to take part in the Montreal expedition, General Wilkinson led his Regulars into the disputed part of West Florida and, without meeting any

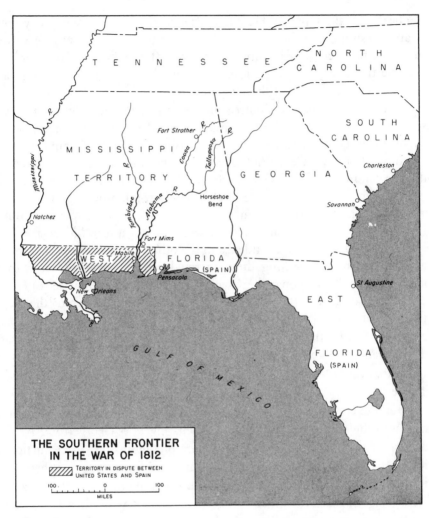

MAP 17

resistance, occupied Mobile, while the Tennessee army was left cooling its heels
in Natchez.

An Indian uprising in that part of the Mississippi Territory soon to become
Alabama saved General Jackson's military career. Inspired by Tecumseh's
earlier successes, the Creek Indians took to the warpath in the summer of 1813
with a series of outrages culminating in the massacre of more than 500 men,
women, and children at Fort Mims. Jackson, with characteristic energy, reas-
sembled his army, which had been dismissed after Congress rejected its services

for an attack on Florida, and moved into the Mississippi Territory. His own energy added to his problems, for he completely outran his primitive supply system and dangerously extended his line of communications. The hardships of the campaign and one near defeat at the hands of the Indians destroyed any enthusiasm the militia might have had for continuing in service. Jackson was compelled to entrench at Fort Strother, on the Coosa River, and remain there for several months until the arrival of a regiment of the Regular Army gave him the means to deal with the mutinous militia. At the end of March 1814 he decided that he had sufficient strength for a decisive blow against the Indians, who had gathered a force of about 900 warriors and many women and children in a fortified camp at the Horseshoe Bend of the Tallapoosa River. Jackson had about 2,000 militia and volunteers, nearly 600 Regulars, several hundred friendly Indians, and a few pieces of artillery. The attack was completely successful. A bayonet charge led by the Regulars routed the Indians, who were ruthlessly hunted down and all but a hundred or so of the warriors were killed. "I lament that two or three women and children were killed by accident," Jackson later reported. The remaining hostile tribes fled into Spanish territory. As one result of the campaign Jackson was appointed a major general in the Regular Army. The campaign against the Creeks had no other effect on the outcome of the war, but for that matter neither had any of the campaigns in the north up to this point.

Fighting also broke out during 1813 along the east coast where a British fleet blockaded the Delaware and Chesapeake Bays, bottling up the American frigates *Constellation* at Norfolk and *Adams* in the Potomac. (*Map 18*) Opposed only by small American gunboats, the British under Admiral Sir John Warren sought "to chastise the Americans into submission," and at the same time to relieve the pressure on Prevost's forces in Canada. With a flotilla, which at times numbered fifteen ships, Rear Adm. Sir George Cockburn, Warren's second-in-command, roamed the Chesapeake during the spring of 1813, burning and looting the prosperous countryside. Reinforced in June by 2,600 Regulars, Warren decided to attack Norfolk, its navy yard and the anchored *Constellation* providing the tempting targets. Norfolk's defenses rested chiefly on Craney Island, which guarded the narrow channel of the Elizabeth River. The island had a 7-gun fortification and was manned by 580 Regulars and militia in addition to 150 sailors and marines from the *Constellation*. The British planned to land an 800-man force on the mainland and, when low tide permitted, march onto the island in a flanking movement. As the tide rose, another 500 men would be rowed across the shoals for a frontal assault. On June 22 the landing party debarked four miles northwest of the island, but the flanking move was

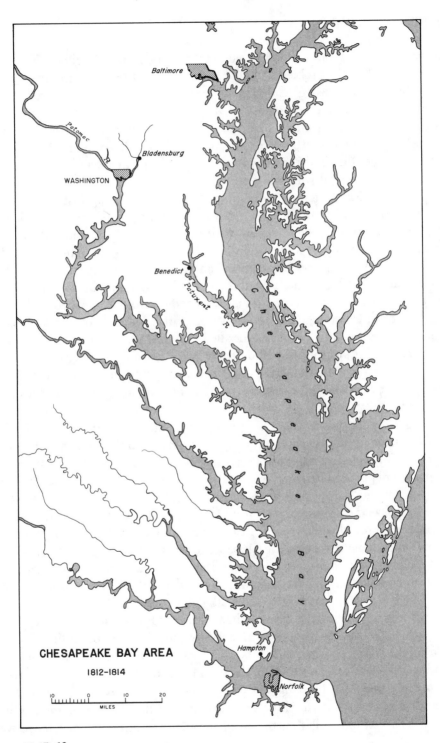

Baltimore

Potomac

WASHINGTON

Bladensburg

Benedict

Patuxent R.

Chesapeake Bay

Hampton

Norfolk

CHESAPEAKE BAY AREA

1812–1814

10   0   10   20
MILES

MAP 18

countered by the highly accurate marksmanship of the *Constellation's* gunners and was forced to pull back. The frontal assault also suffered from well-directed American fire, which sank three barges and threw the rest into confusion. After taking 81 casualties, the British sailed off in disorder. The defenders counted no casualties.

Frustrated at Norfolk, Warren crossed the Roads to Hampton where he overwhelmed the 450 militia defenders and pillaged the town. A portion of the fleet remained in the bay for the rest of the year, blockading and marauding, but the operation was not an unalloyed success. It failed to cause a diversion of American troops from the northern border and, by strengthening popular resentment (Cockburn was vilified throughout the country), helped unite Americans behind the war effort.

The conduct of the war in 1812 and 1813 revealed deficiencies in the administration of the War Department that would plague the American cause to the end. In early 1813 Madison replaced his incompetent Secretary of War William Eustis with John Armstrong, who instituted a reorganization that eventually resulted in the substitution of younger, more aggressive field commanders for the aged veterans of the Revolution. Congress then authorized an expansion of the Army staff to help the Secretary manage the war. In March it re-created the offices of Adjutant General, Inspector General, Surgeon, and Apothecary General and assigned eight topographical Engineers to the staff.

Competent leadership meant little, however, without sufficient logistical support, and logistics, more than any other factor, determined the nature of the military campaigns of the war. Lack of transportation was a major problem. The United States was fighting a war on widely separated fronts that required moving supplies through a wilderness where roads had to be built for wagons and packhorses. For this reason, ammunition and clothing supplies proved inadequate. General Harrison had to depend on homemade cartridges and clothing from Ohio townsmen for his northwestern campaign, and General Scott's Regulars would fight at Chippewa in the gray uniforms of the New York militia. Winter found the troops without blankets, inadequately housed, and without forage for their horses. Most important, the subsistence supply failed so completely that field commanders found it necessary to take local food procurement virtually into their own hands.

Transportation difficulties accounted for only part of the problem. The supply system devised in 1812 proved a resounding failure. Congressional intent notwithstanding, the Quartermaster General had never assumed accountability for the money and property administered by his subordinates or administrative control over his deputies in the south and northwest. Moreover, the functions of his office, never clearly defined, overlapped those of the Commissary General. In a vain attempt to unravel the administrative tangle, Congress created the office of Superintendent General of Military Supplies to keep account of all military stores and reformed the Quartermaster Department, giving the Quartermaster General stricter control over his deputies. In practice, however, the deputies continued to act independently in their own districts.

Both Congress and the War Department overlooked the greatest need for reform as the Army continued to rely on contractors for the collection and delivery of rations for the troops. With no centralized direction for subsistence supply, the inefficient, fraud-racked contract system proved to be one of the gravest hindrances to military operations throughout the war.

The Last Year of the War, 1814

After the setbacks at the end of 1813, a lull descended on the northern frontier. In March 1814 Wilkinson made a foray from Plattsburg with about 4,000 men and managed to penetrate about eight miles into Canada before some 200 British and Canadian troops stopped his advance. It was an even more miserable failure than his attempt of the preceding fall.

In early 1814 Congress increased the Army to 45 infantry regiments, 4 regiments of riflemen, 3 of artillery, 2 of light dragoons, and 1 of light artillery. The number of general officers was fixed at 6 major generals and 16 brigadier generals in addition to the generals created by brevet. Secretary of War Armstrong promoted Jacob Brown, who had been commissioned a brigadier general in the Regular Army after his heroic defense of Sackett's Harbor, to the rank of major general and placed him in command of the Niagara–Lake Ontario theater. He also promoted the youthful George Izard to major general and gave him command of the Lake Champlain frontier. He appointed six new brigadier generals from the ablest, but not necessarily most senior, colonels in the Regular Army, among them Winfield Scott, who had distinguished himself at the battle of Queenston Heights and who was now placed in command at Buffalo.

British control of Lake Ontario, won by dint of feverish naval construction during the previous winter, obliged the Secretary of War to recommend operations from Buffalo, but disagreement within the President's cabinet delayed adoption of a plan until June. Expecting Commodore Chauncey's naval force at Sackett's Harbor to be strong enough to challenge the British Fleet, Washington decided upon a co-ordinated attack on the Niagara peninsula. (*See Map 16.*) Secretary Armstrong instructed General Brown to cross the Niagara

River in the vicinity of Fort Erie and, after assaulting the fort, either to move against Fort George and Newark or to seize and hold a bridge over the Chippewa River, as he saw fit.

Brown accordingly crossed the Niagara River on July 3 with his force of 3,500 men, took Fort Erie, and then advanced toward the Chippewa River, sixteen miles away. There a smaller British force, including 1,500 Regulars, had gathered to oppose the Americans. General Brown posted his army in a strong position behind a creek with his right flank resting on the Niagara River and his left protected by a swamp. In front of the American position was an open plain, beyond which flowed the Chippewa River; on the other side of the river were the British.

In celebration of Independence Day, General Scott had promised his brigade a grand parade on the plain the next day. On July 5 he formed his troops, numbering about 1,300, but on moving forward discovered British Regulars who had crossed the river undetected, lined up on the opposite edge of the plain. Scott ordered his men to charge and the British advanced to meet them. The two lines approached each other, alternately stopping to fire and then moving forward, closing the gaps torn by musketry and artillery fire. They came together first at the flanks, while about sixty or eighty yards apart at the center. At this point the British line crumbled and broke. By the time a second brigade sent forward by General Brown reached the battlefield, the British had withdrawn across the Chippewa River and were retreating toward Ancaster, on Lake Ontario. Scott's casualties amounted to 48 killed and 227 wounded; British losses were 137 killed and 304 wounded.

Brown followed the retreating British as far as Queenston, where he halted to await Commodore Chauncey's fleet. After waiting two weeks for Chauncey, who failed to co-operate in the campaign, Brown withdrew to Chippewa. He proposed to strike out to Ancaster by way of a crossroad known as Lundy's Lane, from which he could reach the Burlington Heights at the head of Lake Ontario and at the rear of the British.

Meanwhile the British had drawn reinforcements from York and Kingston, and more troops were on the way from Lower Canada. Sixteen thousand British veterans, fresh from Wellington's victories over the French in Europe, had just arrived in Canada, too late to participate in the Niagara campaign but in good time to permit the redeployment of the troops that had been defending the upper St. Lawrence. By the time General Brown decided to pull back from Queenston, the British force at Ancaster amounted to about 2,200 men under General Phineas Riall; another 1,500 British troops were gathered at Fort George and Fort Niagara at the mouth of the Niagara River.

As soon as Brown began his withdrawal, Riall sent forward about 1,000 men along Lundy's Lane, the very route by which General Brown intended to advance against Burlington Heights; another force of more than 600 British moved out from Fort George and followed Brown along the Queenston road; while a third enemy force of about 400 men moved along the American side of the Niagara River from Fort Niagara. Riall's advance force reached the junction of Lundy's Lane and the Queenston road on the night of July 24, the same night that Brown reached Chippewa, about three miles distant. Concerned lest the British force on the opposite side of the Niagara cut his line of communications and entirely unaware of Riall's force at Lundy's Lane, General Brown on July 25 ordered Scott to take his brigade back along the road toward Queenston in the hope of drawing back the British force on the other side of the Niagara; but in the meantime that force had crossed the river and joined Riall's men at Lundy's Lane. Scott had not gone far when much to his surprise he discovered himself face-to-face with the enemy.

The ensuing battle, most of which took place after nightfall, was the hardest fought, most stubbornly contested engagement of the war. For two hours Scott attacked and repulsed the counterattacks of the numerically superior British force, which, moreover, had the advantage in position. Then both sides were reinforced. With Brown's whole contingent engaged the Americans now had a force equal to that of the British, about 2,900. They were able to force back the enemy from its position and capture its artillery. The battle then continued without material advantage to either side until just before midnight, when General Brown ordered the exhausted Americans to fall back to their camp across the Chippewa River. The equally exhausted enemy was unable to follow. Losses on both sides had been heavy, each side incurring about 850 casualties. On the American side, both General Brown and General Scott were severely wounded, Scott so badly that he saw no further service during the war. On the British side, General Riall and his superior, General Drummond, who had arrived with the reinforcements, were wounded, and Riall was taken prisoner.

Both sides claimed Lundy's Lane as a victory, as well they might; but Brown's invasion of Canada was halted. Commodore Chauncey, who failed to prevent the British from using Lake Ontario for supply and reinforcements, contributed to the unfavorable outcome. In contrast to the splendid co-operation between Harrison and Perry on Lake Erie, relations between Brown and Chauncey were far from satisfactory. A few days after the Battle of Lundy's Lane the American army withdrew to Fort Erie and held this outpost on Canadian soil until early in November.

Reinforced after Lundy's Lane, the British laid siege to Fort Erie at the beginning of August but were forced to abandon the effort on September 21 after heavy losses. Shortly afterward General Izard arrived with reinforcements from Plattsburg and advanced as far as Chippewa, where the British were strongly entrenched. After a few minor skirmishes, he ceased operations for the winter. The works at Fort Erie were destroyed, and the army withdrew to American soil on November 5.

During the summer of 1814 the British had been able to reinforce Canada and to stage several raids on the American coast. Eastport, Maine, on Passama-quoddy Bay, and Castine, at the mouth of the Penobscot River, were occupied without resistance. This operation was something more than a raid since East-port lay in disputed territory, and it was no secret that Britain wanted a rectifica-tion of the boundary. No such political object was attached to British forays in the region of Chesapeake Bay. (*See Map 18.*) On August 19 a force of some 4,000 British troops under Maj. Gen. Robert Ross landed on the Patuxent River and marched on Washington. At the Battle of Bladensburg, five days later, Ross easily dispersed 5,000 militia, naval gunners, and Regulars hastily gathered together to defend the Capital. The British then entered Washington, burned the Capitol, the White House, and other public buildings, and returned to their ships.

Baltimore was next on the schedule, but that city had been given time to prepare its defenses. The land approach was covered by a rather formidable line of redoubts; the harbor was guarded by Fort McHenry and blocked by a line of sunken gunboats. On September 13 a spirited engagement fought by Mary-land militia, many of whom had run at Bladensburg just two weeks before, delayed the invaders and caused considerable loss, including General Ross, who was killed. When the fleet failed to reduce Fort McHenry, the assault on the city was called off.

Two days before the attack on Baltimore, the British suffered a much more serious repulse on Lake Champlain. After the departure of General Izard for the Niagara front, Brig. Gen. Alexander Macomb had remained at Plattsburg with a force of about 3,300 men. Supporting this force was a small fleet under Commodore Thomas Macdonough. Across the border in Canada was an army of British veterans of the Napoleonic Wars whom Sir George Prevost was to lead down the route taken by Burgoyne thirty-seven years before. Moving slowly up the Richelieu River toward Lake Champlain, he crossed the border and on September 6 arrived before Plattsburg with about 11,000 men. There he waited for almost a week until his naval support was ready to join the attack. With militia reinforcements, Macomb now had about 4,500 men manning a strong line of redoubts and blockhouses that faced a small river. Macdonough had anchored his vessels in Plattsburg Bay, out of range of British guns, but in a position to resist an assault on the American line. On September 11 the British flotilla appeared and Prevost ordered a joint attack. There was no numerical disparity between the naval forces, but an important one in the quality of the seamen. Macdonough's ships were manned by well-trained seamen and gunners, the British ships by hastily recruited French-Canadian militia and soldiers, with only a sprinkling of regular seamen. As the enemy vessels came into the bay the wind died, and the British were exposed to heavy raking fire from Macdonough's long guns. The British worked their way in, came to anchor, and the two fleets began slugging at each other, broadside by broadside. At the end the British commander was dead and his ships battered into submission. Prevost immediately called off the land attack and withdrew to Canada the next day.

Macdonough's victory ended the gravest threat that had arisen so far. More important it gave impetus to peace negotiations then under way. News of the two setbacks—Baltimore and Plattsburg—reached England simultaneously, aggravating the war weariness of the British and bolstering the efforts of the American peace commissioners to obtain satisfactory terms.

New Orleans: The Final Battle

The progress of the peace negotiations influenced the British to continue an operation that General Ross, before his repulse and death at Baltimore, had been instructed to carry out, a descent upon the gulf coast to capture New Orleans and possibly sever Louisiana from the United States. (*See Map 17.*) Major General Sir Edward Pakenham was sent to America to take command of the expedition. On Christmas Day, 1814, Pakenham arrived at the mouth of the Mississippi to find his troops disposed on a narrow isthmus below New Orleans between the Mississippi River and a cypress swamp. They had landed two weeks earlier at a shallow lagoon some ten miles east of New Orleans and had already fought one engagement. In this encounter, on December 23, General Jackson, who had taken command of the defenses on December 1, almost succeeded in cutting off an advance detachment of 2,000 British, but after a 3-hour fight in which casualties on both sides were heavy, he was compelled to retire behind fortifications covering New Orleans.

Opposite the British and behind a ditch stretching from the river to the swamp, Jackson had raised earthworks high enough to require scaling ladders for an assault. The defenses were manned by about 3,500 men with another 1,000 in reserve. It was a varied group, composed of the 7th and 44th Infantry Regi-

BATTLE OF NEW ORLEANS

ments, Major Beale's New Orleans Sharpshooters, LaCoste and Daquin's bat-talions of free Negroes, the Louisiana militia under General David Morgan, a band of Choctaw Indians, the Baratorian pirates, and a motley battalion of fashionably dressed sons and brothers of the New Orleans aristocracy. To support his defenses, Jackson had assembled more than twenty pieces of artillery, including a battery of nine heavy guns on the opposite bank of the Mississippi.

After losing an artillery duel to the Americans on January 1, Pakenham decided on a frontal assault in combination with an attack against the American troops on the west bank. The main assault was to be delivered by about 5,300 men, while about 600 men under Lt. Col. William Thornton were to cross the river and clear the west bank. As the British columns appeared out of the early morning mist on January 8, they were met with murderous fire, first from the artillery, then from the muskets and rifles of Jackson's infantry. Achieving mass through firepower, the Americans mowed the British down by the hundreds. Pakenham and one other general were killed and a third badly wounded. More than 2,000 of the British were casualties; the American losses were trifling.

Suddenly, the battle on the west bank became critical. Jackson did not make adequate preparations to meet the advance there until the British began their movement, but by then it was too late. The heavy guns of a battery posted on the west bank were not placed to command an attack along that side of the river and only about 800 militia, divided in two groups a mile apart, were in position to oppose Thornton. The Americans resisted stubbornly, inflicting greater losses than they suffered, but the British pressed on, routed them, and overran the battery. Had the British continued their advance Jackson's position would have been critical, but Pakenham's successor in command, appalled by the repulse of the main assault, ordered Thornton to withdraw from the west bank and rejoin the main force. For ten days the shattered remnant of Pakenham's army remained in camp unmolested by the Americans, then re-embarked and sailed away.

The British appeared off Mobile on February 8, confirming Jackson's fear that they planned an attack in that quarter. They overwhelmed Fort Bowyer, a garrison manned by 360 Regulars at the entrance to Mobile Harbor. Before they could attack the city itself, word arrived that a treaty had been signed at Ghent on Christmas Eve, two weeks before the Battle of New Orleans.

The news of the peace settlement followed so closely on Jackson's triumph in New Orleans that the war as a whole was popularly regarded in the United States as a great victory. Yet at best it was a draw. American strategy had centered on the conquest of Canada and the harassment of British shipping; but the land campaign failed, and during most of the war the Navy was bottled up behind a tight British blockade of the North American coast.

If it favored neither belligerent, the war at least taught the Americans several lessons. Although the Americans were proud of their reputation as the world's most expert riflemen, the rifle played only a minor role in the war. On the other hand, the American soldier displayed unexpected superiority in gunnery and engineering. Artillery contributed to American successes at Chippewa, Sackett's Harbor, Norfolk, the siege of Fort Erie, and New Orleans. The war also boosted the reputation of the Corps of Engineers, a branch which owed its efficiency chiefly to the Military Academy. Academy graduates completed the fortifications at Fort Erie, built Fort Meigs, planned the harbor defenses of Norfolk and New York, and directed the fortifications at Plattsburg. If larger numbers of infantrymen had been as well trained as the artillerymen and engineers, the course of the war might have been entirely different.

Sea power played a fundamental role in the war. In the west both opponents were handicapped in overland communication, but the British were far more dependent on the Great Lakes for the movement of troops and supplies for the defense of Upper Canada. In the east, Lake Champlain was strategically important as an invasion corridor to the populous areas of both countries. Just as Perry's victory on Lake Erie decided the outcome of the war in the far west, Macdonough's success on Lake Champlain decided the fate of the British invasion in 1814 and helped influence the peace negotiations.

The militia performed as well as the Regular Army. The defeats and humiliations of the Regular forces during the first years of the war matched those of the militia, just as in a later period the Kentucky volunteers at the Thames and the Maryland militia before Baltimore proved that the state citizen soldier could perform well. The keys to the militiaman's performance, of course, were training and leadership, the two areas over which the national government had little control. The militia, occasionally competent, was never dependable, and in the nationalistic period that followed the war when the exploits of the Regulars were justly celebrated, an ardent young Secretary of War, John Calhoun, would be able to convince Congress and the nation that the first line of defense should be a standing army.

CHAPTER 7

The Thirty Years' Peace

When an express rider galloped into Washington on the night of February 13, 1815, with the news that the War of 1812 was over, ended by the treaty signed at Ghent on Christmas Eve 1814, there began the period in American military history sometimes called "The Thirty Years' Peace." Though border warfare with the Indians flared up from time to time, no foreign enemy during these thirty years seriously menaced the peace of the United States.

Toward a Professional Army

Yet in 1815 a long period of freedom from foreign aggression could hardly have been foreseen. After Wellington's victory at Waterloo in June, there was a general expectation in Europe that America would have another war with England. This was reported to Secretary of State James Monroe by Brig. Gen. Winfield Scott, who was in Paris in the summer of 1815 observing the magnificent victory parades of Britain and its allies, collecting every current book, in French and in English, on army management and training, and studying the tactics of the Napoleonic Wars.

The Napoleonic Wars had revived the old tactical issue of column versus line. Linear tactics, well adapted to the highly trained professional armies of the eighteenth century, which aimed to win battles by maneuver, were unsuited to the huge conscript armies under Napoleon. He therefore employed the massed column as the formation for attack, using skirmishers to provide flexibility. In addition, by giving his artillery an unprecedented degree of mobility he was able to mass his firepower at critical points on the battlefield. Yet the issue of massed column versus line had not really been settled, for Napoleon had after all lost the war and the British ascribed their victories to their "thin red lines."

Those who sought to return to the "good old days" while at the same time retaining the best features of Napoleonic warfare found support in the writings of Maj. Gen. Antoine Henri Jomini, who analyzed the Napoleonic Wars in terms of basic principles and of classic, traditional warfare. His first work, *Traité des Grandes Operations Militaires,* published in 1804–05, was early brought to the United States; his greatest work, *Précis de l'Art de la Guerre,* published in 1838, had a profound effect on military thought in America. The influence of Jomini's great contemporary, Maj. Gen. Karl von Clausewitz, was not felt in the United States until long after; the latter's *Vom Krieg,* published posthumously in 1831, was not translated into English until 1873.

The Americans of 1815 were less receptive to the concept of "total war" than were the Americans of the Revolutionary period. In the War of 1812 there had been no surge of revolutionary ardor. Only a small portion of the nation had been directly involved. Neither side had attempted to destroy the other's capacity for continuing the war.

The glory of the victories on the Niagara frontier in 1814 had gone not to the citizen soldier but to the professional. The citizen soldier properly led, as at the Battle of New Orleans, had on occasion done well; but after the war many military realists questioned the ability of the Army to employ him effectively. There were several reasons. It was extremely hard to obtain from state governments accurate figures on how many militiamen were available. Moreover, the states jealously kept control of arming, disciplining, and training their militia. Though training was crucial, the War Department was limited to making recommendations and supplying training manuals. The Army could not enforce the type of rigorous training that had enabled General Scott to convert Regular soldiers—some of them as raw as militiamen—into the professionals who had excited the admiration even of the British at Chippewa and Lundy's Lane.

As soon as President Madison proclaimed the peace in February 1815, the Congress, forced to meet at Blodgett's Hotel because the Capitol lay in blackened ruins, acted promptly to create a small but efficient professional army that was thought adequate—with the addition of the militia—to guard against a repetition of the disasters of the War of 1812. Congress voted a peacetime army of 10,000 men (in addition to the Corps of Engineers), about a third of the actual wartime strength, a figure in marked contrast to the 3,220-man Regular peacetime establishment under President Jefferson. Organization and leadership were improved. The 9 wartime military districts, headed generally by superannuated holdovers from the Revolution, were converted into 2 divisions, a northern with 4 territorial departments and a southern with 5, commanded by officers who had made their reputations in the War of 1812, Maj. Gen. Jacob Brown, Division of the North, and Maj. Gen. Andrew Jackson, Division of the South.

By midsummer 1815, for the first time in nearly a year, President Madison had a full-time Secretary of War. After the forced resignation of Secretary of War John Armstrong at the end of August 1814, mainly as a result of the burning of Washington, Secretary of State James Monroe served as Secretary of War until March 1815 when illness induced him to turn over the office to Secretary of the Treasury Alexander J. Dallas as an additional duty. In the spring of 1815 President Madison appointed William H. Crawford, Minister to France, Secretary of War. By August 1815 he had returned from Paris and was able to take up his duties.

Crawford had a record of distinguished service in the U.S. Senate. He had declined the appointment as Secretary of War later offered to Armstrong, but had maintained a deep interest in the War Department, especially in the General Staff created by Congress in the spring of 1813. Because its purpose was mainly to conduct the housekeeping functions of the Army, it was not a general staff as the term was used a hundred years later, but resembled rather the modern special staff. Under it had been placed the Quartermaster's, Topographical, Adjutant General's, Inspector General's, Ordnance, Hospital, Purchasing, and Pay Departments; the Judge Advocates; the Chaplains; the Military Academy; and the commanding generals of the nine military districts and their logistical staffs. Furthermore, by stationing in Washington at the War Department certain officers of the General Staff—the Adjutant and Inspector General (a dual function performed by one officer) with two assistants, the Commissary General of Ordnance with three assistants, the Paymaster of the Army, and the Assistant Topographical Engineer—Congress had provided a management staff for the Secretary of War, who hitherto had only a few clerks to assist him.

Watching events from Paris in the fall of 1813, Crawford begged Albert Gallatin "For God's sake" to "endeavor to rid the army of old women and blockheads, at least on the general staff." The reorganization of the Army in the spring of 1815 weeded out most of the incompetents. When Crawford took office he recommended to Congress the retention of the General Staff because, as he stated in his recommendation, the history of the early campaigns in the late war had convinced him of "the necessity of giving to the military establishment, in time of peace, the organization which it must have to render it efficient in a state of war."

The only major change he recommended was the addition of the Quartermaster General to the management staff in Washington. He also recommended an increase in the Corps of Engineers. Congress put Crawford's proposals into effect by the act of April 24, 1816, and a few days later authorized the President to employ a "skilful assistant" in the Corps of Engineers, thus securing the services of a brilliant military engineer, General Simon Bernard, who had served under Napoleon. Congress also voted $838,000 for a major program of coast fortification, an effort intended to prevent a repetition of the humiliations suffered in the War of 1812.

At the same time, $115,800 was appropriated for new buildings at the U.S. Military Academy at West Point and $22,171 for the Academy's books, maps, and instruments. Under Crawford's sponsorship, facilities and staff of the Academy were expanded, the curriculum was broadened, regulations for admission were tightened, and provision was made for a Board of Visitors. In September 1816 the cadets first received gray uniforms, honoring (according to tradition) the Regulars of Chippewa and Lundy's Lane, who wore rough gray kersey because they lacked jackets of regulation blue.

Having fostered a peacetime professional army, Crawford might have used his considerable influence with Congress to strengthen it if he had been left in office longer, as he wished, but in the fall of 1816 President Madison asked him to resign and become Secretary of the Treasury in order to bring Henry Clay into the cabinet as Secretary of War. Clay and several others declined the appointment. For more than a year George Graham, the War Department's chief clerk, was Acting Secretary of War. During that period, as the threat from Europe lessened, Congress began to lose interest in the peacetime army. The actual strength had fallen to about 8,200 men at the time John C. Calhoun took the oath as Secretary of War on December 8, 1817. The new Secretary was faced with proposals to cut the Army's authorized strength, abolish the General Staff, and discontinue the Military Academy. But before Calhoun could devote his talents to staving off such proposals, he was faced with an outbreak of Indian warfare on the border between Georgia and the Spanish province of Florida.

The War Hatchet Raised in Florida

The Indians threatening the Georgia frontier were the Lower Creeks, a faction of the Creek Nation which had fled to Florida after being defeated in 1814. Called the "Red Sticks" from their red war clubs, they settled in the swamps and palmetto forests along with Seminole Indians and bands of fugitive Negro slaves and were unrestrained by weak Spanish officials, shut up in their enclaves at St. Augustine on the east coast, St. Marks in central northern Florida, and Pensacola on the west.

The Lower Creeks and Seminoles had been incited to attack American settlers in Georgia by two British adventurers from the Bahamas. One was Lt. Col. Edward Nicholls, who had employed the Indians in his abortive expedition against Mobile in the summer of 1814 and had left them well armed when he sailed away to England in 1815. Another was a trader, Alexander Arbuthnot. Both preached to the Lower Creeks the same false doctrine that the southern part of Georgia, which had been surrendered by the Creeks in the treaty of 1814, had been returned to them by the Treaty of Ghent, and that therefore Americans were settling on lands that belonged to the Indians.

By the fall of 1817 the U.S. Army was attempting to protect the settlers by reinforcing Fort Scott, a log fort built at the southwestern tip of Georgia where the Chattahoochee and Flint Rivers combine to form the Apalachicola, which, flowing through Florida to the Gulf, provided a supply route from Mobile or New Orleans to the fort. At the end of November 1817 an Army keelboat ascending the Apalachicola in advance of supply transports was attacked from the bank by a party of Indians who killed or captured thirty-four of the forty persons aboard—soldiers and wives of soldiers.

The news of the attack, reaching Washington on December 26, 1817, brought on the conflict known as the First Seminole War. Calhoun ordered Maj. Gen. Andrew Jackson to proceed immediately from Nashville to Fort Scott and take command, authorizing him, in case he thought the force on the scene insufficient—800 Regulars and about 1,000 Georgia militia—to request additional militia. Jackson, who had already reported to the War Department that he was expecting trouble in Florida, "The war hatchet having been raised," acted promptly. Calculating that the 3-month Georgia militia might have gone home before he could arrive at Fort Scott, he sent out a call for a thousand 6-month volunteers from West Tennessee. Dispatching to Fort Hawkins, in central Georgia, an officer with $2,000 to buy provisions and ordering further stores to come forward by ship from New Orleans, Jackson, escorted by two mounted companies, set off in advance of the troops.

Riding into Fort Hawkins on the evening of February 9, he was enraged to discover that the contractor who had agreed to supply him with rations had failed to do so. For more than a thousand men, he reported to Calhoun, there was not "a barrel of flour or a bushel of corn." Procuring locally some pigs, corn, and peanuts, he kept going, arriving at Fort Scott on March 9. There he learned that ships loaded with provisions from Mobile had come into the mouth of the Apalachicola. To Jackson it was all-important to protect these boats from Indians who might attack them from the riverbank. He set off next morning with his Georgia militiamen and about 400 Regulars from Fort

Scott on a protective march down the east bank of the Apalachicola. Six days later he was at the river mouth. There he halted his force and ordered Lt. James Gadsden of the Corps of Engineers to build a fort, named Fort Gadsden, for storing the supplies he was expecting from New Orleans.

His supply flotilla, delayed by a gale, did not arrive until March 25. The following day he began his campaign. His objective was a large Indian settlement on the Suwannee River, some 150 miles to the east, where a force of several thousand Indians and Negroes under a Seminole chief, Billy Bowlegs, was said to be preparing for battle. But because Jackson needed a supply base nearer than Fort Gadsden, he decided to take the Spanish fort of St. Marks on the way and arranged for his supplies to be brought by ship to the bay of St. Marks.

Stopping at the Ochlokonee River to make canoes for the crossing and farther along to clean out some Indian villages, on April 7 Jackson took St. Marks, in the process capturing Arbuthnot, whom he imprisoned. In the meantime a brigade of friendly Upper Creek Indians had ridden up, also the first detachment of the Tennessee volunteers. Because of the failure in supply, the main body of Tennesseeans did not catch up with Jackson until April 11, when he was well on the swampy trail to Bowlegs' Town.

The campaign was something of an anticlimax. From Bowlegs' Town the Indians and Negroes had fled, having been warned by Arbuthnot. The only gains were corn and cattle to feed the troops and the capture of a third adventurer from the Bahamas, Robert C. Ambrister, who had been arming and drilling Bowlegs' men. Ambrister was taken back to St. Marks and along with Arbuthnot was tried by a military court and executed. Dismissing the Georgia militia and the Indian brigade, Jackson proceeded west with his Regulars and Tennesseeans. At Fort Gadsden early in May he learned that Indians were assembling in Pensacola. He seized Pensacola, ran up the American flag, and left a garrison there as well as at St. Marks when he returned to Nashville late in May.

Jackson's highhanded actions in the First Seminole War—his invasion of Spanish territory, capture of Spanish forts, and execution of British subjects— might have had serious diplomatic repercussions if Spain or Great Britain had chosen to make an issue of them; but neither nation did. Negotiations with Spain for the purchase of Florida were already under way, and shortly after the return of the forts to Spain, Florida was ceded to the United States in February 1819 by the Adams-Onís Treaty.

For the Army, the most significant aspect of the war had been the breakdown in supply. From the time Jackson rode out of Nashville in late January 1818 until his first encounter with the Indians early in April, he had had to devote all his energies to feeding his troops. The reason had been the failure of civilian contractors. The folly of depending on civilians for so essential an item as rations had been demonstrated by the War of 1812, to Calhoun as well as to the Army. Jackson's experience in the First Seminole War underlined it. At Calhoun's suggestion the Congress in April 1818 required contractors to deliver rations in bulk at depots and provided a better system of transportation and stricter control by the Army. For the first time since the Revolutionary War, the Army had a Subsistence Department, headed by a Commissary General of Subsistence.

John C. Calhoun and the War Department

Calhoun was convinced that the American frontier ought to be protected by Regulars rather than by militia. Calling the militia into active service, he wrote Brig. Gen. Edmund P. Gaines, was "harassing to them and exhausting to the treasury. Protection is the first object, and the second is protection by the regular force." But providing a Regular force capable of protecting the frontiers north, south, and west, as well as the seacoast, was another matter. In 1820 the Congress called upon the Secretary of War to report upon a plan for the reduction of the Army to about 6,000 men. Calhoun suggested that the reduction, if it had to come, could be effected by cutting the enlisted personnel of each company to half strength. In time of war the Army could be quickly expanded to a force of approximately 19,000 officers and men. This was the start of the "expansible army" concept. Congress rejected Calhoun's plan, however, and reduced not only the company strength—in the case of the infantry companies 26 men were dropped, leaving only 42—but also the number of regiments.

The act of March 2, 1821, provided for 7 regiments of infantry and 4 regiments of artillery instead of the existing 8 regiments of infantry, a rifle regiment, a regiment of light artillery, and a corps of artillery comprising 8 battalions. The Ordnance Department was staffed by artillery officers; no ordnance officers were commissioned until 1832. The Northern and Southern Divisions were abolished and replaced by an Eastern and a Western Department, under the respective commands of Brig. Gen. Winfield Scott and General Gaines. Only one major general was provided. Because General Jackson had resigned from the Army to become Governor of Florida, the commission remained with Maj. Gen. Jacob Brown.

To provide a senior line officer in the chain of command, lack of which had been a serious deficiency in the War of 1812, Calhoun brought Brown to Washington in a position which later became known as Commanding General of the Army. Brown held it until his death in 1828, when he was succeeded by

Maj. Gen. Alexander Macomb. When Macomb died in 1841, Maj. Gen. Winfield Scott was appointed. Made brevet lieutenant general in 1847 (the first three-star general since George Washington), Scott served until his retirement in 1861.

In Calhoun's administration other important innovations in Army management were accomplished. Beginning in mid-1822 recruiting depots were opened in major cities, east and west, to enlist men for the Army at large, not for specific units. Though regimental recruiting continued, the General Recruiting Service in its first three years of operation enlisted about 68 percent more men than did the regiments. General Scott prepared a new manual of infantry tactics for Regulars and militia and, on the basis of his research in Paris in 1815, prepared the Army regulations of 1821, going minutely into every detail of the soldier's life, including the ingredients of his soup. The soldier's diet was further improved by the first commissioned Surgeon General, Joseph Lovell, who was appointed by Calhoun. Also, by requiring daily weather reports from all medical officers, in an attempt to find some correlation between weather and army diseases, Lovell provided basic data for the first study of weather in the United States and the most complete data of the sort in the world.

Under Calhoun, the work of seacoast fortification went steadily forward. By 1826 eighteen harbors and ports from the Penobscot River to the mouth of the Mississippi had been fortified with a total of thirty-one works, consisting in general of sloping earthworks covered with grass and backed by stone or brick walls. By 1843 the harbor defense program had been extended to 35 or 40 coastal areas with 69 fortifications either in place or under construction. By then greater emphasis was being placed on heavy artillery (24- and 32-pounder guns and 8-inch howitzers) to keep pace with increasingly heavy naval armaments.

Calhoun early turned his attention to the Military Academy, where Crawford's attempts at rehabilitation had been impeded by controversy stirred up by the arbitrary actions of the superintendent, Capt. Alden Partridge. After Partridge was removed and Bvt. Maj. Sylvanus Thayer was appointed superintendent in July 1817, the Academy became a vital force in maintaining a corps of professionally trained officers. Thayer had been sent by the War Department to Europe in 1815—one of the first of a succession of Army officers sent abroad in the early nineteenth century—to study, among other things, foreign military schools. With Calhoun's support, he organized the West Point cadets into tactical units, created the office of the commandant of cadets, improved the curriculum, and introduced new methods of instruction. For his achievements during his 16-year superintendency, Thayer became known as the father of the Academy. Military education was further advanced in 1824, when, as a result of

U.S. MILITARY ACADEMY, 1828

a proposal by Calhoun for a "school of practice" for men in service, the Artillery School at Fortress Monroe was established—the first of the Army's specialist schools, though unlike most modern schools it instructed not individuals but an entire unit, which was assigned to it for a year's tour of duty. It was closed in 1835 when all the students were sent to Florida to meet the threat of the Second Seminole War, and it was not reopened until 1858.

The first official and complete artillery system for the three categories of artillery—field, siege-and-garrison, and seacoast—was put into effect by Calhoun in 1818, following recommendations by a board of artillery and ordnance officers he had appointed to study the problem. It was based largely on the system of field carriages developed by the famous French artillerist, General Jean Baptiste de Gribeauval. During the next twenty years, growing doubts about the Gribeauval system led succeeding Boards of Ordnance to recommend a newer French system (based on that of the British) called the stock-trail because the carriage used a single trail, of a solid block of wood, rather than the old twin trail. It was simpler than the previous system and introduced interchangeability in carriages and parts. Approved by Secretary of War Joel R. Poinsett and adopted in 1839, it was substantially the artillery system used in the Mexican War. The same board that recommended it also endorsed the introduction of rockets and rocket units into the U.S. Army. The rocket contemplated was patterned after the famous Congreve used by the British in the War of 1812.

Pioneering in the West

In the three decades after 1815, the Army pushed westward ahead of the settlers, surveying, fortifying, and building roads. (*Map 19*) Stockades and forts built and garrisoned in Iowa, Nebraska, and Kansas became the footholds of settlement in the wild frontier; just outside the walls could be found gristmills, sawmills, and blacksmith shops, all of them erected by the troops. Fort Leavenworth, established in 1827 on the Missouri River, was the base for Army expeditions sent out along the Santa Fe and Oregon Trails. An important Army explorer in the 1830's was Capt. Benjamin L. E. Bonneville of the 7th Infantry who on a four years' leave of absence made valuable observations concerning the Pacific coast.

These early expeditions were made by infantrymen using steamboats, wagons, and oxcarts. The discovery that the Indians on the Great Plains were horsemen led the Army in 1832 to organize its first battalion of mounted rangers, which was expanded the following year into a regiment of dragoons—the first cavalry to appear in the Regular Army since 1815.

A western man became Secretary of War in 1831. He was Lewis Cass, former Governor of Michigan, and he was to be the first long-term Secretary since Calhoun. Like Calhoun, he had hardly assumed office when an Indian war broke out. By 1831 American emigrants pouring westward after the opening of the Erie Canal in 1824 were settling on lands in western Illinois from which the Sac and Fox Indians had been pushed out to the prairies west of the Mississippi River. A band of Sac warriors under Chief Black Hawk, called the "British Band" because they had served with the British during the War of 1812, crossed the Mississippi in the spring of 1831 and began burning settlers' houses. General Gaines, commanding the Western Department, moved in with a large body of Regulars and volunteers, and Black Hawk retired across the river. But the chief returned a year later with 500 warriors and 1,500 women and children with the intention of establishing himself on the east bank of the river.

Cass, who knew the importance of impressing the Indians with a show of force, ordered Col. Henry Atkinson, commanding at Jefferson Barracks, Missouri, to take the field with Regulars of the 6th Infantry and also ordered General Scott to bring about 1,000 infantry and artillery from the east coast. The Governor of Illinois called out a large force of militia, most of them mounted. After an inconclusive brush with the Indians, most of the Illinois volunteers returned home. On August 2, 1832, Atkinson with about 500 Regulars and as many volunteers as he had been able to collect caught up with the Indians in southern Wisconsin at the confluence of the Bad Axe River and the Mississippi

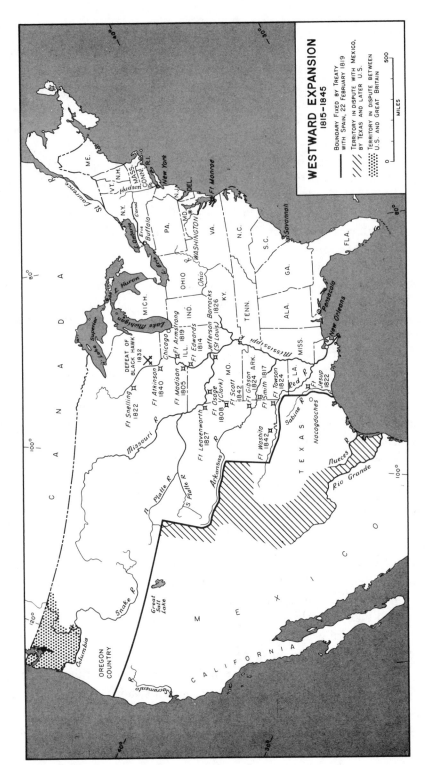

WESTWARD EXPANSION
1815-1845

BOUNDARY FIXED BY TREATY
WITH SPAIN, 22 FEBRUARY 1819

TERRITORY IN DISPUTE WITH MEXICO,
BY TEXAS AND LATER U.S.

TERRITORY IN DISPUTE BETWEEN
U.S. AND GREAT BRITAIN

0   500
MILES

MAP 19

and defeated them decisively, with the help of an Army steamboat carrying a 6-pounder gun firing canister. Five days after the battle, General Scott arrived; but he had with him only a remnant of his forces. Asiatic cholera had broken out aboard his crowded transports on the Great Lakes, killing or disabling one third of the force; others had deserted or could not be brought forward for fear of contagion.

The Second Seminole War

Early in 1832 at the direction of Secretary Cass, the U.S. Indian commissioner in Florida negotiated a treaty with the Seminoles, ratified in 1834, by which the Indians would relinquish their lands in Florida and move to Arkansas. The time limit was eventually set at January 1, 1836. Long before the deadline, the Seminoles, led by a half-breed named Osceola, demonstrated that they would not go peaceably. Outbreaks of violence led the Army to reinforce Fort Brooke on Tampa Bay and Fort King about a hundred miles to the northeast. By December 1835, 9 companies of artillery and 2 of infantry—536 officers and men—were in Florida, under the command of Bvt. Brig. Gen. Duncan L. Clinch.

On the afternoon of December 28, 1835, Osceola with sixty warriors hidden near Fort King killed Wiley Thompson, the agent appointed to superintend the removal, as he was taking a walk outside the fort. The same day another party of warriors attacked a column of 110 Regulars marching from Fort Brooke to Fort King, led by Bvt. Maj. Francis L. Dade and moving at the pace of the oxen drawing their 6-pounder cannon. The Indians massacred all but two men, who escaped severely wounded. The Second Seminole War had begun.

Although the Dade Massacre took place west of a line dividing the Eastern and Western Departments and was therefore in General Gaines' department, President Andrew Jackson and Secretary Cass preferred to give the command to General Scott. Gaines, who was then on an inspection trip at New Orleans, was ordered to the western frontier of Louisiana to take command of all U.S. troops in the region adjoining the boundary with Texas.

General Scott left Washington on January 21, 1836. Stopping in South Carolina and Georgia to arrange for militia and supplies and to set up a depot in Savannah, he did not arrive at his headquarters in Florida near St. Augustine until February 22. Because of logistical troubles and the difficulty of moving troops over primitive, unexplored terrain to Tampa Bay, where he had planned a three-pronged offensive to bottle up the Seminoles in a swamp nearby, it was April 5 before he could begin his campaign at Tampa. By that time, the Seminoles had melted away into the Everglades. Since hot weather had set in, the militiamen, whose three months' term of service had expired, were ready to go home. As a South Carolina militia officer summed up the campaign, "Two months were consumed in preparations and effecting nothing, and the third in marching to Tampa and back again."

Though Scott's experiences in the Second Seminole War resembled in some respects those of Jackson in the First Seminole War eighteen years before, there were two important differences. First, the logistical failure was a failure in transportation, not in supply; the depots had been adequately stocked by the Commissary General of Subsistence, but wagons, roads, and Army maps were lacking. Second, General Scott had to contend with the intrusion of a subordinate commander, General Gaines, who, disregarding orders, brought a large force of Louisiana militiamen from New Orleans by ship to Tampa Bay in February. Supplying this force with rations intended for Scott's troops, Gaines fought an inconclusive battle with the Indians, which he reported as a victory—thus further impeding supply—and returned to New Orleans in March.

During May, General Scott at his headquarters near St. Augustine antagonized the Florida settlers by accusing them of cowardice and also the volunteers by officially requesting Washington that he be sent 3,000 "good troops (not volunteers)." Floridians burned him in effigy and cheered when he was transferred to Georgia at the end of May to put down an uprising of the Creek Nation, which was threatening to spill over from eastern Alabama into Georgia and Florida. There the general got into trouble with Bvt. Maj. Gen. Thomas S. Jesup, in command of operations in Alabama, who won a battle with the Indians before Scott could put his own elaborate plans into effect. In a letter to one of the President's advisers, Jesup charged Scott with unnecessary delay—"the Florida scenes enacted all over again."

The upshot of the controversy with Jesup was Scott's recall to Washington to face a court of inquiry. The court absolved him of all blame for the Florida fiasco, but he was not returned to the Seminole War. Instead, he was given diplomatic missions, for which he had demonstrated his ability during the South Carolina Nullification Crisis in 1833, when he managed to strengthen the federal forts around Charleston without provoking hostilities. He was successful in resolving several conflicts that broke out between American and Canadian settlers on the northern frontier and in persuading 15,000 Cherokee Indians in Georgia to move west peaceably.

The war in Florida continued for six years. General Jesup, commanding from late 1836 to May 1838, was not able either to persuade the Indians to leave Florida or to drive them out. His successor, Bvt. Brig. Gen. Zachary Taylor, adopted a policy of dividing the disaffected region into small districts and searching out the Indians with a pack of bloodhounds provided at one time by the state of Florida—a brief and unsuccessful experiment that aroused a furor in the United States. Taylor's search-and-destroy methods might have produced results, given time, but the War Department insisted on another attempt at negotiation and suspended hostilities. The raids were resumed. Taylor asked to be relieved and was followed by Bvt. Brig. Gen. Walker K. Armistead, who again tried negotiation and failed. In May 1841 Armistead was succeeded by Col. William J. Worth, who brought about a radical change. Hitherto the campaign in Florida had been suspended during the summer season when fever and dysentery were prevalent. Worth campaigned throughout the summer of 1841, preventing the Indians from raising and harvesting crops. By waging a ruthless war of extermination and by destroying food supplies and dwellings, he routed the Indians out of their swamps and hammocks and permitted the war to be officially ended in August 1842.

The Second Seminole War had been guerrilla warfare, of a kind the Army was not equipped to fight. The effort depleted the Regular Army so seriously that in July 1838 its authorized strength had to be increased from around 7,000 to about 12,500 men. A total of about 10,000 Regulars and perhaps 30,000 short-term volunteers had been engaged. Almost 1,600 men had lost their lives in battle or from disease and about $30 million had been spent in order that 3,800 half-starved Indians might be shipped west.

With some of this money and effort, the Army had bought experience, especially in transportation—the most pressing problem of the war. For example, the Quartermaster General had developed a light ponton wagon, lined with India rubber cloth, for crossing rivers. At General Jesup's request, the Secretary of War revived the corps of artificers that had been authorized for the War of 1812. It provided mechanics and laborers to keep wagons and boats in repair. The war taught a great deal about water transportation. Before it was over the Army was turning away from dependence on steamboats hired from private contractors to Army-owned steamboats, more reliable and cheaper in the end. The problem of navigating shallow rivers was solved by building flat-bottomed bateaux. These lessons in transportation were to be put to good use in the Mexican War.

Westward Expansion and the Texas Issue

Army pioneering expeditions from Fort Leavenworth in the 1820's and 1830's had been undertaken mainly for making treaties with the Great Plains Indians and for protecting trading caravans. Beginning in the early 1840's the prime consideration was to help the American settlers pouring westward. In

1842 2d Lt. John C. Fremont of the Corps of Topographical Engineers led an expedition to explore and map the Platte River country for the benefit of emigrants moving over the Oregon Trail; on a second expedition in 1843 he reached Sacramento, Upper California.

In 1842 Fremont reported seeing emigrant parties totaling 64 men and 16 or 17 families. Three years later, when Col. Stephen W. Kearny took five companies of the 1st Dragoons over the Oregon Trail on a march undertaken primarily for the protection of the emigrants, he saw on the trail 850 men and about 475 families in long caravans followed by thousands of cattle.

Some of the pioneers on the Oregon Trail settled in Upper California; but the main stream of American emigration into Mexican territory went to Texas. Between 1825 and 1830 approximately 15,000 emigrants with several thousand Negro slaves poured into Texas. In March of 1836 they proclaimed their independence from Mexico. The Mexicans, under General Antonio Lopez de Santa Ana, moved against the rebels and destroyed the garrison in the Alamo after a siege that lasted thirteen days. American volunteers rushed across the Sabine River to help the Texans. General Gaines, stationed on the western frontier of Louisiana to defend Louisiana and maintain American neutrality, was authorized to cross the Sabine River, generally regarded as the boundary line, but not to go beyond Nacogdoches, fifty miles west of the Sabine, which marked the extreme limit of American claims. He was at the Sabine when General Sam Houston won his victory over Santa Ana at San Jacinto on April 21, 1836. Fired by wild rumors of Mexican reinforcements, Gaines crossed the Sabine with a force of Regulars and in July occupied Nacogdoches, remaining there until recalled in December 1836.

For nearly ten years Texas existed as an independent nation, desiring annexation to the United States but frustrated because annexation had become tied up with the slavery controversy. Northerners saw annexation as an attempt by the South to extend slavery. During this decade Mexico, refusing to recognize Texan independence, made sporadic attempts to recover its lost province. Raids marked by extreme ruthlessness and ferocity by both Texans and Mexicans kept the country along the border in constant turmoil.

CHAPTER 8

The Mexican War and After

Receiving by the new telegraph the news that James K. Polk had been elected to the Presidency in November 1844, President John Tyler interpreted the verdict as a mandate from the people for the annexation of Texas, since Polk had come out strongly in favor of annexation. On March 1, 1845, Congress jointly resolved to admit Texas into the Union and the Mexican Government promptly broke off diplomatic relations. President Polk continued to hope that he could settle by negotiation Mexico's claim to Texas and acquire Upper California by purchase as well. In mid-June, nevertheless, anticipating the Fourth of July acceptance by Texas of annexation, he ordered Bvt. Brig. Gen. Zachary Taylor to move his forces from Fort Jesup on the Louisiana border to a point "on or near" the Rio Grande to repel any invasion from Mexico.

The Period of Watchful Waiting

General Taylor selected a wide sandy plain at the mouth of the Nueces River near the hamlet of Corpus Christi and beginning July 23 sent most of his 1,500-man force by steamboat from New Orleans. Only his dragoons moved overland, via San Antonio. By mid-October, as shipments of Regulars continued to come in from all over the country, his forces had swollen to nearly 4,000, including some volunteers from New Orleans. A company of Texas Rangers served as the eyes and ears of the Army. For the next six months drilling, horse-breaking, and parades, interspersed with boredom and dissipation, went on at the big camp on the Nueces. Then in February Taylor received orders from Washington to advance to the Rio Grande. Negotiations with the Mexican Government had broken down.

The march of more than a hundred miles down the coast to the Rio Grande was led by Bvt. Maj. Samuel Ringgold's battery of "flying artillery," organized in late 1838 on orders from Secretary of War Joel R. Poinsett. It was the last word in mobility, for the cannoneers rode on horseback rather than on limbers and caissons. The rear was brought up by Taylor's supply train of three hundred wagons drawn by oxen. On March 23 the columns came to a road that forked left to Point Isabel, ten miles away on the coast, where Taylor's supply ships were waiting, and led on the right to his destination on the Rio Grande, some eighteen miles southwest, opposite the Mexican town of Matamoros. Sending the bulk of his army ahead, Taylor went to Point Isabel to set up his supply base, fill his wagons, and bring forward four 18-pounder siege guns from his ships.

At the boiling brown waters of the Rio Grande opposite Matamoros he built a strong fort, which he called Fort Texas, mounting his siege guns. At the same time he sent pacific messages to the Mexican commander on the opposite bank. These were countered by threats and warnings, and on April 25, the day after the arrival at Matamoros of General Mariano Arista with two or three thousand additional troops, by open hostilities. The Mexicans crossed the river in some force and attacked a reconnoitering detachment of sixty dragoons under Capt. Seth B. Thornton. They killed eleven men and captured Thornton and the rest, many of whom were wounded.

Taylor reported to President Polk that hostilities had commenced and called on Texas and Louisiana for about 5,000 militiamen. His immediate concern was that his supply base might be captured. Leaving an infantry regiment and a small detachment of artillery at Fort Texas under Maj. Jacob Brown, he set off May 1 with the bulk of his forces for Point Isabel, where he stayed nearly a week strengthening his fortifications. After loading two hundred supply wagons and acquiring two more ox-drawn 18-pounders, he began the return march to Fort Texas with his army of about 2,300 men on the afternoon of May 7. About noon next day near a clump of tall trees at a spot called Palo Alto, he saw across the open prairie a long dark line with bayonets and lances glistening in the sun. It was the Mexican Army.

The Battles of Palo Alto and Resaca de la Palma

General Arista's forces barring the road to Fort Texas stretched out on a front a mile long and were about 4,000 strong. Taylor, who had placed part of his force in the rear to guard the supply wagons, was outnumbered at least two to one; and in terrain that favored cavalry, Arista's cavalry overwhelmingly outnumbered Taylor's dragoons. But the American artillery was superior. Also, among Taylor's junior officers were a number of West Point graduates who were to make their reputations in the Civil War, notably 2d Lt. George G. Meade and 2d Lt. Ulysses S. Grant.

On the advice of the young West Pointers on his staff, Taylor emplaced his two 18-pounder iron siege guns in the center of his line and blasted the advancing Mexicans with canister. His field artillery—bronze 6-pounder guns firing solid shot and 12-pounder howitzers firing shell—in quick-moving attacks threw back Arista's flanks. The Mexicans were using old-fashioned bronze 4-pounders and 8-pounders that fired solid shot and had such short range that their fire did little damage. During the battle Lieutenant Grant saw their cannon balls striking the ground before they reached the American troops and ricocheting so slowly that the men could dodge them.

During the afternoon a gun wad set the dry grass afire, causing the battle to be suspended for nearly an hour. After it was resumed the Mexicans fell back rapidly. By nightfall when both armies went into bivouac, Mexican casualties, caused mostly by cannon fire, numbered about 320 killed and 380 wounded. Taylor lost only 9 men killed and 47 wounded. One of the mortally wounded was his brilliant artilleryman, Major Ringgold.

At daybreak the Americans saw the Mexicans in full retreat. Taylor decided to pursue but did not begin his advance until afternoon, spending the morning erecting defenses around his wagon train, which he intended to leave behind. About two o'clock he reached Resaca de la Palma, a dry river bed about five miles from Palo Alto. There his scouts reported that the Mexicans had taken advantage of his delay to entrench themselves strongly a short distance down the road in a similar shallow ravine known as Resaca de la Guerra, whose banks formed a natural breastwork. Narrow ponds and thick chaparral protected their flanks.

Taylor sent forward his flying artillery, now commanded by Lt. Randolph Ridgely. Stopped by a Mexican battery, Ridgely sent back for help and Taylor ordered in a detachment of dragoons under Capt. Charles A. May. The dragoons overran the Mexican guns but on their return were caught in infantry crossfire from the thickets and could not prevent the enemy from recapturing the guns. The pieces were later captured by American infantrymen. Dense chaparral prevented Taylor from making full use of his artillery. The battle of Resaca de la Palma was an infantry battle of small parties and hand-to-hand fighting.

The Mexicans, still demoralized by their defeat at Palo Alto and lacking effective leadership, gave up the fight and fled toward Matamoros. Their losses at Resaca de la Palma were later officially reported as 547 and were probably much greater. The Americans lost 33 killed and 89 wounded. In the meantime Fort Texas had been attacked by the Mexicans May 3 and had withstood a two-day siege with the loss of only two men, one of them its commander for whom the fort was later renamed Fort Brown.

The panic-stricken Mexicans fleeing to Matamoros crossed the Rio Grande as best they could, some by boats, some by swimming. Many drowned, others were killed by the guns of Fort Texas. If Taylor's Regulars, flushed with victory and yelling as they pursued the enemy, had been able to catch up with Arista, they could probably have taken his demoralized army, complete with guns and ammunition. But Taylor had failed to make any provision for crossing the Rio Grande. He blamed the War Department's failure to provide him with ponton equipment (developed during the Second Seminole War), which he had requested while he was still at Corpus Christi. Since that time, however, he had done nothing to acquire bridge materials or boats, although he had been urged to do so by the West Pointers. Lieutenant Meade reported that "the old gentleman would never listen or give it a moment's attention." Not until May 18, after Taylor had brought up some boats from Point Isabel, was he able to cross into Matamoros. By that time Arista's army had melted away into the interior to rest, recoup, and fight another day.

War Is Declared

On the evening of May 9, the day of the battle of Resaca de la Palma, President Polk received a message from the War Department telling of the attack on Captain Thornton's detachment on April 25. Polk, who was already convinced by the breakdown in negotiations with Mexico that war was justified, immediately drafted a message declaring that a state of war existed between the United States and Mexico. Congress passed the declaration and Polk signed it on May 13. Congress then appropriated $10 million and substantially increased the strength of the Army. After the Second Seminole War the authorized strength had been cut from 12,500 to 8,500. This had been done by reducing the rank and file strength of the regiments, instead of eliminating units, thus firmly establishing the principle of an expansible Army. To meet the needs of the Mexican War the Congress raised the authorized enlisted strength of a company from 64 to 100 men, bringing the rank and file up to 15,540, and added a regiment of mounted riflemen and a company of sappers, miners, and pontoniers. Also, the President was authorized to call for 50,000 volunteers for a term of one year or the duration of the war.

The President went into the war with one object clearly in view—to seize all of Mexico north of the Rio Grande and the Gila River and westward to the Pacific. After discussions with General Scott, the outlines of a three-pronged thrust emerged. (*Map 20*) General Taylor was to advance westward from Matamoros to the city of Monterrey, the key to further progress in northern Mexico. A second expedition under Brig. Gen. John E. Wool was to move from San Antonio to the remote village of Chihuahua in the west, an expedition later directed southward to Saltillo near Monterrey. A third prong under Col. Stephen W. Kearny was to start at Fort Leavenworth

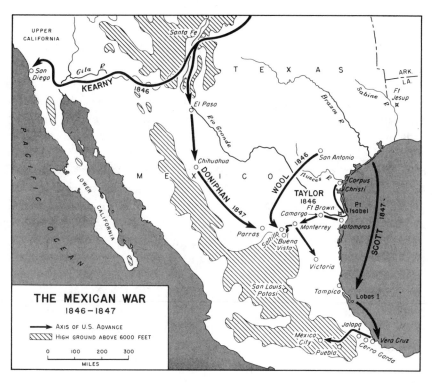

MAP 20

for Santa Fe, ultimately to continue to San Diego on the coast of California; part of Kearny's forces under Col. Alexander W. Doniphan was later sent south through Chihuahua to Parras.

Polk was counting on "a brisk and a short war"; not until July did he and his Secretary of War, William L. Marcy, even begin to consider the possibility of an advance on Mexico City by landing a force on the Gulf near Vera Cruz. General Scott was not so optimistic. He was more aware of the problems of supply, transportation, communications, and mobilization involved in operations against Mexico, a country with a population of seven million and an army of about thirty thousand, many with experience gained by some twenty years of intermittent revolution. Scott's preparations seemed too slow to Polk. Ostensibly for that reason, but also because success in the field might make Scott a too powerful contender for the Presidency, Polk decided not to give him command of the forces in the field. When news came of the victories at Palo Alto and Resaca de la Palma, Polk promoted Zachary Taylor to the brevet rank of major general and gave him command of the army in Mexico.

The Monterrey Campaign

Taylor's plan was to move on Monterrey with about six thousand men via Camargo, a small town on the San Juan River, a tributary of the Rio Grande about 130 miles upriver. From Camargo, where he intended to set up a supply base, a road led southwest about 125 miles to Monterrey in the foothills of the Sierra Madres. His troops were to march overland to Camargo, his supplies to come by steamboat up the Rio Grande. But he could not move immediately because he lacked transportation—partly because of his failure to requisition in time and partly because of the effort required to build more wagons in the United States and to collect shallow-draft steamboats at river towns on the Mississippi and the Ohio and send them across the Gulf of Mexico. Ten steamboats were in operation at the end of July, but wagons did not begin arriving until November, after the campaign was over. To supplement his wagon train, reduced to 175, Taylor had to rely on 1,500 Mexican pack mules and a few native oxcarts.

In manpower Taylor had an embarrassment of riches. May saw the arrival of the first of the three-months militia he had requested on April 26 from the governors of Texas and Louisiana, and with them thousands of additional six-months volunteers from neighboring states recruited by Bvt. Maj. Gen. Edmund P. Gaines, commander of the Department of the West, on his own initiative—a repetition of his impulsive actions in the Second Seminole War. More than 8,000 of these short-term volunteers were sent before Gaines was censured by a court-martial for his unauthorized and illegal recruiting practices and transferred to New York to command the Department of the East. Very few of his recruits had agreed to serve for twelve months. All the rest were sent home without performing any service; in the meantime they had to be fed, sheltered, and transported. In June the volunteers authorized by Congress began pouring into Point Isabel and were quartered in a string of camps along the Rio Grande as far as Matamoros.

By August Taylor had a force of about 15,000 men at Camargo, an unhealthy town deep in mud from a recent freshet and sweltering under heat that rose as high as 112 degrees. Many of the volunteers became ill and more than half were left behind when Taylor advanced toward Monterrey at the end of August with 3,080 Regulars and 3,150 volunteers. The Regulars (with a few volunteers) were organized into the First and Second Divisions, the volunteers mainly into a Field Division, though two regiments of mounted Texans were thought of as the Texas Division. More than a fourth of the troops were mounted, among them the First Mississippi Rifle

Regiment under a West Point graduate recently elected to Congress, Col. Jefferson Davis. The mounted riflemen had percussion rifles; the infantrymen were armed with flintlock muskets. Taylor placed great reliance on the bayonet. He had a low opinion of artillery, and though warned that field pieces were not effective against the stone houses of Mexican towns, he had in addition to his four field batteries only two 24-pounder howitzers and one 10-inch mortar, the latter his only real siege piece.

By September 19 Taylor's army reached Monterrey, a city of stone in a pass of the Sierra Madres leading to the city of Saltillo. It was strongly fortified and defended by more than 7,000 Mexicans with better artillery than the Mexicans had had at Palo Alto—new British 9- and 12-pounder guns. Taylor, encamped on the outskirts of Monterrey, sent out reconnoitering parties accompanied by engineers and on September 20 began his attack. On the north the city was protected by a formidable citadel, on the south by a river; and it was ringed with forts. Taylor sent one of his Regular divisions, with four hundred Texas Rangers in advance, around to the west to cut off the road to Saltillo, and after a miserable night of drenching rain it accomplished its mission the next day, September 21, though at a cost of 394 dead or wounded, a high proportion of them officers. Taylor placed his heavy howitzers and one mortar in position to fire on the citadel and sent the remainder of his forces to close in from the eastern outskirts of the town. By the third day both attacks were driving into the city proper, the men battering down doors of the stone and adobe houses with planks, tossing lighted shells through apertures, and advancing from house to house rather than from street to street—tactics that were to be used a century later by American troops in Italian and German towns.

The climax came when the 10-inch mortar was brought up to lob shells on the great plaza into which the Mexican troops had been driven. On September 24 the Mexican commander offered to surrender on condition that his troops be allowed to withdraw unimpeded and that an eight-week armistice go into effect. Taylor agreed to the proposal. He had lost some 800 men to battle casualties and sickness, besides quantities of arms and ammunition, and he was about 125 miles from his base. Moreover, he believed that magnanimity would advance negotiations for peace which had begun when President Polk allowed General Antonio Lopez de Santa Ana to return to Mexico from exile in Havana to exert his influence in favor of a treaty.

When Polk received the news from Monterrey by courier October 11, he condemned Taylor for allowing the Mexican Army to escape and ordered the armistice terminated. Thereupon, Taylor on November 13 sent a thousand men 68 miles southwestward to occupy Saltillo, an important road center commanding the only road to Mexico City from the north that was practicable for wagons and guns. Saltillo also commanded the road west to Chihuahua and east to Victoria, capital of Tamaulipas, the province that contained Tampico, the second largest Mexican port on the Gulf. The U.S. Navy captured Tampico November 15. On the road to Chihuahua was the town of Parras, where General Wool's expedition of about 2,500 men arrived early in December after a remarkable march from San Antonio. On the way Wool had learned that the Mexican troops holding Chihuahua had abandoned it; accordingly, he joined Taylor's main army. Taylor thus acquired a valuable young engineer who had been scouting with Wool, Capt. Robert E. Lee.

Taylor was planning to establish a strong defensive line, Parras-Saltillo-Monterrey-Victoria, when he learned that most of his troops would have to be released to join General Scott's invasion of Mexico at Vera Cruz, an operation which had been decided upon in Washington in mid-November. Scott arrived in Mexico in late December. He proceeded to Camargo and detached almost all of Taylor's Regulars, about 4,000, and an equal number of volunteers, ordering them to rendezvous at Tampico and at the mouth of the Brazos River in Texas. Taylor, left with fewer than 7,000 men, all volunteers except two squadrons of dragoons and a small force of artillery, was ordered to evacuate Saltillo and go on the defensive at Monterrey.

Enraged, Taylor attributed Scott's motive to politics. Hurrying back to Monterrey from Victoria, he decided to interpret Scott's orders as "advice" rather than as an order. Instead of retiring his forces to Monterrey, he moved 4,650 of his troops (leaving garrisons at Monterrey and Saltillo) to a point about 18 miles south of Saltillo, near the hacienda of Agua Nueva. This move brought him almost 11 miles closer to San Luis Potosi, 200 miles to the south, where General Santa Ana was assembling an army of 20,000. Most of the 200 miles were desert, which Taylor considered impassable by any army; moreover, both he and Scott believed that Santa Ana would make his main effort against Scott's landing at Vera Cruz, the news of which had leaked to the newspapers. On February 8, 1847, Taylor wrote a friend, "I have no fears."

At the time he wrote, Santa Ana was already on the march northward toward Saltillo. Stung by newspaper reports that he had sold out to the Americans, Santa Ana was determined to win a quick victory and he thought he saw his opportunity when his troops brought him a copy of Scott's order depleting Taylor's forces, found on the body of a messenger they had ambushed and killed. Leading his army across barren country through heat, snow, and rain, by February 19 Santa Ana had 15,000 men at a hacienda at the edge of the desert, only 35 miles from Agua Nueva. The hardest battle of the Mexican War was about to begin.

The Battle of Buena Vista

On the morning of February 21 scouts brought the word to General Taylor that a great Mexican army was advancing, preceded by a large body of cavalry swinging east to block the road between Agua Nueva and Saltillo. That afternoon Taylor withdrew his forces up the Saltillo road about 15 miles to a better defensive position near the hacienda Buena Vista, a few miles south of Saltillo. There, about a mile south of the clay-roofed ranch buildings, mountain spurs came down to the road on the east, the longest and highest known as La Angostura; between them was a wide plateau cut by two deep ravines. West of the road was a network of gullies backed by a line of high hills. Leaving General Wool to deploy the the troops, Taylor rode off to Saltillo to look after his defenses there.

By next morning, Washington's Birthday (the password was "Honor to Washington"), the little American army of less than 5,000 troops, most of them green volunteers, was in position to meet a Mexican army more than three times its size. The American main body was east of the road near La Angostura, where artillery had been emplaced, commanding the road. West of the road, the gullies were thought to be sufficient protection.

Santa Ana arrived with his vanguard around eleven o'clock. Disliking the terrain, which by no means favored cavalry, his best arm, he sent a demand for surrender to Taylor, who had returned from Saltillo. Taylor refused. Then Santa Ana planted artillery on the road and the high ground east of it and sent a force of light infantry around the foot of the mountains south of the plateau. About three o'clock a shell from a Mexican howitzer on the road gave the signal for combat; but the rest of the day was consumed mainly in jockeying for position on the mountain spurs, a competition in which the Mexicans came off best, and the placing of American infantry and artillery well forward on the plateau. After a threatening movement on the Mexican left, Taylor sent a Kentucky regiment with two guns of Maj. Braxton Bragg's battery to the high hills west of the road, but no attack occurred there. Toward evening Taylor returned to Saltillo, accompanied by the First Mississippi Rifles and a detachment of dragoons. At nightfall his soldiers, shaken by the size and splendid appearance of the Mexican army, got what sleep they could.

The next day, February 23, the battle opened in earnest at dawn. Santa Ana sent a division up the road toward La Angostura, at the head of the defile, but it was quickly broken up by American artillery and infantrymen, and no further action occurred in that sector. The strongest assault took place on the plateau, well to the east, where Santa Ana launched two divisions, backed by a strong battery at the head of the southernmost ravine. The Americans farthest forward, part of an Indiana regiment supported by three cannons, held off the assault for half an hour; then their commander gave them an order to retreat. They broke and ran and were joined in their flight by adjoining regiments. Some of the men ran all the way back to Buena Vista, where they fired at pursuing Mexican cavalrymen from behind the hacienda walls.

About nine o'clock that morning, when the battle had become almost a rout, General Taylor arrived from Saltillo with his dragoons, Col. Jefferson Davis' Mississippi Rifles, and some men of the Indiana regiment whom he had rallied on the way. They fell upon the Mexican cavalry that had been trying to outflank the Americans north of the plateau. In the meantime Bragg's artillery had come over from the hills west of the road, and the Kentucky regiment also crossed the road to join in the fight. A deafening thunderstorm of rain and hail broke early in the afternoon, but the Americans in the north field continued to force the Mexicans back.

Just when victory for the Americans seemed in sight, Santa Ana threw an entire division of fresh troops, his reserves, against the plateau. Rising from the broad ravine where they had been hidden, the Mexicans of the left column fell upon three regiments—two Illinois and one Kentucky—and forced them back to the road with withering fire, while the right stormed the weak American center. They seemed about to turn the tide of battle when down from the north field galloped two batteries, followed by the Mississippians and Indianans led by Jefferson Davis, wounded, but still in the saddle. They fell upon the Mexicans' right and rear and forced them back into the ravine. The Mexicans' left, pursuing the Illinois and Kentucky regiments up the road, was cut to pieces by the American battery at La Angostura.

That night Santa Ana, having lost 1,500 to 2,000 men killed and wounded, retreated toward San Luis Potosi. The Americans, with 264 men killed, 450 wounded, and 26 missing, had won the battle. A great share of the credit belonged to the artillery; without it, as General Wool said in his report, the army could not have stood "for a single hour." Moving with almost the speed of cavalry, the batteries served as rallying points for the infantry. The fighting spirit of the volunteers, most of them frontiersmen, and the able and courageous leadership of the officers were beyond praise. Perhaps the greatest contribution to the victory had been Zachary Taylor himself. Stationed all day conspicuously

THE MISSISSIPPI RIFLES AT BUENA VISTA

in the center of the battle hunched on his horse "Old Whitey," with one leg hooked over the pommel of his saddle, disregarding two Mexican bullets that ripped through his coat, and occasionally rising in his stirrups to shout encouragement, he was an inspiration to his men, who swore by him. Under such a leader they felt that defeat was impossible.

Taylor knew little of the art of war. He was careless in preparing for battle and neglected intelligence; he often misunderstood the intention of the enemy and underestimated the enemy's strength. But he possessed to a superlative degree physical courage and moral courage, which according to Jomini are the most essential qualities for a general.

Buena Vista ended any further Mexican threat against the lower Rio Grande. On the Pacific coast, Colonel Kearny by December 1846 had reached San Diego after one of the most extraordinary marches in American history, across deserts and rugged mountains, to find that a naval squadron had already seized the California ports. Early in February 1847 a force of Missouri volunteers detached from Kearny's command and led by Col. Alexander W. Doniphan had set out from Santa Fe to pacify the region of the upper Rio Grande. Crossing the river at El Paso, they defeated a large force of Mexicans, mostly militia, at Chihuahua, less than a week after Taylor's victory at Buena Vista. Thus by March 1847, America's hold on Mexico's northern provinces was secure. All that remained was the capture of Mexico City.

The Landing at Vera Cruz

From a rendezvous at Lobos Island almost 50 miles south of Tampico, General Scott's force of 13,660 men, of whom 5,741 were Regulars, set sail on March 2, 1847, for the landing near Vera Cruz—the first major amphibious landing in the history of the U.S. Army. On March 5 the transports were off the coast of their target, where they met a U.S. naval squadron blockading the city. In a small boat Scott, his commanders, and a party of officers including Robert E. Lee, George G. Meade, Joseph E. Johnston, and Pierre G. T. Beauregard ran close inshore to reconnoiter and came near being hit by a shell fired from the island fortress of San Juan de Ulua opposite Vera Cruz, a shell that might have changed the course of the Mexican War and the Civil War as well.

Scott chose for the landing a beach nearly 3 miles south of the city, beyond the range of the Mexican guns. On the evening of March 9, in four hours more than 10,000 men went ashore in landing craft, consisting of 65 heavy surf boats that had been towed to the spot by steamers. The troops proceeded inland over the sand hills with little opposition from the Mexican force of 4,300 behind the city's walls. The landing of artillery, stores, and horses, the last thrown overboard and forced to swim for shore, was slowed by a norther that sprang up on March 12 and blew violently for four days, but by March 22 seven 10-inch mortars had been dragged inland and emplaced about half a mile south of Vera Cruz. That afternoon the bombardment began.

Town and fort replied, and it was soon apparent that the mortars were ineffective. Scott found himself compelled to ask for naval guns from the commander of the naval force, Commodore Matthew C. Perry. The six naval guns—three 32-pounders firing shot and three 8-inch shell guns—soon breached the walls and demoralized the defenders. On March 27, 1847, Vera Cruz capitulated.

Scott's next objective was Jalapa, a city in the highlands about 74 miles from Vera Cruz on the national highway leading to Mexico City. Because on the coast the yellow fever season was approaching, Scott was anxious to move forward to the uplands at once, but not until April 8 was he able to collect enough pack mules and wagons for the advance. The first elements, under Bvt. Maj. Gen. David E. Twiggs, set out with two batteries. One was equipped with 24-pounder guns, 8-inch howitzers, and 10-inch mortars. The other was a new type of battery equipped with mountain howitzers and rockets, officered and manned by the Ordnance Corps. The rocket section, mainly armed with the Congreve, carried for service tests a new rocket, the Hale, which depended for stability not on a stick but on vents in the rear, which also gave it a spin like that of an artillery projectile. The rockets were fired from troughs mounted on portable stands. In addition to his two batteries, General Twiggs had a squadron of dragoons, in all about 2,600 men. He advanced confidently, though warned by Scott that a substantial army commanded by Santa Ana lay somewhere ahead. On April 11, after Twiggs had gone about 30 miles, his scouts brought word that Mexican guns commanded a pass near the hamlet of Cerro Gordo.

The Battle of Cerro Gordo

Near Cerro Gordo the national highway ran through a rocky defile. On the left of the approaching Americans, Santa Ana with about 12,000 men had emplaced batteries on mountain spurs and on the right of the Americans farther down the road his guns were emplaced on a high hill, El Telegrafo. He thus had firm command of the national highway, the only means he thought Scott had of bringing up his artillery.

Fortunately for Twiggs, advancing on the morning of April 12, the Mexican gunners opened fire before he was within range and he was able to pull his forces back. Two days later Scott arrived with reinforcements, bringing his army up to 8,500. A reconnaissance by Capt. Robert E. Lee showed that the rough country to the right of El Telegrafo, which Santa Ana had considered impassable, could be traversed, enabling the Americans to cut in on the Mexican rear. The troops hewed a path through forest and brush, and when they came to ravines, lowered the heavy siege artillery by ropes to the bottom, then hoisted it up the other side. By April 17 they were able to occupy a hill to the right of El Telegrafo, where they sited the rocket battery. Early on the morning of April 18 the battle began.

Though Santa Ana, by then forewarned, had been able to plant guns to protect his flank, he could not withstand the American onslaught. The Mexicans broke and fled into the mountains. By noon Scott's army had won a smashing victory at a cost of only 417 casualties, including 64 dead. Santa Ana's losses were estimated at more than a thousand.

Scott moved next morning to Jalapa. The way seemed open to Mexico City, only 170 miles away. But now he faced a serious loss in manpower. The term of enlistment of seven of his volunteer regiments was about to expire and only a handful agreed to re-enlist. The men had to be sent home at once to minimize the danger of yellow fever when they passed through Vera Cruz. The departure of the volunteers, added to wounds and sickness among the men remaining, reduced the army to 5,820 effectives.

In May Scott pushed forward cautiously to Puebla, then the second largest city in Mexico. Its citizens were hostile to Santa Ana and had lost hope of winning the war. It capitulated without resistance on May 15 to an advance party under General Worth. Scott stayed there until the beginning of August, awaiting reinforcements from Vera Cruz, which by mid-July more than doubled his forces, and awaiting also the outcome of peace negotiations then under way. A State Department emissary, Nicholas P. Trist, had arrived on the scene and made contact with Santa Ana through a British agent in Mexico City. Trist learned that Santa Ana, elected President of Mexico for the second time, would discuss peace terms for $10,000 down and $1,000,000 to be paid when a treaty was ratified. After receiving the down payment through the intermediary, however, Santa Ana made it known that he could not prevail upon the Mexican Congress to repeal a law it had passed after the battle of Cerro Gordo making it high treason for any official to treat with the Americans. It was clear that Scott would have to move closer to the capital of Mexico before Santa Ana would seriously consider peace terms.

Contreras, Churubusco, Chapultepec

For the advance on Mexico City, Scott had about 10,000 men. He had none to spare to protect the road from Vera Cruz to Puebla; therefore his decision to move forward was daring: it meant that he had abandoned his line of communications, as he phrased it, "thrown away the scabbard." On August 7 Scott moved off with the lead division, followed at a day's march by three divisions with a three-mile-long train of white-topped supply wagons bringing up the rear. Meeting no opposition—a sign that Santa Ana had withdrawn to defend Mexico City—Scott by August 10 was at Ayolta, located on a high plateau 14 miles from the city.

The direct road ahead, entering the capital on the east, was barred by strongly fortified positions. Scott therefore decided to take the city from the west by a wide flanking movement to the south, using a narrow muddy road that passed between the southern shores of two lakes and the mountains and skirted a fifteen-mile-wide lava bed, the Pedregal, before it turned north and went over a bridge at Churubusco to the western gates of Mexico City.

The Pedregal had been considered impassable, but Captain Lee found a mule path across its southwestern tip that came out at the village of Contreras.

Scott sent a force under Bvt. Maj. Gen. Gideon J. Pillow to work on the road, supported by Twiggs's division and some light artillery. They came under heavy fire from a Mexican force under General Valencia. Pillow, manhandling his guns to a high position, attacked on August 19, but his light artillery was no match for Valencia's 68-pounder howitzer, nor his men for the reinforcements Santa Ana brought to the scene. American reinforcements made a night march in pouring rain through a gully the engineers had found through the Pedregal and fell upon the Mexicans' rear on the morning of August 20, simultaneously with an attack from the front. In seventeen minutes the battle of Contreras was won, with a loss to Scott of only 60 killed or wounded; the Mexicans lost 700 dead and 800 captured, including 4 generals.

Scott ordered an immediate pursuit, but Santa Ana was able to gather his forces for a stand at Churubusco, where he placed a strong fortification before the town at the bridge and converted a thick-walled stone church and a massive stone convent into fortresses. When the first American troops rode up around noon on August 20 they were met by heavy musket and cannon fire. The Mexicans fought as never before; not until midafternoon could Scott's troops make any progress. At last the fire of the Mexicans slackened, partly because they were running out of ammunition, and the Americans won the day, a day that Santa Ana admitted had cost him one third of his forces. About 4,000 Mexicans had been killed or wounded, not counting the many missing and captured. The battle had also been costly for Scott, who had 155 men killed and 876 wounded.

The victory at Churubusco brought an offer from Santa Ana to reopen negotiations. Scott proposed a short armistice and Santa Ana quickly agreed. For two weeks Trist and representatives of the Mexican Government discussed terms until it became clear that the Mexicans would not accept what Trist had to offer and were merely using the armistice as a breathing spell. On September 6 Scott halted the discussions and prepared to assault Mexico City.

Though refreshed by two weeks of rest, his forces now numbered only about 8,000 men. Santa Ana was reputed to have more than 15,000 and had taken advantage of the respite to strengthen the defenses of the city. And ahead on a high hill above the plain was the Castle of Chapultepec guarding the western approaches.

Scott's first objective, about half a mile west of Chapultepec, was a range of low stone buildings, containing a cannon foundry, known as El Molino del Rey. It was seized on September 8, though at heavy cost from unexpected resistance. At eight o'clock on the morning of September 13, after a barrage from the 24-pounder guns, Scott launched a three-pronged attack over the causeways leading to Chapultepec and up the rugged slopes. Against a hail of Mexican projectiles from above, his determined troops rapidly gained the summit, and though they were delayed at the moat, waiting for scaling ladders to come up, by half past nine o'clock the Americans were overrunning the castle. Scarcely pausing, they pressed on to Mexico City by the two routes available and by nightfall held two gates to the city. Exhausted and depleted by the 800 casualties suffered that day, the troops still faced house-to-house fighting; but at dawn the next day, September 14, the city surrendered.

Throughout the campaign from Vera Cruz to Mexico City General Scott had displayed not only dauntless personal courage and fine qualities of leadership but great skill in applying the principles of war. In preparing for battle he would order his engineers to make a thorough reconnaissance of the enemy's position and the surrounding terrain. He was thus able to execute brilliant flanking movements over terrain that the enemy had considered impassable, notably at Cerro Gordo and the Pedregal, the latter a fine illustration of the principle of surprise. Scott also knew when to break the rules of warfare, as he had done at Puebla when he deliberately severed his line of communications.

"He sees everything and counts the cost of every measure," said Robert E. Lee. Scott on his part ascribed his quick victory over Mexico, won without the loss of a single battle, to the West Pointers in his army, Lee, Grant, and many others. As for the troops, the trained and disciplined Regulars had come off somewhat better than the volunteers, but the army on the whole had fought well. Scott had seen to it that the men fought at the right time and place. Grant summed it up: "Credit is due to the troops engaged, it is true, but the plans and strategy were the general's."

Occupation and Negotiation in Mexico City

For two months the only responsible government in Mexico was the American military government under Scott. The collection of revenues, suppression of disorder, administration of justice, all the details of governing the country were in the hands of the Army. When the Mexicans finally organized a government with which Commissioner Trist could negotiate a peace treaty, dispatches arrived from Washington instructing Trist to return to the United States and ordering Scott to resume the war. Knowing that the Mexicans were now sincerely desirous of ending the war and realizing that the government in Washington was unaware of the situation, both Trist and Scott decided to continue the negotiations.

On February 2, 1848, the Treaty of Guadalupe Hidalgo was signed. It was ratified by the U.S. Senate on March 10, but powerful opposition to it developed

in Mexico. Not until May 30 were ratifications exchanged by the two govern-
ments. Preparations began immediately to evacuate American troops from
Mexico. On June 12 the occupation troops marched out of Mexico City, and on
August 1, 1848, the last American soldiers stepped aboard their transports at
Vera Cruz and quitted Mexican soil.

By the Treaty of Guadalupe Hidalgo the United States agreed to pay
Mexico $15 million and to assume the unpaid claims by Americans against
Mexico. In return Mexico recognized the Rio Grande as the boundary of Texas
and ceded New Mexico (including the present states of Arizona, New Mexico,
Utah, and Nevada, a small corner of present-day Wyoming, and the western
and southern portions of Colorado) and Upper California (the present state
of California) to the United States.

The Army on the New Frontier

The victory over Mexico, as well as the settlement of the Oregon boundary
frontier in June 1846, added to the United States a vast territory that was to
occupy the Army almost exclusively in the postwar years.

The first task was exploration, one in which the Corps of Topographical
Engineers played the leading role. Some knowledge of the new frontier had
been gained by expeditions such as those of Bonneville, Kearny, and Fremont;
more had been gained during the Mexican War by "topogs" attached to
Kearny's march to California and Wool's to Saltillo and after the war by
Maj. William H. Emory's work with the Mexican Boundary Commission, but
much still remained to be done.

The most significant and far-reaching explorations were those to locate
routes for transcontinental railroads. The first effort was directed toward the
southwest, an "ice-free, mountain-free" route. In that area the necessity for
defense against Comanches, Apaches, and Navahoes meant that most of the
Army had to be stationed between San Antonio and Fort Yuma. Forts had
to be constructed, roads built, rivers sought as avenues of supply, and Indian
trails mapped. In 1853 Congress authorized similar explorations on a northern
route to the Pacific from Chicago and a central route from St. Louis.

Railroad construction did not begin until after the Civil War. Emigrants
setting out for the West, in increasing numbers after the discovery of gold in
California in 1849, used wagon trails across plains populated by warlike Indian
tribes. The Army guarded the several transcontinental wagon routes and
managed to keep the tribes in check. During the decade of the fifties there
were no less than twenty-two distinct Indian "wars." Upon a report in 1857

TOPOGRAPHICAL ENGINEERS EXPLORING THE COLORADO RIVER *near Chimney Peak.*

that the Mormons in Utah were defying federal authority, two sizable expeditions were sent from Fort Leavenworth to Utah, but the "Mormon War" never became a reality.

Army expeditions, marching through primitive country where no local procurement was possible, had to carry all requirements, from horseshoe nails to artillery. Supplying the frontier posts, some as far as a thousand miles from inland waterways, entailed great effort. All goods had to be hauled in wagons or carried by pack train. The difficulty of supplying posts in the arid regions of the Southwest led in 1855 to an interesting experiment, strongly backed by Secretary of War Jefferson Davis, in the use of camels as pack animals. Seventy-five were imported from the Middle East and sent to Texas. They showed that they could carry heavy loads, walk surefootedly over ground no wagon could traverse, and subsist by grazing and on little water; but their appearance on the roads stampeded wagon and pack trains, and teamsters hated and feared them. The public and the Army turned against them and the camel experiment ended in failure.

Increasing the Peacetime Army

By the end of 1848 the Army had reverted to a peacetime strength somewhat smaller than the 10,000 authorized in 1815. It was stretched very thin by its manifold duties on the vast new frontier. On the recommendations of General

Scott and Secretary of War George W. Crawford, Congress in June 1850 approved enlarging the companies serving on the frontier to 74 privates, a considerable increase over the 50 in the dragoons, 64 in the mounted rifles, and 42 in the artillery and infantry authorized at the end of 1848. Thereafter 90 of the 158 companies were enlarged, so that by the end of 1850 the Army was authorized 12,927 officers and men.

When Jefferson Davis became Secretary of War in 1853, he strongly urged a larger Army, one that could be expanded to 27,818 men in time of war by enlarging the company to 128 men. Davis desired new mounted regiments for frontier service, because only highly mobile units could hope to handle the Indians. In March 1855 Congress added 4 new regiments to the existing 15 (2 of dragoons, 1 of mounted rifles, 4 of artillery, and 8 of infantry). They were the 1st and 2d Cavalry Regiments and the 9th and 10th Infantry Regiments. The mounted arm thus consisted of dragoons, mounted rifles, and cavalry until the Civil War, when all mounted regiments were called cavalry.

Weapons and Tactics on the Eve of the Civil War

At Davis' insistence the new infantry units were armed with percussion-cap, muzzle-loading rifle muskets instead of smoothbore muskets. Nineteenth century technological developments had made possible an accurate, dependable muzzle-loading rifle with at least as fast a rate of fire as the smoothbore musket. This was partly due to the application of the percussion-cap principle to the rifle and partly to the adoption in 1855 of the Minié ball, a lead projectile tapering forward from its hollow base. To load and fire, the soldier bit open the paper cartridge, poured the powder down the barrel, rammed in the paper to seat the charge, and then rammed the bullet home. He then put the cap in place, full-cocked the piece, aimed, and fired. Sparks from the cap fired the powder. The force of the explosion expanded the hollow base of the bullet to fit the rifling, and the bullet left the barrel spinning, and thus with considerable accuracy. Its effective range was about 400 to 600 yards as compared with 100 to 200 yards for smoothbore muskets. The rate of fire was a theoretical three rounds a minute, though this was seldom attained in practice.

In 1855 the national armories began making only rifles and started converting smoothbores into rifles, but the work took time. By the end of 1858 the Springfield and Harpers Ferry Armories had manufactured only 4,000 of the new type of rifle called the Springfield .58. It was a muzzle-loader. Breechloading, permitting a much more rapid rate of fire, had to await the development of a tight-fitting but easy-moving bolt and a cartridge that would effectively seal the breech. Many breechloaders were on the market in the 1850's and the Army began testing all available models but did not complete its tests before 1861. Effective breech-loading rifles required metallic rather than paper cartridges to prevent escape of gases at the breech. Metallic cartridges were invented in 1856 but were not produced in large numbers until after 1861.

The introduction of rifling into field and coast artillery increased the accuracy and more than doubled the effective range; but rifled guns, which had to await the development of advanced manufacturing techniques, did not immediately supplant the smoothbores. During this period an important smoothbore piece was introduced for the light batteries, the 12-pounder bronze cannon called the "Napoleon" for Napoleon III. Capt. Robert P. Parrott's rifled cannon was developed in 1851 but did not come into use on an appreciable scale until the Civil War. The application of the Minié principle to artillery did much to further the use of rifled artillery, though grape and canister, shell (high explosive and shrapnel), and solid shot, all used in the Mexican War, were still standard.

Rockets declined in favor. The brief experience with them in the Mexican War had not been impressive. After the war, continued experimentation failed to remove faults of eccentricity in flight and instability. The rockets often exploded prematurely, so that troops were reluctant to use them; moreover, they tended to deteriorate in storage. More important than any of these considerations was the fact that the new rifled artillery was decidedly superior to rockets in range and accuracy.

Tactical doctrine did not entirely keep pace with the development of weapons. In an effort in that direction, Secretary Davis prescribed light infantry tactics for all infantry units. In general, this meant reducing the line of the infantry from three to two ranks and placing increased emphasis on skirmishers. Formations, however, were still rigid: men stood shoulder to shoulder (it was almost impossible to load a muzzle-loader lying down) and intervals between units were small. These relatively dense formations would, in the early days of the Civil War, offer inviting targets.

At the U.S. Military Academy during this period, such great names as Robert E. Lee and Dennis Mahan, author of many works on engineering and fortification, appeared on the roster of staff and faculty. The Artillery School of Practice was reopened; and, with the appearance in 1849 of Bvt. Maj. Alfred Mordecai's *Artillery for the United States Land Service,* the Army had for the first time a full, accurate description of its system of artillery. Secretary Davis sent Mordecai, along with Maj. Richard Delafield and Capt. George B. McClellan, to Europe to study all aspects of the Crimean War in particular and

European military institutions and development in general. The study of American military theory was stimulated by the publication in 1846 of Henry Wager Halleck's *Elements of Military Art and Science*. Such volumes as Scott's *Instructions for Field Artillery*, the *General Regulations for the Army of the United States*, *Hardee's Tactics*, and the new volume on infantry tactics sponsored by Davis were made available to Army officers and a few others, although not enough were obtained to furnish copies to the militia. A number of military schools had been founded throughout the country, with the South having a slight edge, an advantage that was to provide officers to the Confederacy when the Civil War broke out.

CHAPTER 9

The Civil War, 1861

During the administration of President James Buchanan, 1857–61, tensions over the issue of extending slavery into the western territories mounted alarmingly and the nation ran its inexorable course toward disunion. Along with slavery, the shifting social, economic, political, and constitutional problems of the fast-growing country fragmented its citizenry. After open warfare broke out in Kansas Territory among slaveholders, abolitionists, and opportunists, the battle lines of opinion hardened rapidly. President Buchanan quieted Kansas by using the Regular Army, but it was too small and too scattered to suppress the struggles that were almost certain to break out in the border states.

In 1859 John Brown, who had won notoriety in "Bleeding Kansas," seized the federal arsenal at Harpers Ferry in a mad attempt to foment a slave uprising within a slaveholding state. Again federal troops were called on to suppress the new outbreak, and pressures and emotions rose on the eve of the 1860 elections. Republican Abraham Lincoln was elected to succeed Buchanan; although he failed to win a majority of the popular vote, he received 180 of the 303 electoral votes. The inauguration that was to vest in him the powers of the Presidency would take place March 4, 1861. During this lame-duck period, Mr. Buchanan was unable to control events and the country continued to lose its cohesion.

Secession, Sumter, and Standing to Arms

Abraham Lincoln's election to the Presidency on November 6, 1860, triggered South Carolina on December 20 to enact an ordinance declaring "the union now subsisting between South Carolina and other States, under the name of the 'United States of America,' is hereby dissolved." Within six weeks, six other deep-South states seceded from the Union and seized federal property inside their borders, including military installations, save Fort Pickens outside Pensacola and Fort Sumter in Charleston Harbor. (*Map 21*) To the seven states that formed the Confederate States of America on February 18, 1861, at Montgomery, Alabama, retention of the forts by the U.S. Government was equivalent to a warlike act. To provide his fledgling government with a military force, on

March 6 the new Confederate Executive, Jefferson Davis, called for a 100,000-man volunteer force to serve for twelve months.

The creation of a rival War Department south of the 35th parallel on February 21 shattered the composition of the Regular Army and disrupted its activities, particularly in Texas, where Maj. Gen. David E. Twiggs surrendered his entire command. With an actual strength of 1,080 officers and 14,926 enlisted men on June 30, 1860, the Regular Army was based on 5-year enlistments. Recruited heavily from men of foreign birth, the United States Army consisted of 10 regiments of infantry, 4 of artillery, 2 of cavalry, 2 of dragoons, and 1 of mounted riflemen. It was not a unified striking force. The Regular Army was deployed within seven departments, six of them west of the Mississippi. Of 198 line companies, 183 were scattered in 79 isolated posts in the territories. The remaining 15 were in garrisons along the Canadian border and on the Atlantic coast.

Created by Secretary of War John C. Calhoun and expanded by Secretary of War Davis in 1853, the departments of the United States Army had become powerful institutions by the eve of the Civil War. Within each of the trans-Mississippi departments a senior colonel or general officer by brevet commanded some 2,000 officers and men. All the states east of the Mississippi constituted the Department of the East, where Bvt. Maj. Gen. John E. Wool controlled 929 Regulars. A department commander was responsible for mobilizing and training militia and volunteer forces called into federal service, and for co-ordinating his resources with any expeditionary force commander who operated inside his territory or crossed through his department. A department commander often doubled in command. He was responsible for the administration of his department as well as for conduct of operations in the field. He often had a dual staff arrangement, one departmental and another for the campaign. For strategic guidance and major decisions he looked to the President and General in Chief; for administrative support he channeled his requirements through the Secretary of War to the appropriate bureau chief. In the modern sense he had no corps of staff experts who could assist him in equating his strategic goals with his logistical needs. In many respects the departmental system was a major reason why the Union armies during the Civil War operated like a team of balky horses.

The 1,676 numbered paragraphs of the U.S. Army Regulations governed the actions of a department commander. The provisions concerning Army organization and tactics were archaic in most cases despite Davis' efforts in 1857 to update the Regulations to reflect the experience of the Mexican War. During the Civil War the Regulations would be slightly modified to incorporate the

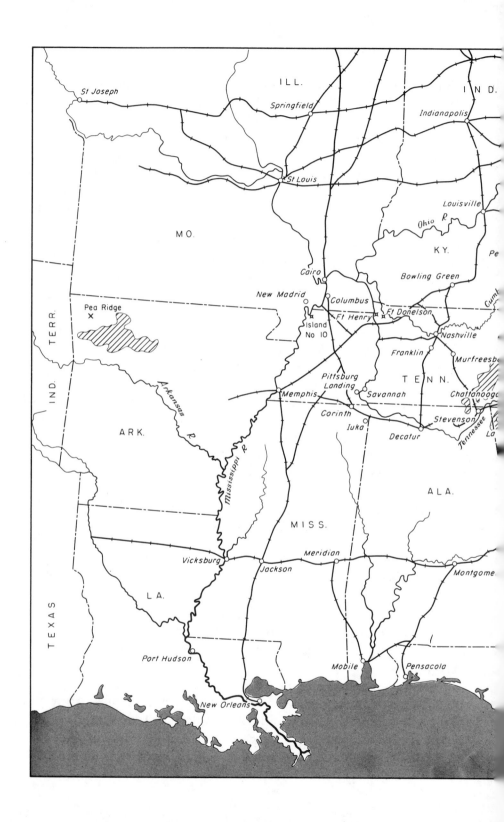

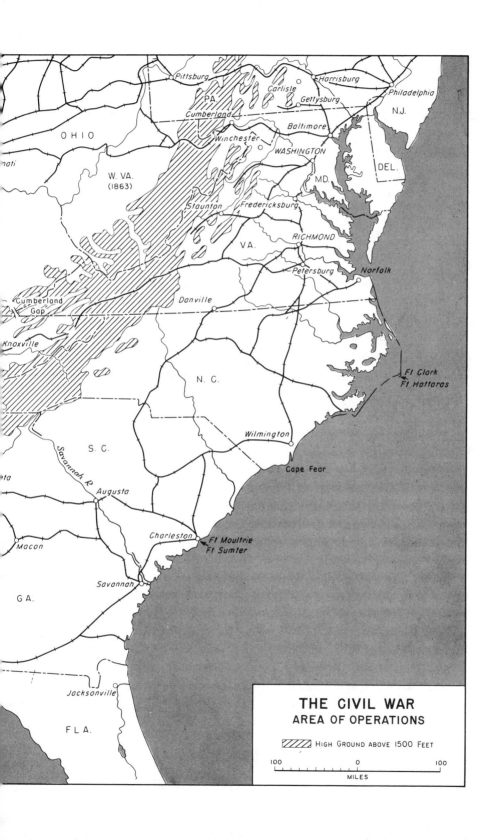

THE CIVIL WAR
AREA OF OPERATIONS

High Ground above 1500 Feet

100   0   100
MILES

military laws passed by two wartime Congresses. In the South these same Regulations would govern the policy and procedures of the Confederate forces.

The roster of the Regular Army was altered considerably by Davis' action in creating a Confederate Army. Of the active officer corps numbering 1,080, 286 resigned or were dismissed and entered the Confederate service. (At least 26 enlisted men are known to have violated their oaths.) West Point graduates on the active list numbered 824; of these, 184 were among the officers who offered their swords to the Confederacy. Of the approximately 900 graduates then in civil life, 114 returned to the Union Army and 99 others sought southern commissions. General in Chief Scott and Col. George H. Thomas of Virginia were southerners who fought for the Union. More serious than their numbers, however, was the high caliber of the officers who joined the Confederacy; many were regimental commanders and three had commanded at departmental level.

With military preparations under way, Davis dispatched commissioners to Washington a few days after Lincoln's inauguration on March 4, 1861, to treat for the speedy takeover of Forts Sumter and Pickens. Informally reassured that the forts would not be provisioned without proper notice, the envoys returned to Montgomery expecting an uneventful evacuation of Sumter. President Lincoln had to move cautiously, for he knew Sumter's supplies were giving out. As each March day passed, Sumter aggravated the harshness of Lincoln's dilemma. In case of war, the fort had no strategic value. If Lincoln reinforced it, Davis would have his act of provocation and Lincoln might drive eight more slaveholding states out of the Union. If Sumter was not succored, the North might cool its enthusiasm for the Union concept and become accustomed to having a confederation south of the Mason-Dixon line.

President Lincoln spent a fortnight listening to the conflicting counsel of his constitutional advisers, and made up his own mind on March 29 to resupply Fort Sumter with provisions only. No effort would be made to increase its military power. By sea he soon dispatched a token expedition and on April 8 notified South Carolina's governor of his decision. The next move was up to the local Confederate commander, Brig. Gen. Pierre G. T. Beauregard. On the 11th, Maj. Robert Anderson, Sumter's commander, politely but firmly rejected a formal surrender demand. At 4:30 the next morning Confederate batteries began a 34-hour bombardment. Anderson's 90-man garrison returned it in earnest, but Sumter's guns were no match for the concentric fire from Confederate artillery. Offered honorable terms on April 14,

Anderson surrendered the federal fort, saluted his U.S. flag with fifty guns, and, with his command, was conveyed to the fleet outside the harbor to be taken to New York City.

Unquestionably, the Confederates fired the first shot of the war, and with that rash act removed many difficulties from Lincoln's path to preserve the Union. On the 15th Lincoln personally penned a proclamation declaring the seven southern states in insurrection against the laws of the United States. To strangle the Confederacy, on the 19th Lincoln declared the entire coast from South Carolina to Texas under naval blockade. To augment the reduced Regular Army, Lincoln asked the governors of the loyal states for 75,000 militiamen to serve for three months, the maximum time permissible under existing laws. With a unanimity which astonished most people, the northern states responded with 100,000 men. Within the eight slave states still in the Union, the militia call to suppress the rebellion was angrily and promptly rejected, and the President's decision to coerce the Confederacy moved Virginia, North Carolina, Tennessee, and Arkansas to join it.

As spring changed into summer the magnitude of the job that the Union had proclaimed for itself—the conquest of an area the size of western Europe, save Scandinavia and Italy, defended by a plucky and proud people and favored by military geography—was imperfectly understood. Although Lincoln later emerged as a diligent student of warfare, he was as yet unversed in the art. His rival, Davis, from the outset knew his military men quite well and thoroughly understood the mechanics of building a fighting force. Yet, as time passed, Davis was to mismanage his government and its military affairs more and more.

Virginia's secession caused Col. Robert E. Lee, Scott's choice to be the Union's field leader, to resign his commission and offer his services to his state. The Confederates moved their capital to Richmond, Virginia, site of the largest iron works in the south and one hundred miles south of the Union capital, Washington. On May 23, Union forces crossed into northern Virginia, occupying Arlington Heights and Alexandria. With Virginia and North Carolina in rebellion, Lincoln extended the naval blockade and called for a large volunteer army backed by an increased Regular force.

Correctly anticipating that Congress in its session to open July 4 would approve his actions, Lincoln, on his own authority, established 40 regiments of U.S. Volunteers (42,034 men) to serve three years or for the duration of the war. He ordered the Regular Army increased by 1 regiment of artillery, 1 of

INSIDE FORT SUMTER *the day after its surrender.*

cavalry, and 8 of infantry (actually, 9 regiments were added), or 22,714 men, and the Navy by 18,000 sailors. The new Regular infantry regiments were each to have 3 battalions of about 800 men, in contrast to the 1-battalion structure in the existing Regular and volunteer regiments. Because the recruits preferred the larger bonuses, laxer discipline, and easy-going atmosphere of the volunteers, most of the newly constituted regiments were never able to fill their additional battalions to authorized strength.

The enthusiastic response to Lincoln's various calls had forced him to ask the governors to scale down the induction of men. The overtaxed camps could not handle the increased manpower. In raising the Army Lincoln used methods that dated back to Washington's day. The combat efficiency and state of training of the new units varied from good to very poor. Some militia regiments were well trained and equipped, others were regiments in name only. The soldiers often elected their own company officers, and the governors commissioned majors and colonels. The President appointed generals. Although many of the newly commissioned officers proved to be enthusiastic, devoted to duty, and eager to learn, incompetents were also appointed. Before the end of 1861, however, officers were being required to prove their qualifications before examining boards; those found unfit were allowed to resign.

Frequently advised by governors and congressmen, Mr. Lincoln selected generals from among leading politicians in order to give himself a broader base of political support. Some political generals, such as John A. Logan and Francis P. Blair, Jr., distinguished themselves, whereas others proved military hindrances. Lincoln gave a majority of the commissions in the first forty volunteer units to Regulars on active duty, to former West Pointers like George B. McClellan who had resigned to pursue a business career, or to those who had held volunteer commissions during the Mexican War. On the other hand, Davis never gave higher than a brigade command to a Confederate volunteer officer until he had proved himself in battle.

Both North and South failed to develop a good system of replacement of individuals in volunteer units. The Confederacy, though hamstrung by its insistence that Texans be commanded by Texans and Georgians by Georgians and by governors' demands for retaining home guards, did devise a regimental system that stood up well until the closing days of the war. Except for Wisconsin, Illinois, and Vermont, the Union armies never had an efficient volunteer replacement system. As battle losses mounted and the ranks of veteran regiments thinned, commanders were forced to send men back to their home states on recruiting duty or face the disbandment of their regiments. Northern governors with patronage in mind preferred to raise new regiments, allowing battle-tested ones to decline to company proportions.

GENERAL LEE. (*Photograph taken after his promotion to lieutenant general.*)

The enlisted Regular Army was kept intact for the duration of the war. Many critics believed that the Regulars should have been used to cadre the volunteer units. But this practice was initially impossible during the summer of 1861 for at least two reasons. Lincoln did not foresee a long war, and the majority of Regulars were needed on the frontier until trained men could replace them. In addition, Lincoln's critics overlooked the breakdown in morale that would have accompanied the breakup of old line regiments, many of which had histories and honors dating back to the War of 1812. An officer holding a Regular commission in 1861 had to resign to accept a commission in the volunteers unless the War Department specifically released him. Most Regulars were loath to resign, uncertain that they would be recalled to active duty after the war. Thus, during 1861 and part of 1862, promotion in the Regular Army was slow. All Regulars could accept commissions in the volunteers by 1862, and in many cases the year that they had spent in small unit command seasoning had its reward in advancing them to higher commands. Ulysses S. Grant and William T. Sherman, both U.S. Military Academy graduates returning from civilian life, asked specifically for volunteer regimental commands at first and soon advanced rapidly to general officer posts.

The Opponents

As North and South lined up for battle, clearly the preponderance of productive capacity, manpower, and agricultural potential lay on the side of the North. Its crops were worth more annually than those of the South, which had concentrated on growing cotton, tobacco, and rice. Between February and May 1861 the Confederate authorities missed the opportunity of shipping baled cotton to England and drawing bills against it for the purchase of arms. In seapower, railroads, material wealth, and industrial capacity to produce iron and munitions the North was vastly superior to the South. This disparity became even more pronounced as the ever-tightening blockade gradually cut off the Confederacy from foreign imports. The North had more mules and horses, a logistical advantage of great importance since supplies had to be carried to the troops from rail and river heads.

According to the census of 1860 the population of the United States numbered 31,443,321 persons. Approximately 23,000,000 of them were in the twenty-two northern states and 9,000,000 in the eleven states that later seceded. Of the latter total, 3,500,000 were slaves. The size of the opposing armies would reflect this disparity. At one time or another about 2,100,000 men would serve in the northern armies, while some 800,000 to 900,000 men would serve the South. Peak strength of the two forces would be about 1,000,000 and 600,000, respectively.

Yet not all the advantages lay with the North. The South possessed good interior lines of communications, and its 3,550-mile coast line, embracing 189 harbors and navigable river mouths, was most difficult to blockade effectively. Possessors of a rich military record in wars against the British, Spanish, Mexicans, and Indians, the southerners initially managed to form redoubtable cavalry units more easily than the North and used them with considerable skill against the invading infantry. As the war moved along, the armies on both sides demonstrated high degrees of military skill and bravery. Man for man they became almost evenly matched, and their battles were among the bloodiest in modern history.

Jefferson Davis hoped that the sympathy or even intervention of European powers might more than compensate for the Confederacy's lack of material resources. This hope, largely illusory from the start, became less and less likely of realization with the emancipation of the slaves, with every Union victory, and with the increasing effectiveness of the blockade.

Militarily, the South's greatest advantage over the North was simply the fact that if not attacked it could win by doing nothing. To restore the Union the Federal forces would have to conquer the Confederacy. Thus the arena of action lay below the strategic line of the Potomac and Ohio Rivers. Here geography divided the theater of war into three interrelated theaters of operations. The eastern theater lay between the Atlantic Ocean and the Appalachian Mountains; the western theater embraced the area from the Appalachians to the Mississippi; and the trans-Mississippi theater ran westward to the Pacific Ocean. (*Map 22*)

In the east, the strategic triangle of northern Virginia shielded invasion routes. Its apex aimed arrowlike at the Federal capital; the Potomac River and the lower Chesapeake Bay formed its right leg; its left bounded on the Blue Ridge and the adjacent Shenandoah Valley; and the base of the triangle followed the basin of the James and Appomattox Rivers, whereon stood Richmond, halfway between the bay and the valley. For three and a half years Federal commanders would be defeated on the legs and in the center of this triangle as they tried to take Richmond and defeat the Army of Northern Virginia under Lee. In three neighboring counties within this triangle more than half a million men would clash in mortal combat; more would die in these counties than in the Revolutionary War, the War of 1812, the War with Mexico, and all the Indian wars combined. To bring the Confederates out of this triangle the North would have to execute an operation aimed at breaking through the base line along the James and Appomattox Rivers.

The hammer for swinging against the anvil of Virginia came from the line of the Ohio River as Union forces moved along the invasion routes of the Green, Cumberland, Tennessee, and Mississippi Rivers. To breach the lower reaches of the Appalachians, the Federals needed the railroad centers at Nashville, Chattanooga, and Atlanta; with them they could strike northward through the Carolinas toward the line of the James. But in the spring of 1861, the anvil and hammer concept had not yet occurred to the military leaders in Washington. Only the General in Chief, Winfield Scott, had a concrete strategic proposal for waging total war. He recommended to Lincoln that time be taken to train an army of 85,000 men and that the naval blockade of the Confederacy be enforced. Then the Army was to advance down the Mississippi to divide and conquer the South. The press ridiculed the strategy, calling it the Anaconda Plan. But few leaders examined the South in terms of its military geography or concentrated on a strategy to prevail over it. Instead, most thought in terms of political boundaries and a short war that would end with the capture of Richmond.

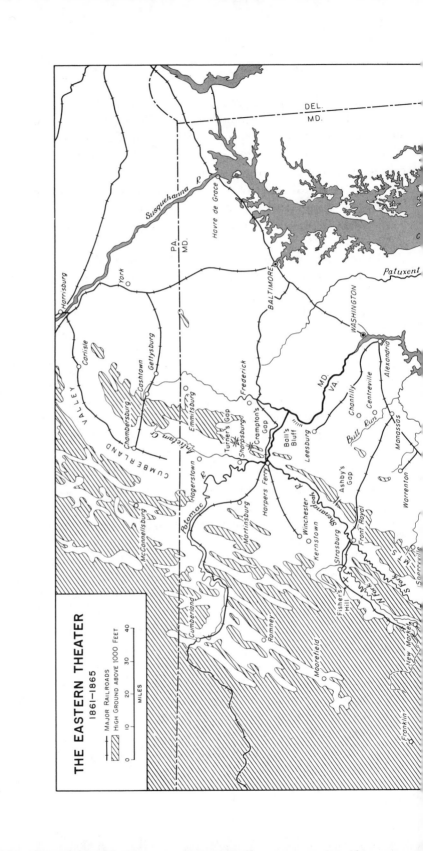

THE EASTERN THEATER
1861–1865

- ┤─┤ MAJOR RAILROADS
- ▨ HIGH GROUND ABOVE 1000 FEET

MILES
0   10   20   30   40

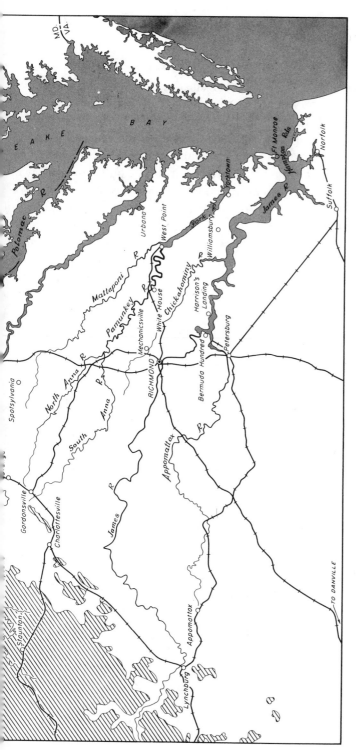

MAP 22

Manassas (Bull Run)

In the early summer of 1861 the partly trained 90-day militia, the almost untrained volunteers, and one newly organized battalion of Regulars—a total force of 50,000 Federals commanded by Brig. Gen. Irvin McDowell—defended the nation's capital. Thirty miles to the southwest, covering the rail and road hub at Manassas, Virginia, General Beauregard posted some 20,000 Confederates, to be joined by 2,000 more within a few days. To the left, on their defensive line along the Potomac, the Confederates stationed another 11,000 men under Brig. Gen. Joseph E. Johnston in the Shenandoah Valley town of Winchester. Opposing Johnston around Martinsburg, with the mission of keeping the Confederates in place, was Maj. Gen. Robert Patterson with 18,000 Federals. On the extreme right of the Confederate northern Virginia defense line was Col. Joseph B. Magruder's force, which had recently repulsed Maj. Gen. Benjamin F. Butler's Union troops at Big Bethel, Virginia, on 10 June, and forced them back into their sanctuary at Fort Monroe.

Big Bethel, the first large-scale meeting engagement of the Civil War, demonstrated that neither opponent was as yet well trained. The Confederates had started preparations earlier to protect northern Virginia and therefore might have had a slight edge on their opponents. General McDowell, only recently a major of Regulars, had less than three months to weld his three types of units—militia, volunteer, and Regular—into a single fighting force. He attempted to do too much himself, and there were few competent staff officers in the vicinity to help him. McDowell's largest tactical unit was a regiment until just before he marched out of Alexandria. Two to four brigades, plus a battery of Regular artillery—the best arm against raw infantry—formed a division. In all, thirteen brigades were organized into five divisions. McDowell parceled out his forty-nine guns among his brigade commanders, who in turn attached them to their regiments. His total force for the advance was 35,732 men, but of these one division of 5,752 men dropped off to guard roads to the rear.

McDowell's advance against Beauregard, on four parallel routes, was hastened by northern opinion, expressed in editorials and Congressional speeches, demanding immediate action. Scott warned Lincoln against undertaking the "On to Richmond" campaign until McDowell's troops had become disciplined units. But Lincoln, eager to use the 90-day militia before they departed, demanded an advance, being aware that the Confederates were also unseasoned and cherishing the belief that one defeat would force the South to quit. Scott, influenced by false intelligence that Beauregard would move immediately on Washington, acceded. Accordingly, McDowell's battle plan and preparations were expedited. The plan, accepted in late June, called for Butler and Patterson to prevent the Confederates facing them from reinforcing Beauregard, while McDowell advanced against Manassas to outflank the southern position. Scott called it a good plan on paper but knew Johnston was capable of frustrating it if given the chance. McDowell's success against the Confederate center depended upon a rapid 30-mile march, if 35,000 Federals were to keep 22,000 Confederates from being reinforced.

On July 16, 1861, the largest army ever assembled on the North American continent up to that time advanced slowly on both sides of the Warrenton pike toward Bull Run. McDowell's march orders were good, but the effect was ruined by one unwise caution to the brigade commanders: "It will not be pardonable in any commander . . . to come upon a battery or breastwork without a knowledge of its position." The caution recalled to McDowell's subordinates the currently sensationalized bugbear of the press of being fooled by "masked batteries," a term originating at Sumter where a certain battery was constructed, masked by a house which was demolished just before the guns opened fire. Accordingly, 35,000 men moved just five miles on the 17th. Next day the Federals occupied Centreville, some four miles east of Stone Bridge, which carried the Warrenton pike over Bull Run. (*Map 23*)

Beauregard's advanced guards made no effort to delay the Federals, but fell back across the battle line, now extending some three miles along the west bank of Bull Run, which meandered from Stone Bridge southeast until it joined the Occoquan stream. The country was fairly rough, cut by streams, and thickly wooded. It presented formidable obstacles to attacking raw troops, but a fair shelter for equally raw troops on the defensive. On the 18th, while McDowell's main body waited at Centreville for the trains to close up, the leading division demonstrated against Beauregard's right around Mitchell's Ford. The Federal infantry retired after a sharp musketry fight, and a 45-minute artillery duel ensued. It was the first exchange of four standard types of artillery ammunition for all muzzle-loading guns, whether rifled or smoothbore. Solid shot, shell, spherical case or shrapnel, and canister from eight Federal guns firing 415 rounds were answered by seven Confederate pieces returning 310 rounds. Steadily withdrawing its guns, the oldest and best drilled unit of the South, the Washington Light Artillery of New Orleans, broke off the fight against well-trained U.S. Regular artillery. Both sides had used rifled artillery, which greatly increased the accuracy and gave a range more than double that of the smoothbores. Yet rifled guns never supplanted the new, easily loaded Napoleons. In the fight, defective Confederate ammunition fired from three new 3-inch iron rifles

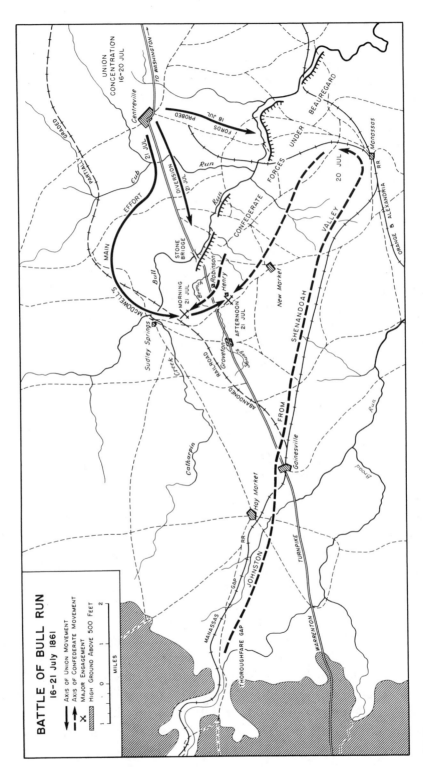

BATTLE OF BULL RUN
16-21 July 1861

Axis of Union Movement

Axis of Confederate Movement

X Major Engagement

High Ground Above 500 Feet

MILES
1   0   1   2

UNION CONCENTRATION 16-20 JUL

TO WASHINGTON

Centreville

PROBED 18 JUL

FORDS

BEAUREGARD

Manassas

Run

21 JUL

Cub

Run

DIVERSION 21 JUL

Run

20 JUL

CONFEDERATE

FORCES UNDER

SHENANDOAH VALLEY

ORANGE & ALEXANDRIA RR

GRADED

PARTIALLY

MAIN EFFORT

STONE BRIDGE

Robinson

MORNING 21 JUL

Henry

New Market

FROM

Bull

McDOWELL'S

Sudley Springs

Creek

Brun

AFTERNOON 21 JUL

ABANDONED RAILROAD

Groveton

Jeffers

Catharpin

Run

Gainesville

Broad

Run

Hay Market

MANASSAS GAP

THOROUGHFARE GAP

JOHNSTON

RR

TURNPIKE

WARRENTON

MAP 23

would not fly point foremost but tumbled and lost range against McDowell's gunners. That the error went undetected for days reveals the haste in which Davis had procured his ordnance.

Sure that his green troops could not flank the Confederate right, McDowell tarried two more fateful days before he attacked in force. Engineers reconnoitered for an undefended ford north of Stone Bridge. Finding no vedettes at the ford near Sudley Springs, McDowell decided to envelop the Confederate left on July 21 and destroy the Manassas Gap Railroad to keep Johnston from reinforcing the outnumbered Beauregard. The idea was excellent, but the timing was slow.

While McDowell frittered away four and a half days before he was ready to envelop in force, new tools of warfare swung the advantages of mobility, surprise, and mass at critical points toward Beauregard. On July 17 spies in Washington told of McDowell's departure from Alexandria. By electric telegraph Beauregard in turn alerted Richmond. Davis, also telegraphing, ordered commanders around Richmond, at Aquia Creek, and at Winchester to concentrate their available strength at Manassas. Johnston lost no time in deceiving Patterson by using Col. J. E. B. Stuart's cavalry as a screen and adroitly maneuvering his infantry away from the valley. Johnston selected the best overland routes for his artillery and cavalry marches and arranged for railroad officials to move his four infantry brigades. Brig. Gen. Thomas Jackson's lead brigade, accompanied by Johnston himself, covered fifty-seven miles in twenty-five hours by road and rail, reaching Beauregard on the 20th.

At daylight on the 21st, McDowell unmasked the first phase of his attack plan. Three brigades of Brig. Gen. Daniel Tyler's division appeared before Stone Bridge, and a huge, 30-pounder Parrott rifle dragged into place by ten horses commenced a slow fire, directed by six cannoneers of the 2d U.S. Artillery. Five brigades in two divisions directly under McDowell's command meanwhile marched on an 8-mile circuitous route toward the undefended ford at Sudley Springs. McDowell's goal was the Confederate left rear and a chance to cut the railroad. At 9:00 a.m. a signal flag wigwag from the Henry house announced the point of the enveloping columns at Sudley's crossing, and the intelligence was immediately relayed to Beauregard and Johnston, who were three miles away on the Confederate right.

The first weight of the Federal attack fell against eleven Confederate companies and two guns. For an hour McDowell's regiments, firing one by one and moving forward cautiously in piecemeal fashion, tried to overrun Beauregard's left flank. The timid tactics gave Beauregard time to redeploy ten regiments across a 3-mile front to form a second defensive line across the north face of the hill behind the Henry house. At 10:30 a.m., as the summer sun grew hotter, a portentous dust cloud, rising ten miles northwest of Manassas, heralded the arrival of Kirby Smith's brigade, the tail of Johnston's reinforcements from the Shenandoah Valley.

For two hours the roar of the battle swelled in volume. Federal musketry crashes and the thunder from the heavier pieces indicated that McDowell was now committing whole brigades, supported by four batteries of artillery. North of the Warrenton turnpike, the Confederate infantry began to lose its brigade cohesion and fall back in disorder. As Beauregard and Johnston rode to the sound of battle, some 10,000 Federals were punishing 7,000 Confederates in the vicinity of the Henry and Robinson houses. Johnston, though senior in command, turned the battle over to Beauregard and galloped off toward Manassas to direct the arrival of reinforcements. Brig. Gen. Barnard E. Bee's brigade was pushed back from its advanced position toward the flat-crested hill behind the Henry house, where Jackson's newly arrived brigade had formed. In rallying his routed troops, Bee shouted: "Look at Jackson's Brigade; it stands like a stone wall! Rally behind the Virginians!" (Out of these words came a nickname that Jackson would carry to his grave, and after his death in 1863 the Confederate War Department officially designated his unit the Stonewall Brigade.) Screened by a wooded area, three brigades regrouped behind Jackson's lines, and the rally became a great equalizer as McDowell's strength dissipated to 9,000 men, with no immediate infantry reserves in sight.

The cloud of dust moved closer to Manassas Junction, but McDowell ignored it and allowed a lull to settle over his front for almost two hours. At 2:00 p.m., having deployed two batteries of Regular artillery directly to his front around the Henry house with insufficient infantry protection, McDowell renewed the battle. By midafternoon the dust had blended sweaty uniforms into a common hue, and more and more cases of mistaken identity were confusing both sides in the smoke of the battle. Then, as part of the confusion, came a fateful episode. To the right front of McDowell's exposed artillery, a line of advancing blue-clad infantry, the 33d Regiment, Virginia Volunteers, suddenly appeared through the smoke. The Federal artillery commander ordered canister, but the chief artillery officer on McDowell's staff overruled the order, claiming that the oncoming blue uniforms belonged to friendly infantry arriving in support. The Virginians advanced to within seventy yards of the Federal guns, leveled their muskets, and let loose. The shock of their volley cut the artillery to shreds, and for the remainder of the day nine Federal guns stood silent, unserved, and helpless between the armies.

About 4:00 p.m., Beauregard, with two additional fresh brigades, advanced his entire line. Shorn of their artillery, the faltering Federal lines soon lost cohesion and began to pull back along the routes they knew; there was more and more confusion as they retired. East of Bull Run, Federal artillery, using Napoleon smoothbores in this initial pullback from the field, proved to the unsuspecting Confederate cavalry, using classic saber-charging tactics, that a determined line of artillerymen could reduce cavalry to dead and sprawling infantry in minutes.

As in so many battles of the Civil War yet to come, there was no organized pursuit in strength to cut the enemy to ribbons while he fled from the immediate area of the battlefield. At Bull Run the Federal withdrawal turned into a panic-stricken flight about 6:30 p.m., when Cub Run bridge, about a mile west of Centreville, was blocked by overturned wagons. Sunset would fall at 7:15 p.m., and President Davis, just arrived from Richmond, had two daylight hours to arrive at a decision for pursuit. In council with Johnston and Beauregard, Davis instructed the whole Confederate right to advance against the Centreville road, but apparently his orders were never delivered or Beauregard neglected to follow them. Davis thus lost a splendid opportunity for seeing in person whether the unused infantry and artillery on the right of his line could have made a concerted effort to destroy McDowell's fleeing forces. Logistically, Federal booty taken over the next two days by the Confederates would have sustained them for days in an advance against Washington.

Strategically, Bull Run was important to the Confederates only because the center of their Virginia defenses had held. Tactically, the action highlights many of the problems and deficiencies that were typical of the first year of the war. Bull Run was a clash between large, ill-trained bodies of recruits, who were slow in joining battle; masked batteries frightened commanders; plans called for maneuvering the enemy out of position, but attacks were frontal; security principles were disregarded; tactical intelligence was nil; and reconnaissance was poorly executed. Soldiers were overloaded for battle. Neither commander was able to employ his whole force effectively. Of McDowell's 35,000 men, only 18,000 crossed Bull Run and casualties among these, including the missing, numbered about 2,708. Beauregard, with 32,000 men, ordered only 18,000 into action and lost 1,982.

Both commanders rode along the front, often interfering in small unit actions. McDowell led his enveloping column instead of directing all his forces from the rear. Wisely, Johnston left the battlefield and went to the rear to hasten up his Shenandoah Valley reserves. Regiments were committed piecemeal. Infantry failed to protect exposed artillery. Artillery was parceled out under infantry command; only on the retreat was the Union senior artillery officer on the scene allowed to manage his guns. He saved 21 guns of the 49 that McDowell had. Beauregard's orders were oral, vague, and confusing. Some were delivered, others were never followed.

The Second Uprising in 1861

The southern victory near Manassas had an immediate and a long-range effect on the efforts of both the northern and the southern states. First, it compelled northern leaders to face up to the nature and scope of the struggle and to begin the task of putting the Union on a full war footing. Second, it made them more willing to give heed to the advice of professional soldiers charged with the task of directing military operations along a vast continental land front extending from Point Lookout, Maryland, to Fort Craig in central New Mexico. Third, Confederate leaders, after their feeling of invincibility quickly wore off, called for 400,000 volunteers, sought critical military items in Europe, and turned to planning operations that might swing the remaining slaveholding states and territories into the Confederacy. Finally, the most potent immediate influence of Bull Run was upon the European powers, which eyed the Confederacy as a belligerent with much potential for political intervention and as a source of revenue. Unless the Federal Navy could make it unprofitable for private merchant ships to deliver arms to southern ports and depart with agricultural goods, speculative capital would flow increasingly into the contraband trade.

Strategically, in 1861 the U.S. Navy made the most important contribution toward an ultimate Union victory. At considerable expense and in haste to make the blockade effective, the Navy by the end of the year had assembled 200 ships of every description, armed them after a fashion, and placed them on station. With new Congressional acts regarding piracy, revenue, confiscation, and enforcement in hand, commanders of this motley fleet intercepted more and more swift blockade runners steaming out of Nassau, Bermuda, and Havana on their three-day run to Wilmington, North Carolina, Charleston, South Carolina, or Savannah, Georgia. In two round trips a blockade runner, even if lost on its third voyage, still produced a considerable profit to its owner. By the end of 1861 such profit was no longer easy, because the Navy had many new fast ships in service, specially fitted for blockade duty.

After 1861 the naval character of the war changed. There was no Civil War on the high seas except for the exciting exploits of three or four Confederate cruisers which raided commercial shipping. As the war progressed, both opponents perfected the nature and construction of ships and naval ordnance for a war that would be fought in coastal waters or inside defensible harbors. The three main weapons, the rifled naval gun, the armored ram, and the torpedo mine, were developed and used in novel ways. To offset the defensive use of these weapons by the South, the Federal Navy beginning in August 1861 landed more and more Army expeditionary forces and gradually obtained footholds in the vicinity of Mobile, Savannah, Charleston, and Wilmington. By the end of the war, joint Navy-Army expeditions would convert the sea blockade into a military occupation and would seal off all major ports in the South.

The defeat at Bull Run was followed by "a second uprising" in the North, greatly surpassing the effort after Sumter's surrender. President Lincoln and Congress set to with a will to raise and train the large Federal armies that would be required to defeat the South, to select competent Army field commanders, and to reorganize and strengthen the War Department. On July 22, 1861, Lincoln called for a 500,000-man force of 3-year volunteers and during the rest of July quickly disbanded the 90-day militiamen. The more experienced entered the newly authorized volunteer force. Meanwhile, the volunteer quota and the increase of Regulars, mobilized after Sumter, had so far progressed that camps and garrisons, established at strategic points along the 1,950-mile boundary with the border states and territories, were bustling with activity. As July ended, Congress authorized the volunteers to serve for the duration of the war and perfected their regimental organization. Four regiments were grouped into a brigade, and three brigades formed a division. The infantry corps structure would be fixed when the President directed. In effect, the Lincoln administration was building a federal force, as opposed to one based on joint state-federal control and support. State governors, given a quota according to a state's population, raised 1,000-man volunteer regiments, bought locally whatever the units needed, shipped them to federal training centers, and presented all bills to the U.S. Government. Accordingly, Congress floated a national loan of $250 million.

Pending the transformation of their volunteer forces, both opponents necessarily suspended major military operations for the remainder of 1861. President Lincoln conferred frequently with General Scott and his military advisers about steps already taken to strengthen Union forces along the continental front. Regular Army units were consolidating their position at Forts Craig and Union to protect the upper Rio Grande valley against any Confederate columns coming from Texas. To protect communication lines to the Pacific and the southwest and to guard federal supplies at Fort Leavenworth, Kansas, and St. Louis, Missouri, Union troops were deployed in eastern Kansas and across central Missouri. In August Union troops fought a drawn battle at Wilson's Creek,

UNION VOLUNTEERS IN CAMP

and Missouri became a state divided against itself. The loss of Kentucky, in Lincoln's judgment, would be "nearly the same as to lose the whole game"; so he carefully respected Kentucky's decision of May to remain neutral. After Bull Run, Illinois, Indiana, and Ohio volunteers were assembled north of the Ohio at exposed river towns to keep watch on the situation in Kentucky. In western Virginia forty counties elected to secede from Virginia and asked for federal troops to assist them in repelling any punitive expeditions emerging from the Shenandoah Valley. Between May and early July 1861, Ohio volunteers, under the command of Maj. Gen. George B. McClellan, occupied the Grafton area of western Virginia, hoping to protect the railroad that linked the Ohio Valley with Baltimore. In a series of clashes at Philippi, Beverly, and along the Cheat River, McClellan's forces checked the invading Confederates, paving the way for West Virginia's entrance into the Union.

Although the border strife intensified in the west, Scott attended to the more important front facing Virginia. The nation's capital was imperiled, the Potomac was directly under Confederate guns, and Maryland and Delaware were being used as recruiting areas for the southern cause. On July 22, Lincoln, following Scott's advice, had summoned McClellan, who was thirty-five years old at the time, to Washington, and assigned him command, under Scott, of all the troops in the Washington area. McClellan's reputation was unrivaled, and the public had acclaimed him for his victories in western Virginia. On August 21 McClellan named his force the Army of the Potomac, and commenced molding it into a formidable machine.

McClellan organized the Army of the Potomac into eleven 10,000-man divisions, each with three brigades of infantry, a cavalry regiment, and four 6-gun batteries. In general this structure was adopted by the other Union armies, and the Confederates deviated from the model only in their cavalry organization. In the Army of Northern Virginia, for example, General Lee treated his cavalry as a tactical arm, grouped first as a division, and later as a cavalry corps. Union cavalry consisted of little more than mounted infantry, carrying out a multitude of duties for the division commander, such as serving as pickets, wagon train escorts, and couriers. McClellan planned, once Lincoln activated corps, to withdraw one-half of the artillery pieces from each infantry division and center them at corps level as a reserve to be deployed under army command. He insisted that the .58-caliber single-shot, muzzle-loading Springfield rifle be the standard weapon of the infantry, and most of the Army of the Potomac possessed it when corps were organized on March 8, 1862.

McClellan completely transformed the military atmosphere around Washington before the end of 1861. But, although he was an able administrator, his critics doubted his abilities as a top field commander. And from the day he activated the Army of the Potomac, McClellan was politically active in trying to oust Scott. Finally, on November 1, the aged and harassed General in Chief, taking advantage of a new law, retired from the Army. That same day, acting on assurances that McClellan could handle two tasks concurrently, Lincoln made McClellan the General in Chief and retained him in command of the Army of the Potomac. By the 9th, basing his action on Scott's earlier groundwork, McClellan carved out five new departments in the west, all commanded by Regular Army officers. In addition, he continued the work of the new Department of New England, where General Butler was already forming volunteer regiments for scheduled seaborne operations off the Carolina capes and in the Gulf of New Mexico.

For the Union cause in Kentucky, the new General in Chief's move came none too soon. As early as September 4, a Confederate force from Tennessee had violated Kentucky's neutrality by occupying the Mississippi River town and railroad terminal of Columbus. The next day Illinois troops under Brig. Gen. Ulysses S. Grant seized Paducah and Smithland, strategic river towns in Kentucky at the confluence of the Tennessee and Cumberland Rivers with the Ohio. After Kentucky declared for the Union on September 20, both sides rapidly concentrated forces in western Kentucky. Maj. Gen. Albert S. Johnston, recently appointed to command Confederate forces in the west, fortified Bowling Green, Kentucky, and extended his defensive line to Columbus. Union troops immediately occupied Louisville and planned advances down the railroad to Nashville and eastward into the Appalachians. By November 15, the commanders of the Department of the Ohio and the Department of the Missouri, dividing their operational boundaries in Kentucky along the Cumberland River, were exchanging strategic plans with McClellan in anticipation of a grand offensive in the spring of 1862.

The outpouring of troops and their preparations for battle disrupted the leisurely pace of the War Department. In their haste to supply, equip, and deploy the second quota of volunteers, a score or more of states competed not only against one another but against the federal government as well. Profiteers demanded exorbitant prices for scarce items, which frequently turned out to be worthless. Unbridled graft and extravagance were reflected in the bills which the states presented to the War Department for payment. After Bull Run a concerted, widespread movement emerged for the dismissal of Secretary of War Simon Cameron, who had failed to manage his office efficiently. Cameron selected Edwin M. Stanton, former Attorney General in President Buchanan's cabinet, as his special counsel to handle all legal arguments justifying the War Department's purchasing policies. Knowing that the cabinet post had considerable potential, Stanton worked hard to restore the War Department's prestige. Behind the scenes Stanton aided his fellow Democrat, McClellan, in outfitting the Army of the Potomac. As the summer faded Stanton, having once scoffed at Lincoln early in the war, ingratiated himself with the President and his key cabinet members by urging his pro-Union views. In January 1862 Lincoln replaced Cameron with Stanton, who immediately set out to make his cabinet position the most powerful in Lincoln's administration.

Self-confident, arrogant, abrupt, and contemptuous of incompetent military leaders, Stanton was also fiercely energetic, incorruptible, and efficient. Respecting few men and fearing none, he did his best to eliminate favoritism and see to it that war contracts were honestly negotiated and faithfully filled. Few men liked Stanton, but almost all high officials respected him. Stanton insisted that the Army receive whatever it needed, and the best available, and no campaign by any Union army would ever fail for want of supplies.

From the day that Stanton took office, the structure of the War Department was centralized to handle the growing volume of business. Each bureau chief reported directly to Stanton, but the responsibility became so heavy that he delegated procurement and distribution matters to three assistant secretaries. Because the Quartermaster General's Department transported men and matériel, operated the depot system, constructed camps, and handled the largest number of contracts, it soon became the most important agency of the general staff. Hard-working, efficient, and loyal, Montgomery C. Meigs as Quartermaster General was an organizing genius, and was one of the few career officers to whom Stanton would listen. To complete his department, Stanton added three major bureaus during the war: the Judge Advocate General's Office in 1862; the Signal Department in 1863; and the Provost Marshal General's Bureau, established in 1863 to administer the draft (enrollment) act. In the same year the Corps of Topographical Engineers was merged with the Corps of Engineers.

Stanton faced mobilization problems and home front crises of unprecedented magnitude. Loyal states were bringing half a million men under arms. Grain, wool, leather, lumber, metals, and fuel were being turned into food, clothing, vehicles, and guns, and thousands of draft animals were being purchased and shipped from every part of the North. A well-managed federal authority was needed to assume the states' obligations, to train volunteer units in the use of their tools of war, and then to deploy them along a vast continental front. By exploiting the railroad, steamship, and telegraph, the War Department provided field commanders a novel type of mobility in their operations. Stanton's major task was to control all aspects of this outpouring of the nation's resources. If war contracts were tainted, the Union soldiers might despair. Moral as well as financial bankruptcy could easily wreck Union hopes of victory. In addition, Stanton had the job of suppressing subversion, of timing the delicate matter of putting Negroes in the Army, and of co-operating with a radical-dominated Congress, a strong-willed cabinet, and a conservative-minded Army. With a lawyer's training, Stanton, like Lincoln, knew little about military affairs, and there was little time for him to learn. Anticipating that President Lincoln would soon call for War Department plans for the spring 1862 offensives, Stanton researched every document he could find on Army administration, consulted his bureau chiefs about readiness, and prepared himself to work with the General in Chief on strategic matters.

When he took office, Stanton found that the War Department had a rival in the form of the Joint Congressional Committee on the Conduct of the War. It had its origins in an investigation of a badly executed reconnaissance at Ball's Bluff on the Potomac, October 21, 1861, in which a volunteer officer and popular former senator, Col. Edward D. Baker, was killed. By subsequently searching out graft and inefficiency, the committee did valuable service, but it also vexed the President, Stanton, and most of the generals during the war. Composed of extreme antislavery men without military knowledge and experience, the committee probed the battles, tried to force all its views regarding statecraft and strategy on the President, and put forward its own candidates for high command. Suspicious of proslavery men and men of moderate views, it considered that the only generals fit for office were those who had been abolitionists before 1861.

As the year ended both North and South were earnestly preparing for a hard war. Both opponents were raising and training huge armies totaling nearly a million men. Fort Sumter and bloody Bull Run were over and each side was gathering its resources for the even bloodier struggles to come.

CHAPTER 10

The Civil War, 1862

In 1862 the armed forces of the United States undertook the first massive campaigns to defeat the southern Confederacy. Better organization, training, and leadership would be displayed on both sides as the combat became more intense. Young American citizen soldiers would find that war was not a romantic adventure and their leaders would learn that every victory had its price.

As the winter of 1861–62 wore on, McClellan exaggerated his difficulties and the enemy's strength, and discounted the Confederacy's problems. He drilled and trained the Army of the Potomac while western forces under his general command accomplished little. Lincoln and the Union waited impatiently for a conclusive engagement. But neither the Union nor the Confederate Army showed much inclination to move, each being intent on perfecting itself before striking a heavy blow.

The President was particularly eager to support Unionist sentiment in east Tennessee by moving forces in that direction. Above all he wanted a concerted movement to crush the rebellion quickly. In an effort to push matters Lincoln issued General War Order No. 1 on January 27, 1862. This order, besides superfluously telling the armies to obey existing orders, directed that a general movement of land and sea forces against the Confederacy be launched on February 22, 1862. Lincoln's issuance of an order for an offensive several weeks in advance, without considering what the weather and the roads might be like, has been scoffed at frequently. But apparently he issued it only to get McClellan to agree to move. Even before Lincoln sent the directive his intentions were overtaken by events in the western theater.

The Twin Rivers Campaign

Students of the Civil War often concentrate their study upon the cockpit of the war in the east—Virginia. The rival capitals lay only a hundred miles apart and the country between them was fought over for four years. But it was the Union armies west of the Appalachians that struck the death knell of the Confederacy.

GENERAL GRANT. (*Photograph taken after his promotion to lieutenant general.*)

These Union forces in late 1861 were organized into two separate commands. Brig. Gen. Don Carlos Buell commanded some 45,000 men from a headquarters at Louisville, Kentucky, while Maj. Gen. Henry W. Halleck with headquarters at St. Louis, Missouri, had 91,000 under his command. These troops were generally raw, undisciplined western volunteers. Logistical matters and training facilities were undeveloped and as Halleck once wrote in disgust to his superior in Washington, "affairs here are in complete chaos."

Affairs were no better among Confederate authorities farther south. Facing Buell and Halleck were 43,000 scattered and ill-equipped Confederate troops under General Albert Sidney Johnston. Charged with defending a line which stretched for more than 500 miles from western Virginia to the border of Kansas, Johnston's forces mostly lay east of the Mississippi River. They occupied a system of forts and camps from Cumberland Gap in western Virginia through Bowling Green, Kentucky, to Columbus, Kentucky, on the Mississippi. Rivers and railroads provided Johnston with most of his interior lines of communications since most of the roads were virtually impassable in winter. To protect a lateral railroad where it crossed two rivers in Tennessee and yet respect Kentucky's neutrality, the Confederates had built Fort Henry on the Tennessee River and Fort Donelson on the Cumberland River just south of the boundary between the two states. On the other hand, hampering the Confederate build-up were southern governors whose states' rights doctrine led them to believe that defense of their respective states had higher priority than pushing forward the needed men and munitions to a Confederate commander, Johnston, at the front.

At the beginning of 1862, Halleck and Buell were supposed to be co-operating with each other but had yet to do so effectively. On his own, Buell moved in mid-January to give token response to Lincoln's desire to help the Unionists in east Tennessee. One of his subordinates succeeded in breaching the

Confederate defense line in eastern Kentucky in a local action near Mill Springs, but Buell failed to exploit the victory.

In Halleck's department, Brig. Gen. Ulysses S. Grant, at the time an inconspicuous district commander at Cairo, Illinois, had meanwhile proposed a river expedition up the Tennessee to take Fort Henry. After some hesitancy and in spite of the absence of assurance of support from Buell, Halleck approved a plan for a joint Army-Navy expedition. On January 30, 1862, he directed 15,000 men under Grant, supported by armored gunboats and river craft of the U.S. Navy under Flag Officer Andrew H. Foote, to "take and hold Fort Henry." The actions of subordinate commanders were at last prodding the Union war machine to move.

Capture of Forts Henry and Donelson

Grant landed his troops below Fort Henry and together with Foote's naval force moved against the Confederate position on February 6. At the Federals' approach the Confederate commander sent most of his men to Fort Donelson. Muddy roads delayed the Union Army's advance, but Foote's seven gunboats plunged ahead and in a short fire fight induced the defenders of Fort Henry to surrender. Indeed, the Confederates had lowered their colors before Grant's infantry could reach the action. The Tennessee River now lay open to Foote's gunboats all the way to northern Alabama.

General Grant was no rhetorician. Sparing with words, he never bombarded his troops with Napoleonic manifestos as McClellan did. After the capture of Fort Henry he simply telegraphed the somewhat surprised Halleck: "I shall take and destroy Fort Donelson on the 8th and return to Fort Henry." But inclement weather delayed the Federal movement until February 12. Then river craft carried some of the troops by water around to Fort Donelson. The rest of the troops moved overland under sunny skies and unseasonably mild temperatures. The springlike weather caused the youthful soldiers to litter the roadside with overcoats, blankets, and tents.

But winter once more descended upon Grant's forces (soon to swell to nearly 27,000 men) as they invested Fort Donelson. Johnston, sure that the fall of this fort would jeopardize his entrenched camp at Bowling Green, hurried three generals and 12,000 reinforcements to Fort Donelson and then retired toward Nashville with 14,000 men. Even without reinforcements, Fort Donelson was a strong position. The main earthwork stood 100 feet above the river and with its outlying system of rifle pits embraced an area of 100 acres. The whole Confederate position occupied less than a square mile. Grant and Foote first attempted to reduce it by naval bombardment, which had succeeded at Fort

Henry. But this time the Confederate defenders handled the gunboats so roughly that they withdrew. Grant then prepared for a long siege, although the bitter cold weather and lack of assault training among his troops caused him to have some reservations.

The Confederates, sensing they were caught in a trap, essayed a sortie on February 15, and swept one of Grant's divisions off the field. But divided Confederate command, not lack of determination or valor on the part of the fighting men, led to ultimate defeat of the attack. The three Confederate commanders could not agree upon the next move, and at a critical moment, Grant ordered counterattacks all along the line. By the end of the day Union troops had captured a portion of the Confederate outer works. Now surrounded by Union forces that outnumbered them almost two to one, the Confederate leaders decided they were in a hopeless situation. In a scene resembling *opéra bouffe,* Brig. Gen. John B. Floyd, who had been Buchanan's Secretary of War and feared execution as a traitor, passed the command to Brig. Gen. Gideon Pillow. Pillow passed the command immediately to Brig. Gen. Simon B. Buckner, who asked Grant, an old friend, for terms. Soon afterward Grant sent his famous message: "No terms except unconditional and immediate surrender can be accepted. I propose to move immediately upon your works."

Some Confederates escaped with Floyd and Pillow, and Col. Nathan Bedford Forrest led his cavalry through frozen backwaters to safety. But the bulk of the garrison "from 12,000 to 15,000 prisoners . . . also 20,000 stand of arms, 48 pieces of artillery, 17 heavy guns, from 2,000 to 4,000 horses, and large quantities of commissary stores" fell into Federal hands.

Poor leadership, violation of the principle of unity of command, and too strict adherence to position defense had cost the South the key to the gateway of the Confederacy in the west. The loss of the two forts dealt the Confederacy a blow from which it never fully recovered. Johnston had to abandon Kentucky and most of middle and west Tennessee. The vital industrial and transportation center of Nashville soon fell to Buell's advancing army. Foreign governments took special notice of the defeats. For the North the victories were its first good news of the war. They set the strategic pattern for further advance into the Confederacy. In Grant the people had a new hero and he was quickly dubbed "Unconditional Surrender" Grant.

Confederate Counterattack at Shiloh

As department commander, Halleck naturally received much credit for these victories. President Lincoln decided to unify command of all the western

THE CIVIL WAR, 1862

armies, and on March 11 Halleck received the command. Halleck, nicknamed "Old Brains," was well known as a master of the theory and literature of war. Lincoln's decision gave him jurisdiction over four armies—Buell's Army of the Ohio, Grant's Army of the Tennessee, Maj. Gen. Samuel Curtis' Army of the Southwest in Missouri and Arkansas, and Maj. Gen. John Pope's Army of the Mississippi. While Pope, in co-operation with Foote's naval forces, successfully attacked New Madrid and Island No. 10 on the Mississippi River, Halleck decided to concentrate Grant's and Buell's armies and move against Johnston at Corinth in northern Mississippi. Grant and Buell were to meet at Shiloh (Pittsburgh Landing) near Savannah on the Tennessee River. Well aware of the Federal movements, Johnston decided to attack Grant before Buell could join him. (*Map 24*) The Confederate army, 40,000 strong, marched out of Corinth on the afternoon of April 3. Muddy roads and faulty staff co-ordination made a shambles of Confederate march discipline. Mixed up commands, artillery and wagons bogged down in the mud, and green troops who insisted upon shooting their rifles at every passing rabbit threatened to abort the whole expedition. Not until late in the afternoon of April 5 did Johnston's army complete the 22-mile march to its attack point. Then the Confederate leader postponed his attack until the next morning and the delay proved costly.

Grant's forces were encamped in a rather loose battle line and apparently anticipated no attack. The position at Shiloh itself was not good, for the army was pocketed by the river at its back and a creek on each flank. Because the army was on an offensive mission, it had not entrenched. Grant has often been criticized for this omission, but entrenchment was not common at that stage of the war. The fact that the principle of security was disregarded is inescapable. Very little patrolling had been carried out, and the Federals were unaware that a Confederate army of 40,000 men was spending the night of April 5 just two miles away. The victories at Forts Henry and Donelson had apparently produced overconfidence in Grant's army, which like Johnston's, was only partly trained. Even Grant reflected this feeling, for he had established his headquarters at Savannah, nine miles downstream.

Johnston's men burst out of the woods early on April 6, so early that Union soldiers turned out into their company streets from their tents to fight. Some fled to the safety of the landing, but most of the regiments fought stubbornly and yielded ground slowly. One particular knot of Federals rallied along an old sunken road, named the Hornet's Nest by Confederates because of the stinging shot and shell they had to face there. Although this obstacle disrupted Johnston's timetable of attack, by afternoon the Confederates had attained local success elsewhere all along the line. At the same time the melee of battle badly

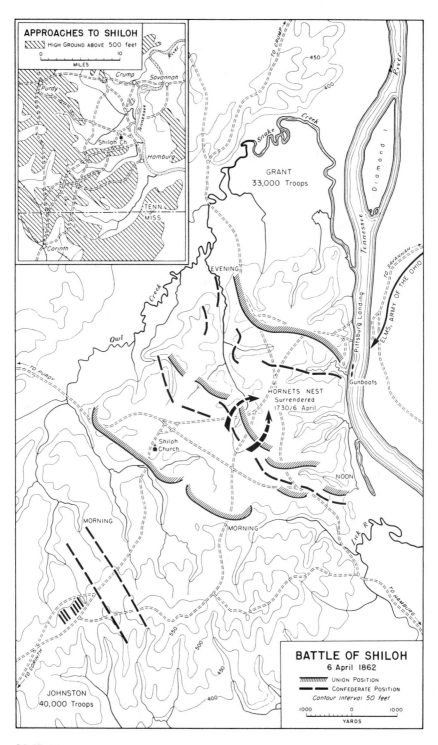

APPROACHES TO SHILOH

High Ground above 500 feet

0   10
MILES

River

Crump

Savannah

Purdy

Tennessee

Shiloh Ch.

Hamburg

TENN.

MISS.

Corinth

TO CRUMP

450

400

Snake *Creek*

GRANT
33,000 Troops

Diamond

Tennessee River

EVENING

Owl *Creek*

TO SAVANNAH

ELMS, ARMY OF THE OHIO

TO PURDY

Pittsburg Landing

Gunboats

HORNETS NEST
Surrendered
1730/6 April

Shiloh
Church

NOON

Lick R.

MORNING

MORNING

550

TO HAMBURG

500

TO CORINTH

450

400

JOHNSTON
40,000 Troops

BATTLE OF SHILOH
6 April 1862

Union Position
Confederate Position
Contour Interval 50 feet

1000   0   1000
YARDS

MAP 24

disorganized the attackers. Johnston's attack formation ·had been awkward from the beginning. He had formed his three corps into one column with each corps deployed with divisions in line so that each corps stretched across the whole battlefront, one behind the other. Such a formation could be effectively controlled neither by army nor corps commanders.

Then, almost at the moment of victory, Johnston himself was mortally wounded while leading a local assault. General Beauregard, Johnston's successor, suspended the attack for the day and attempted to straighten out and reorganize his command. As the day ended, Grant's sixth division, which had lost its way while marching to the battlefield, reached Shiloh along with advance elements of Buell's army.

Next morning Grant counterattacked to regain the lost ground and the Confederates withdrew to Corinth. There was no pursuit. Shiloh was the bloodiest battle fought in North America up to that time. Of 63,000 Federals, 13,000 were casualties. The Confederates lost 11,000. Fortunate indeed for the Federals had been Lincoln's decision to unify the command under Halleck, for this act had guaranteed Buell's presence and prevented Johnston from defeating the Union armies separately. Grant came in for much denunciation for being surprised, but President Lincoln loyally sustained him. "I can't spare this man; he fights."

Halleck was a master of military maxims, but he had failed to concentrate all his forces immediately for a final defeat of Beauregard. As it was, Pope and Foote took Island No. 10 in April, opening the Mississippi as far as Memphis. Halleck, taking personal command of Grant's and Buell's forces, then ponderously advanced toward Corinth. Remembering Shiloh, he proceeded cautiously, and it was May 30 before he reached his objective. Beauregard had already evacuated the town. Meanwhile Capt. David G. Farragut with a naval force and Maj. Gen. Benjamin F. Butler's land units cracked the gulf coast fortifications of the Mississippi and captured New Orleans. By mid-1862, only strongholds at Vicksburg and Port Hudson on the Mississippi blocked complete Federal control of that vital river.

Perryville to Stones River

Despite these early setbacks the Confederate armies in the west were still full of fight. As Federal forces advanced deeper into the Confederacy it became increasingly difficult for them to protect the long lines of river, rail, and road supply and communications. Guerrilla and cavalry operations by colorful

Confederate "wizards of the saddle" like John Hunt Morgan, Joseph Wheeler, and Nathan Bedford Forrest followed Forrest's adage of "Get 'em skeered, and then keep the skeer on 'em." Such tactics completely disrupted the timetable of Federal offensives.

By summer and fall rejuvenated Confederate forces under General Braxton Bragg, Lt. Gen. Edmund Kirby Smith, and Maj. Gen. Earl Van Dorn were ready to seize the initiative. Never again was the South so close to victory, nor did it ever again hold the initiative in every theater of the war.

Over-all Confederate strategy called for a three-pronged advance from the Mississippi River all the way to Virginia. Twin columns under Bragg and Smith were to bear the brunt of the western offensive by advancing from Chattanooga into east Tennessee, then northward into Kentucky. They were to be supported by Van Dorn, who would move north from Mississippi with the intention of driving Grant's forces out of west Tennessee. The western columns of the Confederacy were then to unite somewhere in Kentucky.

At the same time, these movements were to be co-ordinated with the planned invasion of Maryland, east of the Appalachians, by General Robert E. Lee's Army of Northern Virginia. Much depended upon speed, good co-ordination of effort and communications, and attempts to woo Kentucky and Maryland into the arms of the Confederacy. Victory could stimulate peace advocates and the Copperheads in the North to bring peace. Furthermore there was always the possibility that a successful invasion might induce Great Britain and France to recognize the Confederacy and to intervene forcibly to break the blockade. This last hope was a feeble one. Emperor Napoleon III was primarily interested in advancing his Mexican schemes; he considered both recognition and intervention but would not move without British support. Britain, which pursued the policy of recognizing *de facto* governments, would undoubtedly have recognized the Confederacy eventually had it won the war. But the British Government only briefly flirted with the idea of recognition and throughout the war adhered to a policy of neutrality and respect for the Union blockade.

At first things went well for the Confederates in the west. Bragg caught Buell off guard and without fighting a battle forced Federal evacuation of northern Alabama and central Tennessee. But when Bragg entered Kentucky he became engaged in "government making" in an effort to set up a state regime which would bind Kentucky to the Confederacy. Also, the Confederate invasion was not achieving the expected results since few Kentuckians joined Bragg's forces and an attempt at conscription in east Tennessee failed completely.

Buell finally caught up with Bragg's advance at Perryville, Kentucky, on October 7. Finding the Confederates in some strength, Buell began concentrating his own scattered units. The next morning fighting began around Perryville over possession of drinking water. Brig. Gen. Philip H. Sheridan's division forced the Confederates away from one creek and dug in. The battle as a whole turned out to be a rather confused affair as Buell sought to concentrate units arriving from several different directions upon the battlefield itself. Early in the afternoon, Maj. Gen. Alexander M. McCook's Union corps arrived and began forming a line of battle. At that moment Maj. Gen. Leonidas Polk's Confederate corps attacked and drove McCook back about a mile, but Sheridan's troops held their ground. Finally a Union counterattack pushed the Confederates out of the town of Perryville. Buell himself remained at headquarters, only two and a half miles from the field, completely unaware of the extent of the engagement until it was nearly over. The rolling terrain had caused an "acoustic shadow" whereby the sounds of the conflict were completely inaudible to the Federal commander. While the battle ended in a tactical stalemate, Bragg suffered such severe casualties that he was forced to retreat. Coupled with Van Dorn's failure to bypass Federal defenses at Corinth, Mississippi, and carry out his part of the strategic plan, this setback forced the Confederates to abandon any idea of bringing Kentucky into the Confederacy.

By Christmas Bragg was back in middle Tennessee, battered but still anxious to recoup his losses by recapturing Nashville. Buell had been dilatory in pursuing Bragg after Perryville and had been replaced in command of the Army of the Ohio (now restyled the Army of the Cumberland) by Maj. Gen. William S. Rosecrans. In spite of urgent and even threatening letters from the War Department, the new commander would not move against Bragg until he had collected abundant supplies at Nashville. Then he would be independent of the railroad line from Nashville to Louisville, a line of communications continually cut by Confederate cavalry.

On December 26 Rosecrans finally marched south from Nashville. Poorly screened by Union cavalry, his three columns in turn knew little about Confederate concentrations near Murfreesboro, thirty miles southeast of the Tennessee capital. Here Bragg had taken a strong position astride Stones River on the direct route to Chattanooga and proposed to fight it out. Rosecrans moved into line opposite Bragg on the evening of December 30. Both army commanders proceeded to develop identical battle plans—each designed to envelop the opponent's right flank. Bragg's objective was to drive Rosecrans off his communications line with Nashville and pin him against the river. Rosecrans' plan had the same objective in reverse, that of pinning the Confederates against the stream. Victory would probably belong to the commander who struck first and hard.

Insufficient Federal security and Rosecrans' failure to insure that the
pivotal units in his attack plan were also properly posted to thwart Confederate
counterattacks resulted in Confederate seizure of the initiative as the battle of
Stones River opened on December 31. (*Map 25*) At dawn, Maj. Gen. William J.
Hardee's corps with large cavalry support began the drive on the Federal right.
Undeceived by their opponent's device of extra campfires to feign a longer

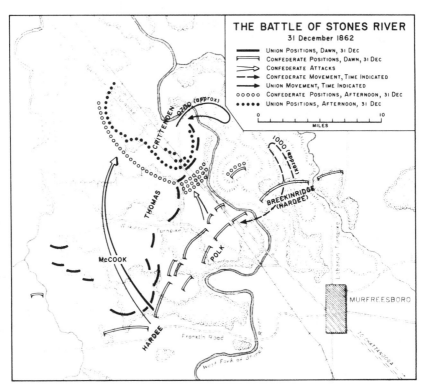

MAP 25

battle line, Confederate attacking columns simply pushed farther around the
Union flank and promptly rolled the defenders back. Applying the principles
of mass and surprise to achieve rapid success, Bragg's battle plan forced Rosecrans
to modify his own. The Union leader pulled back his left flank division, which
had jumped off to attack Maj. Gen. John C. Breckinridge's Confederate units
north of Stones River. While Sheridan's division, as at Perryville, provided
stubborn resistance to General Polk's corps in the center, Hardee's units
continued their drive, which by noon saw the Union battle line bent back
against the Nashville pike. Meanwhile the Confederate cavalry had wrought

havoc among Rosecrans' rear area elements. As was typical of many Civil War battles the attacking columns of Polk and Hardee became badly intermingled. Their men began to tire, and by afternoon repeated Confederate assaults against the constricted Union line along the Nashville pike had bogged down.

That night Rosecrans held a council of war. Some of the subordinate commanders wanted to retreat. Rosecrans and two of his corps commanders, Maj. Gen. Thomas L. Crittenden and Maj. Gen. George H. Thomas, vetoed the scheme. Brigades were then returned to their proper divisions, stragglers rounded up, and various other adjustments made in the Federal position. New Year's Day, 1863, dawned quiet and little action occurred that day.

The sunrise of January 2 revealed Rosecrans still in position. Bragg directed Breckinridge to attack the Union left wing, once more thrown across Stones River on the north. But massed Union artillery shattered the assaults and counterattacking Federals drove Breckinridge's men back to their line of departure. The armies remained stationary on January 3 but Bragg finally withdrew from the battlefield that evening, permitting victory to slip from his grasp. Tactically a draw, Stones River so badly mangled the Army of the Cumberland that it would be immobilized for six months. Yet, more than most other battles of the war, Stones River was a conflict between the wills of the opposing army leaders. Rosecrans, supported by Thomas and others, would not admit himself beaten and in the end won a victory of sorts.

The great Confederate counteroffensives of 1862 had failed in the west, yet Chattanooga, the key to east Tennessee and Georgia, remained in southern hands. Farther west Federal forces had penetrated only slightly into northern Mississippi. The war was simply on dead center in the west at the end of the year.

The Army of the Potomac Moves South

As the year 1862 began in the eastern theater, plans prepared in Washington were aimed at the capture of Richmond rather than destruction of the army commanded by Joseph E. Johnston, now a full general. Precise methods for reaching the Confederate capital differed. President Lincoln favored an overland advance which would always keep an army between the Confederates and Washington. McClellan agreed at first, then changed his views in favor of a waterborne move by the Army of the Potomac to Urbana on the Rappahannock. From there he could drive to Richmond before Johnston could retire from the Manassas area to intercept him. The Washington fortifications, an elaborate system of earthen forts and battery emplacements then in advanced stages of construction, would adequately protect the capital while the field army was away. Johnston, however, rendered this plan obsolete; he withdrew from Manassas to Fredericksburg, halfway between the two capitals and astride McClellan's prospective route of advance. Early in March McClellan moved his army out to the deserted Confederate camps around Manassas to give his troops some field experience. While he was in the field President Lincoln relieved him as General in Chief, doubtless on the ground that he could not command one army in the field and at the same time supervise the operations of all the armies of the United States. Lincoln did not appoint a successor. For a time he and Stanton took over personal direction of the Army, with the advice of a newly constituted Army board consisting of the elderly Maj. Gen. Ethan A. Hitchcock and the chiefs of the War Department bureaus.

When events overtook the Urbana scheme, McClellan began to advocate a seaborne move to Fort Monroe, Virginia (at the tip of the peninsula formed by the York and James Rivers), to be followed by an overland advance up the peninsula. If the troops moved fast, he maintained, they could cover the seventy-five miles to Richmond before Johnston could concentrate his forces to stop them. This plan had promise, for it utilized Federal control of the seas and a useful base of operations at Fort Monroe and there were fewer rivers to cross than by the overland route. Successful neutralization of the *Merrimac* by the *Monitor* on March 9 had eliminated any naval threat to supply and communications lines, but the absence of good roads and the difficult terrain of the peninsula offered drawbacks to the plan. Lincoln approved it, providing McClellan would leave behind the number of men that his corps commanders considered adequate to insure the safety of Washington. McClellan gave the President his assurances, but failed to take Lincoln into his confidence by pointing out that he considered the Federal troops in the Shenandoah Valley to be covering Washington. In listing the forces he had left behind, he counted some men twice and included several units in Pennsylvania not under his command.

Embarkation began in mid-March, and by April 4 advance elements had moved out of Fort Monroe against Yorktown. The day before, however, the commander of the Washington defenses reported that he had insufficient forces to protect the city. In addition, Stonewall Jackson had become active in the Shenandoah Valley. Lincoln thereupon told Stanton to detain one of the two corps which were awaiting embarkation at Alexandria. Stanton held back McDowell's corps, numbering 30,000 men, seriously affecting McClellan's plans.

Jackson's Valley Campaign

While a small Confederate garrison at Yorktown made ready to delay McClellan, Johnston hurried his army to the peninsula. In Richmond Confederate authorities had determined on a spectacularly bold diversion. Robert E. Lee, who had rapidly moved to the rank of general, had assumed the position of military adviser to Jefferson Davis on March 13. Charged with the conduct of operations of the Confederate armies under Davis' direction, Lee saw that any threat to Washington would cause progressive weakening of McClellan's advance against Richmond. He therefore ordered Jackson to begin a rapid campaign in the Shenandoah Valley close to the northern capital. The equivalent of three Federal divisions was sent to the valley to destroy Jackson. Lincoln and Stanton, using the telegraph and what military knowledge they had acquired, devised plans to bottle Jackson up and destroy him. But Federal forces in the valley were not under a locally unified command. They moved too slowly; one force did not obey orders strictly; and directives from Washington often neglected to take time, distance, or logistics into account. Also, in Stonewall Jackson, the Union troops were contending against one of the most outstanding field commanders America has ever produced. Jackson's philosophy of war was:

Always mystify, mislead, and surprise the enemy, if possible; and when you strike and overcome him, never give up the pursuit as long as your men have strength to follow; for an army routed, if hotly pursued, becomes panic-stricken and can then be destroyed by half their number.

By mobility and maneuver, achieved by rapid marches, surprise, deception, and hard fighting, Jackson neutralized and defeated in detail Federal forces three times larger than his own. In a classic campaign between March 23 and June 9, 1862, he fought six battles: Kernstown, McDowell, Front Royal, Winchester, Cross Keys, and Port Republic. All but Kernstown were victories. His presence alone in the Shenandoah immobilized McDowell's corps by keeping these reinforcements from joining McClellan before Richmond.

The Peninsular Campaign: Fair Oaks

When McClellan reached the peninsula in early April he found a force of ten to fifteen thousand Confederates under Maj. Gen. John B. Magruder barring his path to Richmond. Magruder, a student of drama and master of deception, so dazzled him that McClellan, instead of brushing the Confederates aside, spent a month in a siege of Yorktown. But Johnston, who wanted to fight the decisive action closer to Richmond, decided to withdraw slowly up the peninsula. At Williamsburg, on May 5, McClellan's advance elements made contact with the Confederate rear guard under Maj. Gen. James Longstreet, who successfully delayed the Federal advance. McClellan then pursued in leisurely fashion. By May 25, two corps of the Army of the Potomac had turned southwest toward Richmond and crossed the sluggish Chickahominy River.

The remaining three corps were on the north side of the stream with the expectation of making contact with McDowell, who would come down from Fredericksburg. Men of the two corps south of the river could see the spires of the Confederate capital, but Johnston's army was in front of them. (*Map 26*)

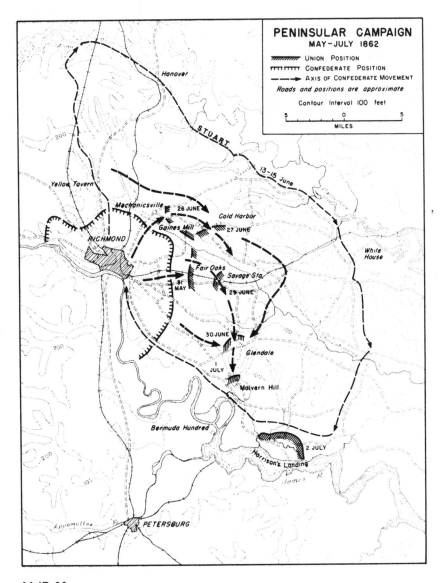

MAP 26

Drenching rains on May 30 raised the Chickahominy to flood stage and seriously divided McClellan's army. Johnston decided to grasp this chance to defeat the Federals in detail. He struck on May 31 near Fair Oaks. His plans called for his whole force to concentrate against the isolated corps south of the river, but his staff and subordinate commanders were not up to the task of executing them. Assaulting columns became confused, and attacks were delivered piecemeal. The Federals, after some initial reverses, held their ground and bloodily repulsed the Confederates.

When Johnston suffered a severe wound at Fair Oaks, President Davis replaced him with General Lee. Lee for his part had no intention of defending Richmond passively. The city's fortifications would enable him to protect Richmond with a relatively small force while he used the main body of his army offensively in an attempt to cut off and destroy the Army of the Potomac. He ordered Jackson back from the Shenandoah Valley with all possible speed.

The Seven Days' Battles

McClellan had planned to utilize his superior artillery to break through the Richmond defenses, but Lee struck the Federal Army before it could resume the advance. Lee's dispositions for the Battle of Mechanicsville on June 26 present a good illustration of the principles of mass and economy of force. On the north side of the Chickahominy, he concentrated 65,000 men to oppose Brig. Gen. Fitz-John Porter's V Corps of 30,000. Only 25,000 were left before Richmond to contain the remainder of the Union Army. When Lee attacked, the timing and co-ordination were off; Jackson of all people was slow and the V Corps defended stoutly during the day. McClellan thereupon withdrew the V Corps southeast to a stronger position at Gaines' Mill. Porter's men constructed light barricades and made ready. Lee massed 57,000 men and assaulted 34,000 Federals on June 27. The fighting was severe but numbers told, and the Federal line broke. Darkness fell before Lee could exploit his advantage, and McClellan took the opportunity to regroup Porter's men with the main army south of the Chickahominy.

At this point McClellan yielded the initiative to Lee. With his line of communications cut to White House—his supply base on the York River—and with the James River open to the U.S. Navy, the Union commander decided to shift his base to Harrison's Landing on the south side of the peninsula. His rear areas had been particularly shaky since Confederate cavalry under Brig. Gen. J. E. B. Stuart had ridden completely around the Federal Army in a daring raid in early June. The intricate retreat to the James, which involved

90,000 men, the artillery train, 3,100 wagons, and 2,500 head of cattle, began on the night of June 27 and was accomplished by using two roads. Lee tried to hinder the movement but was held off by Federal rear guards at Savage Station on June 29 and at Frayser's Farm (Glendale) on the last day of the month.

By the first day of July McClellan had concentrated the Army of the Potomac on a commanding plateau at Malvern Hill, northwest of Harrison's Landing. The location was strong, with clear fields of fire to the front and the flanks secured by streams. Massed artillery could sweep all approaches, and gunboats on the river were ready to provide fire support. The Confederates would have to attack by passing through broken and wooded terrain, traversing swampy ground, and ascending the hill. At first Lee felt McClellan's position was too strong to assault. Then, at 3:00 p.m. on July 1, when a shifting of Federal troops deceived him into thinking there was a general withdrawal, he changed his mind and attacked. Again staff work and control were poor. The assaults, which were all frontal, were delivered piecemeal by only part of the army against Union artillery, massed hub to hub, and supporting infantry. The Confederate formations were shattered because Lee failed to carry out the principle of mass. On the following day, the Army of the Potomac fell back to Harrison's Landing and dug in. After reconnoitering McClellan's position, Lee ordered his exhausted men back to the Richmond lines for rest and reorganization.

The Peninsular Campaign cost the Federal Army some 15,849 men killed, wounded, and missing. The Confederates, who had done most of the attacking, lost 20,614. Improvement in the training and discipline of the two armies since the disorganized fight at Bull Run was notable. Also significant was the fact that higher commanders had not yet thoroughly mastered their jobs. Except in McClellan's defensive action at Malvern Hill, which was largely conducted by his corps commanders, neither side had been able to bring an entire army into co-ordinated action.

Second Manassas

Failure of the Union forces to take Richmond quickly forced President Lincoln to abandon the idea of exercising command over the Union armies in person. On July 11, 1862, he selected as new General in Chief Henry W. Halleck, who had won acclaim for the victories in the west. The President did not at once appoint a successor in the west, which was to suffer from divided command for a time. Lincoln wanted Halleck to direct the various Federal armies in close concert to take advantage of the North's superior strength. If all Federal armies co-ordinated their efforts, Lincoln reasoned, they could strike where the Confederacy was weak or force it to strengthen one army at the expense of another, and eventually they could wear the Confederacy down, destroy the various armies, and win the war.

Halleck turned out to be a disappointment. He never attempted to exercise field command or assume responsibility for strategic direction of the armies. But, acting more as military adviser to the President, he performed a valuable function by serving as a channel of communication between the Chief Executive and the field commanders. He adeptly translated the President's ideas into terms the generals could comprehend, and expressed the soldier's views in language that Mr. Lincoln could understand.

Shortly before Halleck's appointment, Lincoln also decided to consolidate the various Union forces in the Shenandoah Valley and other parts of western Virginia—some 45,000 men—under the victor at Island No. 10, Maj. Gen. John Pope. Pope immediately disenchanted his new command by pointing out that in the west the Federal armies were used to seeing the backs of their enemies. Pope's so-called Army of Virginia was ordered to divert pressure from McClellan on the peninsula. But Jackson had left the valley and Federal forces were scattered. On August 3, Halleck ordered McClellan to withdraw by water from the peninsula to Aquia Creek on the Potomac and to effect a speedy junction at Fredericksburg with Pope. Meanwhile Pope began posting the Army of Virginia along the Orange and Alexandria Railroad to the west of Fredericksburg.

Lee knew that his Army of Northern Virginia was in a dangerous position between Pope and McClellan, especially if the two were to unite. On July 13, he sent Jackson, with forces eventually totaling 24,000 men, to watch Pope. After an initial sparring action at Cedar Mountain on August 9, Jackson and Pope stood watching each other for nearly a week. Lee, knowing that McClellan was leaving Harrison's Landing, had departed Richmond with the remainder of the Army of Northern Virginia and joined Jackson at Gordonsville. The combined Confederate forces outnumbered Pope's, and Lee resolved to outflank and cut off the Army of Virginia before the whole of McClellan's force could be brought to bear.

A succession of captured orders enabled both Lee and Pope to learn the intentions of the other. Pope ascertained Lee's plan to trap him against the Rappahannock and withdrew to the north bank astride the railroad. Lee, learning that two corps from the Army of the Potomac would join Pope within days, acted quickly and boldly. He sent Jackson off on a wide turning movement

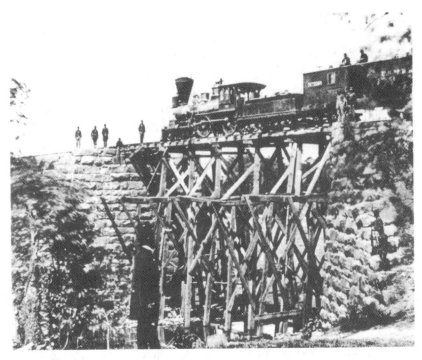

Trestle of the Orange and Alexandria Railroad *built by soldiers.*

through Thoroughfare Gap in the Bull Run Mountains around the northern flank of Pope's army and subsequently followed the same route with the divisions commanded by General Longstreet.

Pope took note of Jackson's move, but first assumed that it was pointed toward the Shenandoah Valley. Then Jackson, covering nearly sixty miles in two days, came in behind Pope at Manassas on August 26, destroyed his supply base there, and slipped away unmolested. Pope marched and counter-marched his forces for two days trying to find the elusive Confederates. At the same time the Union commander failed to take Lee's other forces into account. As a result he walked into Lee's trap on the site of the old battlefield of Manassas, or Bull Run. Pope attacked Jackson, posted behind an abandoned railroad embankment, but again the attack consisted of a series of piecemeal frontal assaults which were repulsed with heavy casualties. By then Porter's V Corps from the Army of the Potomac had reached the field and was ordered to attack Jackson's right (south) flank. By this time also, Longstreet's column had burst through Thoroughfare Gap, and deploying on Jackson's right, it blocked Porter's move.

Next day, August 30, Pope renewed his attacks against Jackson, whom he thought to be retreating. Seizing the opportunity to catch the Federal columns in an exposed position, Lee sent Longstreet slashing along the Warrenton turnpike to catch Pope's flank in the air. The Federal army soon retired from the field and Pope led it back to Washington, fighting an enveloping Confederate force at Chantilly on the way.

Lee, by great daring and rapid movement, and by virtue of having the Confederate forces unified under his command, had successfully defeated one formidable Union army in the presence of another even larger one. Halleck, as General in Chief, had not taken the field to co-ordinate Pope and McClellan, and Pope lost the campaign despite the advantage of interior lines.

President Lincoln, desiring to use McClellan's admitted talents for training and reorganizing the battered eastern armies, had become convinced that bitter personal feelings between McClellan and Pope prevented them from working effectively in the same theater. On September 5, Halleck, upon the President's order, dissolved the Army of Virginia and assigned its units to the Army of the Potomac. He sent Pope to a command in Minnesota. The Union authorities expected that McClellan would be able to devote several months to training and reorganization, but Lee dashed these hopes.

Lee Invades Maryland

Up to this point the Confederates in the east had been following defensive strategy, though tactically they frequently assumed the offensive. But Davis and Lee, for a complicated set of political and military reasons, determined to take the offensive and invade the North in co-ordination with Bragg's drive into Kentucky. Militarily, in the east, an invasion of Maryland would give Lee a chance to defeat or destroy the Army of the Potomac, uncovering such cities as Washington, Baltimore, and Philadelphia, and to cut Federal communications with the states to the west.

The Army of Northern Virginia, organized into 2 infantry commands (Longstreet's consisting of 5 divisions, and Jackson's of 4 divisions) plus Stuart's 3 brigades of cavalry, and the reserve artillery, numbered 55,000 effectives. Lee did not rest after Manassas but crossed the Potomac and encamped near Frederick, Maryland, from which he sent Jackson to capture an isolated Federal garrison at Harpers Ferry. The remainder of Lee's army then crossed South Mountain and headed for Hagerstown, about twenty-five miles northwest of Frederick, with Stuart's cavalry screening the right flank. In the meantime

McClellan's rejuvenated Army of the Potomac, 90,000 men organized into 6 corps, marched northwest from Washington and reached Frederick on September 12.

At this time McClellan had a stroke of luck. Lee, in assigning missions to his command, had detached Maj. Gen. D. H. Hill's division from Jackson and attached it to Longstreet and had sent copies of his orders, which prescribed routes, objectives, and times of arrival, to Jackson, Longstreet, and Hill. But Jackson was not sure that Hill had received the order. He therefore made an additional copy of Lee's order and sent it to Hill. One of Hill's orders, wrapped around some cigars, was somehow left behind in an abandoned camp where it was picked up on September 13 by Union soldiers and rushed to McClellan. This windfall gave the Federal commander an unmatched opportunity to defeat Lee's scattered forces in detail if he pushed fast through the gaps. McClellan vacillated for sixteen hours. Lee, informed of the lost order, sent all available forces to hold the gaps, so that it was nightfall on the 14th before McClellan fought his way across South Mountain.

Lee retreated to Sharpsburg on Antietam Creek where he turned to fight. Pinned between Antietam Creek and the Potomac with no room for maneuver, and still outnumbered since Jackson's force had yet to return to the main body after capturing Harpers Ferry, Lee relied on the advantage of interior lines and the boldness and the fighting ability of his men.

McClellan delayed his attack until September 17, when he launched an un-co-ordinated series of assaults which drove back the Confederates in places but failed to break their line. Heavy fighting swelled across ripe fields and up through rocky glens that became known to history as the West Wood, the Cornfield, the East Wood, Bloody Lane, and Burnside's Bridge. One southerner remembered the attacking Union columns: "With flags flying and the long unfaltering lines rising and falling as they crossed the rolling fields, it looked as though nothing could stop them." But when the massed fire of field guns and small arms struck such human waves, a Union survivor recalled, it "was like a scythe running through our line."

McClellan, like too many leaders during the Civil War, could not bring himself to commit his reserve (the V Corps under Porter) at the strategic moment. Although adored by his men, as one of the veterans wrote after the war, he "never realized the metal that was in his grand Army of the Potomac." Jackson's last division arrived in time to head off the final assaults by Maj. Gen. Ambrose Burnside's corps, and at the end of the day Lee still held most of his line. Casualties were heavy. Of 70,000 Federal troops nearly 13,000 were killed, wounded, or missing, and the 40,000 or more Confederates engaged lost almost as many. Although Lee audaciously awaited new attacks on September 18, McClellan left him unmolested, and that night the Army of Northern Virginia withdrew across the Potomac.

Lincoln's Emancipation Proclamation

Antietam was tactically a draw, but the fact that Lee was forced to call off the invasion made it a strategic victory and gave President Lincoln an opportunity to strike at the Confederacy psychologically and economically by issuing the Emancipation Proclamation on September 22, 1862. Lincoln, while opposed to slavery and its extension to the western territories, was not an abolitionist. He had stated publicly that the war was being fought over union or secession, with the slavery question only incidental, and had earlier overruled several generals who were premature emancipators. But anticipating the total psychological warfare techniques of the twentieth century, he had for some time desired to free the slaves of the Confederate states in order to weaken their economies and to appeal to antislavery opinion in Europe. He had awaited the opportune moment that a Union victory would give him and decided that Antietam was suitable. Acting on his authority as Commander in Chief he issued the Proclamation which stated that all slaves in states or districts in rebellion against the United States on January 1, 1863, would be thenceforward and forever free. The Proclamation set no slaves free on the day it took effect. Negroes in the four slave states still in the Union were not touched, nor were the slaves in those Confederate areas that had not been subjugated by Union bayonets. It had no immediate effect behind the Confederate lines, except to cause a good deal of excitement. But thereafter, as Union forces penetrated the South, the newly freed people deserted the farms and plantations and flocked to the colors.

Negroes had served in the Revolution, the War of 1812, and other early wars, but they had been barred from the Regular Army and, under the Militia Act of 1792, from the state militia. The Civil War marks their official debut in American military forces. Recruiting of Negroes began under the local auspices of Maj. Gen. David Hunter in the Department of the South as early as April 1862. There was a certain appeal to the idea that Negroes might assure their freedom by joining in the battle for it even if they served for lower pay in segregated units under white officers. On July 17, 1862, Congress authorized recruitment of Negroes while passing the antislavery Second Confiscation Act. The Emancipation Proclamation put the matter in a new light, and on May 22, 1863, the War Department established a Bureau of Colored Troops, another innovation of the Civil War since it was an example of Federal volunteer formations without official ties to specific states (others being the various U.S. sharp-shooter regiments and the invalid Veteran Reserve Corps). By the end of the war 100,000 Negroes were enrolled as U.S. Volunteers. Many other Negroes served in state units, elsewhere in the armed forces, and as laborers for the Union Army.

Fiasco at Fredericksburg

After Antietam both armies returned to face each other in Virginia, Lee situated near Culpeper and McClellan at Warrenton. But McClellan's slowness, his failure to accomplish more at Antietam, and perhaps his rather arrogant habit of offering gratuitous political advice to his superiors, coupled with the intense anti-McClellan views of the joint Congressional Committee on the Conduct of the War, convinced Lincoln that he could retain him in command no longer. On November 7 Lincoln replaced him with Burnside, who had won distinction in operations that gained control of ports on the North Carolina coast and who had led the IX Corps at Antietam. Burnside accepted the post with reluctance.

Burnside decided to march rapidly to Fredericksburg and then advance along the railroad line to Richmond before Lee could intercept him. (*Map 27*) Such a move by the army—now 120,000 strong—would cut Lee off from his main base. Burnside's advance elements reached the north bank of the Rappa-hannock on November 17, well ahead of Lee. But a series of minor failures delayed the completion of ponton bridges, and Lee moved his army to high ground on the south side of the river before the Federal forces could cross. Lee's situation resembled McClellan's position at Malvern Hill which had proved the folly of frontal assaults against combined artillery and infantry strongpoints. But Burnside thought the sheer weight of numbers could smash through the Confederates.

To achieve greater ease of tactical control, Burnside had created three headquarters higher than corps—the Right, Center, and Left Grand Divisions under Maj. Gens. Edwin V. Sumner, Joseph Hooker, and William B. Franklin, respectively—with two corps plus cavalry assigned to each grand division. Burnside originally planned to make the main thrust by Center and Left Grand Divisions against Jackson's positions on a long, low-wooded ridge southeast of the town. The Right Grand Division would cross three ponton bridges at Fredericksburg and attack Marye's Heights, a steep eminence about one mile from the river where Longstreet's men were posted. On the morning of December 13, he weakened the attack on the left, feeling that under cover of

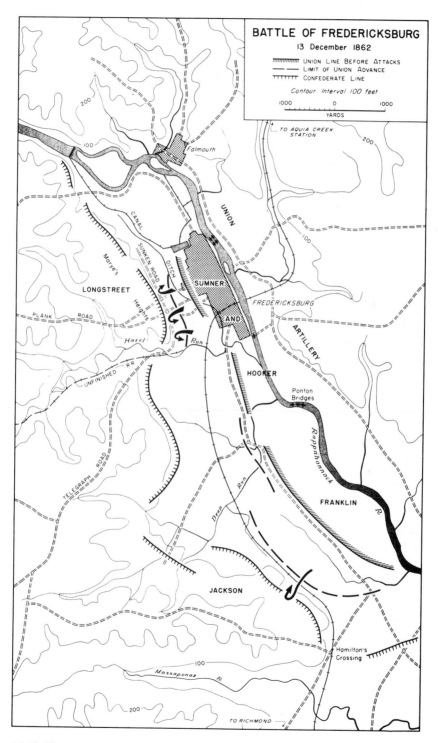

BATTLE OF FREDERICKSBURG
13 December 1862

UNION LINE BEFORE ATTACKS
LIMIT OF UNION ADVANCE
CONFEDERATE LINE

Contour Interval 100 feet

1000   0   1000
YARDS

TO AQUIA CREEK STATION

200

100

Falmouth

200

UNION

CANAL

SUNKEN ROAD

DITCH

Morye's Heights

LONGSTREET

SUMNER

100

FREDERICKSBURG

AND

PLANK ROAD

Hazel Run

ARTILLERY

UNFINISHED RR

HOOKER

Ponton Bridges

Rappahannock

TELEGRAPH ROAD

Deep Run

FRANKLIN

R.

JACKSON

Hamilton's Crossing

100

Massaponax R.

200

TO RICHMOND

MAP 27

147 heavy siege and field guns on the heights on the Union side of the river much could be achieved by a better-balanced attack along the whole line.

Burnside's engineers had begun laying the bridges as early as December 11. But harassment from Confederate sharpshooters complicated the operation, and it was not until the next day that all the assault units were over the river. After an artillery duel on the morning of the 13th, fog lifted to reveal dense Union columns moving forward to the attack. Part of the Left Grand Division, finding a weakness in Jackson's line, drove in to seize the ridge, but as Burnside had weakened this part of the assault the Federals were not able to hold against Confederate counterattacks. On the right, the troops had to cross a mile of open ground to reach Marye's Heights, traverse a drainage canal, and face a fusillade of fire from the infamous sunken road and stone wall behind which Longstreet had placed four ranks of riflemen. In a series of assaults the Union soldiers pushed to the stone wall but no farther. As a demonstration of valor the effort was exemplary; as a demonstration of tactical skill it was tragic. Lee, observing the shattered attackers, commented: "It is well that war is so terrible—we should grow too fond of it."

The Army of the Potomac lost 12,000 men at Fredericksburg while the Army of Northern Virginia suffered only 5,300 casualties. Burnside planned to renew the attack on the following day and Jackson, whose enthusiasm in battle sometimes approached the point of frenzy, suggested that the Confederates strip off their clothes for better identification and strike the Army of the Potomac in a night attack. But Lee knew of Burnside's plans from a captured order and vetoed the scheme. When the Federal corps commanders talked Burnside out of renewing the attack, both armies settled into winter quarters facing each other across the Rappahannock. Fredericksburg, a disastrous defeat, was otherwise noteworthy for the U.S. Army in that the telegraph first saw extensive battlefield use, linking headquarters with forward batteries during the action—a forerunner of twentieth century battlefield communications.

West of the Mississippi

If the major fighting of the Civil War occurred in the "older" populated sections of the United States, the youthful area of the American frontier across the Mississippi saw its share of action also. Missouri and Kansas, and indeed the distant New Mexico Territory (all areas involved in the root causes for the conflict), were touched by the Civil War.

The Southwest was a particularly rich plum, for as one Confederate commander observed: "The vast mineral resources of Arizona, in addition to its affording an outlet to the Pacific, makes its acquisition a matter of some importance to our Govt." Also it was assumed that Indians and the Mormons in Utah would readily accept allegiance to almost any government other than that in Washington.

It was with these motives in mind that early in 1862 Confederate forces moved up the Rio Grande valley and proceeded to establish that part of New Mexico Territory north of the 34th parallel as the Confederate territory of Arizona. Under Brig. Gen. Henry H. Sibley, inventor of a famous tent bearing his name, the Confederates successfully swept all the way to Santa Fe, capital of New Mexico, bypassing several Union garrisons on the way. But Sibley was dangerously overextended, and Federal troops, reinforced by Colorado volunteers, surprised the advancing Confederates in Apache Canyon on March 26 and 28, as they sought to capture the largest Union garrison in the territory at Fort Union.

One of the bypassed Federal columns under Col. Edward R. S. Canby from Fort Craig meanwhile joined the Fort Union troops against the Confederates. Unable to capture the Union posts, unable to resupply his forces, and learning of yet a third Federal column converging on him from California, Sibley began a determined retreat down the Rio Grande valley. By May he was back in Texas and the Confederate invasion of New Mexico was ended. The fighting, on a small scale by eastern standards, provided valuable training for Federal troops involved later in Indian wars in this area. Indeed, while the Confederate dream of a new territory and an outlet to the Pacific was shattered by 1862, Indian leaders in the mountain territories saw an opportunity to reconquer lost land while the white men were otherwise preoccupied. In 1863 and 1864 both Federal and Confederate troops in the southwest were kept busy fighting hostile tribes. (*Map 28*)

In Missouri and Arkansas, fighting had erupted on a large scale by the early spring of 1862. Federal authorities had retained a precarious hold over Missouri when Maj. Gen. Samuel R. Curtis with 11,000 men chased disorganized Confederates back into Arkansas. But under General Van Dorn and Maj. Gen. Sterling Price, the Confederates regrouped and embarked upon a counteroffensive which only ended at Pea Ridge on March 7 and 8. Here Van Dorn executed a double envelopment as half his army stole behind Pea Ridge, marched around three-fourths of Curtis' force, and struck Curtis' left rear near Elkhorn Tavern while the other half attacked his right rear. But in so doing the Confederates uncovered their own line of communications and Curtis' troops turned around and fought off the attacks from the rear. After initial success, Van Dorn and Price were

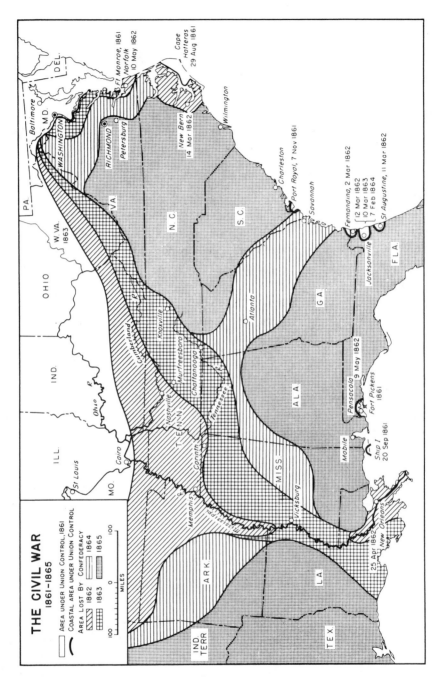

THE CIVIL WAR
1861–1865

Area under Union Control, 1861

Coastal area under Union Control

Area Lost By Confederacy
1862   1864
1863   1865

MILES
100   0   100

PA

DEL.

MD.
Baltimore
WASHINGTON

Ft. Monroe, 1861
Norfolk
10 May 1862

Cape Hatteras
29 Aug 1861

RICHMOND
Petersburg

New Bern
14 Mar 1862

Wilmington

VA.

W. VA.
1863

OHIO

IND.

ILL.

Ohio

St. Louis

MO.

Cairo

N C

S C

Charleston

Port Royal, 7 Nov 1861

Savannah

Fernandina, 2 Mar 1862
12 Mar 1862
10 Mar 1863
7 Feb 1864

St. Augustine, 11 Mar 1862

Cumberland

Knoxville

Nashville

Murfreesboro

Chattanooga

Tennessee

T E N N.

Corinth

Memphis

Mississippi

Vicksburg

ARK.

IND.
TERR.

TEX.

L A

New Orleans

25 Apr 1862

M I S S

Mobile

A L A

Pensacola 9 May 1862

Fort Pickens
1861

Ship I
20 Sep 1861

G A

Atlanta

Jacksonville

F L A

MAP 28

unable to continue the contest and withdrew. For three more years guerrilla warfare would ravage Missouri but the Union grip on the state was secure.

The year 1862, which began with impressive Union victories in the west, ended in bitter frustration in the east. Ten full-scale and costly battles had been fought, but no decisive victory had yet been scored by the forces of the Union. The Federals had broken the great Confederate counteroffensives in the fall only to see their hopes fade with the advent of winter. Apparently the Union war machine had lost its earlier momentum.

CHAPTER 11

The Civil War, 1863

At the beginning of 1863 the Confederacy seemed to have a fair chance of ultimate success on the battlefield. But during this year three great campaigns would take place that would shape the outcome of the war in favor of the North. One would see the final solution to the control of the Mississippi River. A second, concurrent with the first, would break the back of any Confederate hopes for success by invasion of the North and recognition abroad. The third, slow and uncertain in its first phases, would result eventually in Union control of the strategic gateway to the South Atlantic region of the Confederacy—the last great stronghold of secession and the area in which the internecine conflict would come of age as modern total war.

Confusion Over Clearing the Mississippi

When Halleck went east in September 1862 to become General in Chief, his splendid army was divided between Grant and Buell. Grant, with over 60,000 men, remained in western Tennessee guarding communication lines. Buell's army of 56,000, after containing Bragg's invasion of Kentucky, had been taken over by Rosecrans, whose hard-won victory at Murfreesboro at the end of 1862 nevertheless immobilized the Army of the Cumberland for nearly half a year. To the west, only the posts at Vicksburg and Port Hudson prevented the Union from controlling the entire length of the Mississippi and splitting the Confederacy in two. Naval expeditions, under Capt. David G. Farragut, supported by the army, tried to seize Vicksburg in May and again in July 1862, but the Confederates easily repulsed the attempts. In the autumn Grant pressed Halleck to let him get on with the campaign down the Mississippi and finally received the response: "Fight the enemy where you please." But while Halleck and Grant were planning to move against Vicksburg by water and land, Lincoln and Stanton also outlined a similar move, but without consulting the military leaders.

The Chief Executive had long seen the importance of controlling the Mississippi, and in the fall of 1862 he and the Secretary of War prepared plans for a simultaneous advance northward from New Orleans and southward from Tennessee. Somewhat vague orders were drawn up giving command of the northbound expedition to Maj. Gen. Nathaniel Banks, who had replaced Butler as commander of the Department of the Gulf. Command of the southbound expedition was to go to Maj. Gen. John A. McClernand. Both officers were relatively untried, unstable, volunteer officers and politicians who often dabbled in intrigue in order to gain favors. Further, McClernand was to operate within Grant's department but independently of him. When Halleck found out about the Lincoln-Stanton plan, he persuaded the President to put Grant in command of the southbound expedition and to make McClernand one of his subordinates.

Grant's Campaign Against Vicksburg

Grant first tried a combined land and water expedition against Vicksburg in December 1862–January 1863. He sent Maj. Gen. William T. Sherman down river from Memphis, but the Confederates under Van Dorn and Forrest raided and cut the 200-mile-long line of communications. Sherman himself bogged down before Vicksburg, and Grant, perhaps also wishing to keep close rein on McClernand, who ranked Sherman, then determined on a river expedition which he would lead in person. Late in January Grant arrived before Vicksburg. He had upwards of 45,000 men, organized into three corps, the XIII Corps under McClernand, the XV Corps under Sherman, and Maj. Gen. James B. McPherson's XVII Corps. During the ensuing campaign Grant received two more corps as reinforcements to bring his total strength to 75,000 men.

Vicksburg had almost a perfect location for defense. (*Map 29*) At that point on the river, bluffs rose as high as 250 feet above the water and extended for about 100 miles from north to south. North of Vicksburg lay the Yazoo River and its delta, a gloomy stretch of watery, swampy bottom land extending 175 miles from north to south, 60 miles from east to west. The ground immediately south of Vicksburg was almost as swampy and impassable. The Confederates had fortified the bluffs from Haynes' Bluff on the Yazoo, some 10 miles above Vicksburg, to Grand Gulf at the mouth of the Big Black River about 40 miles below. Vicksburg could not be assaulted from the river, and sailing past it was extremely hazardous. The river formed a great U here, and Vicksburg's guns threatened any craft that tried to run by. For the Union troops to attack successfully, they would have to get to the high, dry ground east of town. This would put them in Confederate territory between two enemy forces. Lt. Gen. John C. Pemberton commanded some 30,000 men in Vicksburg, while the Confederate area commander, General Joseph E. Johnston (now recovered from his wound at Fair Oaks), concentrated the other scattered Confederate forces in Mississippi at Jackson, the state capital, 40 miles east of Vicksburg.

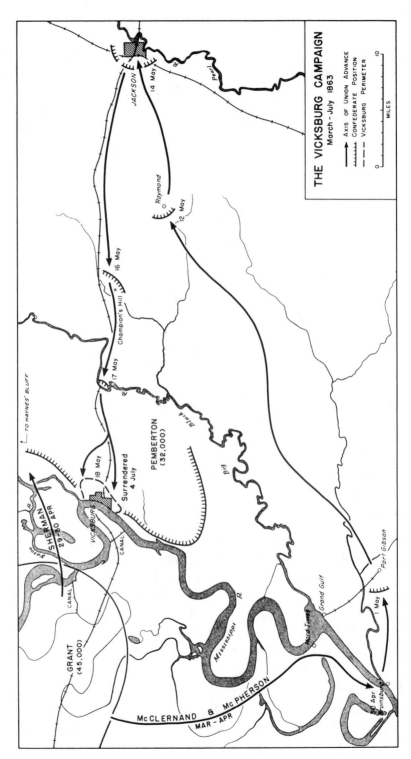

THE VICKSBURG CAMPAIGN
March – July 1863

Axis of Union Advance
Confederate Position
Vicksburg Perimeter

MILES

MAP 29

During late winter and early spring, with the rains falling, the streams high, and the roads at their wettest and muddiest, overland movement was impossible. Primarily to placate discontented politicians and a critical press, Grant made four attempts to reach high ground east of Vicksburg. All four were unsuccessful, foiled either by Confederate resistance or by natural obstacles. One of the more spectacular efforts was digging canals. These projects had as their objective the clearing of an approach by which troops could sail to a point near the high ground without being fired on by Vicksburg's guns, and all failed. That Grant kept on trying in the face of such discouragement is a tribute to his dogged persistence, and that Lincoln supported him is a tribute to his confidence in the general. The trouble was that Grant had been on the river for two months, and by early spring, Vicksburg was no nearer falling than when he came.

On April 4 in a letter to Halleck, Grant divulged his latest plan to capture Vicksburg. Working closely with the local naval commander, Flag Officer David D. Porter, Grant evolved a stroke of great boldness. He decided to use part of his force above Vicksburg to divert the Confederates while the main body marched southward on the west side of the Mississippi, crossed to the east bank, and with only five days' rations struck inland to live off a hostile country without a line of supply or retreat. As he told Sherman, the Union troops would carry "what rations of hard bread, coffee, and salt we can and make the country furnish the balance." Porter's gunboats and other craft, which up to now were on the river north of Vicksburg, were to run past the batteries during darkness and then ferry the troops over the river. Sherman thought the campaign too risky, but the events of the next two months were to prove him wrong.

While Sherman demonstrated near Vicksburg in March, McClernand's and McPherson's corps started their advance south. The rains let up in April, the waters receded slightly, and overland movement became somewhat easier. On the night of April 16 Porter led his river fleet past Vicksburg, whose guns, once the move was discovered, lit up the black night with an eerie bombardment. All but one transport made it safely, and starting on April 30, Porter's craft ferried the troops eastward over the river at Bruinsburg below Grand Gulf. The final march against Vicksburg was ready to begin.

At this time the Confederates had more troops in the vicinity than Grant had but never could make proper use of them. Grant's swift move had bewildered Pemberton. Then too, just before marching downstream, Grant had ordered a brigade of cavalry to come down from the Tennessee border, riding between the parallel north-south railroad lines of the Mississippi Central and Mobile and Ohio. Led by Col. Benjamin H. Grierson, this force sliced the length of the state, cutting railroads, fighting detachments of Confederate cavalry, and finally reaching Union lines at Baton Rouge, Louisiana. Most important, for the few days that counted most, it drew Pemberton's attention away from Grant and kept the Confederate general from discerning the Union's objectives.

Once more divided counsel hampered co-ordination of Confederate strategy. Johnston had been sent west by Davis to take over-all command, an imposing task, for Pemberton's army in Mississippi and Bragg's in Tennessee were widely separated. Things were further confused by Davis' directive to Pemberton to hold Vicksburg at all costs while Johnston recognized the potential trap and ordered him to move directly against Grant. In such a situation Pemberton could do little that was right. He tried to defend too wide an area; he had not concentrated but dispersed his forces at Vicksburg, the Big Black River, and along the railroad line to Jackson, where Johnston was gathering more troops.

After Grant had captured Port Gibson on May 1, and Sherman's corps had rejoined the main force, the Union commander decided that he must defeat Johnston before turning on Vicksburg. He moved northeastward and fought his way into Raymond on May 12, a move which put him squarely between Johnston and Pemberton and in a position to cut the Confederate line of communications. Next day Sherman and McPherson marched against the city of Jackson, with McClernand following in reserve, ready to hold off Pemberton. The leading corps took Jackson on May 14 and drove its garrison eastward. While Sherman occupied the state capital to fend off Johnston, the other two corps turned west against Pemberton and Vicksburg. Pemberton tried too late to catch Grant in open country. He suffered severe defeats at Champion's Hill (May 16) and Black River Bridge (May 17) and was shut up in Vicksburg. In eighteen days' Grant's army had marched 200 miles, had won four victories, and had finally secured the high ground along the Yazoo River that had been the goal of all the winter's fruitless campaigning.

Grant assaulted the Vicksburg lines on May 18 and 22, but as Sherman noted of the attacks: "The heads of columns have been swept away as chaff from the hand on a windy day." The only recourse now was a siege. Grant settled down, and removed McClernand from command after the attack of May 22 during which the corps commander sent a misleading report, then later slighted the efforts of the other corps and publicly criticized the army commander. Grant replaced him with Maj. Gen. Edward O. C. Ord, and ordered the army to implant batteries and dig trenches around the city.

The rest was now a matter of time, as Sherman easily kept Johnston away and the Federals advanced their siegeworks toward the Confederate fortifications. Food became scarce and the troops and civilians inside Vicksburg were soon reduced to eating mules and horses. Shells pounded the city, and the Federal lines were drawn so tight that one Confederate soldier admitted that "a cat could not have crept out of Vicksburg without being discovered." The front lines were so close that the Federals threw primitive hand grenades into the Confederate works. By July 1 the Union troops had completed their approaches and were ready for another assault. But Vicksburg was starving and Pemberton asked for terms. Grant offered to parole all prisoners, and the city surrendered on Independence Day. Since Grant was out of telegraphic contact with Washington, the news reached the President via naval channels on July 7, the day before General Banks' 15,000-man army, having advanced up river from New Orleans, captured Port Hudson. The whole river was now repossessed by the Union, the Confederacy sliced in two. Once more Grant had removed an entire Confederate army from the war—40,000 men—losing only one-tenth that number in the process.

Hooker Crosses the Rappahannock

Events in the western theater in the spring and early summer of 1863 were impressive. Those in the east during the same period were fewer in number but equally dramatic. After the battle of Fredericksburg, Burnside's Army of the Potomac went into winter quarters on the north bank of the Rappahannock, while the main body of Lee's Army of Northern Virginia held Fredericksburg and guarded the railway line to Richmond. During January, Burnside's subordinates intrigued against him and went out of channels to present their grievances to Congress and the President. When Burnside heard of this development, he asked that either he or most of the subordinate general officers be removed. The President accepted the first alternative, and on January 25, 1863, replaced Burnside with Maj. Gen. Joseph Hooker. The new commander had won the sobriquet of "Fighting Joe" for his intrepid reputation as a division and corps commander. He was highly favored in Washington, but in appointing him the President took the occasion to write a fatherly letter in which he warned the general against rashness and overambition, reproached him for plotting against Burnside, and concluded by asking for victories.

Under Hooker's able administration, discipline and training improved. Morale, which had fallen after Fredericksburg, rose as Hooker regularized the furlough system and improved the flow of rations and other supplies to his front-line troops. Abolishing Burnside's grand divisions Hooker returned to the orthodox corps, of which he had seven, each numbering about 15,000 men. One of Hooker's most effective innovations was the introduction of distinctive

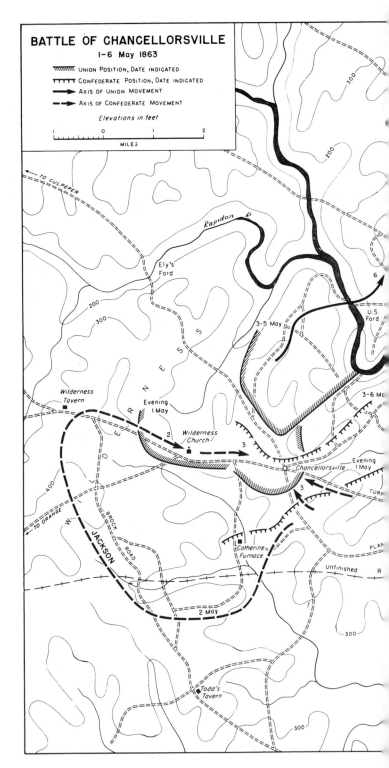

BATTLE OF CHANCELLORSVILLE
1-6 May 1863

▨▨▨▨▨	UNION POSITION, DATE INDICATED
┬┬┬┬┬	CONFEDERATE POSITION, DATE INDICATED
➤	AXIS OF UNION MOVEMENT
➤	AXIS OF CONFEDERATE MOVEMENT

Elevations in feet

```
1        0        1        2
└┴┴┴┴┴┴┴┴┴┴┴┴┴┴┴┴┘
         MILES
```

TO CULPEPER

Rapidan R.

300

200

Ely's
Ford

6

U.S.
Ford

3-5 May

200

300

W I L D E R N E S S

Wilderness
Tavern

Evening
1 May

3-6 May

2

Wilderness
Church

3

Evening
1 May

Chancellorsville

TURN

400

JACKSON

TO ORANGE

BROCK ROAD

3

Catherine
Furnace

PLAN

Unfinished   R

2 May

300

Todd's
Tavern

300

MAP 30

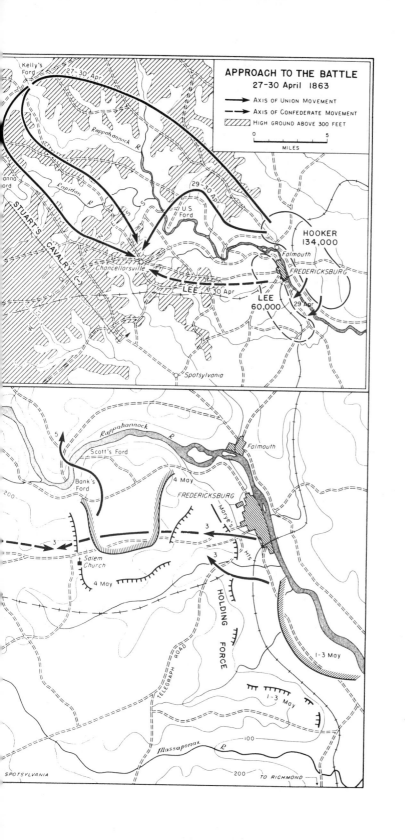

APPROACH TO THE BATTLE
27-30 April 1863

→ AXIS OF UNION MOVEMENT
⇢ AXIS OF CONFEDERATE MOVEMENT
▨ HIGH GROUND ABOVE 300 FEET

0   5
|_____|
MILES

Kelly's Ford

27-30 Apr

Rappahannock R.

29-30 Apr

Rapidan R.

U S Ford

HOOKER
134,000

Falmouth

STUART'S CAVALRY (−)

Chancellorsville

FREDERICKSBURG

LEE 30 Apr

LEE
60,000

29 Apr

Spotsylvania

Rappahannock R.

Scott's Ford

Falmouth

Bank's Ford

4 May

FREDERICKSBURG

200

3

Morye's Hts.

3

Salem Church

3

4 May

HOLDING FORCE

1-3 May

TELEGRAPH ROAD

1-3 May

Massaponax R.

100

SPOTSYLVANIA

200   TO RICHMOND

corps and division insignia. He also took a long step toward improving the cavalry arm of the army, which up to this time had been assigned many diverse duties and was split up into small detachments. Hooker regarded cavalry as a combat arm of full stature, and he concentrated his units into a cavalry corps of three divisions under Brig. Gen. George Stoneman. On the other hand Hooker made a costly mistake in decentralizing tactical control of his artillery to his corps commanders. As a result Union artillery would not be properly massed in the coming action at Chancellorsville.

Hooker had no intention of repeating Burnside's tragic frontal assault at Fredericksburg. With a strength approaching 134,000 men, Hooker planned a double envelopment which would place strong Union forces on each of Lee's flanks. (*Map 30*) He ordered three of his infantry corps to move secretly up the Rappahannock and ford the stream, while two more corps, having conspicuously remained opposite Fredericksburg, were to strike across the old battlefield there. Two more corps were in reserve. The cavalry corps, less one division which was to screen the move up river, was to raid far behind Lee's rear to divert him. Hooker's plan was superb; his execution faulty. The three corps moved quickly up the river and by the end of April had crossed and advanced to the principal road junction of Chancellorsville. They were now in the so-called "Wilderness," a low, flat, confusing area of scrub timber and narrow dirt roads in which movement and visibility were extremely limited. Maj. Gen. John Sedgwick crossed the Rappahannock at Fredericksburg on the 29th, and the two remaining corps moved to within supporting distance of Hooker at Chancellorsville. So far everything had gone according to plan, except that Stoneman's diversion had failed to bother Lee. One of Stuart's brigades kept Stoneman under surveillance while the main body of cavalry shadowed Hooker so effectively that the southern commander knew every move made by the Union army. By the morning of April 30, Lee was aware of what was afoot and knew that he was threatened by double envelopment. Already Hooker was sending his columns eastward toward the back door to Fredericksburg. A less bold and resolute man than Lee would have retreated southward at once, and with such ample justification that only the captious would have found fault. But the southern general, his army numbering only 60,000, used the principles of the offensive, maneuver, economy of force, and surprise to compensate for his inferior numbers. Instead of retreating, he left a part of his army to hold the heights at Fredericksburg and started west for Chancellorsville with the main body.

Chancellorsville: Lee's Finest Battle

When Lee began to move, Hooker simply lost his courage. Over protests of his corps commanders, he ordered the troops back into defensive positions around Chancellorsville. The Federals established a line in the forest, felled trees for an abatis, and constructed earth-and-log breastworks. Their position faced generally south, anchored on the Rappahannock on the east; but in the west it was weak, unsupported, and hanging in the air. Lee brought his main body up and on May 1 made contact with Hooker's strong left. That day Stuart's cavalry discovered Hooker's vulnerable right flank and promptly reported the intelligence to Lee. Conferring that night with Stonewall Jackson, Lee made another bold decision. Facing an army much greater than his own, he decided to divide his forces and further envelop the envelopers. Accordingly, Lee committed about 17,000 men against Hooker's left to hold it in place while Jackson with some 26,000 men made a wide 15-mile swing to get beyond the right flank. At first glance Lee's decision might appear a violation of the principles of mass and concentration, but while Lee's two forces were initially separated their common objective was the Army of the Potomac, and their ultimate routes converged on a common center.

Jackson's force, in a 10-mile-long column, moved out at daybreak of May 2, marching southwest first, then swinging northwest to get into position. The Federals noted that something was happening off to the south but were unable to penetrate the defensive screen; Hooker soon began to think Lee was actually retreating. In late afternoon Jackson turned onto the Orange turnpike near Wilderness Tavern. This move put him west of Hooker's right flank, and since the woods thinned out a little at this point it was possible to form a line of battle. Because time was running short and the hour of the day was late, Jackson deployed in column of divisions, with each division formed with brigades abreast, the same kind of confusing formation Johnston had used at Shiloh. Shortly after 5:00 p.m. Jackson's leading division, shrieking the "rebel yell" and driving startled rabbits and deer before it, came charging out of the woods, rolling up Maj. Gen. Oliver O. Howard's XI Corps in wild rout. The Confederates pressed forward, but fresh Union troops, disorganization of his own men, and oncoming darkness stymied the impatient Jackson. While searching for a road that would permit him to cut off Hooker from United States Ford across the Rappahannock, Jackson fell prey to a mistaken ambush by his own men. The Confederate leader was wounded and died eight days later. During the night of May 2, Stuart, Jackson's successor as corps commander, re-formed his lines. Against Stuart's right, Hooker launched local counterattacks which at first gained some success, but the next morning withdrew his whole line. Once more Hooker yielded the initiative at the moment he had a strong force between Lee's two divided and weaker forces.

Stuart renewed the attack during the morning as Hooker pulled his line back. Hooker was knocked unconscious when a shell struck the pillar of the Chancellor house against which he was leaning. Until the end of the battle he was dazed and incapable of exercising effective command, but he did not relinquish it nor would the army's medical director declare him unfit. Meanwhile Sedgwick, who shortly after Jackson's attack had received orders to proceed through Fredericksburg to Chancellorsville, had assaulted Marye's Heights. He carried it about noon on May 3, but the next day Lee once more divided his command, leaving Stuart with 25,000 to guard Hooker, and moved himself with 21,000 to thwart Sedgwick. In a sharp action at Salem Church, Lee forced the Federals off the road and northward over the Rappahannock. Lee now made ready for a full-scale assault against the Army of the Potomac huddled with its back against the river on May 6, but Hooker ordered retirement to the north bank before the attack. Confederate losses were approximately 13,000; Federal losses, 17,000. But Lee lost far more with the death of Jackson. Actually, Lee's brilliant and daring maneuvers had defeated only one man— Hooker—and in no other action of the war did moral superiority of one general over the other stand out so clearly as a decisive factor in battle. Chancellorsville exemplified Napoleon's maxim: "The General is the head, the whole of the army."

Hooker was a talented tactical commander with a good reputation. But in spite of Lincoln's injunction, "This time, put in all your men," he allowed nearly one-third of his army to stand idle during the heaviest fighting. Here again was a general who could effectively lead a body of troops under his own eyes, but could not use maps and reports to evaluate and control situations that were beyond his range of vision. Hooker, not the Army of the Potomac, lost the battle of Chancellorsville. Yet for the victors, Chancellorsville was a hollow triumph. It was dazzling, a set piece for the instruction of students of the military art ever since, but it had been inconclusive, winning glory and little more. It left government and army on both sides with precisely the problems they had faced before the campaign began.

Lee's Second Invasion of the North

By 1863 the war had entered what Sherman called its professional phase. The troops were well trained and had ample combat experience. Officers had generally mastered their jobs and were deploying their forces fairly skillfully in accordance with the day's tactical principles. Furthermore, the increased range and accuracy of weapons, together with the nature of the terrain, had induced some alterations in tactics, alterations which were embodied in a revised infantry manual published in 1863. Thus, by the third year of the war, battles had begun to take on certain definite characteristics. The battle of Gettysburg is a case in point.

Gettysburg was, first of all, an act of fate—a 3-day holocaust, largely unplanned and uncontrollable. Like the war itself, it sprang from decisions that men under pressure made in the light of imperfect knowledge. It would someday symbolize the war with all the blunders and heroism, hopes and delusions, combativeness and blinding devotion of the American man in arms of that period. With its enormous destruction, tactical maneuvers, and use of weapons, Gettysburg was one of the most dramatic and most typical of the 2,000-odd land engagements of the Civil War.

After the great victory at Chancellorsville, the Confederate cause in the eastern theater looked exceptionally bright. If 60,000 men could beat 134,000, then the Confederacy's inferiority in manpower was surely offset by superior generalship and skill at arms. Vicksburg was not yet under siege, although Grant had ferried his army over to the east bank of the Mississippi. If Davis and Lee were overly optimistic, they could hardly be blamed. Both men favored another invasion of the North for much the same political and military reasons that led to invasion in 1862. Longstreet, on the other hand, was concerned over the Federal threats in the west. He proposed going on the defensive in Virginia and advised taking advantage of the Confederacy's railroads and interior lines to send part of the Army of Northern Virginia to Tennessee to relieve pressure on Vicksburg. But he was overruled and Lee made ready to move into Pennsylvania. By this time Union strategy in the east was clearly defined: to continue operations against Confederate seaports—an attempt to seize Fort Sumter on April 7 had failed—and to destroy Lee's army. President Lincoln's orders made clear that the destruction of the Army of Northern Virginia was the major objective of the Army of the Potomac. Richmond was only incidental.

On June 30, 1863, the Army of the Potomac numbered 115,256 officers and enlisted men, with 362 guns. It consisted of 51 infantry brigades organized into 19 divisions, which in turn formed 7 infantry corps. The cavalry corps had 3 divisions. The field artillery, 67 batteries, was assigned by brigades to the corps, except for army reserve artillery. The Army of Northern Virginia, numbering 76,224 men and 272 guns in late May, comprised 3 infantry corps, each led by a lieutenant general, and Stuart's cavalry division. (The Confederacy was much more generous with rank than was the U.S. Army.) In each corps were 3 divisions, and most divisions had 4 brigades. Of the 15 field artillery battalions of 4 batteries each, 5 battalions were attached to each corps under command of the corps' artillery chiefs.

In early June Lee began moving his units away from Fredericksburg. In his advance he used the Shenandoah and Cumberland Valleys, for by holding the east-west mountain passes he could readily cover his approach route and line of communications. Hooker got wind of the move; he noted the weakening of the Fredericksburg defenses, and on June 9 his cavalry, commanded by Brig. Gen. Alfred Pleasonton, surprised Stuart at Brandy Station, Virginia. Here on an open plain was fought one of the few mounted, saber-swinging, cut-and-thrust cavalry combats of the Civil War. Up to now the Confederate cavalry had been superior, but at Brandy Station the Union horsemen "came of age," and Stuart was lucky to hold his position.

When the Federals learned that Confederate infantrymen were west of the Blue Ridge heading north, Hooker started to move to protect Washington and Baltimore and to attempt to destroy Lee. Earlier, Lincoln had vetoed Hooker's proposal to seize Richmond while Lee went north. As the Army of Northern Virginia moved through the valleys and deployed into Pennsylvania behind cavalry screens, the Army of the Potomac moved north on a broad front to the east, crossing the Potomac on June 25 and 26. Lee, forced to disperse by the lack of supplies, had extended his infantry columns from McConnellsburg and Chambersburg on the west to Carlisle in the north and York on the east.

After Brandy Station, and some sharp clashes in the mountain passes, Stuart set forth on another dramatic ride around the Union army. With only vague instructions and acting largely on his own initiative, he proved of little use to Lee. It was only on the afternoon of July 2 with his troopers so weary that they were almost falling from their saddles, that Stuart rejoined Lee in the vicinity of Gettysburg, too late to have an important influence on the battle. His absence had deprived Lee of prompt, accurate information about the Army of the Potomac. When Lee learned from Longstreet on June 28 that Hooker's men were north of the Potomac, he ordered his widespread units to concentrate at once between Gettysburg and Cashtown.

After Chancellorsville, Lincoln, though advised to drop Hooker, had kept him in command of the Army of the Potomac on the theory that he would not throw away a gun because it has misfired once. But Hooker soon became embroiled with Halleck and requested his own relief. He was replaced by a corps commander, Maj. Gen. George G. Meade, who before dawn on June 28 received word of his promotion and the accompanying problems inherent in assuming command of a great army while it was moving toward the enemy. Meade, who was to command the Army of the Potomac for the rest of the war, started north on a broad front at once but within two days decided to fight a defensive action in Maryland and issued orders to that effect. However, not all his commanders received the order, and events overruled him.

Gettysburg

Outposts of both armies clashed during the afternoon of June 30 near the quiet little Pennsylvania market town of Gettysburg. The terrain in the area included rolling hills and broad shallow valleys. Gettysburg was the junction of twelve roads that led to Harrisburg, Philadelphia, Baltimore, Washington, and the mountain passes to the west which were controlled by Lee. The rest was inevitable; the local commanders sent reports and recommendations to their superiors, who relayed them upward, so that both armies, still widely dispersed, started moving toward Gettysburg. (*Map 31*)

On July 1, Union cavalrymen fought a dismounted delaying action against advance troops of Lt. Gen. Ambrose P. Hill's corps northwest of town. By this stage of the war cavalrymen, armed with saber, pistol, and breech-loading carbine, were often deployed as mounted infantrymen, riding to battle but fighting on foot. The range and accuracy of the infantry's rifled muskets made it next to impossible for mounted men to attack foot soldiers in position. With their superior speed and mobility, cavalrymen, as witnessed in the Gettysburg campaign, were especially useful for screening, reconnaissance, and advance guard actions in which they seized and held important hills, river crossings, and road junctions pending the arrival of infantry. During the morning hours of July 1, this was the role played by Union horsemen on the ridges north and west of Gettysburg.

By noon both the I and the XI Corps of the Army of the Potomac had joined in the battle, and Lt. Gen. Richard S. Ewell's Corps of Confederates had moved to support Hill. The latter, advancing from the north, broke the lines of the XI Corps and drove the Federals back through Gettysburg. The Union infantry rallied behind artillery positioned on Cemetery and Culp's Hills south of the town. Lee, who reached the field about 2:00 p.m. ordered Ewell to take Cemetery Hill, "if possible." But Ewell failed to press his advantage, and the Confederates settled into positions extending in a great curve from northeast of Culp's Hill, westward through Gettysburg, thence south on Seminary

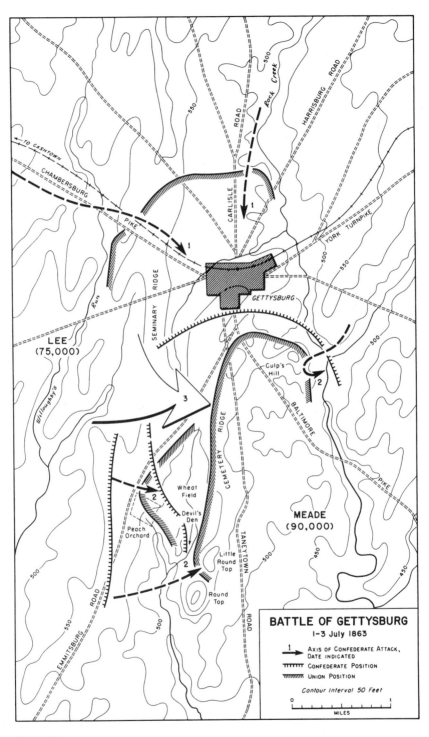

BATTLE OF GETTYSBURG

1–3 July 1863

Axis of Confederate Attack, Date indicated

Confederate Position

Union Position

Contour Interval 50 Feet

0 — MILES — 1

MAP 31

Ridge. During the night the Federals, enjoying interior lines, moved troops onto the key points of Culp's Hill, Cemetery Hill, Cemetery Ridge, and Little Round Top.

Meade had completed his dispositions by the morning of July 2, and his line was strong except in two places. In the confusion, Little Round Top was occupied only by a signal station when the supporting cavalry was dispatched to guard the army trains and not replaced; and the commander of the III Corps, Maj. Gen. Daniel E. Sickles, on his own responsibility moved his line forward from the south end of Cemetery Ridge to higher ground near the Peach Orchard, so that his corps lay in an exposed salient. By early afternoon, seven corps were arrayed along the Union battle line.

On the Confederate side, Lee had not been able to attack early; reconnaissance took time, and Longstreet's leading division did not arrive until afternoon. Generals in the Civil War tried to combine frontal assaults with envelopments and flanking movements, but the difficulty of timing and coordinating the movements of such large bodies of men in broken terrain made intricate maneuvers difficult. The action on the second day at Gettysburg graphically illustrates the problem. Lee wanted Longstreet to outflank the Federal left, part of Hill's corps was to strike the center, while Ewell's corps was to envelop the right flank of Meade's army. The attack did not start until 3:00 p.m. when Longstreet's men, having deployed on unfamiliar ground, under a corps commander that preferred to take a defensive stance, advanced toward Little Round Top. The brigade was the basic maneuver element, and it formed for the attack with regiments in a two-rank line. Divisions usually attacked in columns of brigades, the second 150 to 300 yards behind the first, the third a similar distance behind the second. Skirmishers protected the flanks if no units were posted on either side. But such textbook models usually degenerated under actual fighting conditions, and so it was with Longstreet's attack. Divisions and brigades went in piecemeal, but with savage enthusiasm. Attacks started in close order as most men were using single-shot muzzle-loaders and had to stand shoulder to shoulder in order to get enough firepower and shock effect. But intervals between units soon increased under fire, troops often scattered for cover and concealment behind stone walls and trees, and thereafter units advanced by short rushes supported by fire from neighboring units. Thus, by late afternoon the smoke of battle was thick over the fields south of Gettysburg and the cries of the wounded mingled with the crash of musketry. The whole sector had become a chaos of tangled battle lines.

At this point Meade's chief engineer, Brig. Gen. Gouverneur Warren, discovering that no infantry held Little Round Top, persuaded the commander of the V Corps, Maj. Gen. George Sykes, to send two brigades and some artillery to the hill. They arrived just in time to hold the summit against a furious Confederate assault. When this attack bogged down, Longstreet threw a second division against Sickles' troops in the Peach Orchard and Wheatfield; this cracked the Federal line and drove as far as Cemetery Ridge before Meade's reserves halted it. Lee then ordered his troops to attack progressively from right to left and one of Hill's divisions assaulted Cemetery Ridge in piecemeal fashion, but was driven off. On the north Ewell attacked about 6:00 p.m. and captured some abandoned trenches, but Federals posted behind stone walls proved too strong. As the day ended the Federals held all their main positions. The Confederates had fought hard and with great bravery, but the progressive attack, which ignored the principle of mass, never engaged the Union front decisively at any point. The assaults were delivered against stoutly defended, prepared positions; Malvern Hill and Fredericksburg had shown this tactic to be folly, although perhaps Lee's successes against prepared positions at Chancellorsville led him to overoptimism.

Meade, after requesting the opinions of his corps commanders, decided to defend, rather than attack, on July 3. He also estimated that Lee, having attacked his right and left, would try for his center. He was right. Lee had planned to launch a full-scale, co-ordinated attack all along the line but then changed his mind in favor of a massive frontal assault by 10 brigades from 4 divisions of Longstreet's and Hill's corps against the Union center, which was held by Maj. Gen. Winfield Scott Hancock's II Corps. The assault was to be preceded by a massive artillery barrage.

The infantry's main support during the war was provided by field artillery. Rifled guns of relatively long range were available, but the soldiers preferred the 6-pounder and 12-pounder smoothbores. Rifled cannon were harder to clean; their projectiles were not as effective; their greater range could not always be effectively used because development of a good indirect fire control system would have to await the invention of the field telephone and the radio; and, finally, the rifled guns had flat trajectories, whereas the higher trajectories of the smoothbores enabled gunners to put fire on reverse slopes. Both types of cannon were among the artillery of the two armies at Gettysburg.

At 1:00 p.m. on July 3 Confederate gunners opened fire from approximately 140 pieces along Seminary Ridge in the greatest artillery bombardment witnessed on the American continent up to that time. For two hours the barrage continued, but did little more than tear up ground, destroy a few caissons, and expend ammunition. The Union artillery in the sector, numbering only 80 guns, had not been knocked out. It did stop firing in order to conserve ammunition,

PICKETT'S CHARGE

and the silence seemed to be a signal that the Confederates should begin their attack.

Under command of Maj. Gen. George E. Pickett, 15,000 men emerged from the woods on Seminary Ridge, dressed their three lines as if on parade, and began the mile-long, 20-minute march toward Cemetery Ridge. The assault force—47 regiments altogether—moved at a walk until it neared the Union lines, then broke into a run. Union artillery, especially 40 Napoleons on the south end of the ridge and some rifled guns on Little Round Top, opened fire, enfiladed the gray ranks, and forced Pickett's right over to the north. Despite heavy casualties the Confederates kept their formation until they came within rifle and canister range of the II Corps, and by then the lines and units were intermingled. The four brigades composing the left of Pickett's first line were heavily hit but actually reached and crossed the stone wall defended by Brig. Gen. John Gibbon's 2d Division of the II Corps, only to be quickly cut down or captured. Pickett's survivors withdrew to Seminary Ridge, and the fighting was over except for a suicidal mounted charge by Union cavalry, which Longstreet's right flank units easily halted. Both sides had fought hard and with great valor, for among 90,000 effective Union troops and 75,000 Confederates there were more than 51,000 casualties. The Army of the Potomac lost 3,155 killed, 14,529 wounded, and 5,365 prisoners and missing. Of the Army of Northern Virginia, 3,903 were killed, 18,735 wounded, and 5,425 missing and prisoners. If Chancellorsville was Lee's finest battle, Gettysburg was clearly his worst; yet the reverse did not unnerve him or reduce his effectiveness as a commander. The invasion had patently failed, and he retired at once toward the Potomac. As that river was flooded, it was several days before he was able to cross. Mr. Lincoln, naturally pleased over Meade's defensive victory and elated over Grant's capture of Vicksburg, thought the war could end in 1863 if Meade launched a resolute pursuit and destroyed Lee's army on the north bank of the Potomac. But Meade's own army was too mangled, and the Union commander moved cautiously, permitting Lee to return safely to Virginia on July 13.

Gettysburg was the last important action in the eastern theater in 1863. Lee and Meade maneuvered against each other in Virginia, but there was no more fighting. After Gettysburg and Vicksburg the center of strategic gravity shifted to Tennessee.

The Chickamauga Campaign

One week before the surrender of Vicksburg and the Union victory at Gettysburg, General Rosecrans moved out of Murfreesboro, Tennessee, and headed for Chattanooga, one of the most important cities in the south because of its location. (*See Map 21.*) It was a main junction on the rail line linking Richmond with Knoxville and Memphis. President Lincoln had long recognized the importance of railroads in this area. In 1862 he said, "To take and hold the railroad at or east of Cleveland [near Chattanooga], in East Tennessee, I think fully as important as the taking and holding of Richmond." Furthermore, at Chattanooga the Tennessee River cuts through the parallel ridges of the Appalachian Mountains and forms a natural gateway to either north or south. By holding the city, the Confederates could threaten Kentucky and prevent a Union penetration of the southeastern part of the Confederacy. If the Union armies pushed through Chattanooga, they would be in position to attack Atlanta, Savannah, or even the Carolinas and Richmond from the rear. As Lincoln told Rosecrans in 1863, "If we can hold Chattanooga and East Tennessee I think the rebellion must dwindle and die."

After the spring and summer campaigns in the east, the Davis government in Richmond approved a movement by Longstreet's corps of Lee's army to the west to reinforce the hard-pressed Bragg. Longstreet's move—a 900-mile trip by rail—involving some 10,000–15,000 men and six batteries of artillery, began on September 9. But a force under Burnside, now commanding the Department of the Ohio, which was not part of Rosecrans' command, had penetrated the Cumberland Gap and driven the Confederates from Knoxville; Longstreet had to go around by way of Savannah and Augusta to Atlanta, Georgia, and did not reach Bragg until September 18. The rail network was rickety, and Longstreet's soldiers quipped that such poor rolling stock had never been intended to carry such good soldiers. Movement of Longstreet's troops from Virginia was nevertheless an outstanding logistical achievement for the Confederacy.

Rosecrans had meanwhile reached the north bank of the Tennessee River near Stevenson, Alabama, on August 20. By September 4 his forces were across and on their way toward Chattanooga. After months of delay Rosecrans had accomplished the feat of completely outmaneuvering Bragg without a major battle. He planned to get in behind Bragg from the southwest and bottle him up in Chattanooga, but the Confederate general saw through the scheme and slipped away southward, carefully planting rumors that his army was demoralized and in flight. Rosecrans then resolved to pursue, a decision that would have been wise if Bragg has been retreating in disorder.

There were few passes through the mountains and no good lateral roads. Rosecrans' army was dispersed in three columns over a 40-mile front in order to make use of the various passes. Bragg concentrated his army about September 10 at Lafayette, Georgia, some twenty miles south of Chattanooga. As his force was three times as large as any one of the Union columns, Bragg hopefully anticipated that he could defeat Rosecrans in detail. But his intelligence service failed him: he thought there were two, rather than three Union columns, and prepared plans accordingly. He first planned to strike what he thought was Rosecrans' right—actually the center—then the left, but his subordinates did not support him promptly, and the attacks were made in desultory fashion. Thus, twice in three days Bragg missed a fine opportunity to inflict a serious reverse upon the Federals because of his subordinates' failure to carry out orders.

By September 12 Rosecrans was at last aware that Bragg was not retreating in disorder but was preparing to fight. The Union commander ordered an immediate concentration, but this would take several days and in the meantime his corps were vulnerable. Although Bragg was usually speedy in executing attacks, this time he delayed, awaiting the arrival of Longstreet's corps. He intended to push Rosecrans southward away from Chattanooga into a mountain cul-de-sac where the Federals could be destroyed.

By September 17 Bragg was poised just east of Chickamauga Creek. (*Map 32*) (Chickamauga, translated from Cherokee into English, means "River of Death.") When Longstreet's three leading brigades arrived on September 18, Bragg decided to cross the Chickamauga and attack. But the Federals, with two corps almost concentrated, defended the fords so stoutly that only a few units got over that day. During the night more Confederates slipped across, and by morning of the 19th about three-fourths of Bragg's men were over.

Rosecrans' third corps went into the line on the 19th, and now Bragg faced a much stronger force than he had expected. The heavily wooded battlefield had few landmarks, and some units had difficulty maintaining direction. Fighting continued throughout much of the day, but by nightfall the Federals still controlled the roads to Chattanooga. That night Lee's "Warhorse," Longstreet, arrived in person with two more brigades. He went looking for Bragg to report to him and lost his way in the woods. Encountering some soldiers, he asked them to identify their unit. When they replied with numbers—Confederate divisions were named for their commanders—he realized he was within

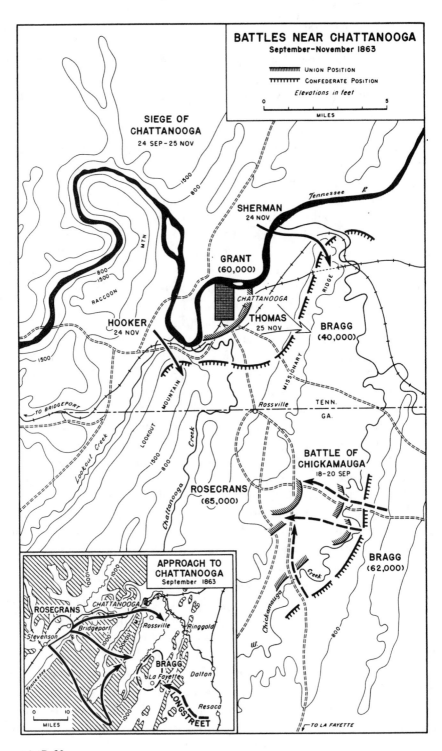

BATTLES NEAR CHATTANOOGA
September–November 1863

|||||||||| UNION POSITION
TTTTTTTT CONFEDERATE POSITION
Elevations in feet

0   5
MILES

SIEGE OF
CHATTANOOGA
24 SEP–25 NOV

Tennessee R.

SHERMAN
24 NOV

GRANT
(60,000)

1500
800

RACCOON

CHATTANOOGA

RIDGE

HOOKER
24 NOV

THOMAS
25 NOV

BRAGG
(40,000)

MTN

LOOKOUT MOUNTAIN

MISSIONARY

TO BRIDGEPORT

Rossville

TENN.
GA.

Lookout Creek

Chattanooga Creek

BATTLE OF
CHICKAMAUGA
18–20 SEP

ROSECRANS
(65,000)

BRAGG
(62,000)

Chickamauga Creek

APPROACH TO
CHATTANOOGA
September 1863

ROSECRANS

CHATTANOOGA

Bridgeport

LOOKOUT MTN.

Rossville

Ringgold

Stevenson

BRAGG

La Fayette

Dalton

Tennessee R.

LONGSTREET

Resaca

0   10
MILES

TO LA FAYETTE

MAP 32

Union lines, hastily rode off in the darkness, and eventually found Bragg. During the night Rosecrans regrouped and dug in.

Bragg decided to renew the attack the next day and to attack progressively from his right to left (sometimes known in military parlance as "oblique order"). He reorganized the Army of Tennessee into two wings under Polk and Longstreet with little regard for its existing corps organization. The attack began about 9:00 a.m. and hit Thomas' corps first. The Union line held until Rosecrans received an erroneous report that one of his units was not supported, and ordered another unit to move in and help. In the ensuing confusion, orders designated a unit which was already in line of battle. When this force obediently abandoned its position, Longstreet, just beginning his attack, saw the hole and drove into it at once. Thomas' right flank was bent back and most of the Union right wing simply melted from the field and streamed in rout back toward Chattanooga. Rosecrans, considering himself defeated, retired to Chattanooga to organize it for defense. Thomas, with about two-thirds of the disorganized army, stood fast and checked vicious attacks by Longstreet and Polk until nightfall. This resolute stand and the valorous performance of the U.S. 19th Infantry won for Thomas and that unit the title "Rock of Chickamauga." A Confederate remembered that afternoon how "the dead were piled upon each other in ricks, like cord wood, to make passage for advancing columns. The sluggish Chickamauga ran red with human blood."

Bragg concluded that no decisive results could be attained that day. Polk, Longstreet, and Forrest pleaded with him to push the routed Federals and recapture Chattanooga. But 18,000 casualties (the Federals had lost only 1,500 less) so unnerved Bragg that he permitted Thomas to withdraw unmolested from the field to a blocking position extending from Missionary Ridge west to Lookout Mountain. Next day Thomas retired into Chattanooga. Polk wrote to President Davis of Bragg's "criminal negligence," and Forrest a week later insubordinately told the army commander, "You have played the part of a damned scoundrel, and are a coward and if you were any part of a man I would slap your jaws." Yet nothing could erase completely the fact that the Confederates had won a great victory and had Rosecrans' army bottled up in a trap.

Grant at Chattanooga

Rosecrans' army, having started out offensively, was now shut up in Chattanooga, as Bragg took up positions on Lookout Mountain and Missionary Ridge. The Union commander accepted investment and thus surrendered his freedom of action. Burnside, at Knoxville, was too far away to render immediate aid. There were no strong Confederate units north of Chattanooga, but Rosecrans' line of communications was cut away. The Nashville and Chattanooga Railroad, instead of running directly into the city, reached the river at Stevenson, crossed at Bridgeport southwest of Chattanooga, and ran through Confederate territory into town. River steamers could get to within only eight miles of Chattanooga; beyond, the Tennessee River was swift and narrow. Supplies therefore came over the mountains in wagons, but starting September 30 Confederate cavalry under Maj. Gen. Joseph Wheeler, one of Bragg's cavalry corps commanders, raided as far north as Murfreesboro. Though heavily and effectively opposed in his effort to tear up the railroad, he managed to destroy many precious Union supply wagons. With the mountain roads breaking down under the heavy traffic in wet weather, rations within Chattanooga ran short. Men went hungry, and horses and mules began to die of starvation. Rosecrans prepared to reopen his line of communications by means of an overland route to the west. But this route was dominated by Confederate troops on Raccoon and Lookout Mountains. Additional troops to clear these strongpoints were required if the Army of the Cumberland was to survive.

Washington finally awoke to the fact that an entire Union army was trapped in Chattanooga and in danger of capture. In a midnight council meeting on September 23, the President met with Secretary Stanton, General Halleck, and others to determine what could be done. As General Meade was not then active in the east, they decided to detach two corps, or about 20,000 men, from the Army of the Potomac and send them by rail to Tennessee under the command of General Hooker, who had been without active command since his relief in June. The forces selected included 10 artillery batteries with over 3,000 mules and horses. The 1,157–mile journey involved four changes of trains, owing to differing gauges and lack of track connections, and eclipsed all other such troop movements by rail up to that time. The troops began to entrain at Manassas Junction and Bealton Station, Virginia, on September 25 and five days later the first trains arrived at Bridgeport, Alabama. Not all of the troops made such good time—for the majority of the infantry the trip consumed about nine days. And movement of the artillery, horses, mules, baggage, and impedimenta was somewhat slower. Combined with a waterborne movement of 17,000 men under Sherman from Mississippi, the reinforcement of the besieged Rosecrans was a triumph of skill and planning.

Chickamauga had caused Stanton and his associates to lose confidence in Rosecrans. For some time Lincoln had been dubious about Rosecrans, who, he said, acted "like a duck hit on the head" after Chickamauga, but he did not immediately choose a successor. Finally, about mid-October, he decided to

UNION TRANSPORTS ON THE TENNESSEE RIVER

unify command in the west and to vest it in General Grant, who still commanded the Army of the Tennessee. In October Stanton met Grant in Louisville and gave him orders which allowed him some discretion in selecting subordinates. Grant was appointed commander of the Military Division of the Mississippi, which embraced the Departments and Armies of the Ohio, the Cumberland, and the Tennessee, and included the vast area from the Alleghenies to the Mississippi River north of Banks' Department of the Gulf. Thomas replaced Rosecrans, and Sherman was appointed to command Grant's old army.

Now that Hooker had arrived, the line of communications, or the "cracker line" to the troops, could be reopened. Rosecrans had actually shaped the plan, and all that was needed was combat troops to execute it. On October 26 Hooker crossed the Tennessee at Bridgeport and attacked eastward. Within two days he had taken the spurs of the mountains, other Union troops had captured two important river crossings, and the supply line was open once more. Men, equipment, and food moved via riverboat and wagon road, bypassing Confederate strongpoints, to reinforce the besieged Army of the Cumberland.

In early November Bragg weakened his besieging army by sending Longstreet's force against Burnside at Knoxville. This move reduced Confederate strength to about 40,000 at about the same time that Sherman arrived with two army corps from Memphis. The troops immediately at hand under Grant—Thomas' Army of the Cumberland, two corps of Sherman's Army of the Tennessee, and two corps under Hooker from the Army of the Potomac—now numbered about 60,000. Grant characteristically decided to resume the offensive with his entire force.

The Confederates had held their dominant position for so long that they seemed to look on all of the Federals in Chattanooga as their ultimate prisoners. One day Grant went out to inspect the Union lines and he reached a point where Union and Confederate picket posts were not far apart. Not only did his own troops turn out the guard, but a smart set of Confederates came swarming out, formed a neat military rank, snapped to attention, and presented arms. Grant returned the salute and rode away. But plans were already afoot to divest the Confederates of some of their cockiness.

Grant planned to hit the ends of the Confederates' line at once. Hooker would strike at Lookout Mountain, and Sherman moving his army upstream, across the river from Chattanooga, and crossing over by pontons, would hit the upper end of Missionary Ridge. While they were breaking the Confederate flanks, Thomas' men could make limited attacks on the center, and the Army of the Cumberland's soldiers, already nursing a bruised ego for the rout at Chickamauga, realized that in the eyes of the commanding general they were second-class troops.

Hooker took Lookout Mountain on November 24. On the same day Sherman crossed the Tennessee at the mouth of Chickamauga Creek and gained positions on the north end of Missionary Ridge. The next day his attacks bogged down as he attempted to drive southward along the Ridge. To help Sherman, Grant directed the Army of the Cumberland to take the rifle pits at the foot of the west slope of Missionary Ridge. These rifle pits were the first of three lines of Confederate trenches. Thomas' troops rushed forward, seized the pits, and then, having a score to settle with the Confederates positioned above them, took control of this phase of the battle. Coming under fire from the pits above and in front of them, the Federals simply kept on going. When Grant observed this movement he muttered that someone was going to sweat for it if the charge ended in disaster. But Thomas' troops drove all the way to the top, and in the afternoon Hooker swept the southern end of the ridge. The Federals then had the unusual experience of seeing a Confederate army disintegrate into precipitate retreat and beckoned to their Northern comrades: "My God! Come and see them run!" Grant pursued Bragg the next day, but one Confederate division skillfully halted the pursuit while Bragg retired into Georgia to regroup.

The battles around Chattanooga ended in one of the most complete Union victories of the war. Bragg's army was defeated, men and matériel captured, and the Confederates driven south. The mountainous defense line which the Confederates had hoped to hold had been pierced; the rail center of Chattanooga was permanently in Union hands; and the rich, food-producing eastern Tennessee section was lost to the Confederacy. Relief had come at last for the Union sympathizers in eastern Tennessee. With Chattanooga secured as a base, the way was open for an invasion of the lower South.

CHAPTER 12

The Civil War, 1864–1865

From Bull Run to Chattanooga, the Union armies had fought their battles without benefit of either a grand strategy or a supreme field commander. During the final year of the war the people of the North grew restless, and as the election of 1864 approached, many of them advocated a policy of making peace with the Confederacy. President Lincoln never wavered. Committed to the policy of destroying the armed power of the Confederacy, he sought a general who could pull all the threads of an emerging strategy together, and then concentrate the Union armies and their supporting naval power against the secessionists. After Vicksburg in July 1863, Lincoln leaned more and more toward Grant as the man whose strategic thinking and resolution would lead the Union armies to final victory.

It is the strategic moves of the armies during the last year of the war, rather than the tactical details, that are most instructive.

Strategy of Annihilation and Unity of Command

Acting largely as his own General in Chief after McClellan's removal in early 1862, Mr. Lincoln had watched the Confederates fight from one ephemeral victory to another inside their cockpit of northern Virginia. In the western theater, Union armies, often operating independently of one another, had scored great victories at key terrain points. But their hold on the communications base at Nashville was always in jeopardy as long as the elusive armies of the Confederacy could escape to fight another day at another key point. The twin, un-co-ordinated victories at Gettysburg and Vicksburg, 900 airline miles apart, only pointed up the North's need for an over-all strategic plan and a general who could carry it out.

Having cleared the Mississippi River, Grant wrote to Halleck and the President about the opportunities now open to his army. Grant first called for the consolidation of the autonomous western departments and the co-ordination of their individual armies. After this great step, he proposed to isolate the area west of the line Chattanooga-Atlanta-Montgomery-Mobile. Within this region, Grant urged a "massive rear attack" that would take Union armies in the Gulf Department under Maj. Gen. Nathaniel P. Banks and Grant's Army of the Tennessee to Mobile and up the Alabama River to Montgomery. The U.S. Navy would play a major role in this attack. Simultaneously, Rosecrans was to advance overland through Chattanooga to Atlanta. All military resources within this isolated area would be destroyed.

Lincoln vetoed Grant's plan in part by deferring the Mobile-Montgomery phase. The President favored a demonstration by Banks up the Red River to Shreveport in order to show the American flag to Napoleon III's interlopers in Mexico, and Banks' Department of the Gulf was left out of the consolidation of the other western commands under Grant in October 1863.

After his own victory at Chattanooga in November, Grant wasted few hours in writing the President what he thought the next strategic moves should be. As a possible winter attack, Grant revived the touchy Mobile campaign while the Chattanooga victors were gathering strength for a spring offensive to Atlanta. Grant reasoned that Lee would vacate Virginia and shift strength toward Atlanta. For the Mobile-Montgomery plan, Grant asked for Banks' resources in the Gulf Department. Lincoln again balked because the Texas seacoast would be abandoned. Grant's rebuttal explained that Napoleon III would really be impressed with a large Army-Navy operation against Mobile Bay. The Red River campaign, Grant believed, would not deter Napoleon III. The President told Grant again that he had to heed the demands of Union diplomacy, but at the same time he encouraged Grant to enlarge his strategic proposals to include estimates for a grand Federal offensive for the coming spring of 1864.

Grant's plan of January 1864 projected a four-pronged continental attack. In concert, the four armies were to move on Atlanta, on Mobile—after Banks took Shreveport—on Lee's communications by a campaign across the middle of North Carolina on the axis New Bern–Neuse River–Goldsboro–Raleigh–Greensboro, and on Lee's Army of Northern Virginia in the hope of defeating it in an open battle. Lincoln opposed the North Carolina phase, fearing that Grant's diversion of 60,000 effective bayonets from formations covering Washington was too dangerous. Lincoln knew that Lee's eyes were always fixed on the vast amount of supplies in the depots around the Washington area.

Though Lincoln scuttled some of Grant's professional schemes, he never lost his esteem for Grant's enthusiasm and intelligence. In February 1864 Congress revived Scott's old rank of lieutenant general, to which Grant was promoted on March 9. Lincoln relieved Halleck as General in Chief, ordered Grant to Washington to assume Halleck's post, and during March the President, the new General in Chief, and the Secretary of War ironed out top-level command arrangements which had plagued every President since the

War of 1812. Lincoln and Stanton relinquished powerful command, staff, and communications tools to Grant. Stanton, greatly impressed with Grant's public acclaim, cautioned his General Staff Bureau chiefs to heed Grant's needs and timetables.

In twentieth century terms, Grant was a theater commander. As General in Chief, he reported directly to the President and Secretary of War, keeping them informed about the broad aspects of his strategic plans and telling them in advance of his armies' needs. Grant removed himself from the politics of Washington and established his headquarters in northern Virginia. Though he planned to go quickly to troubled spots, Grant elected to accompany Meade's Army of the Potomac in order to assess Lee's moves and their effects on the other columns of the Union Army. By rail or steamboat, Grant was never far from Lincoln, and in turn the President visited Grant frequently. To tie his far-flung commands together, Grant employed a vast telegraph system.

In a continental theater of war larger than Napoleon's at its zenith, Grant's job, administratively, eventually embraced four military divisions, totaling seventeen subcommands, wherein 500,000 combat soldiers would be employed. At Washington, Halleck operated a war room for Grant and eased his heavy burden of studying the several Army commanders' detailed field directives by preparing brief digests, thus saving the General in Chief many hours of reading detailed reports. Bearing the then nebulous title of "Chief of Staff, U.S. Army," Halleck had a major job in keeping Grant informed about supply levels at base depots and advance dumps in Nashville, St. Louis, City Point, Washington, Philadelphia, Louisville, and New York City. Under Stanton, Quartermaster General Montgomery C. Meigs, the most informed logistician and supply manager of his day, dispatched men and munitions to Grant's subcommands according to a strategic timetable. As the spring offensive progressed, Stanton, Halleck, and Meigs gave Grant a rear-area team that grasped the delicate balance between theater objectives and the logistical support required to achieve them.

Grant spent the month of April on the Rapidan front developing his final strategic plan for ending the war. In essence, he recapped all of his views on the advantages to be gained from his victories in the western theater. He added some thoughts about moving several Federal armies, aided by naval power when necessary, toward a common center in a vast, concentrated effort. He planned to stop the Confederates from using their interior lines. He intended to maneuver Lee away from the Rapidan Wilderness and defeat the Army of Northern Virginia in open terrain by a decisive battle. Another Union force collected from the Atlantic seaport towns of the deep South was to cut the James-Appomattox River line to sever Lee's rail and road links with the other parts of the Confederacy. Simultaneously, Sherman's group of armies would execute a wide wheeling movement through the South to complete the envelopment of the whole country east of the Mississippi. Banks was still scheduled to make the attack through Mobile. As Lincoln described the plan, "Those not skinning can hold a leg."

By mid-April 1864 Grant had issued specific orders to each commander of the four Federal armies that were to execute the grand strategy. In round numbers the Union armies were sending 300,000 combat troops against 150,000 Confederates defending the invasion paths. Meade's Army of the Potomac and Burnside's independent IX Corps, a combined force of 120,000 men, constituted the major attack column under Grant's over-all direction. The enemy had 63,000 troops facing Grant along the Rapidan. Two subsidiary thrusts were to support Meade's efforts. Commanding a force of 33,000 men, Butler with his Army of the James was to skirt the south bank of the James, menace Richmond, take it if possible, and destroy the railroads below Petersburg. Acting as a right guard in the Shenandoah Valley, Maj. Gen. Franz Sigel's 23,000 Federals were to advance on Lee's rail hub at Lynchburg, Virginia. With the northern Virginia triangle under attack, in the continental center of the line Sherman's 100,000 men were to march on Atlanta, annihilating Joseph E. Johnston's 65,000 soldiers, and devastating the resources of central Georgia. On the continental right of the line, Banks was to disengage as soon as possible along the Red River and with Rear Adm. David C. Farragut's blockading squadron in the Gulf of Mexico make a limited amphibious landing against Mobile. The day for advance would be announced early in May.

In rising from regimental command to General in Chief, Grant had learned much from experience, and if he sometimes made mistakes he rarely repeated them. Not a profound student of the literature of warfare, he had become, by the eve of his grand campaign, one of those rare leaders who combine the talents of the strategist, tactician, and logistician and who marry those talents to the principle of the offensive. His operations, especially the "rear mass attack," were models of the execution of the principles of war. He was calm in crisis; reversals and disappointments did not unhinge his cool judgment. He mastered the dry-as-dust details of a logistical system and used common sense in deciding when to use the horse-drawn wagon, the railroad, or the steamboat in his strategic moves. Above all, Grant understood and applied the principle of modern war that the destruction of the enemy's economic resources is as necessary as the annihilation of the enemy's armies.

Lee Cornered at Richmond

On the morning of May 4, 1864, Meade and Sherman moved out to execute Grant's grand strategy. The combat strength of the Army of the Potomac, slimmed down from seven unwieldy corps, consisted of three infantry corps of 25,000 rifles each and a cavalry corps. Commanding the 12,000-man cavalry corps was Maj. Gen. Philip H. Sheridan, an energetic leader brought east by Grant on Halleck's recommendation. Meade again dispersed his cavalry, using troopers as messengers, pickets, and train guards, but young Sheridan, after considerable argument, eventually succeeded in concentrating all of his sabers as a separate combat arm. Grant reorganized Burnside's IX Corps of 20,000 infantrymen, held it as a strategic reserve for a time, and then assigned the IX Corps to Meade's army. Lee's army, now 70,000 strong, was also organized into a cavalry and three infantry corps.

Grant and Lee were at the height of their careers and this was their first contest of wills. Having the initiative, Grant crossed the Rapidan and decided to go by Lee's right, rather than his left. (*Map 33*) First, Grant wanted to rid himself of the need to use an insecure railroad with limited capacity back to Alexandria, Virginia. Second, he wanted to end the Army of the Potomac's dependence on a train of 4,000 wagons; the Army's mobility was hobbled by having to care for 60,000 animals. Finally, Grant wanted to use the advantages of Virginia's tidewater rivers and base his depots on the Chesapeake Bay. He was willing to accept the risk inherent in moving obliquely across Lee's front in northern Virginia.

With little room for maneuver, Grant was forced to advance through the Wilderness, where Hooker had come to grief the year before. As the army column halted near Chancellorsville to allow the wagon trains to pass the Rapidan, on May 5 Lee struck at Meade's right flank. Grant and Meade swung their corps into line and hit hard. The fighting in the battle of the Wilderness, consisting of assault, defense, and counterattack, was close and desperate in tangled woods and thickets. Artillery could not be brought to bear. The dry woods caught fire and some of the wounded died miserably in the flame and smoke. On May 6 Lee attacked again. Longstreet's I Corps, arriving late in battle but as always in perfect march order, drove the Federals back. Longstreet himself received a severe neck wound, inflicted in error by his own men, that took him out of action until October 1864. Lee, at a decisive moment in the battle, his fighting blood aroused to a white heat, attempted to lead an assault in person; but men of the Texas brigade with whom Lee was riding persuaded

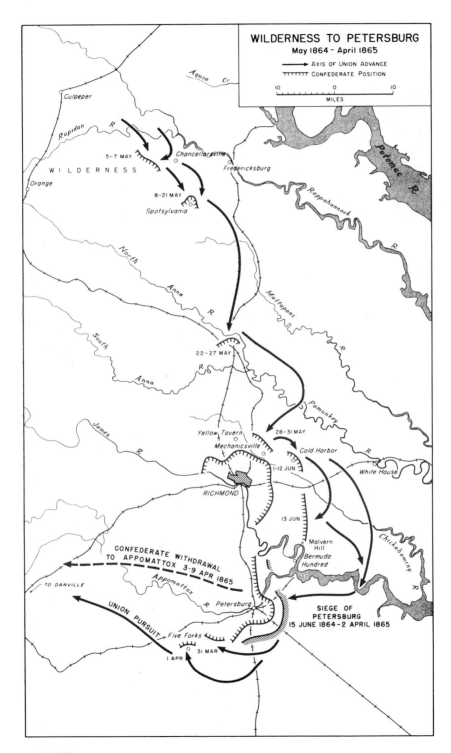

WILDERNESS TO PETERSBURG
May 1864 - April 1865

→ AXIS OF UNION ADVANCE
⊥⊥⊥⊥⊥ CONFEDERATE POSITION

10   0   10
MILES

Culpeper

Aquia Cr.

Rapidan R.

5-7 MAY

WILDERNESS

Chancellorsville

Fredericksburg

Orange

8-21 MAY

Spotsylvania

Rappahannock R.

Potomac R.

North Anna R.

South Anna

Mattaponi R.

22-27 MAY

R.

James R.

Pamunkey

Yellow Tavern

Mechanicsville

28-31 MAY

Cold Harbor

White House

RICHMOND

1-12 JUN

13 JUN

Malvern Hill

Bermuda Hundred

Chickahominy R.

CONFEDERATE WITHDRAWAL
TO APPOMATTOX 3-9 APR 1865

TO DANVILLE

Appomattox R.

Petersburg

SIEGE OF
PETERSBURG
15 JUNE 1864-2 APRIL 1865

UNION PURSUIT

Five Forks

1 APR   31 MAR

MAP 33

the southern leader to go to the rear and direct the battle as their Army commander. On May 7 neither side renewed the battle.

Now came the critical test of Grant's execution of strategy. He had been worsted, though not really beaten, by Lee, a greater antagonist than Bragg, Joseph E. Johnston, and Pemberton. After an encounter with Lee, each of the former Army of the Potomac commanders, McClellan, Burnside, and Hooker, had retired north of the Rappahannock River and postponed any further clashes with that great tactician. But Grant was of a different breed. He calmly ordered his lead corps to move south toward Spotsylvania as rapidly as possible to get around Lee's flank and interpose the Army of the Potomac between Lee and Richmond.

Lee detected Grant's march and, using roads generally parallel to Grant's, also raced toward the key road junction at Spotsylvania. J.E.B. Stuart's cavalry harassed and slowed Grant; Lee arrived first and quickly built strong earth-and-log trenches over commanding ground which covered the roads leading to Richmond. In this crossroads race, Sheridan's cavalry would have been useful, but Meade had dissipated the cavalry corps' strength by deploying two divisions of horse to guard his already well-protected trains. Sheridan and Meade argued once again over the use of cavalry, and the General in Chief backed Sheridan, allowing him now to concentrate his cavalry arm. Grant gave Sheridan a free hand in order to stop Stuart's raids. Leading his corps southward in a long ride toward Richmond, its objective a decisive charge against Stuart, Sheridan did the job. He fought a running series of engagements that culminated in a victory at Yellow Tavern, in which the gallant Stuart was mortally wounded. The South was already short of horses and mules, and Sheridan's 16-day raid ended forever the offensive power of Lee's mounted arm.

For four days beginning May 9 Meade struck repeatedly at Lee's roadblock at Spotsylvania but was beaten back. Twice the Federals broke through the trenches and divided Lee's army, but in each case the attackers became disorganized. Supporting infantry did not or could not close in, and Confederate counterattacks were delivered with such ferocity that the breakthroughs could be neither exploited nor held. On the morning of the 11th, Grant wrote Halleck: "I propose to fight it out on this line if it takes all summer." On May 20, having decided the entrenchments were too strong to capture, Grant sideslipped south again, still trying to envelop Lee's right flank.

With smaller numbers, Lee skillfully avoided Grant's trap and refused to leave entrenched positions and be destroyed in open battle. Lee retired to the North Anna River and dug in. Grant then continued to move south, to his left, in a daring and difficult tactical maneuver. Butler had meanwhile advanced

up the peninsula toward Richmond, but
Beauregard outmaneuvered him in May
and bottled up Butler's men at Bermuda
Hundred between the James and Appomattox Rivers. Eventually Butler and
Banks, who did not take Mobile, were
removed from command for their failure to carry out their assignments in the
grand strategy.

Lee easily made his way into the
Richmond defenses with his right flank
on the Chickahominy and his center
at Cold Harbor, the site of the Gaines'
Mill action in 1862. The front extended
for eight miles. On June 3 Grant assaulted Lee's center at Cold Harbor.
Though bravely executed, the attack was
badly planned. The Confederates re-

GUNS AND AMMUNITION *stored at
City Point.*

pulsed it with gory efficiency, and Grant later regretted that he had ever
made the attempt. Cold Harbor climaxed a month of heavy fighting in which
Grant's forces had casualties totaling about 55,000 as against about 32,000 for
those of Lee. After Cold Harbor, Grant executed a brilliant maneuver in the
face of the enemy. All Union corps were on the north bank of the deep, wide
James by June 14 and crossed over a 2,100-foot ponton bridge, the longest up to
that time in modern history. Having established a new and modern base depot
at City Point, complete with a railroad line to the front, Grant on June 18, 1864,
undertook siege operations at Petersburg below Richmond, an effort which
continued into the next year.

After forty-four days of continuous fighting, Lee was fixed finally in
position warfare, a war of trenches and sieges, conducted ironically enough
by two masters of mobile warfare. Mortars were used extensively, and heavy
siege guns were brought up on railway cars. Grant still sought to get around
Lee's right and hold against Lee's left to prevent him from shortening his line
and achieving a higher degree of concentration. When Lee moved his lines to
counter Grant, the two commanders were, in effect, maneuvering their
fortifications.

Now that Lee was firmly entrenched in front of Grant, and could spare
some men, he decided to ease the pressure with one of his perennial raids up
the Shenandoah Valley toward Washington. Confederate Maj. Gen. Jubal A.

Early's corps in early July advanced against Maj. Gen. David Hunter, who had replaced Sigel. Hunter, upon receiving confused orders from Halleck, retired up the valley. When he reached the Potomac, he turned west into the safety of the Appalachians and uncovered Washington. Early saw his chance and drove through Maryland. Delayed by a Union force on July 9 near Frederick, he reached the northern outskirts of Washington on July 11 and skirmished briskly in the vicinity of Fort Stevens. Abraham Lincoln and Quartermaster General Meigs were interested spectators. At City Point, Grant had received the news of Early's raid calmly. Using his interior waterway, he embarked the men of his VI Corps for the capital, where they landed on the 11th. When Early realized he was engaging troops from the Army of the Potomac, he managed to escape the next day.

Grant decided that Early had eluded the Union's superior forces because they had not been under a single commander. He abolished four separate departments and formed them into one, embracing Washington, western Maryland, and the Shenandoah Valley. In August, Sheridan was put in command with orders to follow Early to the death. Sheridan spent the remainder of the year in the valley, employing and co-ordinating his infantry, cavalry, and artillery in a manner that has won the admiration of military students ever since. He met and defeated Early at Winchester and Fisher's Hill in September and shattered him at Cedar Creek in October. To stop further raids and prevent Lee from feeding his army on the crops of that fertile region, Sheridan devastated the Shenandoah Valley.

Sherman's Great Wheel to the East

On March 17, 1864, Grant had met with Sherman at Nashville and told him his role in the grand strategy. Sherman, like Grant, held two commands. As Division of the Mississippi commander, he was responsible for the operation and defense of a vast logistical system that reached from a communications zone at St. Louis, Louisville, and Cincinnati to center on a large base depot at Nashville. Strategically, Nashville on the Cumberland River rivaled Washington, D.C., in importance. A 90-mile military railroad, built and operated by Union troops, gave Nashville access to steamboats plying the Tennessee River. Connected with Louisville by rail, Nashville became one vast storehouse and corral. If the city was destroyed, the Federal forces would have to fall back to the Ohio River line. Wearing his other hat, Sherman was a field commander, with three armies under his direction.

With the promise of the return of his two crack divisions from the Red River expedition by May 1864 and with a splendid administrative system working behind him, Sherman was ready to leave Chattanooga in the direction of Atlanta. (*Map 34*) His mission was to destroy Johnston's armies and capture Atlanta, which after Richmond was the most important industrial center in the Confederacy. With 254 guns, Sherman matched his three small armies, and a separate cavalry command—a total force of more than 100,000 men—against Joseph E. Johnston's Army of Tennessee and the Army of Mississippi including Wheeler's cavalry, consisting of 65,000 men.

Sherman moved out on May 4, 1864, the same day the Army of the Potomac crossed the Rapidan. Johnston, realizing how seriously he was outnumbered, decided to go on the defensive, preserve his forces intact, hold Atlanta, and delay Sherman as long as possible. There was always the hope that the North would grow weary of the costly struggle and that some advocate of peaceful settlement might defeat Abraham Lincoln in the election of 1864. From May 4 through mid-July, the two forces maneuvered against each other. There were daily fights but few large-scale actions. As Sherman pushed south, Johnston would take up a strong position and force Sherman to halt, deploy, and reconnoiter. Sherman would then outflank Johnston, who in turn would retire to a new line and start the process all over again. On June 27 Sherman, unable to maneuver because the roads were muddy and seriously concerned by the unrest in his armies brought about by constant and apparently fruitless marching, decided to assault Johnston at Kennesaw Mountain. This attack against prepared positions, like the costly failure at Cold Harbor, was beaten back. Sherman returned to maneuver and forced Johnston back to positions in front of Atlanta.

Johnston had done his part well. He had accomplished his missions and had so slowed Sherman that Sherman covered only 100 miles in 74 days. Johnston, his forces intact, was holding strong positions in front of Atlanta, his main base; but by this time Jefferson Davis had grown impatient with Johnston and his tactics of cautious delay. In July he replaced him with Lt. Gen. John B. Hood, a much more impetuous commander.

On July 20, while Sherman was executing a wide turning movement around the northeast side of Atlanta, Hood left his fortifications and attacked at Peach Tree Creek. When Sherman beat him off, Hood pulled back into the city. While Sherman made ready to invest, Hood attacked again and failed again. Sherman then tried cavalry raids to cut the railroads, just as Johnston had during the advance from Chattanooga, but Sherman's raids had as little success as Johnston's. Sherman then began extending fortifications on August 31. Hood, who had dissipated his striking power in his assaults, gave up and retired to

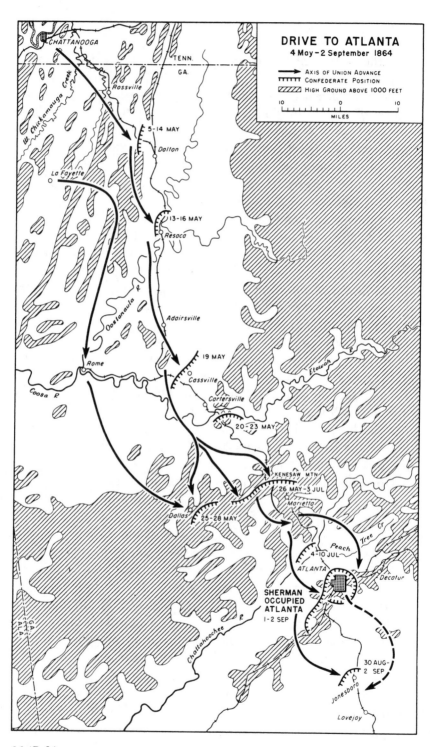

DRIVE TO ATLANTA
4 May – 2 September 1864

AXIS OF UNION ADVANCE
CONFEDERATE POSITION
HIGH GROUND ABOVE 1000 FEET

10   0   10
MILES

CHATTANOOGA

TENN.
GA.

Rossville

W. Chickamauga Creek

5-14 MAY
Dalton

La Fayette

13-16 MAY
Resaca

Oostanaula R.

Adairsville

19 MAY
Cassville

Rome

Coosa R.

Cartersville

Etowah R.

20-23 MAY

KENESAW MTN
26 MAY-3 JUL

Marietta

Dallas

25-28 MAY

Peach Tree Cr.

4-10 JUL

ATLANTA

Decatur

SHERMAN
OCCUPIED
ATLANTA
1-2 SEP

Chattahoochee R.

GA. R.R.

30 AUG-
2 SEP

Jonesboro

Lovejoy

MAP 34

northwest Alabama, and Sherman marched into Atlanta on the first two days of September. Sherman hoped that Mobile had fallen, and a shorter line for his supplies by way of Montgomery, Alabama, or still better by the lower Chattahoochee to Columbus, Georgia, was open. Admiral Farragut had entered Mobile Bay on August 5, 1864, but had no troops to take Mobile itself.

The fall of Atlanta gave President Lincoln's campaign for re-election in 1864 a tremendous boost. In addition, the psychological lift given the Union by Admiral Farragut's personal heroism in the battle of Mobile Bay greatly added to Lincoln's prestige.

Atlanta was only a halfway point in Sherman's vast wheel from the western theater toward the rear of Lee's Army of Northern Virginia. Abandoning the idea of catching up with Hood, Sherman by telegraph outlined his next strategic move to Lincoln and Grant in early September 1864. Sherman's two proposals proved him an able strategist as well as a consummately bold and aggressive commander. To defend Nashville, he suggested that he send two corps, 30,000 men, back to Thomas, where that commander would raise and train more men and be in position to hold Tennessee if Hood came north. To carry the offensive against the economic heart of the Confederacy, Sherman recommended that he himself take four corps—62,000 men—cut his own communications, live off the country, and march to the seacoast through Georgia, devastating and laying waste all farms, railways, and storehouses in his path. Whether he arrived at Pensacola, Charleston, or Savannah, Sherman reasoned he could hold a port, make contact with the U.S. Navy, and be refitted by Stanton and Meigs. Meigs promised to do the logistical job, and Lincoln and Grant, though their reaction to the plan was less than enthusiastic, accepted it in a show of confidence in Sherman.

Before marching out of Atlanta, Sherman's engineers put selected buildings to the torch and destroyed all railroads in the vicinity. On November 12, moving away from the Nashville depots toward Savannah, the Division of the Mississippi troops broke telegraphic contact with Grant. They had twenty days' emergency rations in their wagons, but planned to replenish them by living off the country. Operating on a 60-mile-wide front, unimpeded by any Confederate force, Sherman's army systematically burned and destroyed what it did not need. The march became something of a rowdy excursion. Sherman's campaign, like Sheridan's in the Shenandoah, anticipated the economic warfare and strategic aerial bombardments of the twentieth century. Yet the victims of his methods could hardly be blamed if they regarded Sherman's strategy as an excuse for simple thievery.

On December 10 Sherman, having broken the classic pattern by moving away from his logistical base, arrived in front of Savannah. Confederate forces evacuated the seaport on December 21 and Sherman offered it to the nation as a Christmas present. Awaiting him offshore was Meigs' floating seatrain, which enabled him to execute the last phase of Grant's strategy, a thrust north toward the line of the James River.

Thomas Protects the Nashville Base

Sherman, as the western theater commander, did not learn of Nashville's fate until he reached Savannah. He had planned Nashville's defense well enough by sending his IV and XXII Corps under Maj. Gen. John M. Schofield to screen Hood's northward move from Florence, Alabama. Schofield was to allow Thomas some time to assemble 50,000 men and strengthen Nashville. The aggressive Hood with his 30,000 men had lost a golden opportunity to trap Schofield at Spring Hill, Tennessee, on November 29, 1864. Unopposed, the Union troops made a night march across Hood's front to escape capture. Bitterly disappointed, Hood overtook Schofield the next day at Franklin.

Grant's continental timetable could have at this point been upset by Hood. Booty at Nashville might carry Hood to the Ohio or allow him to concentrate with Lee before Richmond. But Franklin turned into one of the Confederacy's most tragic battles. It commenced about 3:30 p.m. on November 30 and ended at dusk as Hood threw 18,000 of his veterans against a solidly entrenched force of Federals. Like Pickett's charge at Gettysburg, Hood's frontal assault gained nothing. He lost over 6,000 men, including 13 general officers. At nightfall Schofield brought his troops in behind Thomas' defenses at Nashville.

Hood was in a precarious position. He had been far weaker than Thomas to begin with; the battle of Franklin had further depleted his army; and, even worse, his men had lost confidence in their commander. The Federals in Nashville were securely emplaced in a city which they had been occupying for three years. Hood could do little more than encamp on high ground a few miles south of Nashville and wait. He could not storm the city; his force was too small to lay siege; to sidestep and go north was an open invitation to Thomas to attack his flank and rear; and to retreat meant disintegration of his army. He could only watch Thomas' moves.

Thomas, the Rock of Chickamauga, belonged to the last bootlace school of soldiering. In comparison with Grant and Sherman, he was slow; but he was also thorough. He had gathered and trained men and horses and was prepared to attack Hood on December 10, but an ice storm the day before made movement impossible. Grant and his superiors in Washington fretted at the delay, and the General in Chief actually started west to remove Thomas. But on December 15 Thomas struck like a sledgehammer in an attack that militarily students have regarded as virtually faultless.

Thomas' tactical plan was a masterly, co-ordinated attack. His heavily weighted main effort drove against Hood's left flank while a secondary attack aimed simultaneously at Hood's right. Thomas provided an adequate reserve and used cavalry to screen his flank and extend the envelopment of the enemy left. Hood, on the other hand, was overextended and his thin line was concave to the enemy, denying him the advantage of interior lines. Hood's reserve was inadequate, and his cavalry was absent on a minor mission.

The two-day battle proceeded according to Thomas' plan as the Federals fixed Hood's right while slashing savagely around the Confederate left flank. They broke Hood's first line on December 15, forcing the southerners to retire to a new line two miles to the rear. The Federals repeated their maneuver on the 16th, and by nightfall the three-sided battle had disintegrated into a rout of Hood's army. Broken and defeated, it streamed southward, protected from hotly pursuing Union cavalry only by the intrepid rear-guard action of Forrest's horsemen. The shattered Army of the Tennessee reached Tupelo, Mississippi, on January 10, 1865. It no longer existed as an effective fighting force; Hood was relieved of command and his scattered units were assigned to other areas of combat. The decisive battle of Nashville had eliminated one of the two great armies of the Confederacy from a shrinking chessboard.

Lee's Last 100 Days

President Lincoln was delighted with Savannah as a Christmas present, and in his congratulatory letter to Sherman and Grant the Commander in Chief said that he would leave the final phases of the war to his two leading professional soldiers. Accordingly, from City Point, Grant directed Sherman, on December 27, 1864, to march overland toward Richmond. At 3:00 p.m. on December 31, Sherman agreed to execute this last phase of Grant's continental sweep. In the final 100 days of the war, the two generals would clearly demonstrate the art of making principles of warfare come alive and prove that each principle was something more than a platitude. Each commander had a common objective: Grant and Meade would continue to hammer Lee. Sherman was to execute a devastating invasion northward through the Carolinas toward a juncture with Meade's Army of the Potomac, then on the line of the James River. Their strategy was simple. It called for the massing of strength and exemplified an economy of force. It would place Lee in an unmaneuverable position, cutting him off from all other Confederate commanders. Surprise would be achieved by reuniting all of Sherman's original corps when Schofield, moving from central Tennessee by rail, river, and ocean transport, arrived at the Carolina capes. Solidly based on a centralized logistical system with protected Atlantic sea trains at their side, Grant and Sherman were ready to end Lee's stay in Richmond.

Robert E. Lee, the master tactician, divining his end, wrote to Davis that the Confederates would have to concentrate their forces for a last-ditch stand. In February 1865 the Confederate Congress conferred supreme command of all Confederate armies on Lee, but it was an empty honor. Lee could no longer control events. Sherman moved through Columbia, South Carolina, in February, took Wilmington, North Carolina, the Confederacy's last port, then pushed on. Johnston, newly reappointed to a command, had the mission of stopping Sherman's forces, but could not. At Richmond and Petersburg toward the end of March, Grant renewed his efforts along a thirty-eight-mile front to get at Lee's right (west) flank. By now Sheridan's cavalry and the VI Corps had returned from the Shenandoah Valley, and the total force immediately under Grant numbered 101,000 infantry, 14,700 cavalry, and 9,000 artillery. Lee had 46,000 infantry, 6,000 cavalry, and 5,000 artillery.

On March 29 Grant began his move to the left. Sheridan and the cavalry pushed out ahead by way of Dinwiddie Court House in order to strike at Burke's Station, the intersection of the Southside and Danville Railroads, while Grant's main body moved to envelop Lee's right. But Lee, alerted to the threat, moved west. General A.P. Hill, who never stood on the defense if there was a chance to attack, took his corps out of its trenches and assaulted the Union left in the swampy forests around White Oak Road. He pushed General Warren's V Corps back at first, but Warren counterattacked and by March 31 had driven Hill back to his trenches. Next day Sheridan advanced to Five Forks, a road junction southwest of Petersburg, and there encountered a strong Confederate force under General Pickett—cavalry plus two infantry divisions—which Lee had dispatched to forestall Sheridan. Pickett attacked and drove Sheridan back to Dinwiddie Court House, but there Sheridan dug in and halted him. Pickett then entrenched at Five Forks instead of pulling back to make contact with Hill, whose failure to destroy Warren had left a gap between him and Pickett, with Warren's corps in between. Sheridan, still formally the commander of the Army of the Shenandoah, had authority from Grant to take control of any nearby infantry corps of the Army of the Potomac. He wanted Warren to fall upon Pickett's exposed rear and destroy him, but Warren moved too slowly, and Pickett consolidated his position. Next day Sheridan attacked again but failed to destroy Pickett because Warren had moved his corps too slowly and put most of it in the wrong place. Sheridan, another devotee of the offensive principle who would not tolerate failure to engage the enemy, summarily relieved Warren of command.

Grant renewed his attack against Lee's right on April 2. The assault broke the Confederate line and forced it back northward. The Federals took the line of the Southside Railroad, and the Confederates withdrew toward Petersburg. Lee then pulled Longstreet's corps away from the shambles of Richmond to hold the line, and in this day's action Hill was killed. With his forces stretched thin, Lee had to abandon Richmond and the Petersburg fortifications. He struck out and raced west toward the Danville Railroad, hoping to get to Lynchburg or Danville, break loose, and eventually join forces with Johnston. But Grant had him in the open at last. He pursued relentlessly and speedily, with troops behind (east of) Lee and south of him on his left flank, while Sheridan dashed ahead with the cavalry to head Lee off. A running fight ensued from April 2 through 6. Ewell's corps was surrounded and captured at Sayler's Creek. Lee's rations ran out; his men began deserting and straggling. Finally, Sheridan galloped his men to Appomattox Court House, squarely athwart Lee's line of retreat.

Lee resolved that he could accomplish nothing more by fighting. He met Grant at the McLean House in Appomattox on April 9, 1865. The handsome, well-tailored Lee, the very epitome of southern chivalry, asked Grant for terms. Reserving all political questions for his own decision, Lincoln had authorized Grant to treat only on purely military matters. Grant, though less impressive in his bearing than Lee, was equally chivalrous. He accepted Lee's surrender, allowed 28,356 paroled Confederates to keep their horses and mules, furnished rations to the Army of Northern Virginia, and forbade the soldiers of the Army of the Potomac to cheer or fire salutes in celebration of victory over their old antagonists. Johnston surrendered to Sherman on April 26, twelve days after the assassination of the President. The last major trans-Mississippi force gave up the struggle on May 26, and the grim fighting was over.

Attrition in manpower had forced both South and North to turn from volunteers to conscription in order to keep their armies up to effective strength. The Confederate government had enacted a draft law as early as April 1862. Late in that year Union governors were no longer able to raise enough troops for the Federal armies and on March 3, 1863, Congress passed the Enrollment Act, an outright assertion of national conscription by the central government. This law made able-bodied males between 20 and 45 years of age liable for national

TRENCHES BEFORE PETERSBURG

military service. The Enrollment Act was not popular, as bloody draft riots in New York demonstrated after Gettysburg. Both the Confederate and the U.S. laws were undemocratic in that they did not apply equally to all individuals. They provided for exemptions that allowed many to escape military service entirely. Comparatively few men were ever drafted into the Federal service, but by stimulating men to volunteer the Enrollment Act had its desired effect.

The principal importance of the Enrollment Act of 1863, however, does not lie in the effect it had on manpower procurement for the Civil War. This measure established firmly the principle that every citizen is obligated to defend the nation and that the Federal government can impose that obligation directly on the citizen without mediation of the states. In addition, the act recognized that the previous system of total reliance on militia and volunteers would not suffice in a modern, total war.

Dimensions of the War

Viewing the war in its broadest context, a historian could fairly conclude that a determined general of the North had bested a legendary general of the South, probably the most brilliant tactician on either side, because the Union could bring to bear a decisive superiority in economic resources and manpower.

Lee's mastery of the art of warfare staved off defeat for four long years, but the outcome was never really in doubt. Grant—and Lincoln—held too many high cards. And during the last year of the war, the relations between the Union's Commander in Chief and his General in Chief set an unexcelled example of civil-military co-ordination.

In this costly war, the Union Army lost 138,154 men killed in battle. This figure seems large, but it is scarcely half the number—221,374—who died of other causes, principally disease, bringing the total Union dead to 359,528. Men wounded in action numbered 280,040. Figures for the Confederacy are incomplete, but at least 94,000 were killed in battle, 70,000 died of other causes, and some 30,000 died in northern prisons.

With the advent of conscription, mass armies, and long casualty lists, the individual soldier seemed destined to lose his identity and dignity. These were the days before regulation serial numbers and dog tags (although some soldiers made individual tags from coins or scraps of paper). But by the third year of the war various innovations had been introduced to enhance the soldier's lot. Union forces were wearing corps badges which heightened unit identification, *esprit de corps*, and pride in organization. The year 1863 saw the first award of the highest United States decoration, the Medal of Honor. Congress had authorized it on July 12, 1862, and the first medals were given by Secretary Stanton in 1863 to Pvt. Jacob Parrott and five other soldiers. They had demonstrated extraordinary valor in a daring raid behind the Confederate lines near Chattanooga. The Medal of Honor remains the highest honor the United States can bestow upon any individual in the armed services.

Throughout the western world, the nineteenth century, with its many humanitarian movements, evidenced a general improvement in the treatment of the individual soldier, and the U.S. soldier was no exception. The more severe forms of corporal punishment were abolished in the U.S. Army in 1861. Although Civil War medical science was primitive in comparison with that of the mid-twentieth century, an effort was made to extend medical services in the Army beyond the mere treatment of battle wounds. As an auxiliary to the regular medical service, the volunteer U.S. Sanitary Commission fitted out hospital ships and hospital units, provided male and, for the first time in the U.S. Army, female nurses, and furnished clothing and fancier foods than the regular rations. Similiary, the U.S. Christian Commission augmented the efforts of the regimental chaplains and even provided, besides songbooks and Bibles, some coffee bars and reading rooms.

The Civil War forced changes in the traditional policies governing the burial of soldiers. On July 17, 1862, Congress authorized the President to establish national cemeteries "for the soldiers who shall die in the service of the country." While little was done during the war to implement this Congressional action, several battlefield cemeteries—Antietam, Gettysburg, Chattanooga, Stones River, and Knoxville—were set up, ". . . as a final resting place for those who here gave their lives . . ." in lieu of some nameless corner of a forgotten field.

As the largest and longest conflict of the nineteenth century in the western world, save for the Napoleonic struggle, the American Civil War has been argued and analyzed for the more than a hundred years since the fighting stopped. It continues to excite the imagination because it was full of paradox. Old-fashioned, in that infantry attacked in the open in dense formations, it also foreshadowed modern total war. Though not all the ingredients were new, railroads, telegraph communications, steamships, balloons, armor plate, rifled weapons, wire entanglements, the submarine, large-scale photography, and torpedoes—all products of the burgeoning industrial revolution—gave new and awesome dimensions to armed conflict.

CHAPTER 13

Darkness and Light
The Interwar Years, 1865–1898

With the end of the Civil War, the great volunteer army enlisted for that struggle was quickly demobilized and the U.S. Army became once again a Regular organization. During the ensuing period the Army faced a variety of problems, some old and some new. These included, besides demobilization, occupation duty in the South, a French threat in Mexico, domestic disturbances, Indian troubles, and, within the Army itself, the old awkward relationship between the line and the staff departments. Despite a relative isolation from civilian society during the period 1865–98, the Army developed professionally, experimented with new equipment of various kinds, and took halting steps toward utilizing the period's new technology in weapons. In a period of professional introspection, the Army still contributed to the nation's civil progress.

Demobilization, Reorganization, and the French Threat in Mexico

The military might of the Union was put on display late in May 1865, when Meade's and Sherman's armies participated in a grand review in Washington, Sherman's army alone taking six and one-half hours to pass the reviewing stand on Pennsylvania Avenue. It was a spectacle well calculated to impress on Confederate and foreign leaders alike that only a strong government could field such a powerful force. But even as these troops were preparing for their victory march, the War Department sent Sheridan to command an aggregate force of about 80,000 men in the territory west of the Mississippi and south of the Arkansas, of which he put about 52,000 in Texas. There Sheridan's men put muscle behind previous diplomatic protests against the presence of French troops in Mexico. The French had entered that country several years earlier ostensibly to collect debts, but since 1864 had maintained their puppet Maximilian on a Mexican throne in the face of opposition from

Mexican patriot forces under Benito Juárez. While the Civil War lasted, the United States had been unable to do more than protest this situation, for even a too vigorous diplomacy might have pushed France into an alliance with the South. Now stronger measures seemed necessary.

The military might in being in May 1865 was ephemeral, for the volunteers wanted to go home and Congress wanted to decrease the size of the Army. Because of the needs of occupation in the South and the French threat in Mexico, demobilization was spread over a period of eighteen months instead of the three in which it could have been accomplished. Nevertheless, it was rapid. On May 1, 1865, there were 1,034,064 volunteers in the Army, but by November 15, 800,963 of them had been paid, mustered out, and transported to their home states by the Quartermaster Corps. A year later there were only 11,043 volunteers left in the service, most of whom were United States Colored Troops. These were almost all mustered out by late October 1867.

General Grant, the General in Chief, wanted to increase the Regular Army, kept small during the Civil War, to 80,000 men, but neither Secretary Stanton nor Congress would agree. Congress, on July 28, 1866, voted an establishment of 54,302 officers and enlisted men. Actual strength reached about 57,000 on September 30, 1867, a peak for the whole period down to 1898. In 1869 Congress cut the number of infantry regiments to 25 and the authorized strength to 45,000; in 1876 the regimental tables of organization were reduced so as to limit the total authorized force to 27,442, an authorization that remained virtually stationary until the Spanish-American War. A significant effect of the Civil War on the new organization of the Army was a provision in the 1866 act for four Negro infantry regiments, which were reduced to two in 1869, and two Negro cavalry regiments, though most of their officers would be white. In 1877, Henry O. Flipper of Thomasville, Georgia, became the first Negro graduate of West Point and was assigned to one of these regiments, the 10th Cavalry.

Demobilization was not so rapid that Napoleon III was unaware of the strength of U.S. forces in being. In the spring of 1867 he finally withdrew his troops from Mexico and left Maximilian to die before a *juarista* firing squad. While there were other factors that help explain the French emperor's action, and historians are not agreed on his motives, he could not have ignored the determination to enforce the Monroe Doctrine embodied in Sheridan's show of force, especially since Maj. Gen. John M. Schofield was then on a special mission in France to make this point clear.

Reconstruction

The Civil War settled once and for all the questions of slavery and of state sovereignty, but the problems of reconstruction remained after Appomattox and with them the Army's involvement in southern affairs. The nation had to be put back together, and the peace had to be won or the sacrifices of a terrible war would have been in vain. The Army had a principal role in reconstruction from the very beginning. As the Union armies advanced in the South, civil government collapsed, except in Sherman's military district, and the Army found itself acting in place of the civil government by extending the function of its provost marshals from policing troops to policing and, in effect, governing the occupied areas. The duties of these provost marshals ranged from establishing garbage regulations to trying to determine the loyalty of southern citizens. Near the end of the war, Congress created the Bureau of Refugees, Freedmen, and Abandoned Lands—the Freedmen's Bureau—and put it under the Army. Its primary purpose was to protect and help the former slaves. In late 1865 most of the governmental functions of the provost marshals were transferred to this bureau, which was headed by Maj. Gen. Oliver O. Howard, a professional officer with antislavery convictions of long standing. As early as 1862, President Lincoln appointed military governors, who were civilians functioning with military support, in Tennessee, Louisiana, and North Carolina.

After Lincoln's death, President Andrew Johnson went ahead with his own reconstruction plans. He declared the Civil War formally at an end in April 1866, liberally pardoned most former Confederates upon their taking a loyalty oath, and then permitted them to re-establish civil government. The leniency of this program, some historians now maintain, led the Army, under Grant, with Stanton in the War Department, to look to Congress rather than to the President, the Commander in Chief, for aid in protecting the Union forces in the South from harassment. Congress, at the same time, was in fundamental disagreement with the President's course. It therefore asserted its supremacy in a series of legislative acts, undoing all that President Johnson had done and placing the South under military control.

The Congress set forth its basic plan in the Command of the Army Act (actually a part of the Army Appropriations Act of 1867) and the Tenure of Office and the First Reconstruction Acts of March 1867. The first of these provided that all Presidential orders to the Army should be issued through the General in Chief, whose headquarters would be in Washington, and who could be removed only with Senate approval. Similarly, the Tenure of Office Act denied the President authority to remove Cabinet officers without approval of the Senate. The first of these acts sought to make Grant rather than the President supreme over the Army, while the Tenure of Office Act sought to keep Stanton in the War Department and the next year provided the principal basis for the impeachment of President Johnson when he suspended the Secretary from office without the Senate's consent.

The First Reconstruction Act divided the South into five military districts. The commanders of these districts were major generals who reported directly to Washington. This was an interesting command relationship, for it was customary to divide the country into geographical commands called divisions, whose subordinate parts were called departments. In March 1867, however, there were only two divisions, the Missouri and the Pacific, with the rest of the country divided into the five military districts of the South and into departments which, like the five districts, reported directly to Washington. As time went by, the Army created additional geographical divisions, and in 1870 a Division of the South comprising three territorial departments administered military affairs in what had been the five reconstruction districts. There is a difference of opinion as to how much the First Reconstruction Act removed control of the reconstruction forces from President Johnson, although Grant advised Sheridan, one of the district commanders, that these commanders, rather than the Executive in Washington, were the sole interpreters of the act. In July 1867, Congress incorporated this interpretation in the Third Reconstruction Act, which declared that "no district commander . . . shall be bound in his action by any opinion of any civil officer of the United States." As a consequence of the First and Third Reconstruction Acts, some historians regard the reconstruction forces as virtually a separate army under Congressional control, thus distinguishing them from the forces in the territorial divisions and departments which remained clearly under the President.

Under the Reconstruction Acts the district commanders had to cope with such matters as horse stealing, moonshining, rioting, civil court proceedings, regulating commercial law, public education, fraud, removing public officials, registering voters, holding elections, and the approving of new state constitutions by registered voters. This occupation duty absorbed somewhat more than one-third of the Army's strength in 1867. As the southern states were restored to the Union under the reconstruction governments, military rule came to an end and civil authorities assumed full control of state offices. This process was largely completed in 1870.

With the ending of Congressional reconstruction, the Army's direct supervision of civil affairs in the South came to an end and the number of troops on occupation duty, which already had fallen off markedly, was reduced still further. Now its mission was to preserve the new state governments by continuing its protection of the Negroes and their white allies upon whom the governments rested, policing elections, helping to apprehend criminals, and keeping the peace in conflicts between rival state officials. The Ku Klux Klan, a postwar organization that had a considerable membership by 1870–71, became an object of special concern to the Army, as it did to the Congress, because of the Klan's terroristic efforts to deliver the South from Negro-Radical Republican control. Consequently, one of the most important Army functions in this period was support of federal marshals in an effort to suppress the Klan. This became an Army responsibility despite the restoration of state militia forces under the reconstruction governments as a means of relieving some of the burden on the Regular troops, which were spread thin. Since many of these new militia forces consisted of Negroes, they were not very effective against white terrorists, who directed some of their acts against the militiamen themselves. These militia forces mainly performed general police duty and watched over elections and voting. Eventually, because of the opposition of white southerners to Negroes in uniform, the Negro militia forces were disbanded.

In April 1877, as a result of the compromise by which Rutherford B. Hayes became President after the disputed election of 1876, the last of the troops on reconstruction duty in the South were transferred to other duty and the federal military occupation of the South came to an end. The Army's role in the South in the years 1865–77 was without precedent in the United States.

Domestic Disturbances

Aside from the Indian wars and Sheridan's show of force on the Mexican border, the Army engaged in no conventional military operations of any consequence until the Spanish-American War, that is, for a period of over thirty years. There were, however, a number of domestic disturbances in which armed forces were used, not only in the South during the reconstruction period but elsewhere as well. Indeed, by 1878, when Congress forbade the use of federal troops without authorization by either "the Constitution or . . . Congress," there had been literally hundreds of instances of their use by federal marshals in strikes, enforcement of local laws, collection of revenues, and arrests of offenders.

In the summer of 1877 the Hayes administration used troops in the wave of railway strikes that marked the country's first great national labor dispute. These strikes spread to a dozen or more states and led to a number of requests for federal help. Thereupon, the Hayes administration pursued a policy of moving troops only to protect federal property or upon the request of a governor or federal judge. The Army stripped every post in Maj. Gen. Winfield Scott Hancock's Military Division of the Atlantic of its available men and also obtained troops from other posts. Additionally, President Hayes used some marines. The President had his own source of information during the strikes in Signal Corps observer-sergeants at weather stations, who reported to Washington at intervals concerning conditions as they saw them in their localities.

Under the circumstances of their use, federal troops came into only limited contact with mobs during the 1877 strikes. They nevertheless contributed greatly to the restoration of order, as Hancock reported, "by their presence alone." The positive results were not due to the size of the forces, for with only about 24,000 troops in the entire Army in 1877 only a small detachment could be used at any one place. But these Regular troops were well disciplined and, taking their cue from the President himself, they acted with considerable restraint in putting down the strikes, neither losing a single soldier nor causing the death of any civilian.

Although the Army became involved in other strike duty in the succeeding years of the century, the best-known instance was in the Pullman, or railway, strike of 1894 which, though centered in Chicago, also affected other parts of the country. President Grover Cleveland's order hastily putting troops in Chicago against the wishes of Governor John Peter Altgeld provided that they should execute the orders and processes of federal courts, prevent obstructions to the movement of the mails, and generally enforce U.S. laws. In fact, they put down the strike. Other governors also protested the use of federal troops in their states. Maj. Gen. Nelson A. Miles, who commanded the 2,000 federal troops in Chicago (and who had advised against using them in the strike), did not use his men effectively, perhaps because he broke them up in small detachments in support of policemen and marshals at scattered points. New orders, however, required him to concentrate his forces and authorized him to fire upon rioters after a proper warning. A small company of Regular troops under his command did fire upon a mob in Hammond, Indiana, on July 8, 1894, when about to be overwhelmed by many times their own number. At least one rioter was killed and more than a dozen rioters were wounded in this action.

The violence was actually much less in 1894 than in 1877, but with only about 28,000 officers and enlisted men in the Army, Schofield, the Commanding General, reported that while his troops performed their duty "promptly and effectively," the situation taxed them "nearly to the limit." He might have added that, at least in California, both sailors and marines were used. The

United States Supreme Court unanimously sustained President Cleveland's actions in Chicago during the 1894 strike, with the result that a legal precedent was set for using federal troops within a state without its consent.

The National Guard Movement

Despite the use of Regular troops in notable instances, the organized militia under state control saw more strike duty than the Regulars in the years after the Civil War. The volunteer militia organizations that had existed since the colonial period became, in effect, the only real militia in existence in those years. The events of the seventies in particular led many persons to fear another insurrection, and as a result legislation was introduced to improve and to provide better arms for the organized militia. In 1879, in support of this effort, the National Guard Association came into being in St. Louis, and between 1881 and 1892 every state revised its military code to provide for an organized militia, which most states, following the lead of New York, called the National Guard. As such, it was by 1898 the principal reserve standing behind the Regular Army.

There was a certain martial enthusiasm in the seventies and eighties, despite the general antimilitarism of the period, that swelled the ranks of the Guard. Also, the Guard attracted some persons because it was a fraternal group that appealed to the manly virtues of physical fitness, duty, and discipline; and it attracted many because it was a kind of social club whose members enjoyed a local prestige. Although organized by states, the Guard had roots in the new nationalism of the period, as may be seen in its very name. Despite this new interest in the Guard, and although the War Department supported the Guard's proposal for a new militia act, apathy, states' rights, and antimilitarism prevented Congress from enacting the desired legislation. Through the efforts of the National Guard Association, the Guard nevertheless succeeded in securing an act in 1887 that doubled the $200,000 annual federal grant for firearms that the militia had enjoyed since 1808.

Isolation and Professional Development

The industrial unrest of the seventies and later was a manifestation of the growing industrialization and urbanization of the nation in the last decades of the nineteenth century, but while labor organizations grew as never before they were of relatively little influence until much later. Meanwhile, perhaps partly as a reaction to the terrible experiences of the Civil War, the ideals and philosophy of what Samuel P. Huntington calls "business pacifism" became dominant. Among other things, business pacifism rejected things military as outmoded in an industrial world designed to produce and sell goods, and it made an impression upon both intellectuals and the popular mind. It manifested itself as either indifference or outright hostility to the Regular Army, affected military appropriations, and philosophically separated the Army from the people. In the late sixties and in the seventies, as Army appropriations fell off (and in 1877 were not even made until November) the Army became isolated from the society at large. It became isolated not only socially, but physically as well, for much of the Army was on lonely duty in the West. Those years, according to William Addleman Ganoe, were "The Army's Dark Ages." They caused the Army and the Navy as well to look inward and to develop a truly military viewpoint that differed fundamentally from business pacifism and civilian liberal thought in general.

Paradoxically, in Huntington's words, the post-Civil War years were actually "the most fertile, creative, and formative in the history of the American armed forces." It took such a period of peace to develop the professionalism that would find employment in the world wars of the next century. In the Army, this professionalism took shape largely under the impetus of two men, General William T. Sherman and Col. Emory Upton, who were helped by other reformers of lesser rank. Their contemporary, Rear Adm. Stephen B. Luce, was similarly the architect of a new professionalism in the Navy.

Sherman's fame, of course, rests upon his record in the Civil War, but he was also the Commanding General of the Army for almost fifteen years from 1869, when he succeeded Grant, to 1883, when Sheridan succeeded him—a record second only to that of Winfield Scott. Unlike Grant and two of the other five Commanding Generals before him, Sherman remained out of politics and thus began the tradition of political neutrality, which would be adhered to long after his time, although not religiously. In this and other ways he oriented the thought of the professional soldier. As Commanding General he became the architect for a system of postgraduate schools beyond the Military Academy through which an officer could learn the skills of his own branch of the service and finally the principles of higher command.

Emory Upton, a protégé of Sherman, was the most influential of the younger officers who worked to reform the Army. He was graduated from West Point in 1861 and was brevetted a major general during the Civil War. After the war he prepared a new system of infantry tactics; served as commandant of cadets at the Military Academy, 1870–75; went on a mission to study the armies of Asia and Europe, which left him especially impressed by the German military system; and then became superintendent of theoretical instruction in the Artillery School at Fort Monroe. His best known writings, *The Armies of Asia and Europe* (1878) and *The Military Policy of the United States* (1904), argued for numerous reforms. The second of these two books was unfinished at the time of his death by suicide in 1881, but was put in order by an associate and, circulating in the Army, became influential long before its publication. It presented a case for a strong Regular military force based upon U.S. experience and subsequently provided the Regular Army with intellectual ammunition for shooting down the arguments of militia advocates, for whom John A. Logan provided a text in his posthumously published *Volunteer Soldier of America* (1887). In Upton's view, a wartime army should consist entirely of Regular formations, which meant that all volunteers should serve under Regular officers. Upton borrowed this plan for an expansible Regular Army from John C. Calhoun. Without giving due weight to the strength of tradition, he wanted the United States to abandon its traditional dual military system and replace it with a thoroughgoing professional army on the German model.

The Military Academy at West Point was at the base of the pyramidal structure of the Army educational system. Unfortunately, much of the vitality went out of the instruction at West Point after 1871 with the departure of Dennis Hart Mahan, the intellectual godfather of the postwar reformers. Although the War Department removed West Point from control of the Corps of Engineers in 1866, the Academy continued to provide a heavily mathematical training and to turn out military technicists but at the same time lost its former eminence as an engineering school. As time went by, the technical content of the curriculum in both the Military Academy and the Naval Academy was reduced, but by 1900 the effort to combine basic military and liberal arts subjects set both institutions off from other collegiate institutions and from the mainstream of education in the United States.

The period of reduced emphasis on technicism at the Military Academy saw the rise of the special postgraduate technical schools that Sherman favored. When the Engineers lost their responsibility for West Point in 1866, a group of engineer officers founded the Essayons Club, which became the Engineer School of Application in 1885. In 1868 Grant revived Calhoun's Artillery School at Fort Monroe, which had been closed since 1860. Also in 1868, a signal school of instruction opened at Fort Greble and, in 1869, moved to Fort Whipple (later Fort Myer), where it continued until 1885. In 1881, Sherman founded the School of Application for Infantry and Cavalry at Fort Leavenworth. Although at its beginning this school was little different from any of the other branch schools, it eventually fulfilled Sherman's hopes and evolved, with much of the credit due Col. Arthur L. Wagner, into the General Service and Staff College.

The Medical Department under the Surgeon General, George Miller Sternberg, founded the Army Medical School in 1893.

Included in the act of 1866 that fixed the organization of the postwar Army was a provision authorizing the President to detail as many as twenty officers to teach military science in schools of higher learning. This supplemented the part of the Morrill Act of 1862 that had provided for military instruction in land-grant colleges. By 1893 the number of instructors had increased to one hundred. In this program can be seen the beginnings of the Reserve Officers' Training Corps, although it would not be organized as such for many years.

Another significant aspect of the developing military professionalism of the years following the Civil War was the founding of professional associations and journals. Notable among them were the United States Naval Institute, founded in 1873, whose *Proceedings* would become well known; the Military Service Institution of the United States, whose *Journal* would become a casualty of World War I; the United States Cavalry Association, which published the *Cavalry Journal;* and the Association of Military Surgeons, which published *The Military Surgeon.* In 1892 the Artillery School at Fort Monroe founded *The Journal of the United States Artillery;* and in 1893 a group of officers at Fort Leavenworth founded the Infantry Society, which became the United States Infantry Association the following year and later published the *Infantry Journal.* Earlier, in 1879, *United Service* began publication as a journal of naval and military affairs. Still earlier, in 1863, the *Army and Navy Journal,* as it came to be called, began a long run. It was not a professional journal like the others mentioned, but along with its social and other items about service personnel it carried articles, correspondence, and news of interest to military people that helped bind its readers together in a common professional fraternity.

Before the Civil War the Army had no professional personnel system in the modern sense. Traditionally, most officers came into the service from the Military Academy at the lowest rank and received promotions on the basis of seniority. The war, however, made at least the need for a retirement system evident, and in 1861 Congress provided for compulsory retirement for incapacity. In 1862 and 1870 it provided that after thirty years' service an officer might retire either voluntarily or compulsorily at the President's discretion. Finally, in 1882, legislation made retirement compulsory at age sixty-four, which prompted the retirement of Sherman, Meigs, and Surgeon General Joseph K. Barnes. Beginning in 1890, promotions for all officers below the rank of major were by examination, thus insuring a minimum level of professional competence. In the mid-nineties, the Army instituted systematic character and efficiency reports for all officers.

Line and Staff

There was no end, during the years between the Civil War and the turn of the century, to the old controversy between the line of the Army and the staff departments. The controversy had its roots in a legally divided responsibility and received nourishment from a conception of war as a science and as the natural purpose of the military. Although Congress made Grant a full general in 1866, and although Sherman and Sheridan both held that rank after him neither these officers (except only Grant during postwar reconstruction) nor their successors were able to avoid the basic organizational frustrations of the office of Commanding General. The problem was inevitable because, as Army regulations put it as late as 1895, the military establishment in the territorial commands was under the Commanding General for matters of discipline and military control, while the Army's fiscal affairs were conducted by the Secretary of War through the staff departments. At the same time, no statutory definition of the functions of the Commanding General existed except to a limited extent late in the century in the matter of research and development. In practice this situation also diluted the Commanding General's control of the territorial departments, since obviously the distribution and diversion of logistical support for these departments by the staff heads and the Secretary of War would affect troop operations.

Basic to the controversy was an assertion of the primacy of the line over the staff departments, for which there was a theoretical foundation in the developing conception of war as a science and the practice of that science as the sole purpose of military forces. Since the Army existed only to fight, it followed that its organization, training, and every activity should be directed to the single end of efficiency in combat. Therefore, the staff departments, which represented technicism, existed only to serve the purposes of the line, which represented professionalism. From that proposition it followed that the line, in the person of the Commanding General, should control the staff. It also followed that the Army should not become involved, as it did, in such activities as the advancement of science or exploration.

"The regular Army now is a very curious compound," Sherman observed in 1874 in hearings on a bill to reduce the Army. As the Commanding General, he had "no authority, control or influence over anything but the cavalry, artillery, and infantry, and such staff officers as are assigned by their respective chiefs, approved by the Secretary of War, and attached to these various bodies for actual service." To him the three services that he named were "the Army of the United States," while the rest simply went "to make up the military peace establishment." If the Army had to be pruned, he advised pruning the branches of this peace establishment, not the active regiments. To a question about who commanded the engineer battalion, he replied that "God only knows, for I do not." In his opinion the Ordnance Department was "the softest place in the Army." Sons and nephews wanted to go into it, he declared, "especially young men with influential congressional friends." As for the 450 men of the "signal detachment," Sherman regarded them as "no more soldiers than the men at the Smithsonian Institution. They are making scientific observations of the weather, of great interest to navigators and the country at large. But what does a soldier care about the weather? Whether good or bad, he must take it as it comes."

Sherman's view was that of the Army command and of the line, but it did not prevail. In 1894, the situation in which heads of the staff departments spent their entire careers with their specialty and became technical rather than military experts was modified by the requirement that thereafter appointments to the staff departments should be from the line of the Army. This left the basic command problem still unresolved.

Technical Development

The record of the Army's technical development in the years down to the end of the century was not one of marked and continuous progress in every field, for it was hampered by military conservatism, insufficient funds, and the nation's slowness in adapting inventive genius to the art of war. Yet there was considerable progress. In transportation, with the extension of the trans-Mississippi railroads, it became possible to move whole wagon trains by lashing the wagons to flatcars and transporting the mules in closed cars. In ordnance there was progress, however slow, and there were notable beginnings, some of them of vast potential, in signal communications.

The Army was about as slow in adopting new weapons as it was in solving the problem of command that had plagued it for so long. Although Henry and Spencer breech-loading repeating rifles using rim-fire cartridges were used during the Civil War, the typical Civil War infantry shoulder arm was a muzzle-loading rifle musket. In the years immediately following the war, the Ordnance Department, faced with a shortage of funds, converted thousands of Civil War muzzle-loaders to breechloaders. Desiring a better weapon, however, the Army convened a board in 1872 to examine and test existing weapons. After the board had examined over a hundred weapons the Army adopted the single-shot Model 1873 Springfield breechloader. This fired a center-fire, .45-caliber cartridge, the caliber that the Ordnance Department selected as most desirable for all rifles, carbines, and pistols. The 1889 model of this gun, which embodied its final modifications, was the last of the Army's single-shot, large-caliber, black-powder rifles and the principal shoulder arm of the National Guard as late as 1898.

The Springfield remained in service even after the adoption of newer weapons and despite the trend toward smokeless powder and repeating arms abroad. U.S. manufacturers were slow to develop the new powder, which had several clear advantages. It burned progressively, gradually increasing the velocity of the bullet as it traveled through the barrel. In addition, its increasing pressures permitted a refinement in the rifling that gave a greater spin to the bullet and produced a higher velocity and a flatter trajectory.

When smokeless powder became available in the United States, a board in 1890 recommended adoption of the Danish .30-caliber, bolt-action Krag-Jörgensen rifle, which fired smokeless cartridges and had a box magazine holding five cartridges. The Army adopted the Krag, as it came to be known, in 1892, but Congress delayed production at the Springfield Armory for two years until tests of fourteen American models failed to turn up a superior weapon. By 1897 the Krag had been issued throughout the Regular Army. When its manufacture was discontinued in 1904, the original 1892 model had been twice modified, in 1896 and 1898.

Of the several types of the early machine gun available during the Civil War, the most successful was the Gatling gun, which the Army did not adopt until 1866, when the war was over. Even the advocates of this gun failed to recognize its usefulness as an infantry weapon, but instead looked upon it as either auxiliary to artillery or as a useful weapon for defending bridges.

In artillery as in shoulder arms American technical genius lagged behind that of Europe, where breech-loading artillery using smokeless powder became common in the late nineteenth century. Other European improvements were explosive shells and recoil-absorbing devices, which permitted refiring without reaiming after every shot and opened the way to sophisticated sighting mechanisms and to indirect fire. Also, the year before the Spanish-American War the French invented their famous 75-mm. gun. The U.S. Army nevertheless adopted some good rifled breechloaders, the 3.2-inch rifle being the standard light field piece. These new guns replaced the old smoothbores and steel replaced iron in their construction, but they still used black powder. The Army also had begun to experiment with steel carriages, pneumatic or hydraulic brakes, and mechanisms for elevating, traversing, and sighting artillery pieces.

The progress that had been made in artillery and armor plate was at least partly the result of the work of several boards. The first of these was the joint Army-Navy Gun Foundry Board, provided by the Naval Appropriations Act of 1883. Its purpose was to consider the problem of how American industry could produce both armor plate and armor-piercing guns, upon which a modern navy depended, that would be comparable to the products of European industry. After touring European armament factories, the board recommended that the government award generous contracts to U.S. companies to stimulate their development of steels and forgings, and that the government itself assemble the new materials into weapons at both the Naval Gun Factory and Army arsenals.

The new interest in the Navy in those years resulted in a need to examine coastal fortifications, which would have to be improved if new ships were not to be tied down to defense of the principal harbors. As a consequence the Endicott Board was set up in 1885 to plan for restoration of the coastal fortifications. Neither the world situation nor the existing naval technology justified the estimated cost of implementing the board's recommendations, but in 1888 Congress voted an initial appropriation and established a permanent body, the Board of Ordnance and Fortification, to supervise programs concerned with preparing coastal fortifications. This board was significant as the first War Department-wide agency for supporting research and development and as an attempt to place the important staff departments partly under the control of the Commanding General. Moreover, its failure served to point up the defects in the War Department's organization. The board remained in existence until 1920, but in 1890 and 1891 engineer expenditures and in 1892 ordnance expenditures were removed from the board's supervision. The actual work on the fortifications that followed was never completed, but during the nineties the Army abandoned the old forts around the principal harbors in favor of earthworks, armor-plated concrete pits, and great 10-inch and 12-inch disappearing rifles.

During the years after the Civil War there were several significant, some even germinal, developments in signal communications under the Signal Corps, or the Signal Service as it was known for many years. In 1867 the War Department restored electric field telegraphy to the Signal Corps, which had lost responsibility for it about three years earlier; and the corps quickly developed a new flying or field telegraph train, using batteries, sounders, and insulated wire. Then after constructing a telegraph line along the east coast in 1873 as an aid to the Life-Saving Service, the Signal Corps built long telegraph lines in both the Southwest and Northwest to provide communication between isolated military posts. These also provided facilities for transmitting weather reports. By 1881 these lines extended for slightly more than 5,000 miles.

In the late seventies, within a year or two of Alexander Graham Bell's patenting of the telephone, the Army was using it experimentally at Fort Whipple and between that post and Signal Corps offices in Washington. By 1889 a field-telephone kit, combining the Bell telephone, a Morse key, and a battery, had been developed but was believed to be too expensive for manufacture and issue at that time. About three years later, of ninety-nine garrisoned posts, fifty-nine had telephone equipment, some belonging to the Signal Corps and some rented from the Bell Telephone Company. At about the same time that the Army began using the telephone, it also became interested in the heliograph and found it to be particularly useful in the Southwest. There were also experiments as early as 1878 with homing pigeons.

Perhaps most significant of all the Signal Corps experimentation and developments of the period was the reintroduction of balloons into the Army in the early nineties for the first time since the Civil War. In 1893 the Signal Corps exhibited a military balloon at the World's Columbian Exposition in Chicago, and in 1896 it organized a model balloon train at Fort Logan, Colorado. Here were the beginnings that would lead without interruption to the development of Army aviation.

The backwardness of the United States in military technology in the nineties, despite some important developments, would be misleading unless one looked beyond the specific military facts to examine the nation's industrial base. The United States was already an industrial giant. In 1890, only twenty-nine years after the beginning of the Civil War, the United States pulled ahead of Great Britain in the production of both pig iron and steel and thus became the world's leading producer. Moreover, in the decade of the nineties, the United States also surpassed Great Britain in coal production. In total manufactures, the nation's share jumped from less than 20 percent of the world volume in 1880 to more than 35 percent in 1913. With such an industrial base and potential, the Army of the nineties had no real need for concern.

Civil Accomplishment

The U.S. Army performed a variety of highly useful civil functions in the interwar years, despite the new professionalism that decried such activities as contrary to the natural purpose of an army. Upon the purchase of Alaska from Russia in 1867 the Army assumed responsibility for Alaskan affairs, excepting in

MEMBERS OF THE GREELY EXPEDITION. *Lieutenant Greely is fourth from the left, front row.*

matters concerning customs, commerce, and navigation which became a responsibility of the Treasury Department. This situation continued until June 1877 when the Army withdrew from Alaska, partly because of the cost of maintaining a garrison in so remote a place, and left the Treasury Department in charge. For the next twenty years the Army's principal role in Alaska was in support of various explorations conducted by Army personnel, which had begun at least as early as 1869 when Capt. Charles W. Raymond of the Army Engineers explored the Yukon. Thereafter there were other explorations in the Yukon, the region of the Copper and Tanana Rivers, and to Point Barrow by, variously, 1st Lt. Frederick Schwatka of the 3d Cavalry, 2d Lt. William R. Abercrombie of the 2d Infantry, 2d Lt. Henry T. Allen of the 2d Cavalry, and 1st Lt. Patrick Henry Ray of the Signal Corps.

Ray's expedition to Point Barrow, 1881–83, was successful in carrying out various meteorological and other observations. It returned safely, but the companion Lady Franklin Bay expedition to Ellesmere Island, 1881–84, under 1st Lt. Adolphus Washington Greely of the Signal Corps, was not nearly so fortunate. Although the Greely expedition reached a point farther north than any prior expedition and carried out its scientific observations, all but seven members of the party died before rescue (and one person died afterward) through failure of prearranged plans for receiving supplies. The Greely expedition grew out of the plans of Signal Corps 1st Lt. Henry W. Howgate for an Arctic colony at Lady Franklin Bay, and out of the proposals of the international polar conference in Hamburg in 1879 for a chain of meteorological stations about the North Pole. The Ray expedition stemmed from the Hamburg conference.

EARLY SIGNAL CORPS WEATHER OFFICE, *Washington, D.C.*

After the Civil War, the rivers and harbors work of the Corps of Engineers increased considerably, contributing substantially to development of the nation's water resources. Other notable contributions of the Engineers were their construction of public buildings, including supervision of the final work on the Washington Monument and on the State, War, and Navy Building, together with Brig. Gen. Thomas Lincoln Casey's planning and supervision from 1888 to 1895 of the construction of what is now the main building of the Library of Congress. Beginning in 1878, the Engineers provided an officer to serve by Presidential appointment as one of the three governing commissioners of the District of Columbia.

Of the four great surveys undertaken in the United States prior to establishment of the Geological Survey in the Interior Department in 1879, the Corps of Engineers had responsibility for two. They were the King Survey, 1867–72, which made a geological exploration of the 40th parallel; and the Wheeler Survey, 1871–79, as the geographical survey west of the 100th meridian was called. The latter was more of a military survey in the tradition of the old Corps of Topographical Engineers than was the former, which was essentially a civilian undertaking. Both of these surveys nevertheless collected specimens of great use to scientists in the fields of botany, zoology, paleontology, and related disciplines.

Although the Navy was largely responsible for interoceanic canal surveys in the post-Civil War years, the first United States Isthmian Canal Commission, appointed by President Grant in 1872, had Brig. Gen. Andrew A. Humphreys, Chief of Engineers, as one of its three members. In 1874 Maj. Walter McFarland,

Corps of Engineers, went out, with naval assistance, to examine the Nicaragua and Atrato-Napipi canal routes; and in 1897 Col. Peter C. Hains of the Engineers was one of the members appointed by President William McKinley to the Nicaragua Canal Commission.

In the years from 1870 to 1891 the War Department organized and operated under the Signal Corps the nation's first modern weather service using both leased telegraph lines and, after they were built, the Army's own military lines for reporting simultaneous observations to Washington. Under Brig. Gen. Albert J. Myer, the Chief Signal Officer, the service gained international renown, but partly because of the hostility of the War Department and the Army to the essentially civil character of the weather service and to its cost, Congress in 1890 directed transfer of the service to the Department of Agriculture, where it became the Weather Bureau in 1891. This loss of the weather service marked a general decline in the role of the military services in the cause of science. Although the Signal Corps retained responsibility for military meteorology, the Army had little need of it until World War I.

Of all the Army's civil contributions, those of its Medical Department, with immeasurable implications for the entire society, may well have been the most important. Indeed, medical research in the Army, in which a few outstanding men were predominant, did not reflect the decline in research that affected the other military branches of the period. One of the most notable of the Army's medical contributions was the Army Medical Library, or the Surgeon General's Library, which, though founded in 1836, did not come into its own until after 1868, when Assistant Surgeon John Shaw Billings began to make it into one of the world's great medical libraries. Similarly, in the same period, Billings developed the Army Medical Museum, which had been founded during the Civil War, into what would become in fact a national institute of pathology.

George Sternberg, who became the Surgeon General in 1893, was the leading pioneer in bacteriology in the United States and a worthy contemporary of Louis Pasteur and Robert Koch. Sternberg's official duties provided some opportunity for his studies, although he performed most of his research independently, some of it in the Johns Hopkins Hospital in Baltimore under the auspices of the American Public Health Association. He was appreciated by all except the more conservative of his colleagues who resisted the germ theory to about the same degree as physicians in private practice.

The more than three decades from the end of the Civil War to the Spanish-American War took the Army through a period of isolation and penury in which it engaged in no large war but in which it had opportunity for introspection. It took advantage of this opportunity and in professional ways that would mean much to its future success moved from darkness and near despair into the light of a new military day. Yet as the century drew to a close, the Army had yet another war to fight before it would see accomplished at least some of the reforms toward which the new military professionalism looked. Meanwhile, it became caught up in numerous Indian campaigns, or Indian wars, as they are now called.

CHAPTER 14

Winning the West: The Army in the Indian Wars, 1865–1890

Perhaps because of a tendency to view the record of a military establishment in terms of conflict, the U.S. Army's operational experience in the quarter century following the Civil War has come to be known as the Indian wars. Previous struggles with the Indian, dating back to colonial times, had been limited as to scope and opponent and took place in a period when the Indian could withdraw or be pushed into vast reaches of uninhabited and as yet unwanted territory to westward. By 1865 this safety valve was fast disappearing; routes of travel and pockets of settlement had multiplied across the western two-thirds of the nation, and as the Civil War closed, white Americans in greater numbers and with greater energy than before resumed the quest for land, gold, commerce, and adventure that had been largely interrupted by the war. The showdown between the older Americans and the new—between two ways of life that were basically incompatible—was at hand. The besieged red man, with white civilization pressing in and a main source of livelihood—the buffalo—threatened with extinction, was faced with a fundamental choice: surrender or fight. Many chose to fight, and over the course of some twenty-five years the struggle ranged over the plains, mountains, and deserts of the American West, a guerrilla war characterized by skirmishes, pursuits, massacres, raids, expeditions, battles, and campaigns, of varying size and intensity. Given its central role in dealing with the Indian, the Army made a major contribution to continental consolidation.

The Setting and the Challenge

After Appomattox the Army had to muster out over a million volunteers and reconstitute a Regular establishment that had languished during the Civil War when bounties and short enlistments made service in the volunteers more profitable. There were operational commitments to sustain during and after the transition, some an outgrowth of the war just ended, others the product of internal and external situations that could not be ignored. Whereas the prewar Army of the 1850's was essentially a frontier Army, the postwar Army became something more. To defense of the frontier were added military occupation of the southern states, neutralization of the Mexican border during Napoleon's colonial enterprise under Maximilian, elimination of a Fenian (Irish Brotherhood) threat to Canada in the Northeast, and dispersion of white marauders in the border states. But these and other later involvements were passing concerns. The conflict with the red man was the overriding consideration in the next twenty-five years until Indian power was broken.

Unfortunately, the military assets released from other tasks were lost through reductions in force instead of being diverted to frontier defense. For even though the country during the Indian campaigns could not be said to be at peace, neither Congress nor the war-weary citizens in the populous Atlantic states were prepared to consider it in a state of war. And in any case, there was strong sentiment against a large standing army as well as a widely held belief that the Indian problem could be settled by other than military means.

As the postwar Army took shape, its strength began a decade of decline, dropping from an 1867 level of about 57,000 to half that in the year that General Custer was killed, then leveling off at an average of about 26,000 for the remaining years up to the War with Spain. Effective strength always lay somewhere below authorized strength, seriously impaired, for example, by high rates of sickness and desertion.

Because the Army's military responsibilities were of continental proportions, involving sweeping distances, limited resources, and far-flung operations, an administrative structure was required for command and control. The Army was, therefore, organized on a territorial basis, with geographical segments variously designated as divisions, departments, and districts. There were frequent modifications of organization, rearrangements of boundaries, and transfers of troops and posts to meet changing conditions. (*Map 35*)

Development of a basic defense system in the trans-Mississippi West had followed the course of empire; territorial acquisition and exploration succeeded by emigration and settlement brought the whites increasingly into collision with the Indians and progressively raised the need for military posts along the transcontinental trails and in settled areas.

The annexation of Texas in 1845, the settlement of the Oregon boundary dispute in 1846, and the successful conclusion of the Mexican War with the cession to the United States in 1848 of vast areas of land, all drew the outlines of the major task facing the Army in the West in the middle of the nineteenth century. During the period between the Mexican and Civil Wars the Army

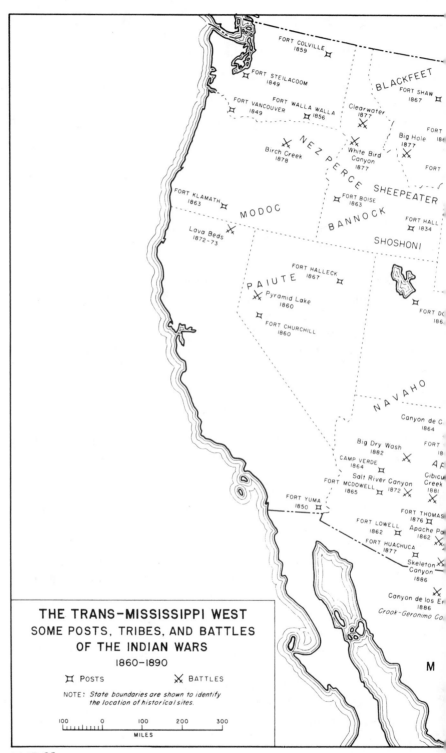

FORT COLVILLE 1859

FORT STEILACOOM 1849

BLACKFEET

FORT SHAW 1867

FORT WALLA WALLA 1856

FORT VANCOUVER 1849

Clearwater 1877

FORT

N E Z   P E R C E

Big Hole 1877

White Bird Canyon 1877

Birch Creek 1878

FORT

SHEEPEATER

FORT KLAMATH 1863

FORT BOISE 1863

MODOC

BANNOCK

FORT HALL 1834

Lava Beds 1872-73

SHOSHONI

FORT HALLECK 1867

P A I U T E

Pyramid Lake 1860

FORT DO 186

FORT CHURCHILL 1860

N A V A H O

Canyon de C. 1864

Big Dry Wash 1882

FORT 18

CAMP VERDE 1864

A F

Salt River Canyon 1872

Cibicu Creek 1881

FORT MCDOWELL 1865

FORT YUMA 1850

FORT THOMAS 1876

FORT LOWELL 1862

Apache Pa 1862

FORT HUACHUCA 1877

Skeleton Canyon 1886

Canyon de los Er 1886

Crook-Geronimo Co

M

THE TRANS-MISSISSIPPI WEST
SOME POSTS, TRIBES, AND BATTLES
OF THE INDIAN WARS
1860-1890

Ⴟ POSTS   ✕ BATTLES

NOTE: *State boundaries are shown to identify
the location of historical sites.*

100   0   100   200   300
MILES

MAP 35

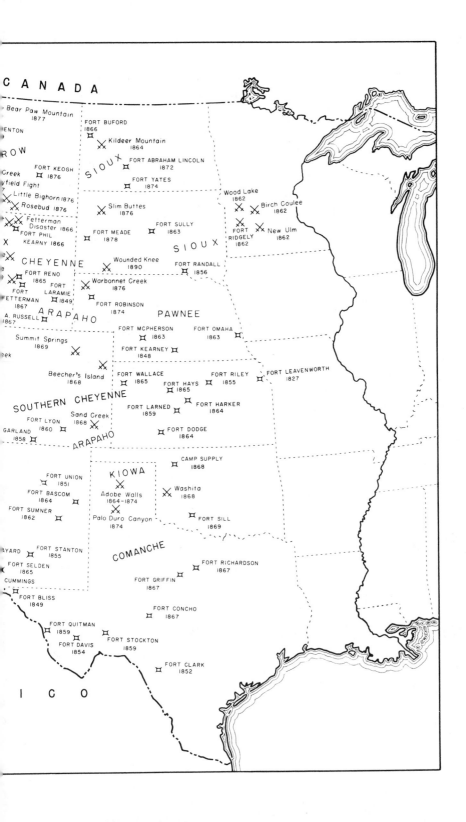

established a reasonably comprehensive system of forts to protect the arteries of white travel and areas of white settlement across the frontier. At the same time, operations were launched against Indian tribes that represented actual or potential threats to movement and settlement.

Militarily successful in some cases, these operations nevertheless hardened Indian opposition, prompted wider red provocation, and led to the delineation of an Indian barrier to westward expansion extending down the Great Plains from the Canadian to the Mexican border. Brig. Gen. William S. Harney, for example, responded to the massacre of Lt. John L. Grattan's detachment by Sioux with a punishing attack on elements of that tribe on the Blue Water in Nebraska in 1855. Farther south Col. Edwin V. Sumner hit the Cheyennes on the Solomon Fork in Kansas in 1857, and Bvt. Maj. Earl Van Dorn fought the Comanches in two successful battles, at Rush Spring in future Oklahoma and Crooked Creek in Kansas, in 1858 and 1859, respectively.

In the Southwest between the wars, Army units pursued Apaches and Utes in New Mexico Territory, clashing with the Apaches at Cieneguilla and Rio Caliente in 1854 and the Utes at Poncha Pass in 1855. There were various expeditions against various branches of the elusive Apaches involving hard campaigning but few conclusive engagements such as the one at Rio Gila in 1857. It was in this region in 1861 that Lt. George N. Bascom moved against Chief Cochise, precipitating events that opened a quarter century of hostilities with the Chiricahua Apaches.

In the Northwest, where numerous small tribes existed, there were occasional hostilities between the late 1840's and the middle 1860's. Their general character was similar to operations elsewhere: white intrusion, Indian reaction, and white counteraction with superior force. The more important events involved the Rogue River Indians in Oregon between 1851 and 1856 and the Yakima, Walla Walla, Cayuse, and other tribes on both sides of the Cascade Mountains in Washington in the last half of the 1850's. The Army, often at odds with civil authority and public opinion in the area, found it necessary on occasion to protect Indians from whites as well as the other way around.

The Regular Army's frontier mission was interrupted by the onset of the Civil War, and the task of dealing with the Indians was transferred to the volunteers. Although the red man demonstrated an awareness of what was going on and took some satisfaction from the fact that white men were fighting each other, there is little evidence that he took advantage of the transition period between removal of the Regulars and deployment of the volunteers. The so-called Great Sioux Uprising in Minnesota in 1862 that produced active campaigning in the Upper Missouri River region in 1863 and 1864 was spontaneous, and other clashes around the West were the result, not of the withdrawal of the Regular Army from the West, but of the play of more fundamental and established forces. In any case, by 1865 Army strength in the frontier departments was about double what it had been at the time of Fort Sumter. The volunteers were generally able to keep pace with a continuing and gradually enlarging westward movement by developing further the system of forts begun by their predecessors.

Thus the regional defense systems established in the West in the 1850's and 60's provided a framework for the deployment of the Army as it turned from the Civil War to frontier responsibilities. In the late summer of 1866 the general command and administrative structure for frontier defense comprised the Division of the Missouri, containing the Departments of Arkansas, Missouri, Dakota, and the Platte; the Division of the Pacific, consisting of the Departments of California and the Columbia; and the independent Department of the Gulf, whose area included Texas.

The Army's challenge in the West was one of environment as well as adversary, and in the summer of 1866 General Grant sent a number of senior officer inspectors across the country to observe and report on conditions. The theater of war was uninhabited or only sparsely settled, and its great distances and extreme variations of climate and geography accentuated manpower limitations, logistical and communications problems, and the difficulties of movement. The extension of the rail system only gradually eased the situation. Above all, the mounted tribes of the Plains were a different breed from the Indians the Army had dealt with previously in the forested areas of the East. Despite the fact that the Army had fought Indians in the West in the period after the Mexican War, much of the direct experience of its officers and men had been lost during the Civil War years. Until frontier proficiency could be re-established, the Army would depend upon the somewhat intangible body of knowledge that marks any institution, fortified by the seasoning of the Civil War.

Of the officers who moved to the forefront of the Army in the Indian wars, few had frontier and Indian experience. At the top levels at the outset, Grant as a captain had had only a taste of the loneliness of the frontier outpost. Western duty was unknown to Sherman, and, while Sheridan had served about five years in the Northwest as a junior officer, neither Nelson A. Miles nor Oliver Otis Howard knew frontier service of any kind. Wesley Merritt, George Armstrong Custer, and Ranald S. Mackenzie all graduated from West Point into the Civil War, and John Gibbon had only minor involvement in the Seminole War and some garrison duty in the West. Alfred Sully, also a veteran of the Seminole War and an active campaigner against the Sioux during Civil

War years, fell into obscurity, while Philip St. George Cooke was overtaken by age and Edward R. S. Canby's experience was lost prematurely through his death at Indian hands. George Crook almost alone among the Army leaders at the upper levels of the Indian wars had pre-Civil War frontier experience, dating from 1852, that he could bring back to the West in 1866.

Thus to a large degree the officers of the Indian wars were products of the Civil War. Many brought outstanding records to the frontier, but this was a new conflict against an unorthodox enemy. Those who approached their new opponent with respect and learned his ways became the best Indian fighters and in some cases the most helpful in promoting a solution to the Indian problem. Some who had little respect for the "savages" and placed too much store in Civil War methods and achievements paid the penalty on the battlefield. Capt. William J. Fetterman was one of the first to fall as the final chapter of the Indian wars opened in 1866.

The Bozeman Trail

While the Civil War was still in progress, gold was discovered in Montana and fortune seekers flocked to the area. Lines of communications to the fields around Virginia City lay along circuitous routes and pressure mounted for more direct access. The Army explored the possibilities and adopted a route, pioneered by John Bozeman, extending from Fort Laramie on the North Platte River and Oregon Trail, northwestward along the eastern base and around the northern shoulder of the Big Horn Mountains. Unfortunately, the trail cut through hunting grounds reserved to the Sioux, Northern Cheyennes, and Arapahoes by treaty in 1865.

The Indians resisted white incursions and Maj. Gen. Patrick E. Connor's Powder River Expedition failed to stop their depredations. In 1866 the government, under public pressure and officially attracted to the gold resources as a means of relieving the financial strains of the Civil War, opened new negotiations, but with indifferent results. A few friendly chiefs signed a new agreement at Fort Laramie, but others led by Red Cloud of the Sioux stalked out defiantly when Col. Henry B. Carrington marched in with a battalion of the 18th Infantry, on his way to establish posts along the Bozeman Trail even before agreement with the Indians had been reached.

Although motivated by a sense of justice, treaty-making with the Indians more often than not constituted an exercise in futility for both parties. On the Indian side the tribes were loosely knit societies of individualists living a nomadic existence under leaders whose control and influence fluctuated with the fortunes of war. A treaty was no more binding than the degree of power, authority, and allegiance a leader might muster at any given time, Washington's understanding to the contrary. On the white side, although the authority of negotiating officials was unquestioned, the power to enforce treaty provisions on highly independent westering whites was another thing, and as breach after breach provoked the red man to action the Army was invariably called in to protect the offending citizens and punish the Indians.

Colonel Carrington's battalion of about 700 men departed Fort Laramie in June 1866 for the Big Horn country. Despite Red Cloud's threat to oppose the move, several families, including the commanding officer's, accompanied the force. At Fort Reno on Powder River, some miles beyond the end of the telegraph, Carrington with a Regular company relieved two companies of the 5th U.S. Volunteers, former Confederate prisoners who became so-called galvanized Yankees when they agreed to frontier Indian service in exchange for their freedom. Farther northwestward, 225 miles from Fort Laramie, he selected a site on the Piney tributary of Powder River to construct his headquarters post—Fort Phil Kearny. Five companies remained there while the remaining two were sent another 90 miles out to establish Fort C. F. Smith at the northern edge of the Big Horns.

Fort Phil Kearny became the focus of enemy attention and during its brief existence remained virtually in a state of siege. On December 21, 1866, the Indians attacked a wood train six miles from the fort. Captain Fetterman, who had been brevetted lieutenant colonel in Civil War actions and now boasted that with eighty men he could ride through the whole Sioux Nation, asked to lead a relief column. Indian decoys demonstrated invitingly before the rescue party, withdrawing gradually over Lodge Trail Ridge northwest of the post. Fetterman fell for the ruse and, against Carrington's orders, with eighty men at his back crossed the ridge. In a carefully executed ambush the Indians wiped out the entire force, including two civilians who had gone along to try out their new Henry repeating rifles, weapons far superior to the Springfield muzzle-loaders carried by the infantrymen and the Spencer carbines carried by the cavalrymen in the detail.

The Army was more successful in two other notable actions on the Bozeman Trail. In August 1867 the Indians launched separate but apparently co-ordinated attacks against a haying detail near Fort Smith and a wood detail outside Fort Kearny. In the Hayfield Fight 19 soldiers and 6 civilians, under Lt. Sigismund Sternberg, equipped with converted breech-loading Springfields and several repeating rifles, held off vastly superior odds with a loss of only 3 killed and 3 wounded. In the Wagon Box Fight, Capt. James Powell, with 31 men similarly armed and stationed behind wagon boxes removed from their running gear, held off an investing force of several thousand Sioux and Cheyennes for a good four hours, withstanding mounted and dismounted attacks by several hundred warriors at various times with only 3 killed and 2 wounded.

It is risky to deal in statistics concerning Indian participation and casualties in western campaigns. Accounts vary widely, are founded on shaky evidence, and require some balancing and juggling merely to reach a general order of magnitude, much less an accurate assessment of the facts in a given situation. There is no doubt that the Sioux and Cheyennes suffered serious casualties in the Hayfield and Wagon Box fights. For the Army, however, these were defensive engagements and it lacked sufficient force in the Upper Plains to undertake offensive operations. At the same time there was sentiment in the East to treat with rather than chastise the Indians. The government withdrew the garrisons and abandoned the Montana road in July 1868.

The Southern Plains

The Army during the Indian wars was habitually unable to balance resources with requirements, both because of limited manpower and because of the continental size of the theater of operations. As Lt. Gen. William T. Sherman, commanding the Division of the Missouri, put it, "Were I or the department commanders to send guards to every point where they are clamored for, we would need alone on the plains a hundred thousand men, mostly of cavalry. Each spot of every road, and each little settlement along five thousand miles of frontier, wants its regiment of cavalry or infantry to protect it against the combined power of all the Indians, because of the bare possibility of their being attacked by the combined force of all the Indians."

It was the good fortune of both the Army and the citizen in the West that the Indians rarely acted in concert within or between tribes, although had they done so the Army might have been able regularly to employ large units instead of dispersing troops in small detachments all over the frontier, and might also have had better luck in forcing the elusive opponent to stand and fight. But troops and units were at a premium, so much so in 1868 that Maj. Gen. Philip H. Sheridan decided to try an unusual expedient to carry out his responsibilities in the Department of the Missouri.

Sheridan directed Maj. George A. Forsyth to "employ fifty first-class hardy frontiersmen, to be used as scouts against the hostile Indians, to be commanded by yourself." Recruited at Forts Harker and Hays in Kansas, the command took the field in late August in a region frequented by Comanches, Kiowas,

Southern Cheyennes, and Arapahoes, augmented by some Sioux roaming south of the Platte. The tribes were restive. The Kansas Pacific Railroad was advancing through their country, frightening the buffalo—their source of food, clothing, and shelter—and attracting white settlement. The Cheyennes were still smoldering over the massacre of some 200 of Black Kettle's band, including women and children, by Col. John M. Chivington and his Colorado volunteers on Sand Creek in 1864, and had demonstrated their mistrust of the whites when Maj. Gen. Winfield Scott Hancock penetrated their area with a large and presumably peaceful expedition in 1867.

Forsyth and the Indians collided on the Arickaree Fork of the Republican River at dawn on September 17, 1868, when a combined war party of about 600 Cheyennes, Sioux, and Arapahoes attacked him in a defensive position on a small island in the river bed. The Indians pressed the fight for three days, wounding Forsyth and upwards of 20 of his scouts and killing his second in command, Lt. Frederick H. Beecher, and his surgeon and 3 scouts. Among Indian casualties in this Battle of Beecher Island was the influential Cheyenne leader Roman Nose. The first rescue force on the scene was Capt. Louis H. Carpenter's company of Negro troopers of the 10th Cavalry Regiment.

By the late 1860's the government's policy of removing Indians from desirable areas (graphically represented by the transfer of the Five Civilized Tribes from the Southeast to Oklahoma—the Cherokees called it the "Trail of Tears") had run its course and was succeeded by one of concentrating them on reservations. The practice of locating tribes in other than native or salubrious surroundings and of joining uncongenial bands led to more than one Indian war. Some bands found it convenient to accept reservation status and government rations during the winter months, returning to the warpath and hunting trail in the milder seasons. Many bands of many tribes refused to accept the treaties offered by a peace commission and resisted the government's attempt to confine them to specific geographical limits; it fell to the Army to force compliance. In his area, General Sheridan now planned to hit the Indians in their permanent winter camps.

While a winter campaign presented serious logistical problems, it offered opportunities for decisive results. If the Indians' shelter, food, and livestock could be destroyed or captured, not only the warriors but their women and children were at the mercy of the Army and the elements, and there was little left but surrender. Here was the technique of total war, a practice that raised certain moral questions for many officers and men that were never satisfactorily resolved.

Sheridan devised a plan whereby three columns would converge on the wintering grounds of the Indians just east of the Texas Panhandle, one from Fort Lyon in Colorado, one from Fort Bascom in New Mexico, and one from Camp Supply in Oklahoma. The 7th Cavalry Regiment under Lt. Col. George Armstrong Custer fought the major engagement of the campaign. Custer found the Indians on the Washita River and struck Black Kettle's Cheyenne village with eleven companies from four directions at dawn on November 29, 1868, as the regimental band played "Garry Owen." A fierce fight developed which the Indians continued from surrounding terrain. By mid-morning Custer learned that this was only one of many villages of Cheyennes, Arapahoes, Kiowas, and Comanches extending for miles along the Washita. Facing such odds, Custer hastened to destroy the village and its supplies and horses, used an offensive maneuver to deceive the enemy, and under cover of darkness withdrew from the field, taking 53 women and children as prisoners. The 7th lost 21 officers and men killed and 13 wounded in the Battle of the Washita; the Indians perhaps 50 killed and as many wounded.

The Kiowas and Comanches did not lightly relinquish their hunting grounds and forsake their way of life. Some lived restlessly on a reservation in Indian Territory around Fort Sill, others held out. Sherman, now Commanding General of the U.S. Army, Sheridan, commanding the Division of the Missouri, and their field commanders were forced into active compaigning before these tribes were subdued. In 1871 reservation Kiowas raided into Texas, killing some teamsters of a government wagon train. General Sherman, visiting at Fort Sill, had the responsible leaders—Satanta, Satank, and Big Tree—arrested in a dramatic confrontation on the post between armed Indians and soldiers in which only Sherman's coolness prevented an explosion. Satank was later killed attempting escape, while Satanta and Big Tree were tried and imprisoned for two years. Again in custody in 1876, Satanta took his own life.

There were other incidents on the Southern Plains before the Indians there were subjugated. An Army campaign in 1874, involving about 3,000 troops under Col. Nelson A. Miles' over-all command, was launched in five columns from bases in Texas, New Mexico, and Indian Territory against the Texas Panhandle refuge of the Plains tribes. On September 24 Col. Ranald S. Mackenzie and the 4th Cavalry found the winter camp of the Comanches, Kiowas, Cheyennes, and Arapahoes in a last stronghold, the deep Palo Duro Canyon on the Staked Plains. Mackenzie's surprise attack separated the Indians from their horses and belongings, and these were destroyed. With winter coming on the Indians had little alternative to the reservation.

The Northwest

Not all the Indian wars were fought with Plains tribes. The Army engaged in wars with several Pacific slope tribes in the 1870's, and the operations were widely scattered over the mountainous northwestern quarter of the trans-Mississippi West.

The Modoc War of 1872–73 began when the Modocs, who had been placed on a reservation in southern Oregon with the more numerous and traditionally unfriendly Klamaths, returned without permission to their home in the Lost River country on the California border. When the Army attempted in November of 1872 to take them back to the reservation, fighting broke out and the Indians retreated into a natural fortress—the Lava Beds at the southern end of Tule Lake. Over the course of six months there were four engagements in which Regular and volunteer troops with superior strength and weapons incurred heavier losses than their opponents. Extended efforts by a peace commission made little headway and ended in tragedy when two of the members, Brig. Gen. Edward R. S. Canby and Reverend Eleaser Thomas, both unarmed, were shot while in conference with the Indians. The Modocs finally surrendered and four of their leaders, including Canby's murderer, Captain Jack, were hanged.

The practice of uprooting the Indians from their homeland was also the cause of the Nez Perce War in 1877. The Nez Perces had been friendly to the whites from the days of their contact with Lewis and Clark. Although they ceded some of their lands to the whites, they refused to give up the Wallowa Valley in northeastern Oregon. White encroachment increased, stiffening the lines of political pressure back to Washington and leading inevitably to decisions favorable to white settlement and removal of the Nez Perces to the Lapwai Reservation across the Snake River in Idaho. Some elements of the tribe complied, but Chief Joseph and his people did not and the Army was ordered to move them. An inevitable course of events and irresponsible actions by both reds and whites made hostilities unavoidable.

In a remarkable campaign that demonstrated the unique capabilities of guerrilla forces and the difficulties that formal military units have in dealing with them, the Nez Perces led the Army on a 1,300-mile chase over the Continental Divide, punctuated by a number of sharp engagements. The Indians used the terrain to great advantage, fighting when circumstances favored them, sideslipping around opposing forces or breaking contact when the situation dictated it. They lived off the land, while the Army was tied to supply trains that were vulnerable to Indian attack. But their freedom of

SURRENDER OF CHIEF JOSEPH

movement was hindered by their women and children, while Army superiority in strength and weapons gradually began to tell. Indian rifles were no match for howitzers and Gatling guns, and Indian mobility could not outstrip the Army's use of the telegraph to alert additional forces along the Nez Perce line of flight. The battles of White Bird Canyon, Clearwater, Big Hole, Canyon Creek, and Bear Paw Mountain involved hundreds of troops and numerous units under Howard, Gibbon, Samuel D. Sturgis, and Miles. There were heavy casualties on both sides before Chief Joseph, in a poignant speech, surrendered. "Hear me, my Chiefs," were his closing words to Generals Howard and Miles, "my heart is sick and sad. From where the sun now stands I will fight no more forever."

In 1878 and 1879 Army forces took the field against various bands of Indians in mountain areas of the Northwest. Operations against the Bannocks, Sheepeaters, and Utes were relatively minor. The Bannock War was caused by white intrusion on the Camas Prairie in Idaho, where camas roots were a prime source of food for the Indians. The Sheepeater War, also centered in Idaho, broke out when the Indians were charged wtih several murders they probably did not commit. The Ute War in northwestern Colorado grew out of the misguided methods and impractical idealism of Indian Agent Nathan C.

Meeker. All of these clashes represented a last convulsion against fate for the tribes involved, while for the Army they meant hard campaigning and casualties.

The Southwest

The Apaches were among the Army's toughest opponents in the Indian wars. The zone of operations embraced the territories of Arizona and New Mexico, western Texas, and Mexico's northern provinces, and, despite the fact that hostile Apaches were relatively few in number and the theater was essentially a secondary one, they tied down sizable forces over a long period of time.

Post-Civil War Apache troubles extended from the late 1860's, when the Army campaigned against Cochise, on through the seventies and eighties, when Victorio and Geronimo came to the fore. On the Army side the important factor was the assignment of Bvt. Maj. Gen. George Crook to the Southwest, where he served two tours between 1871 and 1886. Crook was an able administrator as well as an outstanding soldier, and proved to be a relentless opponent of the Indian on the battlefield and a steadfast friend off it. As commander of the Department of Arizona he organized at key locations a number of mobile striking forces under experienced frontier officers and launched them in a concerted campaign supported by mule pack trains. Acting under an 1866 Congressional act, which authorized the Army to enlist up to a thousand Indian scouts (they came from traditionally friendly tribes like the Crow and Pawnee or from friendly elements of warring tribes), Crook also employed Apache scouts. Converging columns and persistent pursuit brought results, and he left Arizona in relative quiet when he went to the Department of the Platte in 1875.

But the quiet in the Southwest did not last long. Largely at the instigation of politicians, merchants, contractors, and other self-serving whites, several bands of mutually uncongenial Apaches were transferred from desirable areas to the unhealthy San Carlos Reservation in the Arizona lowlands. As a result, much of what Crook had accomplished was undone as disgruntled Apaches again turned to raiding and killing. In the summer of 1881, for example, an Apache medicine man stirred the Indians to heights of religious fervor that led to a sharp clash on Cibicu Creek with troops commanded by Col. Eugene A. Carr, one of the Army's most experienced Indian fighters. The action was highlighted by perhaps the most notable instance of disaffection when the Indian scouts with the command turned on the Regulars.

GERONIMO (*left center*) AT THE CONFERENCE WITH GENERAL CROOK (*second from right, seated*), *1886*.

Throughout the Indian wars there was constant friction between the War and the Interior Departments over the conduct of Indian affairs. A committee of the Continental Congress had first exercised this responsibility. In 1789 it was transferred to the Secretary of War, and in 1824 a Bureau of Indian Affairs was created in the War Department. When the Department of the Interior was established in 1849, the Indian bureau was transferred to that agency. Thus administration of Indian affairs was handled by one department while enforcement lay with another. As General Crook put it to a Congressional committee in 1879: "As it is now you have a divided responsibility. It is like having two captains on the same ship."

Crook returned to Arizona in 1882 to restore confidence among the Apaches in white administration, move them along the paths of civilization, and spar constantly with the Indian bureau. On the military side, he took the field against dwindling numbers of hostiles, co-operating with Mexican officials and authorized to cross the international boundary in pursuit of the renegades. Crook met with Geronimo in the Sierra Madre Mountains in March of 1886 and negotiated a surrender that brought in all but Geronimo and a few followers who backed out at the last moment. When Washington failed to back the field commander in the conditions on which he had negotiated the surrender, Crook asked to be relieved. Nelson A. Miles replaced him, and Lt. Charles B. Gatewood entered

Geronimo's mountain fastness to arrange a surrender and bring the Apache campaigns to a close.

The Northern Plains

All of the elements of the clash of red and white civilizations were present in the events leading to final subjugation of the Indians. The mounted tribes of the Great Plains were astride the main corridors of westward expansion, and this was the area of decision. The treaty of 1868 had set aside the Great Sioux Reservation in South Dakota and the Army had abandoned the Bozeman Trail, leaving the Powder River region as unceded Indian country. The Sioux and their allies were thus north of the main transcontinental artery along the Platte. Although the arrangement worked for several years, it was doomed by the irresistible march of civilization. The Sioux rejected white overtures for a right-of-way for the Northern Pacific Railroad, and when surveyors went ahead anyway they ran into Indian resistance, which led to the dispatch in 1873 of a large military expedition under Col. David S. Stanley up the Yellowstone Valley. The next year General Sheridan sent Custer and the 7th Cavalry on a reconnaissance through the Black Hills, within the Sioux Reservation. When geologists with the expedition found gold, the word spread rapidly and prospectors filtered into the area despite the Army's best efforts to keep them out. Another treaty was broken and, band by band, angry reservation Indians slipped away to join nontreaty recalcitrants in the unceded Powder River region of Wyoming and Montana.

In December 1875 the Indian bureau notified the Sioux and Cheyennes that they had to return to the reservation by the end of the following month. Since the Indians were in winter quarters in remote areas and would have had little chance against the elements, they did not obey. As the deadline passed, the Commissioner of Indian Affairs appealed to the Army to force compliance. Sheridan, mindful of his success with converging columns against the Southern Plains tribes, determined upon a similar campaign in the north.

Columns were organized to move on the Powder River area from three directions. Brig. Gen. Alfred H. Terry marched westward from Fort Abraham Lincoln in Dakota Territory, his principal element the 7th Cavalry under Custer. Col. John Gibbon moved eastward from Fort Ellis in western Montana with a mixed force of infantry and cavalry, while Brig. Gen. George Crook moved northward from Fort Fetterman on the North Platte in Wyoming with a force heavily weighted in cavalry. In March 1876 a part of Crook's force under Col. Joseph J. Reynolds had entered the valley of the Powder and surprised a

Cheyenne-Sioux camp, but Reynolds had failed to press an initial advantage and had withdrawn without punishing the Indians. In June, with the major campaign under way, Crook made the first contact. The Sioux and Cheyennes learned of his approach along Rosebud Creek, and some 1,500 warriors moved to meet him. Crook had fifteen companies of cavalry and five of infantry, about 1,000 men, plus another 300 friendly Indians and civilians. The two forces met on roughly equal terms on the 17th in heavy fighting. Tactically, neither side carried the field conclusively enough to claim a victory. Strategically, Crook's withdrawal to a supply base to southward gave the Battle of the Rosebud the complexion of a defeat for the Army, especially in view of developments on the Little Bighorn River about fifty miles to northwestward, which his continued advance might have influenced decisively.

While Crook was moving northward to his collision on the Rosebud, Terry and Gibbon, marching from east and west, had joined forces on the Yellowstone River at its confluence with the Powder, where a supply base serviced by river steamer was established. Terry sent out the 7th Cavalry to scout for Indian sign, and Maj. Marcus A. Reno with six companies (the cavalry "company" was not called a "troop" until 1883) reconnoitered up the Powder, across the Tongue River, and into the valley of the Rosebud. Here on June 17 Reno found a fresh trail leading west out of the valley and across the Wolf Mountains in the direction of the Little Bighorn. He was unaware, and was thus unable to inform his superiors, that Crook was also in the Rosebud valley and had been engaged and blocked by a large force of Indians not far upstream on this very same day.

Terry held a council of war aboard the steamer *Far West* to outline his plan. Custer's 7th Cavalry would move south up the Rosebud, cross the Wolf Mountains, and enter the Little Bighorn valley from the south. Gibbon, joined by Terry, would ascend the Bighorn River and its tributary, the Little Bighorn, from the north, trapping the Indians between the two forces.

As it happened, Custer moved at least a day early for the co-operative action envisioned in Terry's plan. On June 25, 1876, the 7th crossed the Wolf Mountains and moved into the valley of the Little Bighorn. Custer was confident of his capability to handle whatever he ran up against, convinced that the Indians would follow their usual practice of scattering before a show of force, and completely unaware that he was descending upon one of the largest concentrations of Indians ever assembled on the Plains—perhaps as many as 12,000 to 15,000 Sioux and Northern Cheyennes, with between 3,000 and 4,000 warriors under such leaders as Crazy Horse, Sitting Bull, Gall, Crow King, Lame Deer, Hump, and Two Moon.

Around noon of this Sunday in June, Custer sent Capt. Frederick W. Benteen with three companies to scout to the left of the command, not an unusual move for a force still attempting to fix the location of an elusive enemy and expecting him to slip away on contact. About 2:30 p.m., still two miles short of the river, when the upper end of an Indian village came into view, Custer advanced three more companies under Major Reno with instructions to cross the river and charge the Indian camp. With five companies Custer moved off to the right, still screened by a fold of ground from observing the extent of his opposition, perhaps with the thought of hitting the Indians from the flank—of letting Reno hold the enemy by the nose while he, Custer, kicked him in the seat of the pants. As he progressed, Custer rushed Sgt. Daniel Kanipe to the rear to hurry the pack train and its one-company escort forward, and shortly afterward dispatched Trumpeter John Martin with a last message to Benteen informing him that a "big village" lay ahead and to "be quick—bring packs."

The main phase of the Battle of the Little Bighorn lasted about two hours. Reno, charging down the river with three companies and some Arickara scouts, ran into hordes of Indians, not retreating, but advancing, perhaps mindful of their creditable performance against Crook the week before, and certainly motivated by a desire to protect their women and children and cover a withdrawal of the villages. Far outnumbered, suffering heavy casualties, and in danger of being overrun, Reno withdrew to the bluffs across the river and dug in.

Custer and his five companies—about 230 strong—moved briskly along the bluffs above the river until, some four miles away, beyond supporting distance and out of sight of the rest of the command, they were brought to bay and overwhelmed by an Indian force that outnumbered them by perhaps 20 to 1. When the last man had fallen and the dead had been plundered, the Indians turned their attention to Reno once again.

While the Indians had been chiefly absorbed on the Custer section of the field, Benteen's battalion and the pack train and its escorting company had moved up and gone into a defensive perimeter with Reno's force. An attempt to move in force in Custer's direction, despite a complete lack of knowledge of his location and situation, failed; the Reno defensive position was reoccupied and remained under attack until dark of the 25th and on through daylight hours of the 26th. The siege was finally lifted with the arrival of the Terry-Gibbon column on June 27th.

The Custer disaster shocked the nation and was the climax of the Indian wars. The Army poured troops into the Upper Plains and the Indians scattered, some, like Sitting Bull's band, to Canada. But gradually, under Army pressure or seeing the futility of further resistance, the Indians surrendered and returned to the reservation.

The last gasp of the Indian wars occurred in 1890 and grew out of the fervor of the Ghost Dance religion. The Sioux were particularly susceptible to the emotional excitement and the call of the old way of life represented in these ceremonies, and their wild involvement frightened the agent on the Sioux Reservation into calling for military protection. The 7th Cavalry, now commanded by Col. James W. Forsyth, moved to Wounded Knee Creek on the Pine Ridge Agency where, on December 29, 1890, the regiment attempted to disarm Big Foot's band. An Indian's rifle was discharged into the air as two soldiers disarmed him, precipitating a battle in which more than 150 Indians, including women and children, were killed and a third as many wounded, while 25 soldiers were killed and another 37 wounded.

The Battle of Wounded Knee was the last Indian engagement to fall in the category of warfare; later incidents were more in the realm of civil disturbance. The nineteenth century was drawing to a close and the frontier was rapidly disappearing. Territories were being replaced by states, and people, settlements, government, and law were spreading across the land. The buffalo were gone and the Indians were confined to reservations and dependent upon the government for subsistence. An expanded rail system was available to move troops quickly to trouble spots, and the Army could now concentrate its forces at the larger and more permanent posts and relinquish numerous smaller installations that had outgrown their usefulness. By 1895 the Army was deployed more or less equally around the country on the basis of regional rather than operational considerations.

In the quarter century of the Indian wars the Army met the Indian in over a thousand actions, large and small, all across the American West. It fought these wars with peacetime strength and on a peacetime budget, while at the same time it helped shape Indian policy, contributed to the red man's acculturation, and was centrally involved in numerous other activities that were part and parcel of westward expansion and of the nation's attainment of its "manifest destiny." Operations against the Indians seasoned the Army and forged a core of experienced leaders who would serve the republic well as it moved onto the world scene at the turn of the century.

CHAPTER 15

Emergence to World Power
1898–1902

In the latter part of the nineteenth century the United States, hitherto largely provincial in thought and policies, began to emerge as a new world power. Beginning in the late 1880's more and more Americans displayed a willingness to support involvement of the nation in frankly imperialistic ventures, justifying this break with traditional policy on strategic, economic, religious, and emotional grounds. Much of the energy that had been channeled earlier into internal development of the country, and especially into westward expansion along the frontier (which, according to the Census Bureau, ceased to exist as of 1890), was now diverted to enterprises beyond the continental limits of the United States. It was only a matter of time before both the Army and the Navy were to be called upon to support and protect the new American interests overseas.

A New Manifest Destiny

This new manifest destiny first took the form of vigorous efforts to expand long-established American trade and naval interests overseas, especially in the Pacific and Caribbean. Thus, in the Pacific the United States took steps to acquire control of coaling and maintenance stations for a growing steam-propelled fleet. In 1878 the United States obtained the right to develop a coaling station in Samoa and in 1889, to make this concession more secure, recognized independence of the islands in a tripartite pact with Great Britain and Germany. In 1893, when a new native government in Hawaii threatened to withdraw concessions, including a site for a naval station at Pearl Harbor, American residents tried unsuccessfully to secure annexation of the islands by the United States. Development of a more favorable climate of opinion in the United States in the closing years of the century opened the way for annexation of Hawaii in 1898 and Eastern Samoa (Tutuila) in 1899.

In the same period, the Navy endeavored with little success to secure coaling stations in the Caribbean, and Americans watched with interest abortive efforts of private firms to build an isthmian canal in Panama. American businessmen promoted establishment of better trade relations with Latin American countries, laying the groundwork for the future Pan American Union. And recurrent diplomatic crises, such as that with Chile in 1891–92, arising from a mob attack on American sailors in Valparaiso, and with Great Britain over the Venezuelan–British Guiana boundary in 1895, drew further attention to the southern continent.

Trouble in Cuba

While economic and strategic motives contributed significantly to the new manifest destiny, it was traditional American humanitarian concern for the oppressed peoples of Cuba that ultimately proved most important in launching the United States on an imperialistic course at the turn of the century. Cuba's geographic proximity to the United States and strategic location had long attracted the interest of American expansionists. Yet they were a small minority, and only when the Cubans rebelled against the repressive colonial policies of Spain did the attention of most Americans turn to the Caribbean island. This was true in 1868, when Cubans revolted against the Spanish regime in a rebellion destined to last for a decade, and again in 1895, when they rose up once more against continuing repression by the mother country. Many Americans soon favored some kind of intervention, but President Grover Cleveland was determined that the United States should adhere to a policy of strict neutrality. Events in Cuba, however, soon were to make this position increasingly difficult to maintain.

When after almost a year of costly fighting the Spanish had failed to suppress the rebellion, they turned to harsher measures. To carry these out the Madrid Government appointed a new Captain-General for Cuba, Valeriano Weyler, an officer with a reputation as an able soldier. Weyler arrived in Havana in early February 1896 with additional troops and immediately instituted new tactics designed to isolate the insurrectionist forces—entrenchments, barbed-wire fences, and, at narrow parts of the island, lines of blockhouses. Simultaneously, he inaugurated a policy of *reconcentrado,* herding women, children, and old people from the countryside into detention camps and garrisoned towns, where thousands died from disease and starvation. Weyler's methods gave newspapers in the United States, especially those practicing a newly fashionable yellow journalism, opportunity for renewed attacks on Spanish policies in Cuba. They portrayed the Spanish general as an inhuman "butcher" inflicting his cruel tactics on high-minded patriots struggling bravely for freedom from the oppression of an out-dated Old World authoritarianism.

In early 1896 both houses of Congress adopted by overwhelming majorities concurrent resolutions proposing that the United States grant belligerent status to the insurgents and employ its good offices to gain Spain's recognition of Cuban independence. Politicians, both in and out of Congress, saw in the Cuban situation an opportunity to gain popular support in the upcoming election of 1896. And a few expansion-minded American leaders perceived the insurrection as a chance to acquire naval bases in the Caribbean and open the way further for the country to play a more prominent role in world affairs. But neither Cleveland, nor his successor as President in 1897, William McKinley, wanted a war with Spain.

The Republican party platform of 1896, however, committed McKinley to a policy of using the nation's "influences and good offices to restore peace and give independence . . ." to Cuba. Consistent with this pledge, the newly elected President, in the face of a crescendo of demands for immediate American intervention, worked courageously and patiently, seeking to find a diplomatic solution that would satisfy the Cuban insurrectionists yet avoid a conflict between the United States and Spain.

In early February 1898, after serious rioting in Havana, the jingoistic New York *Journal* published a private letter written by Enrique Dupuy de Lôme, the Spanish Minister in Washington, to a Spanish editor then traveling in the United States. This communication, which a Cuban official in the Havana Post Office had stolen and passed on to the newspaper, expressed de Lôme's adverse personal reaction to McKinley's message to Congress in December 1897. The President was, he thought, "weak and a bidder for admiration of the crowd . . . a would-be politician who tries to leave a door open behind himself while keeping on good terms with the jingoes in his party." For the majority of Americans this unprecedented insult to a President was only further confirmation of the arrogance and insolence with which they felt Spain regularly conducted its Cuban policies. Even de Lôme's prompt resignation did little to calm the storm of indignation that swept the country. Nevertheless when Spain, at American insistence, somewhat reluctantly offered an apology, McKinley was inclined to accept it. Privately he was horrified at the possibility that what he viewed as a strictly personal matter might lead to war.

Despite this development McKinley still might have achieved a diplomatic solution had the American battleship *Maine* not been sunk on February 15, 1898, in Havana harbor as a result of a mysterious explosion, with a loss of 260 lives. The vessel was in the port ostensibly on a courtesy call—but actually to provide closer protection for American citizens in Cuba—dispatched there rather **reluctantly by McKinley upon the advice of the American consul in Havana.**

A naval investigating commission appointed by the President announced on March 25 that the *Maine* had gone down as a result of an external explosion, which to most Americans indicated Spanish treachery. But McKinley, in reporting to Congress on the commission's verdict, once again counseled "deliberate consideration" and, on March 27, sent to Madrid a new plan for peaceful settlement of the Cuban problem. The Spanish reply on March 31 agreed to end the *reconcentrado* policy and arbitrate the *Maine* disaster, but procrastinated on granting the insurrectionists an immediate armistice and refused to accept mediation by McKinley or to promise eventual independence for Cuba.

In spite of this discouraging response from Spain, the President continued to move slowly, leaving the door open for last-minute negotiations. Twice he postponed his war message to Congress before finally delivering it on April 11. Eight days later Congress passed a joint resolution proclaiming Cuba independent and authorizing the President to take necessary measures to expel the Spanish from the island. It included a significant amendment by Senator Teller of Colorado forbidding annexation of Cuba. With this authorization McKinley immediately ordered a blockade of Cuba, and an American naval squadron promptly took up a position off Havana. On April 25 Congress declared a state of war had existed since April 21. So began the conflict with Spain which McKinley and Cleveland had tried so hard to avoid—a war for which, despite the months of negotiation preceding its outbreak, the country was militarily most ill prepared.

Mobilizing for War

The extent of unpreparedness for overseas combat varied considerably in the two military services. In the decade preceding the war, the Navy, thanks to the efforts of career officers such as Rear Adm. Stephen B. Luce and Capt. Alfred T. Mahan, and to Benjamin Tracy, Secretary of the Navy in Harrison's administration, and also to the willingness of Congress, in a period of expanding overseas interests and relative prosperity, to appropriate the necessary funds, had carried out an extensive construction and modernization program. During the same period, the Naval War College at Newport, Rhode Island (established in 1885 through the efforts of Admiral Luce), had provided the Navy with a strong corps of professional officers trained in the higher levels of warfare and strategy, including the far-ranging doctrines of Mahan.

The Army was not so fortunate. With an average size in the quarter of a century preceding 1898 of only about 26,000 officers and men, most of whom were scattered widely across the country in company- and battalion-size organizations, the Army never had an opportunity for training and experience in the operation of units larger than a regiment. And while the individual soldier was well trained, the Army lacked a mobilization plan, a well-knit higher staff, and experience in carrying on joint operations with the Navy. The National Guard, with somewhat more than 100,000 members, was composed mostly of infantry units. Still lacking a consistent program of supervision by the Regular forces, most Guard units were poorly trained and disciplined, understrength, and inadequately equipped. Thus, typically, although most Regulars by 1898 were armed with Krag-Jörgensen rifles firing smokeless powder cartridges, most Guardsmen were still equipped with Springfield rifles which could fire only black powder ammunition.

Despite obvious deficiencies, the Guard might have supplied many of the units used in the conflict had it not been for other factors that made it difficult to employ Guardsmen on short notice in overseas theaters of war. Under existing law, there was some question as to whether it was legal for Guard units to serve abroad. Furthermore, Guard organization varied greatly from state to state, and most Guardsmen objected to any move that would place them under control of the Regular Army for the sake of achieving greater uniformity in organization. The War Department proposed to form a new federal volunteer force with officers appointed by the President. But again the Guard opposed this, and Congress in the mobilization act of April 22, 1898, settled for a makeshift arrangement providing for a wartime force composed of both Regular and volunteer units organized into brigades, divisions, and army corps. Some Guard units did, in effect, serve under an arrangement whereby if enough members of a state unit volunteered for service, they were kept together to form a comparable federal volunteer unit.

Although the act of April 22 provided for 125,000 volunteers, popular demand soon led Congress to increase this number by 75,000 and authorize additional special volunteer forces, including 10,000 enlisted men "possessing immunity from diseases incident to tropical climates"—the so-called Immunes. Simultaneously it also authorized more than doubling the size of the Regular Army to nearly 65,000. By war's end in August 1898, the Regular forces numbered 59,000 and the volunteers, 216,000, a total of 275,000.

Mobilizing, equipping, and supplying these wartime forces placed a severe burden upon the War Department. With neither a military planning staff nor the funds necessary to plan for war in peacetime, the department inevitably was ill prepared for any kind of major mobilization or military operation.

Further complicating matters was a basic disagreement within the department concerning the strategy to be followed and the way mobilization should
be carried out.

To the extent the United States had a strategy for conduct of the war against
Spain in the Caribbean, it consisted of maintaining a naval blockade of Cuba
while native insurgent forces carried on a harassing campaign against Spanish
troops on the island. Supporters of this policy—Captain Mahan was among its
more articulate advocates—believed that it would lead eventually to surrender
of the Spanish forces and the freeing of Cuba. No direct clash between American
and Spanish troops was visualized; American land forces would simply occupy
Cuba as soon as the Spanish departed.

More or less in conformity with this strategy, Maj. Gen. Nelson Miles,
Commanding General of the Army, proposed to assemble, train, and equip a
small force of about 80,000, using the Regular Army as a nucleus. There would
be ample time for mobilizing this force, since Miles deemed it unwise to land
any troops in Cuba before the end of the unhealthy rainy season in October.
The first step was to concentrate the entire Regular Army at Chickamauga Park,
Georgia, where it could receive much-needed instruction in combined arms
operations.

So deliberate and cautious a plan, however, was, by mid-April 1898, not
in harmony with the increasing public demand for immediate action against
the Spanish. With an ear to this demand, Secretary of War Russell M. Alger,
who had been a general officer in the Civil War and subsequently had pursued
a political career for thirty years, ignored the advice of General Miles. He
ordered the Regular infantry regiments to go to New Orleans, Tampa, and
Mobile, where presumably they would be ready for an immediate descent
on Cuba. (*Map 36*) (Later some infantry troops did go to Chickamauga Park,
where they trained with the Regular cavalry and artillery concentrated there.)

The decision to mobilize large volunteer forces compounded the problems
of equipping, training, and supplying the wartime Army. In the spring and
summer of 1898, thousands of enthusiastic volunteers, a few with some militia
training but most only raw recruits, poured into newly established camps
in the South—located there so as to be near Cuba and, at the same time, help
the soldiers to become accustomed to semitropical climatic conditions. But
a taste of military life in the training camps soon curbed the enthusiasm of
most volunteers, for there they found chronic shortages of the most essential
equipment—even of such basic items as underwear, socks, and shoes—a steady
diet of badly prepared food, unbelievably poor sanitary conditions, inadequate

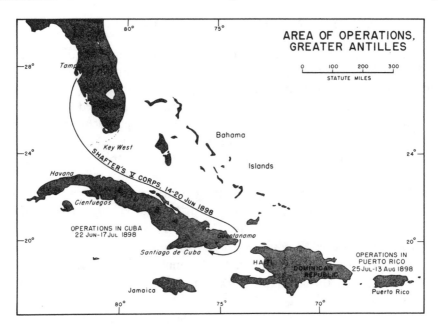

MAP 36

medical facilities, and a lack of up-to-date weapons. Red tape and poor management in the War Department's supply bureaus (the Ordnance Department possibly excepted) continued to delay correction of some of the worst deficiencies and combined with the shortage of capable volunteer officers to limit the effectiveness and quality of training received in the camps.

A similar general inefficiency characterized the War Department's conduct of actual operations against Spain. Since Congress had provided no machinery in the department for peacetime co-ordination of foreign policy with the country's military posture, the nation went to war without any kind of over-all plan of operations or even adequate intelligence about the enemy or the Cuban insurgents. Suddenly confronted in April 1898 with the necessity for launching overseas amphibious attacks on hostile shores—under the best circumstances always a difficult type of operation, requiring careful planning and close interservice co-operation—the War Department bureaus and the Army high command found themselves almost totally unprepared. Given time, they might have devised at least adequate operational plans; but public opinion, political pressures, and the trend of events demanded the launching of an immediate expedition against the Spanish in Cuba.

Victory at Sea: Naval Operations in the Caribbean and Pacific

Fortunately, it turned out that the really decisive fighting of the war fell to the much better prepared Navy, although last-minute alterations in its strategic plan for dealing with the Spanish Fleet seriously threatened to reduce its effectiveness. Shortly after the war began, rumors circulated that an enemy fleet under Admiral Pascual Cervera y Topete was approaching the Atlantic coast of the United States. An alarmed public demanded that measures be taken to defend the Atlantic seaboard. In deference to this demand, the Navy Department in late April 1898 withheld some of its best fighting ships from Rear Adm. William T. Sampson's North Atlantic Squadron, sent to blockade Cuba. These ships, formed into a "flying squadron" under Commodore Winfield S. Schley, set up a watch for Cervera. This move was in conflict with the provisions in the Navy's strategical plan for a war with Spain. Based upon Mahan's doctrines, the plan called for maintaining Sampson's squadron at full strength in the Caribbean, ready to intercept any Spanish fleet sent out to relieve Cuba.

In the western Pacific, meantime, the Navy was able to adhere to its strategical plan—the latest version of which had been completed in June 1897. Worked out after 1895 by officers at the Naval War College in collaboration with the Office of Naval Intelligence, this plan, known to President McKinley and the high officials in the Navy Department, provided for an attack on the Philippines, leading to destruction of Spanish warships there, capture of Manila, and blockade of the principal Philippine ports. The basic objectives of the plan were to weaken Spain by cutting off revenues from the Philippines and to place the United States in the position of having something to offer the Spanish as an inducement to make peace after Cuba had been freed.

Active Navy preparation for war began in January 1898, and in late February Theodore Roosevelt, as Acting Secretary of the Navy (Secretary John D. Long was ailing), cabled orders to American naval commanders, instructing them to get their squadrons in readiness to carry out existing war plans against Spain. Commodore George Dewey of the Asiatic Squadron received instructions to assemble his ships at Hong Kong, where they could take on coal and supplies preparatory to an attack on the Philippines.

Thus, on April 24, when McKinley finally ordered the Asiatic Squadron to execute the war plan against the Philippines Dewey was ready. He sailed into Manila Bay on the night of April 30 and next morning located the Spanish warships at Cavite. In a few hours and without loss of a single

American life, he sank or disabled the entire Spanish Fleet. In the days immediately following, he also silenced the land batteries defending Manila harbor, but the city itself continued to resist. (*See Map 44.*)

Since Dewey's 1,700 men were barely sufficient to maintain his own naval squadron, he requested dispatch of land forces from the United States to take Manila. In the two months before their arrival, he blockaded the port and gave assistance to Emilio Aguinaldo, Filipino insurgent leader, who, with Dewey's aid, had returned to the Philippines from exile in Hong Kong. Aguinaldo undertook guerrilla operations to keep the Spanish land forces in the vicinity of Manila. Dewey had to deal as well with the ticklish problem of British, French, and German naval contingents in Manila Bay, which arrived ostensibly to protect their nationals from the insurgents, but actually also to help uphold any claims their governments might advance to Filipino territory should the United States fail to take control over the islands. Most troublesome was the German squadron under Rear Adm. Otto von Diederichs, but Dewey's patience and firmness prevented a serious incident, and Berlin withdrew its fleet when it became apparent that the United States was not going to abandon the Philippines.

Operations in the Caribbean

As in the Pacific so also in the Caribbean the course of naval developments would determine when and where the Army undertook operations against Spanish land forces. During the early part of May 1898, the whereabouts of the Spanish Fleet under Admiral Cervera remained a mystery. Lacking this information, the Army could not fix precisely the point where it would launch an attack. Nevertheless, the War Department pushed preparations at Tampa, Florida, for an expedition under General Miles to be put ashore somewhere near Havana. But persistent rumors of the approach of the Spanish Fleet to Cuban waters delayed this expedition while the Navy searched further for Cervera. News at last reached Washington near the end of May that the Spanish admiral had skillfully evaded the American naval blockade and, on the 19th of the month, had slipped into the bay at Santiago de Cuba. (*See Map 36.*)

The Navy, at first not at all certain that it was actually Cervera's fleet in Santiago, sent Admiral Sampson to inspect the harbor. As soon as the American naval commander had ascertained that the four cruisers and several smaller war vessels were indeed Spanish, he bombarded the forts at the entrance to Santiago Bay. Unable to silence them, Sampson decided against trying to run the heavily mined harbor entrance. Instead, he sent Lt. (jg) Richmond P. Hobson to bottle up the enemy fleet by sinking the collier *Merrimac* athwart the channel. When this bold project failed, Sampson requested land forces to seize the Spanish batteries, at the same time dispatching marines ashore to secure a site for a naval base east of Santiago. In the first land skirmish of the Cuban campaign, the marines quickly overcame enemy resistance and established the base at Guantánamo Bay.

Upon receipt of Sampson's request for land forces, the War Department, already under strong public pressure to get the Army into action, ordered Maj. Gen. William R. Shafter to embark with the V Corps from Tampa as soon as possible to conduct operations against Santiago in co-operation with the Navy. This corps was the only one of the eight that the War Department had organized for the war that was anywhere near ready to fight. Composed chiefly of Regular Army units, it had been assembling at Tampa for weeks when the order came on May 31 for its embarkation; it would require another two weeks to get the corps and its equipment on board and ready to sail for Cuba.

The slow pace of preparation and loading of the expedition was attributable to many factors. There was no over-all plan and no special staff to direct it. Although selected because of its port facilities and proximity to Cuba, Tampa, from the logistical point of view, proved to be a poor choice for marshaling a major military expedition. With only one pier for loading ships and a single-track railroad connecting with mainline routes from the north, the resulting backup of freight cars for miles delayed shipment of much needed supplies and equipment. Incoming soldiers waited interminably in uncomfortable railroad cars. When freight cars finally did reach the port area, there were no wagons to unload them and no bills of lading to indicate what was in them. When it came to loading the ships, of which there were not enough to carry the entire corps, supplies and equipment were put on board with little regard for unloading priorities in the combat zone should there be enemy resistance during the landings.

In spite of the confusion and inefficiency at Tampa, by June 14 nearly 17,000 men were ready to sail. On board were 18 Regular and 2 volunteer infantry regiments; 10 Regular and 2 volunteer cavalry squadrons, serving dismounted; 1 mounted cavalry squadron; 6 artillery batteries; and a machine gun (Gatling gun) company. The expedition comprised a major part of the Regular forces, including all of the Regular Negro combat regiments. Moving out from Tampa on the morning of the 14th, the V Corps joined its naval convoy next day off the Florida Keys and by June 20 had reached the vicinity of Santiago.

TRANSPORTS AT TAMPA

While the troops on board endured tropical heat, unsanitary conditions, and cold rations—the canned beef was especially unpalatable—Shafter and Sampson conferred on how to proceed against the Spanish in Santiago. Sampson wanted the Army to storm the fort on the east side of the bay entrance, driving the Spanish from their guns. Then his fleet could clear away the mines and enter Santiago Bay to fight Cervera's squadron. Lacking heavy artillery, Shafter was not sure his troops could take the fort, which crowned a steep hill. He decided instead to follow the suggestion of General Calixto Garcia, the local insurgent leader, and land his forces at Daiquirí, east of Santiago Bay. (*Map 37*)

On June 22, after heavy shelling of the landing areas, the V Corps began disembarking amid circumstances almost as confused and hectic as those at Tampa. Captains of many of the chartered merchant ships resisted bringing their vessels close inshore. Their reluctance slowed the landing of troops and equipment, already handicapped by a shortage of lighters (the Navy could not spare the additional ones needed). Horses, simply dropped overboard to get ashore on their own, swam out to sea in some instances and were lost. An alert enemy defense might well have taken advantage of the chaotic conditions

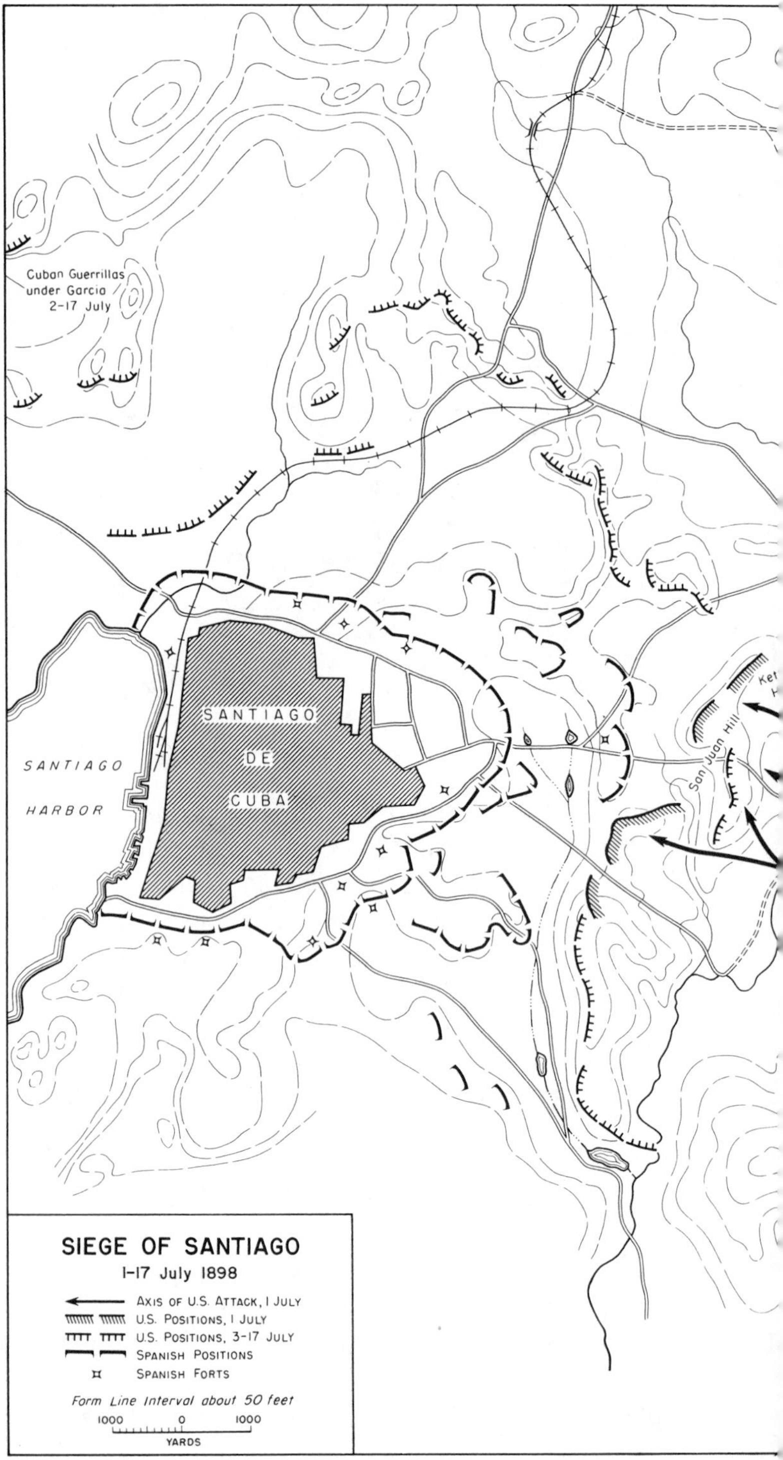

Cuban Guerrillas under Garcia 2–17 July
SANTIAGO HARBOR
SANTIAGO DE CUBA
San Juan Hill
SIEGE OF SANTIAGO
1–17 July 1898
Axis of U.S. Attack, 1 July
U.S. Positions, 1 July
U.S. Positions, 3–17 July
Spanish Positions
Spanish Forts
Form Line Interval about 50 feet
1000 0 1000
YARDS

MAP 37

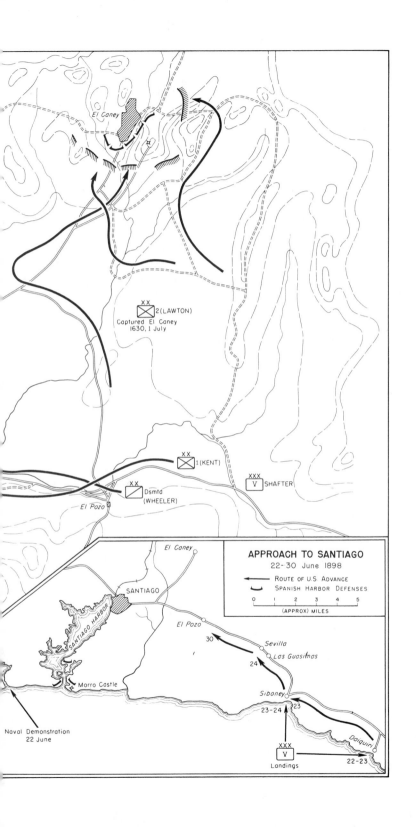

El Caney

XX
⊠ 2 (LAWTON)
Captured El Caney
1630, 1 July

XX
⊠ 1 (KENT)

XXX
▢ V SHAFTER

XX
▢ Dsmtd
(WHEELER)

El Pozo

APPROACH TO SANTIAGO
22-30 June 1898

⟵ ROUTE OF U.S. ADVANCE
⟜ SPANISH HARBOR DEFENSES

0   1   2   3   4   5
(APPROX) MILES

El Caney

SANTIAGO

SANTIAGO HARBOR

El Pozo

30

Sevilla

Las Guasímas

24

Morro Castle

Siboney

23-24   23

Naval Demonstration
22 June

Daiquiri

XXX
▢ V
Landings

22-23

to oppose the landings effectively. But the Spanish, though they had more than 200,000 troops in Cuba—some 36,000 of them in Santiago Province—did nothing to prevent Shafter's men from getting ashore. Some 6,000 landed on June 22 and most of the remaining 11,000 on the two days following. In addition, some 4,000 to 5,000 insurgents under General Garcia supplemented the American force.

The Battle of Santiago

Once ashore, elements of the V Corps moved westward toward the heights of San Juan, a series of ridge lines immediately east of Santiago, where well-entrenched enemy troops guarded the land approaches to the city. On June 23, Brig. Gen. Henry W. Lawton, commanding the vanguard, advanced along the coast from Daiquirí to occupy Siboney, which then became the main base of operations. The next day, Brig. Gen. Joseph Wheeler, the Confederate Army veteran, pushed inland along the road to Santiago with dismounted cavalry to seize Las Guásimas, after a brief skirmish with rear guard elements of a retiring Spanish force. This move brought American units within five miles of the San Juan Heights, where they paused for a few days while General Shafter assembled the rest of his divisions and brought up supplies. Even in this short time, Shafter could observe the debilitating effects of tropical climate and disease on his men. He was aware, too, that the hurricane season was approaching. Consequently, he decided in favor of an immediate attack on the defenses of Santiago.

Shafter's plan was simple: a frontal attack on the San Juan Heights. For this purpose, he deployed Brig. Gen. Jacob F. Kent's infantry division on the left and Wheeler's dismounted cavalry on the right, the entire force with supporting elements comprising some 8,000 troops. But before he made the main advance on the heights Lawton's infantry division with a supporting battery of artillery—more than 6,500 men—was to move some two miles north to seize the fortified village of El Caney, cutting off Santiago's water supply and, if necessary, intercepting rumored Spanish reinforcements. This action completed—Shafter thought it would take about two hours—Lawton was to turn southwestward and form on the right flank of Wheeler's division for participation in the main assault. A brigade which had just landed at Siboney was to advance meanwhile along the coast in a feint to deceive the enemy.

The attack, which moved out at dawn on July 1, soon became badly disorganized because of poor co-ordination, difficult terrain, and tropical heat. The corpulent Shafter, virtually prostrated by the heat, had to leave the direction of the battle to others. At a stream crossing on the crowded main trail to

San Juan Heights enemy gunners scored heavily when a towed Signal Corps balloon pinpointed the front of the advancing line of troops. And Lawton's division, delayed in its seizure of El Caney by a stubborn enemy defense, misplaced artillery, and the necessity of withdrawing a volunteer unit armed only with telltale black powder, did not rejoin the main force until after the assault had ended. Despite these unexpected setbacks, Kent's and Wheeler's divisions at midday launched a strong frontal attack on the Spanish forward defensive positions. Cavalry units of Wheeler's division, including the 9th Cavalry and part of the 10th, both Negro regiments, and the volunteer Rough Riders, who were commanded by Lt. Col. Theodore Roosevelt, seized Kettle Hill, separate from the central heights. Then Kent's infantry regiments, sup-

THE SIGNAL CORPS BALLOON *at Santiago.*

ported by the unorthodox employment of Gatling guns in the attack, stormed up San Juan Hill in the main ridge line, driving the Spanish from blockhouse and trench defenses and compelling them to retire to a strongly fortified inner line. Thus the day ended with the Americans having achieved most of their initial objectives. But the cost was high—nearly 1,700 casualties sustained since the start of operations against Santiago.

Concerned with the increasing sickness that was further thinning the ranks of the V Corps and faced by a well-organized Spanish second line of defense, General Shafter cabled Secretary Alger on July 3 that he was considering withdrawing about five miles to higher ground between the San Juan River and Siboney. The shift would place his troops in a position where they would be less exposed to enemy fire and easier to supply. Alger replied that "the effect upon the country would be much better" if Shafter continued to hold his advanced position.

The V Corps commander then again sought to get the Navy to enter Santiago Bay and attack the city. But neither the Navy Department nor President McKinley was willing to sanction this move. Just when the whole matter threatened to become an embarrassing public debate between the two services, the Spanish themselves resolved the issue.

Deteriorating conditions within Santiago—lack of food and ammunition were seriously affecting the health and morale of the defending forces—convinced the defenders that the city must soon fall. While Cervera considered flight from the port hopeless, he had no recourse but to attempt it. Officials in both Havana and Madrid had ordered him, for reasons of honor, to escape when Santiago appeared about to surrender. Finally, on the morning of July 3, while Sampson and Shafter conferred ashore, Cervera made his dash for the open sea, hoping to reach the port of Cienfuegos on the south coast of Cuba. As soon as the Spanish Fleet appeared, Sampson's squadron, temporarily under command of Commodore Schley, gave chase and in less than two hours destroyed Cervera's fleet; four cruisers were crippled and run ashore and one destroyer was beached and another sunk.

A few days later, General Shafter persuaded the Spanish leaders in Santiago that they had no choice except to surrender. On July 16 they signed the unconditional terms demanded by the McKinley administration, which provided for surrender of 11,500 troops in the city and some 12,000 others in the vicinity of Santiago. The formal surrender ceremony took place on the following day.

During preparations for the Santiago campaign, General Miles personally had been overseeing organization of a second expedition to seize Puerto Rico. On July 21 he sailed from Guantánamo with more than 3,000 troops. His original strategy was to land first at Cape Fajardo in the northeast part of the island, where he could establish a base of operations for a subsequent advance westward to the capital, San Juan. For reasons not entirely clear, but probably because of a desire not to have to co-operate with the Navy in the attack on San Juan, Miles, while still at sea, changed his plans and on July 25 landed forces first at Guánica on the southeastern coast. Meeting virtually no opposition, the Americans shortly occupied the port of Ponce. In early August, after arrival of more than 10,000 additional troops from ports in the United States, General Miles, using Ponce as a base of operations, launched a four-column drive toward San Juan. There was little bloodshed—casualties for the campaign totaled fewer than fifty—and, in fact, most Puerto Ricans welcomed the American troops. The campaign ended on August 13 when word reached the island that Spain had signed a peace protocol the previous day.

Back in Cuba, meanwhile, conditions for the Army were much less pleasant. Spread of malaria, typhoid, and yellow fever among Shafter's troops at Santiago threatened to have far deadlier consequences than had the actual fighting. Concern over this problem led to the drafting of a joint letter by a number of Shafter's senior officers, proposing immediate evacuation of the Army from Cuba. Addressed to the commanding general, this round robin letter unfortunately came to the attention of the press before it reached Shafter. Hence, Washington officials read it in the newspapers before learning of its content from the general himself. Naturally the whole episode, coming at the time when peace negotiations were beginning, caused a sensation. Although acutely embarrassing for the Army and General Shafter, the incident did have the salutary effect of hastening measures to evacuate thousands of troops to Montauk Point, Long Island, where the Army Medical Department already had taken steps to establish an isolated detention camp. Here those who had contracted tropical infections received the necessary treatment. And out of the Army's nearly disastrous experience with the debilitating effects of disease and climate in Cuba came the impetus for the Medical Corps' notable project to determine the causes of yellow fever, inaugurating a long-term program of research and study into what henceforth would be a permanent concern of the Army—the maintenance of the health and effectiveness of American troops in a tropical environment.

The Fall of Manila

In another tropical setting halfway around the world from Cuba the final military episode of the war took place. During May and June 1898 Admiral Dewey, while awaiting the arrival in the Philippines of land forces from the United States, kept in contact with the insurgent leader, General Aguinaldo. The Filipino forces occupied lines on the land side of Manila, preventing the Spanish garrison from moving beyond the immediate outskirts of the city.

Although the Americans and the Philippine insurgents shared a common interest in bringing about the defeat of the Spanish, relations between them tended to deteriorate during the period of waiting. The most important reason was a fundamental difference in objectives. The goal of the insurgents, who controlled most areas outside the towns and cities on Luzon and the other important islands, was immediate independence for the Philippines. But after some hesitation the McKinley administration and more and more Americans were coming around to the view that the United States ought to retain the islands. Once Aguinaldo became aware of this he endeavored to counteract it by taking steps to establish a revolutionary government with himself as president. On August 6 he appealed to foreign governments to recognize the independence of the Philippines. Hence by late summer there was serious doubt as to just what might be expected from the increasingly hostile insurgent forces.

In the interim, the long-awaited ground forces needed to complete the campaign in the Philippines began arriving in the Manila area. By the end of July 1898, some 13,000 volunteer and 2,000 Regular troops, constituting the VIII Corps under Maj. Gen. Wesley Merritt, had reached the islands. These troops had embarked from west coast ports (chiefly San Francisco) with a minimum of the confusion and difficulty that had characterized the launching of the Cuban expedition. In spite of the long voyage across the Pacific, they were in good condition and ready to start operations against the Spanish as soon as enough troops could be moved into the vicinity of Manila.

By early August General Merritt had 11,000 troops of the VIII Corps in lines immediately to the rear of those occupied by the insurgents, ready to attack the city. Inside the Philippine capital and in fortified lines just beyond the city walls were about 10,000 to 15,000 Spanish troops. Although their leaders were fully aware of the relative hopelessness of the situation, efforts of Dewey and Merritt to secure a peaceful surrender failed because the Spanish Government in Madrid insisted that the garrison should make at least a token show of resistance.

On the morning of August 13 the VIII Corps launched an assault on Manila. As the tide receded, American units moved quickly to the beaches on the south side of the city and then, supported by concentrated fire from Dewey's ships, advanced through the insurgent lines. By prior arrangement, somewhat reluctantly agreed to by Aguinaldo, the insurgents were to retire as the Americans moved toward the Spanish entrenchments. But in carrying out this difficult maneuver, Americans and insurgents unintentionally became intermixed and some troops—presumably for the most part insurgents—began firing on the Spanish lines. Momentarily, this flare-up threatened to thwart the enemy's plan to offer only token resistance, but quick action by American officers brought the firing under control and the garrison surrendered. Operations at Manila cost the Americans a total of 17 killed and 105 wounded.

Formal surrender ceremonies came the following day—actually two days after the government in Madrid had signed a peace protocol ending hostilities. News of the protocol had not yet reached Manila because the cable Dewey cut when he first entered Manila Bay still had not been repaired.

After negotiations in Paris in the fall of 1898, the United States and Spain signed a treaty on December 10 ending the war. By its terms Spain gave up sovereignty over Cuba, which became an independent state, ceded Puerto Rico and Guam to the United States, and accepted $20 million in payment for the Philippines. Thus fatefully did Americans commit the nation to a new role as a colonial power in the Far East, with momentous future consequences that few at the turn of the century could anticipate.

The Philippine Insurrection, 1899–1902

Signing of the Treaty of Paris brought only a brief pause in military operations for the Army in the Philippines. With defeat and departure of the Spanish, the Americans inherited the complex problems of governing a populous Far Eastern archipelago about which they still knew relatively little. Even with full co-operation of all the heterogeneous peoples of differing cultures living in the islands, the task would have been formidable. Leaders of the native nationalist movement were no more ready to accept American rule peacefully than Spanish.

In the period following the fall of Manila while peace negotiations were in progress an uneasy truce existed between the insurgents and the American occupation forces. Under leadership of Aguinaldo, the insurgents established a provisional republic with a capital at Malolos, northeast of Manila, and organized a congress which began preparing a constitution. After the United States in January 1899 officially proclaimed possession of the Philippines and its intention to extend political control over all the islands, the insurgent congress ratified the constitution, formally establishing a Filipino republic, and prepared to resist the Americans.

The circumstances surrounding the start of fighting on the night of February 4, 1899, are vague. An insurgent patrol apparently deliberately challenged without provocation an American guard post near Manila. Since the incident occurred on the eve of ratification of the Treaty of Paris by the United States Senate, it is conceivable that the insurgents may have wished by this surprise move to inflict an embarrassing setback on the Americans before reinforcements could arrive in the Philippines, hoping thus to influence the vote on the treaty. Or it may simply have been a spontaneous outburst, stemming from Aguinaldo's known inability to exercise very tight discipline over his loosely organized army. Whatever the reason, the VIII Corps reacted promptly and decisively. Against an estimated 40,000 insurgents in the Manila area, Maj. Gen. Elwell S. Otis, who had replaced General Merritt, could commit only about 12,000 of his 21,000 troops, since the remainder were volunteers scheduled to go home for early demobilization. Nevertheless, in extensive operations around the Philippine capital in the several days immediately following the attack on the 4th, the VIII Corps drove back the insurgents at all points, inflicting some 3,000 casualties, and then, late in the month, thwarted what appeared to be the beginning of a widespread uprising in the city, potentially fraught with the most serious consequences.

Although the insurgents suffered a severe setback in these first major engagements of the Philippine Insurrection, they continued more or less organized resistance on a smaller scale for more than two years, with spasmodic outbursts in the Visayas, the islands immediately south of Luzon. The Americans also met resistance from the predominantly Moslem Moro peoples residing in Mindanao and the Sulu Archipelago in the southern Philippines, areas where even the Spanish during their long period of rule had never exercised effective control.

When news of the insurrection reached Washington it quickly dispelled any doubts the McKinley administration might have had concerning the need for more troops in the Philippines to establish effective American control. The War Department responded promptly, arranging to raise ten additional federal volunteer regiments and, at the same time, ordering immediate dispatch of much needed Regular units to the islands. By late summer of 1899, more than 35,000 additional troops had joined the VIII Corps and more were on the way. Before it ended more than 100,000 American soldiers took part in some phase of the Philippine Insurrection.

Short of firearms and ammunition, the insurgents depended primarily upon unconventional tactics. Avoiding open confrontation with the better armed and organized Americans whenever possible, they relied upon surprise attacks and ambush, where bolo knives and other more primitive weapons could be employed with the most devastating effect. Resort to guerrilla operations enabled the insurgents to exploit their superior knowledge of the jungle and the mountainous country in which much of the fighting took place. To cope with these tactics, the Army found itself drawing upon its long experience in fighting the western Indians. Hampered logistically by the lack of roads and by rough terrain in the interior, the Americans had to depend primarily upon small arms fire and the bayonet in repelling hit-and-run insurgent attacks. Keeping the poorly organized and poorly co-ordinated insurgent bands under constant pursuit and pressure, VIII Corps troops gradually extended their control over most of Luzon and the other important islands.

Beginning in April 1899, the Army carried out a series of carefully co-ordinated offensives, aimed at securing control of the important population centers and lines of communications as a first step in establishing stable government and restoring normal economic activities. Immediately after the outbreak of insurgent hostilities in February, American columns had pushed north, south, and east from Manila, capturing the rebel capital at Malolos, and securing the Pasig River, which cut the main line of communications between insurgent forces in north and south Luzon. Now in April, General Otis sent General Lawton, veteran of the Santiago campaign, south toward Santa Cruz in the Laguna de Bay area and Maj. Gen. Arthur MacArthur north up the central plain from Malolos toward San Fernando. By mid-May, the success of these drives had seriously undermined insurgent ability to continue organized resistance and forced Aguinaldo to flee to the mountains in northern Luzon. Advent of the rainy season and shortage of manpower halted further operations until fall.

In the autumn of 1899, General Otis launched a three-pronged drive in north central Luzon against Aguinaldo's remaining forces. Moving up on the right, Lawton recaptured San Isidro and approached San Fabian on Lingayen Gulf; MacArthur, in the center, seized Tarlac and reached Dagupan; Brig. Gen. Loyd Wheaton, on the left, went by ship from Manila to San Fabian, moving inland to defeat the insurgents at San Jacinto, and then linked up with MacArthur at Dagupan. Aguinaldo again managed to escape, but eventually was captured in March 1901 through a ruse skillfully carried out by a small party of Filipino scouts and American soldiers led by Brig. Gen. Frederick Funston.

Operations in the winter of 1899–1900 cleared insurrectionist remnants from the Manila region and permanently secured important lines of communications in central Luzon. By March 1900 the Army also controlled southern Luzon and the Visayas. In May, Otis, believing the insurrection virtually over, requested his own relief and General MacArthur replaced him. Events proved Otis mistaken, for the Army had to continue in the field for many more months, dealing with sporadic but persistent resistance in numerous small engagements. The guerrilla warfare was bitter and costly, resulting in more casualties for the Army than in the entire preceding fifteen months of extensive military operations. In early 1902, unrest among the Moros in Mindanao and the Sulu Archipelago intensified, and was by no means really settled when President Theodore Roosevelt announced on July 4 the formal end of the Philippine Insurrection.

The Boxer Uprising

Acquisition of the Philippines tended to stimulate further a growing interest in China among Americans for both commercial and humanitarian reasons. One important argument advanced for retaining the Philippines was that they would serve as a convenient way station in carrying on trade and protecting American interests in the Manchu empire. The dominant problem in China at the end of the nineteenth century was its threatened partition by the Great Powers. Both the Americans and the British opposed this, and in

September 1899 the United States announced it had secured agreement from the interested powers for maintenance of an Open Door policy in their relations with China.

The already extensive exploitation of their country by foreign states, however, had aroused widespread resentment among younger Chinese. They formed the nucleus of a secret group called Boxers by Westerners which, with tacit support of the Dowager Empress, undertook a campaign against foreign influences and foreigners. By early 1900 this movement had brought much of China to the verge of revolution. Boxers in the northern provinces attacked and killed hundreds of Chinese Christians and foreigners, mostly missionaries. The wave of violence was climaxed by murder of the German Minister on June 20. In fear for their lives in what appeared to be the beginning of a general uprising, most remaining foreigners as well as many Chinese converts fled to the foreign legations area in Peking, defended by a composite force of some 600 soldiers and civilians. Soon they were besieged there by a much larger force of Boxers assisted by Chinese imperial troops.

Although the McKinley administration disliked the idea of becoming involved in an election year in an international incident with overtones of entangling foreign alliances, it agreed to join with the other powers in taking such steps as seemed necessary to rescue their beleaguered nationals. In establishing the limits of American diplomatic co-operation with the intervening powers, Secretary of State John Hay admonished the United States Minister that ". . . we have no policy in China except to protect with energy American interests and especially American citizens. . . . There must be no alliances." And on July 3 Hay circulated a second Open Door note among the interested powers, stating that it was the policy of the United States "to seek a solution which may bring about permanent safety and peace to China, preserve Chinese territorial and administrative entity, protect all rights guaranteed to friendly powers by treaty and international law, and safeguard for the world the principle of equal and impartial trade with all parts of the Chinese Empire."

Already in June the Navy's China squadron, under Rear Adm. Louis Kempff, had joined with other foreign naval units in bombardment of the Taku forts guarding Tientsin, the port city nearest to Peking, and had supplied a contingent for an international landing force composed of marines and other available troops. Formed into a rescue column, including more than a hundred Americans, this force had encountered overwhelming opposition and failed to break through to Peking. The powers then had taken immediate steps to organize a large relief expedition to drive through to the Chinese capital.

Because of the Philippine Insurrection the United States had sizable Army units available fairly near China. It could therefore contribute one of the larger contingents to the international relief force. Although General MacArthur, commanding in the Philippines, was somewhat reluctant to weaken his already overextended forces, he agreed to dispatch to China immediately the 9th Infantry and later the 14th Infantry and some artillery units. Other units, including the 6th Cavalry, came directly from the United States. Using Manila as a base and Nagasaki, Japan, as an advance port, the United States eventually assembled some 2,500 soldiers and marines in China under command of Maj. Gen. Adna R. Chaffee. On July 13, elements of this force, officially designated the China Relief Expedition, participated with troops from several other nations in the attack on Tientsin, which surrendered on the same day.

By early August, an allied force of some 19,000, including British, French, Japanese, Russian, German, Austrian, Italian, and American troops, was ready to move out of Tientsin toward Peking, some seventy miles distant. Fighting a number of sharp skirmishes en route, this force reached the Manchu capital on August 12 and prepared immediately to assault the gates leading into the Outer City. Lacking effective central direction, the relief expedition's attack was poorly executed. The Russian contingent prematurely forced an entrance into the Outer City on August 13, only to be thrown into confusion and require rescue by other allied troops. The next day, in a more carefully co-ordinated assault, elements of the U.S. 14th Infantry scaled the so-called Tartar Wall and provided cover for the British as they entered the Outer City in force, relieving the legations compound. Then on August 15, Capt. Henry J. Reilly's Light Battery F of the U.S. 5th Artillery shattered the gates leading into the Inner City with several well-placed salvos, opening the way for the allied troops to occupy the center of Peking. Although American troops had suffered comparatively light losses—slightly more than 200 killed and wounded—they did not take part in subsequent military operations, which consisted primarily of suppressing scattered Boxer elements and rescuing foreigners in the provinces. The McKinley administration, anxious to avoid further involvement in China, wanted to get Army units back to the Philippines before winter.

In a few months all resistance had ended and the Dowager Empress sued for peace, offering to pay an indemnity and reaffirm previously existing commercial concessions. During prolonged negotiations an international army of occupation to which the United States contributed a small contingent of Regulars remained in north China. It was withdrawn in September 1901 under terms of the Boxer Protocol. This agreement also provided that the powers maintain a fortified legation in Peking, garrison the Tientsin-Peking railway—an American contingent served as a part of this force until 1938—and receive reparations of $333 million. Of this amount the United States claimed only $25 million. In a few years it became apparent that even this sum was more than was needed to indemnify claims of American nationals and in 1907, and again in 1924, the United States returned portions totaling nearly $17 million to China, which placed the money in a trust fund for education of Chinese youths in both countries.

Participation of the United States in the Boxer Uprising at the beginning of the twentieth century marked the first time since the American Revolution that the country had joined with other powers in an allied military operation. The intervention in China represented one more instance of the gradual change taking place at the turn of the century in the traditional policies and attitudes of the United States in world affairs as a result of the triumph of imperialism. As they entered the new century most Americans still believed that despite the acquisition of overseas colonies the nation could continue to adhere to the historic principles of isolationism. Developments in the early years of the twentieth century would demonstrate, however, that the nation had to make changes and adjustments in many long-established institutions and policies—including those relating to military defense of the country—to meet the requirements of its new status as a world power.

Suggested Readings

by

Brig. Gen. William A. Stofft

Editors' note. In place of the lengthy general bibliography found in earlier editions of this volume, the editors are substituting a personal essay by the Chief of Military History on the subject of reading history. Bibliographic information on the volumes mentioned in this essay, along with that for other general works recommended by the editors, is appended below.

These remarks are addressed to this volume's principal audience—future officers of the United States Army. Taking advantage of your goodwill and general interest in a new subject, I want to suggest that developing a habit of reading military history is both useful and rewarding. Many of our great captains of war read military history in their spare time. I believe that, like them, you will discover that a familiarity with histories that carefully and clearly analyze our country's military past will provide you with a new and special perspective on your profession.

Some of the books I'm going to mention are classics and appear elsewhere in this volume's formal bibliography. Others do not, but they all rate a place on my personal suggested reading list. Not only are they among my own favorites, they also serve a major intention of the Army: to stimulate a lasting interest in military history among Army officers. As the Army's leaders have frequently put it, an understanding of military history is essential in our future military leaders.

Before I give you my personal reading list, let me urge you to take advantage of the many fine military journals available to Army officers to keep themselves abreast of the latest trends in our profession. Begin with the fine periodicals published by the various branch schools. For generations, officers have gained valuable insights from studying the pages of *Infantry, Armor, Field Artillery,* and the rest. For a broader view of military matters, I recommend that you pick up the Command and General Staff College's *Military Review,* which specializes in articles about combined arms war, and the Army War College's *Parameters,* which will provide you with a useful survey of current thinking on military strategy and theory.

My personal recommendations begin with three volumes that introduce the student to the battlefield, the epicenter of the soldier's profession. *The Face of Battle, Company Commander,* and *Seven Firefights in Vietnam,* all superb books, approach the battlefield from different perspectives, but each analyzes the performance of the individual soldier under fire and convincingly demonstrates both the reality of fear and the overriding influence of military discipline and leadership on the outcome of battle. I promise they will linger long in your memory.

Every officer needs some notion of how the art of war has evolved throughout western history. I'd suggest that you start by sampling the work of four modern masters of our craft. Sir John Winthrop Hackett distilled a lifetime study into the brilliant chapters of his brief survey, *Profession of Arms*. Bernard Brodie is especially recommended for his examination of the philosophical dimensions of warfare in his masterful *War and Politics*. J. F. C. Fuller focuses on the evolution of military operations in his *The Decisive Battles of the Western World;* while the authors in Peter Paret's collection, *Makers of Modern Strategy: Military Thought From Machiavelli to the Nuclear Age,* concentrate on the strategy of war in the West. Taken together, these insightful and beautifully written analyses create the essential context in which American military history must be placed.

Knowledge of our own military past has benefited greatly from the work of gifted historians who have specialized in interpreting the American approach to war. Four of the best in terms of originality and clarity of thought are Walter Millis, who in his *Arms and Men* describes the evolution of American military institutions in the context of the nation's social and economic forces; T. Harry Williams, who examines the effects of military organization on strategy in his short but provocative *Americans at War: The Development of the American Military System;* Samuel P. Huntington, who presents a classic interpretation of the role of the professional soldier in a free society in *The Soldier and the State;* and Russell Weigley, who demonstrates the grand sweep of America's military past in *The American Way of War: A History of United States Military Strategy and Policy* and *History of the United States Army.*

Military historians have always and with good reason depended on the biographer's craft to help define the role of great commanders. Here are six of the best: Flexner's *George Washington,* Freeman's *Lee's Lieutenants,* Henderson's *Stonewall Jackson,* Pogue's *George C. Marshall,* Blumenson's *The Patton Papers,* and the articles in Roger Spiller's concise and informative *Dictionary of Military Biography.* The student often finds biography a particularly human introduction to the complexities of our military past. These authors reveal in fascinating detail the personalities of these great captains, the times in which they lived, and the changing face of war.

I've discovered not only that novelists and poets can illuminate the essential truths of our profession in memorable ways, but that fictionalized accounts of warfare can often provide a unique and broad perspective on the nature of conflict. Remarque's *All Quiet on the Western Front* and Forester's *The General,* masterworks of fiction, cut through the confusion of the Great War with unequaled precision and poignancy. Shaara's *Killer Angels* puts you with great immediacy into the mind of the Civil War commander, providing thereby an impressive lesson in military leadership. *Once an Eagle*, Myrer's realistic portrait of the modern Army officer, makes the point well that his training in peacetime is the key to a soldier's success in war. Finally, let me press on you the *Book of War Poetry* compiled by the Oxford University Press. Here we see in distilled form and beautiful language the inner convictions, along with the doubts and fears, that have possessed the warrior over time.

It's a source of pride to me and, I hope, of inspiration to those of you who plan to make the study of military history a part of your Army career that some important books in our field are the work of serving Army officers. General Dave Palmer's insights into military strategy shine through his study of the Vietnam War, *Summons of the Trumpet*, and of the American Revolution, *The Way of the Fox*, while General John Galvin shares his special knowledge of modern tactics in *Air Assault: The Development of Airmobile Warfare*. Although Col. Robert Doughty's *The Seeds of Disaster: The Development of French Army Doctrine, 1919–1939*, Col. Harold Nelson's *Leon Trotsky and the Art of Insurrection*, and Lt. Col. Harold Winton's *To Change an Army* focus on other armies in other times, they address issues that have broad implications for our own Army today. Nelson has joined with the distinguished military history professor Jay Luvaas to produce several books that I am convinced will stand the test of time. The Army War College guides to the battles of Gettysburg, Antietam, and Chancellorsville are proving invaluable to those of us who, by means of staff rides, use the experience of great commanders of the past to prepare us for future tests. Finally, the novelist's skills have enabled Lt. Col. Jim McDonough in his *Platoon Leader* and Maj. H. W. Coyle in his *Team Yankee: A Novel of World War III* to add new perspectives to issues that you will be encountering as serving officers.

Let me conclude by urging you to dip into three books that newspaper critics were once prone to call "good reads": William Prescott's *The Conquest of Mexico*, Cecil Woodham-Smith's *The Reason Why: The Charge of the Light Brigade*, and Matthew Brennan's *Brennan's War*. Good reads they certainly are, but beware: they are also solid and serious examples of the historian's craft, and they just might hook you for life on reading military history.

GENERAL WORKS

The Battlefield
Cash, John A., Albright, John N., and Sandstrum, Allan W. *Seven Firefights in Vietnam*. Washington: Government Printing Office, 1970.

Esposito, Vincent, ed. *The West Point Atlas of American Wars*. 2 vols. New York: Frederick A. Praeger, 1959.

Keegan, John. *The Face of Battle*. New York: Viking Press, 1976.

MacDonald, Charles B. *Company Commander*. New York: Ballantine Books, 1966.

Western Military History

Brodie, Bernard. *War and Politics*. New York: Macmillan, 1973.

Doughty, Robert A. *The Seeds of Disaster: The Development of French Army Doctrine 1919–1939*. Hamden, Conn.: Anchor Books, 1985.

Fuller, J. F. C. *The Decisive Battles of the Western World, and Their Influence Upon History*. London: Eyre and Spottiswoode, 1954.

———. *A Military History of the Western World*. 3 vols. New York: Funk and Wagnalls, 1954–56.

Hackett, Sir John Winthrop. *Profession of Arms*. Washington: Government Printing Office, 1988.

Nef, John U. *War and Human Progress: An Essay on the Rise of Industrial Civilization*. New York: Norton, 1968.

Nelson, Harold W. *Leon Trotsky and the Art of Insurrection, 1905–1917*. London: Frank Cass, 1988.

Paret, Peter, Craig, Gordon A., and Gilbert, Felix, eds. *Makers of Modern Strategy: Military Thought From Machiavelli to the Nuclear Age*. Princeton: Princeton University Press, 1986.

Preston, Richard A., Wise, Sydney F., and Werner, Hermon O. *Men in Arms: A History of Warfare and Its Relationships With Western Society*. New York: Frederick A. Praeger, 1962.

Ropp, Theodore. *War in the Modern World*. Durham: Duke University Press, 1959.

Winton, Harold R. *To Change an Army: General Sir John Burnett-Stuart and British Armored Doctrine, 1927–1938*. Lawrence: University Press of Kansas, 1988.

American Military Thought

Hagen, Kenneth J., and Roberts, William R., eds. *Against All Enemies: Interpretations of American Military History From Colonial Times to the Present*. New York: Greenwood Press, 1986.

Hammond, Paul. *Organizing for Defense: The American Military Establishment in the Twentieth Century*. Princeton: Princeton University Press, 1961.

Heller, Charles E., and Stofft, William A., eds. *America's First Battles, 1776–1965*. Lawrence: University Press of Kansas, 1986.

Huntington, Samuel P. *The Soldier and the State: The Theory and Politics of Civil-Military Relations*. Cambridge: Belknap Press, 1959.

Millett, Allan R., and Maslowski, Peter. *For the Common Defense: A Military History of the United States of America*. New York: The Free Press, 1984.

Millis, Walter. *Arms and Men: A Study in American Military History*. New York: Putnam, 1956.

Nelson, Otto L., Jr. *National Security and the General Staff*. Washington: Combat Forces Press, 1946.

Weigley, Russell F. *The American Way of War: A History of United States Military Strategy and Policy*. Bloomington: Indiana University Press, 1977.

———. *History of the United States Army*. 2d ed. Bloomington: Indiana University Press, 1984.

Williams, T. Harry. *Americans at War: The Development of the American Military System*. Baton Rouge: Louisiana State University Press, 1960.

Specialized Studies in American Military History

Ambrose, Stephen. *Duty, Honor, Country: A History of West Point*. Baltimore: Johns Hopkins University Press, 1966.

Ball, Harry P. *Of Reasonable Command: A History of the U.S. Army War College*. Carlisle Barracks, Pa.: Alumni Association of the U.S. Army War College, 1983.

Coffman, Edward. *The Old Army: A Portrait of the American Army in Peacetime, 1784–1898*. New York: Oxford University Press, 1986.

Galvin, John R. *Air Assault: The Development of Airmobile Warfare.* New York: Hawthorne Books, 1969.

Huston, James A. *The Sinews of War: Army Logistics, 1775–1953.* Washington: Government Printing Office, 1966.

Janowitz, Morris. *The Professional Soldier: A Social and Professional Portrait.* Glencoe, Ill.: The Free Press, 1960.

Nalty, Bernard. *Strength for the Fight: A History of Black Americans in the Military.* New York: The Free Press, 1986.

Nelson, Harold W., and Luvaas, Jay. *The U.S. Army War College Guide to the Battle of Gettysburg.* Carlisle, Pa.: South Mountain Press, 1986.

———. *The U.S. Army War College Guide to the Battle of Antietam.* Carlisle, Pa.: South Mountain Press, 1987.

———. *The U.S. Army War College Guide to the Battle of Chancellorsville.* Carlisle, Pa.: South Mountain Press, 1988.

Nenninger, Timothy K. *The Leavenworth Schools and the Old Army: Education, Professionalism, and the Officer Corps of the United States Army, 1881–1918.* Westport, Conn.: Greenwood Press, 1978.

Palmer, Dave R. *Summons of the Trumpet: U.S.-Vietnam in Perspective.* Novato, Calif.: Presidio Press, 1978.

———. *The Way of the Fox: American Strategy in the War for America, 1775–1783.* Westport, Conn.: Greenwood Press, 1975.

Military Biography

Blumenson, Martin. *The Patton Papers.* 2 vols. Boston: Houghton Mifflin, 1974.

Flexner, James. *George Washington.* 4 vols. Boston: Little, Brown, 1965–72.

Freeman, Douglas Southall. *Lee's Lieutenants: A Study in Command.* 3 vols. New York: Scribners, 1942–44.

Henderson, George F. R. *Stonewall Jackson and the American Civil War.* New York: Longmans, Green, 1900.

Pogue, Forrest C. *George C. Marshall.* 4 vols. New York: Viking, 1987.

Spiller, Roger J., et al., eds. *Dictionary of American Military Biography.* 3 vols. Westport, Conn.: Greenwood Press, 1984.

Bibliography

Higham, Robin, and Mrozek, Donald, eds. *A Guide to the Sources of United States Military History.* Hamden, Conn.: Archon Books, 1975 (with Supplements I, 1981, and II, 1984).

Jessup, John E., Jr., and Coakley, Robert W., eds. *A Guide to the Study and Use of Military History.* Washington: Government Printing Office, 1970.

Further Readings

Brennan, Matthew. *Brennan's War.* Novato, Calif.: Presidio Press, 1985.

Coyle, H.W. *Team Yankee: A Novel of World War III.* Novato, Calif.: Presidio Press, 1987.

Forester, C. S. *The General.* Baltimore: Nautical and Aviation, 1987 .

McDonough, James R. *Platoon Leader.* Novato, Calif.: Presidio Press, 1985.

Myrer, Anton. *Once an Eagle.* New York: Dell, 1970.

Prescott, William H. *The Conquest of Mexico.* New York: Modern Library, 1931.

Remarque, Erich M. *All Quiet on the Western Front.* New York: Fawcett, 1987.

Shaara, Michael. *Killer Angels: A Novel About the Four Days at Gettysburg.* New York: McKay, 1974.

Stallworthy, Jon, ed. *Oxford Book of War Poetry.* New York: Oxford University Press, 1984.

Woodham-Smith, Cecil. *The Reason Why: The Charge of the Light Brigade.* New York: Dutton, 1960.

CHAPTER BIBLIOGRAPHIES

Chapter 1: Introduction

Recommended Readings

Brodie, Bernard. *War and Politics.* New York: Macmillan, 1973.
Craven, W. Frank. *Why Military History?* The Harmon Memorial Lectures in Military History, no. 1. Colorado Springs: U.S. Air Force Academy, 1959.
Howard, Michael. "The Use and Abuse of Military History." *Journal of the Royal United Service Institution* 107, no. 625 (February 1962): 4–10.
Weigley, Russell F. *The American Way of War: A History of United States Military Strategy and Policy.* Bloomington: Indiana University Press, 1977.
————. *Towards an American Army: Military Thought From Washington to Marshall.* New York: Columbia University Press, 1962.

Other Readings

Herring, Pendleton. *The Impact of War: Our American Democracy Under Arms.* New York: Farrar & Rinehart, 1941. Chapters 1–3 and 10.
Howard, Michael, ed. *The Theory and Practice of War.* New York: Frederick A. Praeger, 1966.
Huntington, Samuel P. *The Soldier and the State: The Theory and Politics of Civil-Military Relations.* Cambridge: Harvard University Press, Belknap Press, 1959.
Millis, Walter. *Arms and Men: A Study in American Military History.* New York: Putnam, 1956.
Paret, Peter, Craig, Gordon A., and Gilbert, Felix. *Makers of Modern Strategy From Machiavelli to the Nuclear Age.* Princeton: Princeton University Press, 1986.
Ropp, Theodore. *War in the Modern World.* New York: Collier Books, 1962.
Smith, Louis. *American Democracy and Military Power: A Study of Civil Control of the Military Powers in the United States.* Chicago: University of Chicago Press, 1951.
Williams, T. Harry. *Americans at War: The Development of the American Military System.* New York: Collier Books, 1962.

Chapter 2: The Beginnings

Recommended Readings

Anderson, Fred. *A People's Army: Massachusetts Soldiers and Society in the Seven Years' War.* Chapel Hill: University of North Carolina Press, 1984.
Ferling, John E. *A Wilderness of Miseries: War and Warriors in Early America.* Westport: Greenwood Press, 1980.
Leach, Douglas E. *Arms for Empire: A Military History of the British Colonies in North America.* New York: Macmillan, 1973.
————. *Roots of Conflict: British Armed Forces and Colonial Americans, 1677–1763.* Chapel Hill: University of North Carolina Press, 1986.
Mahon, John K. "Anglo-American Methods of Indian Warfare, 1676–1794." *Mississippi Valley Historical Review* 45 (1958): 254–75.
Malone, Patrick M. "Changing Military Technology Among the Indians of Southern New England, 1600–1677." *American Quarterly* 25 (March 1973): 48–63.
Shy, John W. *Toward Lexington: The Role of the British Army in the Coming of the Revolution.* Princeton: Princeton University Press, 1965. Pp. 3–44.

Other Readings

Crane, Verner W. *The Southern Frontier, 1679–1732.* Durham: Duke University Press, 1928.

Fregault, Guy. *Canada: The War of Conquest.* Translated by Margaret Cameron. New York: Oxford University Press, 1969.

Gipson, Lawrence H. *The British Empire Before the American Revolution.* 15 vols. New York: A. A. Knopf, 1963–70. Vols. 6–8.

Hunt, George T. *The Wars of the Iroquois.* Madison: University of Wisconsin Press, 1940.

Leach, Douglas E. *The Northern Colonial Frontier, 1607–1763.* New York: Holt, Rinehart, and Winston, 1966.

————. *Flintlock and Tomahawk: New England in King Philip's War.* New York: W. W. Norton, 1958.

Pargellis, Stanley. *Lord Loudon in North America.* New Haven: Yale University Press, 1933.

Peckham, Howard H. *The Colonial Wars, 1689–1763.* Chicago: University of Chicago Press, 1964.

Rawlyk, George A. *Yankees at Louisburg.* Orono: University of Maine Press, 1967.

Shea, William Lee. *The Virginia Militia in the Seventeenth Century.* Baton Rouge: Louisiana State University Press, 1983.

Stacey, Col. C. P. *Quebec 1759: The Siege and the Battle.* New York: St. Martin's Press, 1959.

Vaughn, Alden T. *New England Frontier: Puritans and Indians, 1620–1675.* Boston: Little, Brown, 1965.

Wright, J. Leitch, Jr. *Anglo-American Rivalry in North America.* Athens: University of Georgia Press, 1971.

Chapter 3: The American Revolution: First Phase

Recommended Readings

Flexner, James T. *George Washington in the American Revolution, 1775–1783.* Boston: Little, Brown, 1968. Pp. 9–216.

Higginbotham, Don. *The War of American Independence: Military Attitudes, Policies, and Practices.* New York: Macmillan, 1971. Pp. 25–174.

Mackesy, Piers. *The War for America, 1775–1783.* Cambridge: Harvard University Press, 1964. Pp. 1–102.

Middlekauff, Robert. *The Glorious Cause: The American Revolution, 1763–1789.* New York: Oxford University Press, 1982.

Tourtellot, Arthur B. *William Diamond's Drum: The Beginnings of the War of the American Revolution.* Garden City: Doubleday, 1959.

Ward, Christopher. *The War of the Revolution.* 2 vols. New York: Macmillan, 1952. 1:3–318.

Other Readings

Alden, John R. *General Gage in America.* Baton Rouge: Louisiana State University Press, 1948.

Boatner, Mark M. *Encyclopedia of the American Revolution.* Rev. ed. New York: David McKay, 1974.

Brown, Wallace. *The Good Americans: The Loyalists in the American Revolution.* New York: William Morrow, 1969.

Freeman, Douglas Southall. *Planter and Patriot.* George Washington: A Biography, vol. 3. New York: Scribner, 1948–57.

French, Allen. *The First Year of the Revolution.* Boston: Houghton Mifflin, 1934.

Gross, Robert A. *The Minutemen and Their World.* New York: Hill & Wang, 1976.

Gruber, Ira D. *The Howe Brothers and the American Revolution.* New York: Atheneum, 1972.

Robson, Eric. *The American Revolution in Its Political and Military Aspects, 1763–1783.* London: Batchworth Press, 1955.

Chapter 4: The Winning of Independence

Recommended Readings

Billias, George Athan, ed. *George Washington's Generals*. New York: William Morrow, 1964.
Freeman, Douglas Southall. *Leader of the Revolution*. George Washington: A Biography, vol. 4. New York: Scribner, 1948–57.
———. *Victory With the Aid of France*. George Washington: A Biography, vol. 5. New York: Scribner, 1948–57.
Higginbotham, Don, ed. *Reconsiderations on the Revolutionary War: Selected Essays*. Westport: Greenwood Press, 1978.
Hoffman, Ronald, and Albert, Peter J., eds. *Arms and Independence: The Military Character of the American Revolution*. Charlottesville: University of Virginia Press, 1984.
Mackesy, Piers. *The War for America, 1775–1783*. Cambridge: Harvard University Press, 1964. Pp. 103 to end, especially pp. 510–16.
Peckham, Howard H. *The War for Independence: A Military History*. 2 vols. New York: Macmillan, 1958.
Shy, John. *A People Numerous and Armed*. New York: Oxford University Press, 1976.
Wallace, Willard. *Appeal to Arms—A Military History of the American Revolution*. New York: Harper, 1951.
Ward, Christopher. *The War of the Revolution*. 2 vols. New York: Macmillan, 1952. Vol. 2.
Wright, Robert K., Jr. *The Continental Army*. Washington: Government Printing Office, 1983.

Other Readings

Billias, George A., ed. *George Washington's Opponents: British Generals and Admirals of the American Revolution*. New York: William Morrow, 1969.
Bowler, R. Arthur. *Logistics and the Failure of the British Army in America, 1775–1783*. Princeton: Princeton University Press, 1975.
Buel, Richard, Jr. *Dear Liberty: Connecticut's Mobilization for the Revolutionary War*. Middletown: Wesleyan University Press, 1980.
Carp, E. Wayne. *To Starve the Army at Pleasure: Continental Army Administration and American Political Culture, 1775–1783*. Chapel Hill: University of North Carolina Press, 1984.
Cress, Lawrence D. *Citizens in Arms: The Army and Militia in American Society to the War of 1812*. Chapel Hill: University of North Carolina Press, 1982.
Dann, John C., ed. *The Revolution Remembered: Eyewitness Accounts of the War for Independence*. Chicago: University of Chicago Press, 1983.
Larrabee, Harold A. *Decision at the Chesapeake*. New York: C. N. Porter, 1964.
Rossie, Jonathan G. *The Politics of Command*. Syracuse: Syracuse University Press, 1975.
Royster, Charles. *A Revolutionary People at War: The Continental Army and American Character, 1775–1783*. Chapel Hill: University of North Carolina Press, 1979.
U.S. Air Force Academy. *Military History of the American Revolution, Proceedings of the Sixth Military History Symposium, USAF Academy, 1974.* Washington: Government Printing Office, 1976.

Chapter 5: The Formative Years, 1783–1812

Recommended Readings

Bird, Harrison. *War for the West, 1790–1813*. New York: Oxford University Press, 1971.
Coakley, Robert W. *The Role of Federal Military Forces in Domestic Disorders, 1789–1878*. Washington: Government Printing Office, 1988.
Crackel, Theodore J. *Mr. Jefferson's Army: Political and Social Reform of the Military Establishment, 1801–1809*. New York: New York University Press, 1987.

Guthman, William H. *March to Massacre: A History of the First Seven Years of the United States Army, 1784–1791.* New York: McGraw-Hill, 1970.
Jacobs, James R. *The Beginnings of the U.S. Army, 1783–1812.* Philadelphia: The University of Pennsylvania Press, 1962.
Kohn, Richard H. *Eagle and Sword: The Federalists and the Creation of the Military Establishment in America, 1783–1802.* New York: The Free Press, 1975.
May, Ernest R., ed. *The Ultimate Decision: The President as Commander in Chief.* New York: George Braziller, 1960. Chapter 1.
Perkins, Bradford. *Prologue to War: England and the United States.* Berkeley: University of California Press, 1961.
Prucha, Francis P. *The Sword of the Republic: The United States Army on the Frontier, 1783–1840.* New York: Macmillan, 1969. Chapters 1–5.
Stagg, J. C. A. *Mr. Madison's War: Politics, Diplomacy, and Warfare in the Early American Republic, 1783–1830.* Princeton: Princeton University Press, 1983.

Other Readings

Adams, Henry. *The Formative Years.* Edited and condensed by Herbert Agar. Boston: Houghton Mifflin, 1947.
Callahan, North. *Henry Knox: General Washington's General.* New York: Rinehart, 1958.
Cleaves, Freeman. *Old Tippecanoe: William Henry Harrison.* New York: Scribner, 1939.
DeVoto, Bernard, ed. *Journals of Lewis and Clark.* Boston: Houghton Mifflin, 1953.
Jacobs, James R. *The Beginnings of the U.S. Army, 1783–1812.* Princeton: Princeton University Press, 1947.
Knopf, Richard C., ed. *Anthony Wayne, A Name in Arms: The Wayne-Knox-Pickering-McHenry Correspondence.* Pittsburgh: University of Pittsburgh Press, 1960.
Van Every, Dale. *Final Challenge: The American Frontier, 1804–1845.* New York: William Morrow, 1965.

Chapter 6: The War of 1812

Recommended Readings

Brandt, Irving. *James Madison: Commander in Chief, 1812–1836.* Indianapolis: Bobbs-Merrill, 1961. Chapters 9–28.
Gilpin, Alex R. *The War of 1812 in the Old Northwest.* East Lansing: Michigan State University Press, 1958. Especially Chapters 3–7 and 10–11.
Horseman, Reginald. *The Causes of the War of 1812.* Philadelphia: The University of Pennsylvania Press, 1962.
James, Marquis. *Andrew Jackson: The Border Captain.* Indianapolis: Bobbs-Merrill, 1933. Chapters 9–20.
Kimball, Jeffrey. "The Battle of Chippewa: Infantry Tactics in the War of 1812." *Military Affairs* (Winter 1967–68), pp. 169–86.
Lord, Walter. *The Dawn's Early Light.* New York: Norton, 1972.
Mahon, John K. *The War of 1812.* Gainsville: University of Florida Press, 1972.
May, Ernest, ed. *The Ultimate Decision: The President as Commander in Chief.* New York: George Braziller, 1960. Chapter 2.
Remini, Robert V. *Andrew Jackson and the Course of American Empire, 1767–1821.* New York: Harper & Row, 1977.
Risch, Erna. *Quartermaster Support of the Army: A History of the Corps, 1775–1939.* Washington: Government Printing Office, 1962. Chapter 5.

Other Readings

Adams, Henry. *The War of 1812.* Edited by H. A. DeWeerd. Washington: Infantry Journal Press, 1944.
Brooks, Charles B. *The Siege of New Orleans.* Seattle: University of Washington Press, 1961.
Coles, Harry L. *The War of 1812.* Chicago: University of Chicago Press, 1965.
Hitsman, J. MacKay. *The Incredible War of 1812.* Toronto: University of Toronto Press, 1965.
Mahan, Alfred T. *Sea Power in Its Relation to the War of 1812.* New York: Scribner, 1903.
Mason, Philip, ed. *After Tippecanoe: Some Aspects of the War of 1812.* East Lansing: Michigan State University Press, 1963.
Muller, Charles. *The Darkest Day, 1812: The Washington-Baltimore Campaign.* Philadelphia: Lippincott, 1963.
Prucha, Francis P. *The Sword of the Republic: The United States Army on the Frontier, 1783–1840.* New York: Macmillan, 1969. Chapter 6.
Stagg, J. C. A. *Mr. Madison's War: Politics, Diplomacy, and Warfare in the Early American Republic, 1783–1830.* Princeton: Princeton University Press, 1983.

Chapter 7: The Thirty Years' Peace

Recommended Readings

Elliott, Charles Winslow. *Winfield Scott: The Soldier and the Man.* New York: Macmillan, 1937. Chapters 24–27.
Falk, Stanley L. "Artillery for the Land Service: The Development of a System." *Military Affairs* 28, no. 3 (Fall 1964): 97–110.
James, Marquis. *The Life of Andrew Jackson.* Indianapolis and New York: Bobbs-Merrill, 1938. Chapter 18.
Mahon, John K. *History of the Second Seminole War, 1835–1842.* Gainesville: University of Florida Press, 1967.
Prucha, Francis P. *The Sword of the Republic: The United States Army on the Frontier, 1783–1846.* New York: Macmillan, 1969.
Rippy, J. Fred. *Joel Poinsett, Versatile American.* Durham: Duke University Press, 1935. Chapters 12 and 13.
Schubert, N. Frank. *Vanguard of Expansion: Army Engineers in the Trans-Mississippi West, 1819–1879.* Washington: Government Printing Office, 1981.
White, Leonard D. *The Jeffersonians: A Study in Administrative History, 1801–1829.* New York: Macmillan, 1951. Chapters 17, 18, and 34.

Other Readings

Beers, Henry P. *The Western Military Frontier, 1815–1846.* Philadelphia, 1935.
Forman, Sidney. *West Point.* New York: Columbia University Press, 1950.
Peters, Virginia Bergman. *The Florida Wars.* Hamden: Archon Books, 1979.
Remini, Robert V. *Andrew Jackson and the Course of American Empire, 1767–1821.* New York: Harper & Row, 1977.
Sprague, John T. *The Origin, Progress, and Conclusion of the Florida War.* Quadricentennial ed. Gainesville: University of Florida Press, 1964.
Walton, George H. *Sentinel of the Plains: Fort Leavenworth and the American West.* Englewood Cliffs: Prentice-Hall, 1973.

Chapter 8: The Mexican War and After

Recommended Readings

Bauer, K. Jack. *The Mexican War, 1846–1848*. New York: Macmillan, 1974.
———. *Zachary Taylor: Soldier, Planter, Statesman of the Old Southwest*. Baton Rouge: Louisiana State University Press, 1985.
Connor, Seymour V., and Faulk, Odie B. *North America Divided: The Mexican War, 1846–1848*. New York: Oxford University Press, 1971.
Dufour, Charles L. *The Mexican War: A Compact History, 1846–1848*. New York: Hawthorne Books, 1968.
Elliott, Charles Winslow. *Winfield Scott: The Soldier and the Man*. New York: Macmillan, 1937. Chapters 35–41.
Nichols, Edward J. *Zach Taylor's Little Army*. Garden City: Doubleday, 1963.
Risch, Erna. *Quartermaster Support of the Army: A History of the Corps, 1775–1939*. Washington: Government Printing Office, 1962. Chapters 6–8.
Strode, Hudson. *Jefferson Davis, American Patriot*. New York: Harcourt, 1955. Chapters 11, 12, 16, and 17.
Utley, Robert M. *Frontiersmen in Blue: The United States Army and the Indian, 1848–1865*. New York: Macmillan, 1967.

Other Readings

Bill, Alfred Hoyt. *Rehearsal for Conflict: The War With Mexico, 1846–1848*. New York: Knopf, 1947.
Goetzmann, William H. *Army Exploration in the American West, 1803–1863*. New Haven: Yale University Press, 1959.
Henry, Robert Selph. *The Story of the Mexican War*. Indianapolis and New York: Bobbs-Merrill, 1959.
Johannsen, Robert W. *To the Halls of the Montezumas: The Mexican War in the American Imagination*. New York: Oxford University Press, 1985.
Lavender, David. *Climax at Buena Vista*. Philadelphia: Lippincott, 1966.
Singletary, Otis A. *The Mexican War*. Chicago: University of Chicago Press, 1960.
Smith, George Winston, and Judah, Charles. *Chronicles of the Gringos: The U.S. Army in the Mexican War, 1846–1848: Accounts of Eyewitnesses and Combatants*. Albuquerque: University of New Mexico Press, 1968.

Chapter 9: The Civil War, 1861

Recommended Readings

Catton, Bruce. *The Coming Fury*. The Centennial History of the Civil War, vol. 1. Garden City: Doubleday, 1963.
Davis, William C. *The Deep Waters of the Proud*. The Imperiled Union, 1861–1865, vol. 1. Garden City: Doubleday, 1982. Chapters 1–6.
Foote, Shelby. *Fort Sumter to Perryville*. The Civil War: A Narrative, vol. 1. New York: Random House, 1958. Chapters 1–2.
Freeman, Douglas Southall. *Manassas to Malvern Hill*. Lee's Lieutenants: A Study in Command, vol. 1. New York: Scribner, 1942–44. Chapters 1–10.
Longstreet, James. *From Manassas to Appomattox: Memoirs of the Civil War in America*. Edited by James I. Robinson. Reprint ed. Milwood: Kraus, 1968. Chapters 1–4.
McPherson, James M. *Battle Cry of Freedom*. New York: Oxford University Press, 1988.
Thomas, Emory M. *The Confederate Nation*. New York: Harper, 1979. Chapters 1–6.

Wilshin, Francis F. *Manassas (Bull Run) National Battlefield Park, Virginia.* U.S. National Park Service Historical Handbook Series no. 15. Rev. ed. Washington: Government Printing Office, 1957.

Other Readings

Davis, William C. *Battle of Bull Run: A History of the First Major Campaign of the Civil War.* Garden City: Doubleday, 1977.
Esposito, Vincent J., ed. *The West Point Atlas of American Wars.* Vol. 1, 1689–1900. New York: Holt, Rinehart, and Winston, 1978. Maps 17–24.
Jones, Virgil Carrington. *The Civil War at Sea.* New York: Holt, Rinehart, and Winston, 1960. Vol. 1, Chapters 1–24.
Mitchell, Joseph B. *Military Leaders of the Civil War.* New York: Putnam, 1972.
Nevins, Allan. *Ordeal of the Union.* 2 vols. New York: Scribner, 1947.
———. *The Improvised War, 1861–1862.* The War for the Union, vol. 1. New York: Scribner, 1959.

Chapter 10: The Civil War, 1862

Recommended Readings

Catton, Bruce. *Mr. Lincoln's Army.* Garden City: Doubleday, 1951.
———. *Glory Road.* Garden City: Doubleday, 1954. Chapters 1–2.
Cullen, Joseph P. *The Peninsular Campaign: McClellan and Lee Struggle for Richmond.* Harrisburg: Stackpole, 1973.
Davis, William C. *The Deep Waters of the Proud.* The Imperiled Union, 1861–1865, vol. 1. Garden City: Doubleday, 1982. Chapters 7–20.
Freeman, Douglas Southall. *Manassas to Malvern Hill.* Lee's Lieutenants: A Study in Command, vol. 1. New York: Scribner, 1942–44. Chapters 10–43.
———. *Cedar Mountain to Chancellorsville.* Lee's Lieutenants: A Study in Command, vol. 2. New York: Scribner, 1942–44. Chapters 1–23.
Sword, Wiley. *Shiloh: Bloody April.* New York: William Morrow, 1974.
Tanner, Robert G. *Stonewall in the Valley: Thomas J. "Stonewall" Jackson's Shenandoah Valley Campaign, Spring 1862.* Garden City: Doubleday, 1976.
Williams, Kenneth P. *Lincoln Finds a General: A Military Study of the Civil War.* 5 vols. New York: Macmillan, 1949–59. Vol. 1, Chapters 4–13; Vol. 2, Chapters 14–16; Vol. 3, Chapters 5–15; and Vol. 4, Chapters 10–11.
Williams, T. Harry. *Lincoln and His Generals.* New York: Knopf, 1952. Chapters 4–8.

Other Readings

Blackerby, H. C. *Blacks in the Blue and the Grey: Afro-American Service in the Civil War.* Tuscaloosa: Portals Press, 1979.
Dowdy, Clifford. *The Seven Days: The Emergence of Lee.* New York: Little, Brown, 1964.
Esposito, Vincent J., ed. *The West Point Atlas of American Wars.* Vol. 1, 1689–1900. New York: Holt, Rinehart, and Winston, 1978. Maps 25–83.
Luvaas, Jay, and Nelson, Harold W. *The U.S. Army War College Guide to the Battle of Antietam: The Maryland Campaign in 1862.* Carlisle: South Mountain Press, 1987.
Jones, Virgil Carrington. *The Civil War at Sea.* New York: Holt, Rinehart, and Winston, 1960. Vol. 1, Chapters 25–28, and Vol. 2, Chapters 1–16.
Sears, Stephen. *Landscape Turned Red: The Battle of Antietam.* New Haven: Ticknor and Fields, 1983.
Stackpole, Edward J. *From Cedar Mountain to Antietam.* Harrisburg: The Stackpole Co., 1959.

Vandiver, Frank E. *Rebel Brass: The Confederate Command System*. Baton Rouge: Louisiana State University Press, 1956.

Chapter 11: The Civil War, 1863

Recommended Readings

Carter, Samuel III. *The Final Fortress: The Campaign for Vicksburg, 1862–1863*. New York: St. Martin, 1980. Chapters 8–23.
Catton, Bruce. *Glory Road*. Garden City: Doubleday, 1954. Chapters 3–6.
Coddington, Edwin B. *The Gettysburg Campaign: A Study in Command*. New York: Charles Scribner's Sons, 1984.
Foote, Shelby. *Fredericksburg to Meridian*. The Civil War: A Narrative, vol. 1. New York: Random House, 1963. Chapters 3–9.
Freeman, Douglas Southall. *Cedar Mountain to Chancellorsville*. Lee's Lieutenants: A Study in Command, vol. 2. New York: Scribner, 1942–44. Chapters 25–36.
———. *Gettysburg to Appomattox*. Lee's Lieutenants: A Study in Command, vol. 3. New York: Scribner, 1942–44. Chapters 1–18.
Montgomery, James. *The Shaping of a Battle: Gettysburg*. Philadelphia: Chilton, 1959.
Stackpole, Edward J. *Chancellorsville: Lee's Greatest Battle*. Harrisburg: The Stackpole Co., 1958.
Williams, Kenneth P. *Lincoln Finds a General: A Military Study of the Civil War*. 5 vols. New York: Macmillan, 1949–59. Vol. 4, Chapters 10–13, and Vol. 5.
Williams, T. Harry. *Lincoln and His Generals*. New York: Knopf, 1967. Chapters 9–12.

Other Readings

Coakley, Robert W. *The Role of Federal Military Forces in Domestic Disorders, 1789–1878*. Washington: Government Printing Office, 1988.
Editors of *Military Affairs*. *Military Analysis of the Civil War*. Milwood, N.Y.: KTO Press, 1977.
Esposito, Vincent J., ed. *The West Point Atlas of the Civil War*. Vol. 1. 1689–1900. New York: Holt, Rinehart, and Winston, 1978. Maps 84–116.
Funk, Arville L. *The Morgan Raid in Indiana and Ohio, 1863*. Corydon, Ind.: ALFCO Publications, 1978.
Jones, Virgil Carrington. *The Civil War at Sea*. New York: Holt, Rinehart, and Winston, 1960. Vol. 2, Chapters 17–24, and Vol. 3, Chapters 1–7.
Nelson, Harold W., and Luvaas, Jay, eds. *The U.S. Army War College Guide to the Battle of Gettysburg*. Carlisle: South Mountain Press, 1986.
Tucker, Glenn. *Chickamauga: Bloody Battle in the West*. Dayton: Morningside, 1975.
Wiley, Bell. *The Life of Billy Yank: The Common Soldier of the Union*. Baton Rouge: Louisiana State University Press, 1978.
———. *The Life of Johnny Reb: The Common Soldier of the Confederacy*. Baton Rouge: Louisiana State University Press, 1978.

Chapter 12: The Civil War, 1864–1865

Recommended Readings

Catton, Bruce. *A Stillness at Appomattox*. New York: Simon & Schuster, Washington Square Press, 1970.
Dowdy, Clifford. *Lee's Last Campaign*. New York: Little, Brown, 1960.
Freeman, Douglas Southall. *Gettysburg to Appomattox*. Lee's Lieutenants: A Study in Command, vol. 2. New York: Scribner, 1942–44. Chapters 18–36.

Glatthaar, Joseph T. *The March to the Sea and Beyond: Sherman's Troops in the Savannah and Carolinas Campaigns.* New York: New York University Press, 1985.

Kinchen, Oscar A. *Confederate Operations in Canada and in the North: A Little-Known Phase of the American Civil War.* North Quincy: Christopher, 1970.

Thomas, Emory M. *The Confederate Nation.* New York: Harper, 1979. Chapters 11–12.

Williams, T. Harry. *Lincoln and His Generals.* New York: Knopf, 1967. Chapters 9–12.

Other Readings

Beringer, Richard E., et al. *Why the South Lost the Civil War.* Athens: University of Georgia Press, 1986.

Carter, Samuel. *The Siege of Atlanta.* New York: St. Martin, 1973.

Davis, Burke. *Sherman's March.* New York: Random House, 1980.

Jones, Virgil Carrington. *The Civil War at Sea.* New York: Holt, Rinehart, and Winston, 1960. Vol. 3, Chapters 8–26.

Sommers, Richard J. *Richmond Redeemed: The Siege of Petersburg.* Garden City: Doubleday, 1981.

Chapter 13: Darkness and Light: The Interwar Years, 1865–1898

Recommended Readings

Abrahamson, James L. *America Arms for a New Century: The Making of a Great Military Power.* New York: The Free Press, 1981.

Ambrose, Stephen. *Upton and the Army.* Baton Rouge: Louisiana State University Press, 1964.

Coakley, Robert W. *The Role of Federal Military Forces in Domestic Disorders, 1789–1878.* Washington: Government Printing Office, 1988.

Cooper, Jerry M. *The Army and Civil Disorder: Federal Military Intervention in Labor Disputes, 1877–1900.* Westport: Greenwood Press, 1980.

Foner, Jack D. *The United States Soldier Between Two Wars: Army Life and Reforms, 1865–1898.* New York: Humanities Press, 1970.

Gates, John M. "The Alleged Isolation of U.S. Army Officers in the Late 19th Century." *Parameters: Journal of the U.S. Army War College,* September 1980, pp. 32–45.

Gluckman, Arcadi. *United States Muskets, Rifles and Carbines.* Harrisburg: The Stackpole Co., 1959. Pp. 227–33, 405–09, and 438–44.

Huntington, Samuel P. *The Soldier and the State: The Theory and Politics of Civil-Military Relations.* Cambridge: Harvard University Press, Belknap Press, 1957. Pp. 222–69.

Leckie, William H. *The Buffalo Soldiers: A Narrative of the Negro Cavalry in the West.* Norman: University of Oklahoma Press, 1967.

Risch, Erna. *Quartermaster Support of the Army: A History of the Corps, 1775–1939.* Washington: Government Printing Office, 1962. Pp. 453–514.

Other Readings

Bruce, Robert V. *1877: Year of Violence.* Indianapolis: Bobbs-Merrill, 1959.

Caswell, John E. *Arctic Frontiers: United States Explorations in the Far North.* Norman: University of Oklahoma Press, 1956. Pp. 42–122 and *passim.*

Hill, Jim Dan. *The Minute Man in Peace and War: A History of the National Guard.* Harrisburg: The Stackpole Co., 1964. Pp. 99–137.

Hume, Edgar Erskine. *Victories of Army Medicine: Scientific Accomplishments of the Medical Department of the United States Army.* Philadelphia: Lippincott, 1943. Pp. 22–30 and 45–57.

Sefton, James E. *The United States Army and Reconstruction, 1865–1877.* Baton Rouge: Louisiana State University Press, 1967.

Thomas, Benjamin P., and Hyman, Harold M. *Stanton: The Life and Times of Lincoln's Secretary of War.* New York: Knopf, 1962. Pp. 402–640.

Todd, A. L. *Abandoned: The Story of the Greely Arctic Expedition, 1881–1884.* New York: McGraw-Hill, 1961.

Chapter 14: Winning the West:
The Army in the Indian Wars, 1865–1890

Recommended Readings

Andrist, Ralph K. *The Long Death: The Last Days of the Plains Indians.* New York: Macmillan, 1962.

Connell, Evan S. *Son of the Morning Star.* San Francisco: North Point Press, 1984.

Fowler, Arlen L. *The Black Infantry in the West, 1869–1891.* Westport: Greenwood Press, 1971.

Leckie, William H. *The Buffalo Soldiers: A Narrative of the Negro Cavalry in the West.* Norman: University of Oklahoma Press, 1967.

National Park Service. *Soldier and Brave: Military and Indian Affairs in the Trans-Mississippi West, Including a Guide to Historic Sites and Landmarks.* New York: Harper & Row, 1963.

Rickey, Don. *Forty Miles a Day on Beans and Hay: The Enlisted Soldier Fighting the Indian Wars.* Norman: University of Oklahoma Press, 1963.

Utley, Robert M. *Frontier Regulars: The United States Army and the Indian, 1866–1891.* New York: Macmillan, 1973.

―――. *Frontiersmen in Blue: The United States Army and the Indian, 1848–1865.* New York: Macmillan, 1967.

Wooster, Robert. *The Military and United States Indian Policy.* New Haven: Yale University Press, 1988.

Other Readings

Athearn, Robert G. *Forts of the Upper Missouri.* Englewood Cliffs: Prentice-Hall, 1967.

Beal, Merrill D. *"I Will Fight No More Forever": Chief Joseph and the Nez Perce War.* Seattle: University of Washington Press, 1963.

Brown, Dee. *Fort Phil Kearny: An American Saga.* New York: Putnam, 1962.

Leckie, William H. *The Military Conquest of the Southern Plains.* Norman: University of Oklahoma Press, 1963.

Murray, Keith A. *The Modocs and Their War.* Norman: University of Oklahoma Press, 1959.

Nye, Wilbur S. *Carbine and Lance: The Story of Old Fort Sill.* Norman: University of Oklahoma Press, 1937.

Olson, James C. *Red Cloud and the Sioux Problem.* Lincoln: University of Nebraska Press, 1965.

Prucha, Francis P. *The Great Father: The United States Government and the American Indians.* Lincoln: University of Nebraska Press, 1984.

Thrapp, Dan L. *The Conquest of Apacheria.* Norman: University of Oklahoma Press, 1967.

Utley, Robert M. *The Last Days of the Sioux Nation.* New Haven: Yale University Press, 1963.

Chapter 15: Emergence to World Power, 1898–1902

Recommended Readings

Cosmas, Graham A. *An Army for Empire: The U.S. Army in the Spanish American War.* Columbia: University of Missouri Press, 1971.

Gates, John M. *Schoolbooks and Krags: The U.S. Army in the Philippines, 1898–1902.* Westport: Greenwood Press, 1973.

Grenville, John A. S., and Young, George Berkeley. *Politics, Strategy, and American Diplomacy: Studies in Foreign Policy, 1873–1917.* New Haven: Yale University Press, 1966. Chapters 7–10.

Langley, Lester D. *The Banana Wars: United States Intervention in the Caribbean, 1898–1934.* 2d ed. Lexington: University Press of Kentucky, 1985.

Linn, Brian. "Provincial Pacification in the Philippines, 1900–1901: The First District, Department of Northern Luzon." *Military Affairs* 51, no. 2 (April 1987): 62–66.

Morgan, H. Wayne. *America's Road to Empire: The War With Spain and Overseas Expansion.* America in Crisis series. Edited by Robert A. Devine. New York: John Wiley, 1965. Especially Chapters 4 and 5.

Purcell, Victor. *The Boxer Uprising: A Background Study.* Cambridge: Cambridge University Press, 1963. Especially Chapter 12.

Risch, Erna. *Quartermaster Support of the Army: A History of the Corps, 1775–1939.* Washington: Government Printing Office, 1962. Chapter 12.

Trask, David F. *The War With Spain in 1898.* New York: Macmillan, 1981.

Other Readings

Alger, Russell A. *The Spanish-American War.* New York: Harper, 1901.

Heller, Charles E., and Stofft, William A., eds. *America's First Battles, 1776–1965.* Lawrence: University Press of Kansas, 1986. Chapter 5, "San Juan Hill and El Caney, 1–2 July 1898" by Graham A. Cosmas.

Sexton, William T. *Soldiers in the Sun.* Harrisburg: Military Service, 1939. 2d ed., 1944, retitled: *Soldiers in the Philippines: A History of the Insurrection.*

Tan, Chester C. *The Boxer Catastrophe.* New York: Columbia University Press, 1955.

Index